Alfred Tennyson: The Critical Legacy

Acknowledgments

AS THE CRITICS OF CULTURE are quick to point out, no book is produced in a vacuum, and no author can claim exclusive rights to its preparation. *Alfred Tennyson: The Critical Legacy* was a project that competed for attention with the students, faculty, and staff of Alvernia College, whose friendships I value and to whom I owe much both professionally and personally. Among the many people who assisted me, I feel an obligation to single out Ms. Roberta Rohrbach of the Franco Library at Alvernia, a librarian and researcher extraordinaire when it comes to locating copies of long-out-of-print volumes and journals. James Hood of Guilford College, who read the draft of this volume with critical acumen, has helped me immensely, though he is certainly not responsible for any errors or faulty judgments that remain. Finally, I would also like to thank James Walker and James Hardin of Camden House for their willingness to let someone — whose duties as a college president must take precedence over his scholarly pursuits — have the time necessary to work on this project.

Introduction

IN 1855, CHARLES TENNYSON, Baron d'Eyncourt of Bayons Manor, found himself once more embarrassed by one of his unsuitable relatives. Throughout most of his life he had become accustomed to treating the family of his Uncle George with open disdain. But now he was totally exasperated with his nephew Alfred's latest volume, *Maud, and Other Poems*. "Horrid rubbish indeed!" he wrote to a correspondent. "What a discredit it is that British taste and Poetry should have such a representative before the Nations of the Earth and Posterity! For a Laureate will so appear. Posterity will, it is hoped, have a sound judgment on such matters, and if so what an age this must appear when such trash can be tolerated and not only tolerated but enthusiastically admired!" (Ricks 233).

Posterity has not come to share Uncle Charles's judgment. The Bayons branch of the family never reconciled themselves to the fame achieved by their poor relation who had been elevated (quite unfairly in their view) to become England's poet laureate in 1850. The English public, however, and England's queen found in Tennyson the voice of their deepest hopes and fears. He was not simply one of England's poet laureates; in his own day, and for a century after, his name became synonymous with the term.

No poet has ever or since been more closely associated with his times than Alfred Tennyson. The Victorians were captivated by his poetry. He could make them weep over the plight of the poor fisherman Enoch Arden or fire their idealism with his portrait of the perfect ruler in his Arthurian epic *Idylls of the King*. He could stir up controversy with poetic tracts such as *The Princess* or experimental verse such as *Maud*. And above all, he could offer readers the possibility of hope emerging from grief as he did in his signatory accomplishment, *In Memoriam A. H. H.* As Leonée Ormond observes, when he accepted the invitation to become Queen Victoria's poet laureate, Tennyson was profoundly aware of the temperament of his countrymen. He did not simply become *a* poet laureate; rather he became "the greatest of all laureates, the man with whom the title itself will always be most closely associated" (Ormond 109). He was, as Joanna Richardson describes him in the title of her critical biography, the "pre-eminent Victorian."

Hence, it is not surprising that Tennyson's reputation has risen, fallen, and risen again as critics during the twentieth century continued to reassess and reinterpret the Victorian Age. His early works were criticized as trivial and introspective by a generation raised to appreciate the poetry of the

Augustans and Sir Walter Scott. By mid-century he had risen to a position of prominence enjoyed by few poets in their lifetime. As the century closed, a new generation was finding fault not only with his artistry but also with what they considered his priggish morality, while those who were growing old with him continued to treat him with the reverence accorded to sages and saints. For a half-century after his death, his reputation suffered the same fate as other Victorians at the hands of their children and grandchildren who found the promises of optimism and belief in progress demolished and dispelled by the tragedy of world war and the emergence of modernism. The rise in the Victorians' reputation during the middle of the twentieth century saw a concurrent rise in Tennyson's stature, though the hostile trends late-century critics displayed toward more politically conservative Victorian writers has had an effect on the Victorian laureate's reputation. At the same time, some of his poems have risen or fallen in stature — a trend reflecting as much on the tastes of the twentieth century as it does on Tennyson.

Alfred Tennyson: The Critical Legacy focuses on ways critics have approached Tennyson's poetry and judgments they have made about his work. Such a book is possible because so much has been written about Tennyson, and so much scholarly work has been done to provide authentic texts and detailed biographical information. Anyone wishing to understand Tennyson's reputation should first be familiar with the history of the texts used to present his works to twentieth-century readers, the major sources for biographical information, and the important bibliographical studies that precede and complement the present study.

For more than half of the twentieth century, scholars relied on the multivolume edition of Tennyson's poetry, commonly known as the Eversley Edition, published by Macmillan & Co. in 1907–8 under the supervision of the poet's elder son, Hallam. Because Hallam Tennyson had access to his father's notes and private papers, and because his father had reviewed and revised many of these poems before he died, these volumes were considered definitive. Unfortunately, when Tennyson died, he left his papers to Trinity College, Cambridge, establishing a perpetual ban on their publication. Scholars could examine these papers, but could not quote from them; so, for nearly a century, critics were forced to resort to cryptic allusions to variant readings or additional stanzas not included in Hallam Tennyson's edition. Hallam's editorial commentary in the Eversley edition was modest, further exasperating those who might have wanted to do serious study of the poet's creative process.

In 1963, after the revival of interest in Tennyson made it possible for young scholars to devote serious attention to his work, George O. Marshall compiled *A Tennyson Handbook* (1963), providing details about publication history, background, plot, and theme. While this book still serves as a useful guide to understanding individual poems, Marshall's work was supplanted in less than a decade by one of the great achievements of twentieth-century editing, Christopher Ricks's *The Poems of Tennyson* (1969). This volume contains variant readings, extensive textual notes, brief critical commentaries, and sound background on the poet and his times. Ricks was limited in his work by the prohibition the Tennyson family had placed on using the poet's manuscripts deposited at Trinity College, Cambridge. His frustration at having to complete his work without quoting from the manuscripts at Trinity was shared by many who used this first edition. Fortunately, the prohibition was lifted several years later. Diligently, Ricks prepared a second edition, issued in three volumes in 1987. It is unquestionably the finest source of information about the poet's literary career, and the starting point for serious students of Tennyson's work.

The removal of the ban on copying and quoting has had other beneficial effects. Since 1986 Christopher Ricks and Aidan Day have been compiling copies of these papers and other collections in a monumental thirty-volume *Tennyson Archives* (1986–). Additionally, distinguished Tennyson scholars Marion Shaw and Susan Shatto, both associated at one time or another with the Tennyson Research Centre and its publications staff, used the newly available manuscripts at Trinity College to produce a superb variorum edition of *In Memoriam* (1982). The volume contains a detailed commentary on the composition process and extensive notes on textual variants, supplementing the work of earlier scholars who either had to guess at Tennyson's methods or write circumspectly about what they had discovered in the Trinity manuscripts. Shatto produced a variorum edition of *Maud* in 1986, applying the same high standards she and Shaw had demonstrated in their edition of Tennyson's elegy.

In the days prior to computer-assisted search capability, the publication of concordances was often welcomed by scholars needing to identify key words and phrases in a poet's work. Two major concordances of Tennyson's work are available, Daniel B. Brightwell's *A Concordance to the Entire Works of Alfred Tennyson* (1869) and Arthur E. Baker's *A Concordance to the Poetical and Dramatic Works of Alfred, Lord Tennyson* (1914). Unfortunately, the first is incomplete, since it does not index works published during the last quarter-century of the poet's life; the second is more helpful, but it is keyed to the Eversley edition, not the newer and more comprehensive Ricks edition.[1]

Tennyson's letters have been edited ably by two distinguished scholars of the Victorian period, Cecil Y. Lang and Edgar Shannon. Unfortunately, the three volumes of *The Letters of Alfred Lord Tennyson* (1981–90) contain little important information about Tennyson's poetic theory and less about his private life than one might hope to find. There is not much, either, in James Hoge's editions of the *Letters of Emily Lady Tennyson* (1974) or *Lady Tennyson's Journal* (1981) to shed additional light on the poet's life and works that is not at least hinted at in the monumental two-volume *Memoir* produced by the poet's son Hallam Tennyson in 1897. That book contains reminiscences of Tennyson by contemporaries (most are flattering portraits), but a more balanced assessment of the poet by fellow Victorians can be found in John D. Jump's *Tennyson: The Critical Heritage* (1967) and Norman Page's *Tennyson, Interviews and Recollections* (1983). Additional information about the family is available in Sir Charles Tennyson and Hope Dyson's *The Tennysons: Background to Genius* (1974).

Books, articles, and notes about Tennyson's poetry and plays are catalogued regularly in annual publications such as the *MLA Bibliography*, the *Humanities Index* (formerly *Humanities & Social Science Index*) and, to a much more limited extent in the *Readers Guide to Periodicals Index*. Fortunately, the systematic study of Tennyson criticism has been aided by several important bibliographies that point readers to sources not easily identifiable in more generalized, comprehensive bibliographies. Theodore G. Ehrsam, Robert H. Deily, and Robert M. Smith include a chapter on Tennyson in *Bibliographies of Twelve Victorian Authors* (1936), a book of great use to scholars for more than two decades but now superseded by more comprehensive and recent compilations. Similarly, the essays by Paull F. Baum and E. D. H. Johnson in the two editions of *The Victorian Poets: A Guide to Research* published by Harvard University Press (1956, 1968) are enlightening for their scholarly assessment of the poet's reputation, but are limited in their usefulness in identifying sources for further study.

Nearly a half-century of scholarship on Tennyson is catalogued in the five volumes of *Bibliographies of Studies in Victorian Literature,* begun by William Darby Templeman and Samuel Chew and continued by others working with the University of Illinois Press; individual volumes, published at roughly ten-year intervals, list critical work published between 1932 and 1984. Since the 1970s, the editors of *Victorian Poetry* have commissioned respected scholars to compile annotated listings of "the year's work" on Victorian writers. Tennyson has been well served by the efforts of Joseph Sendry and Linda K. Hughes, whose commentary on contemporary scholarship is a valuable resource for scholars wishing to keep up with the flood of publications about Tennyson. The Tennyson Centre in Lincoln subsidized publication of a two-volume catalogue of primary and secondary sources in their collection (Nancie Campbell, *Tennyson in Lincoln: A Catalogue of the Collections in the Research Centre,* 2 vols., 1971). Peter Revel and Sian Allsobrook's *A Catalogue of the Tennyson Collection in the Library of University College, Cardiff* (1972) identifies materials in this major repository outside Cambridge and Lincoln. Many other major research libraries, including Harvard University, have substantial collections of Tennysoniana.

During the twentieth century, a baker's dozen of bibliographies listing critical studies of Tennyson's works were published. The most comprehensive, Kirk Beetz's *Tennyson: A Bibliography, 1827–1982* (1984), contains over four thousand entries. Some scholars have criticized this work for notable omissions and paucity of commentary; fortunately, Arthur Sherbo's "Additions to the Beetz Tennyson Bibliography" (1993) corrects many of the deficiencies by publishing a list of dozens of works not included in Beetz's volume. Despite its shortcomings, Beetz's work remains the single best source for identifying Tennyson scholarship published before 1983. John Dixon Hunt's chapter on Tennyson in A. E. Dyson's *English Poetry: Select Bibliographical Guides* (1971) is more heavily annotated than Beetz's book, and closer to my own study in providing some analysis of critics' biases. Though not organized chronologically, it provides a good idea of how Tennyson was viewed before 1970. Other specialized, selected bibliographies that scholars and students may find useful are Sir Charles Tennyson and Christine Fall's *Alfred Tennyson: An Annotated Bibliography* (1967), Aletha Andrew's *An Annotated Bibliography and Study of the Contemporary Criticism of Tennyson's "Idylls of the King," 1859–1886* (1993), and Marion Shaw's *An Annotated Critical Bibliography of Alfred, Lord Tennyson* (1989).

Tennyson's reputation has been the subject of several articles and monographs, and has occupied the attention of most of his biographers as well. Thomas Lounsbury's *The Life And Times of Tennyson: From 1809 to 1850* (1915) contains detailed discussion on the impact reviewers had on Tennyson's decision to revise early poems, and sometimes caustic commentary on the unfair judgments of some of these critics. Edward T. Cook writes briefly about the subject in "The Second Thoughts of Poets" (1919), finding that Tennyson paid careful attention to criticism, even from those who seemed to take pleasure in savaging his work. Amy Cruse's *Victorians and Their Reading* (1935) takes a slightly different tack, focusing on ways the general public affected the laureate's decisions regarding his choice of subjects and his decision to revise work that did not meet with popular approval. W. D. Paden's "Tennyson and the Reviewers (1829–1835)" (1940) is an excellent analysis of the reception of the 1830 and 1833 volumes. In *The Athenaeum: A Mirror of Victorian Culture* (1941), Leslie Marchand studies in detail the way reviewers in one influential journal treated Tennyson's work, demonstrating how critical opinion shifted in the poet's favor over a half-century. Edgar Shannon's 1943 *PMLA* article and his 1952 monograph *Tennyson and the Reviewers* are the best sources for understanding the poet's reaction to reviews of his work and to learn how, despite his protests to the contrary, Tennyson took seriously criticisms leveled at him. Shannon adeptly challenges assertions of earlier critics and sets the record straight about the true impact of contemporary critics on Tennyson's early work. *Tennyson and the Reviewers* also contains an extensive bibliography that will be of valuable assistance to those wishing to explore this topic.

Focused studies of Tennyson's reputation have appeared from time to time. John Eidson's *Tennyson in America: His Reputation and Influence from 1827 to 1858* (1943) and Marjorie Bowden's *Tennyson in France* (1930) are more detailed than most, and are helpful for those wishing to see how foreigners reacted to the appearance of new works by the poet. Barbara Clark's 1987 Memorial Address to the Tennyson Society, printed as "Tennyson Across the Atlantic" in the *Tennyson Research Bulletin,* expands Eidson's study to include twentieth-century critics and lovers of Tennyson's work. Earlier studies are more limited but nonetheless useful. Hamilton W. Mabie's "The Influence of Tennyson in America" (1892) is useful for those interested in seeing how an American contemporary assessed his countrymen's reaction to Tennyson's work. Charles W. Moulton's compilation of excerpts from various reviews and reminiscences in volume 8 of *The Library of Literary Criticism of English and American Authors* (1905) suggests how widely Tennyson's influence penetrated readers in the United States. Clyde Ryals's "The Poet as Critic: Appraisals of Tennyson by his Contemporaries" (1962) brings together comments from the poet's friends and others whose opinions shaped criticism during the last half of the nineteenth century. Similarly, Isobel Armstrong's *Victorian Scrutinies* (1972) is a collection of reviews by Victorian critics of works by Tennyson and others; it includes key reviews of the 1830, 1833, and 1842 volumes, as well as commentaries on *The Princess* and *In Memoriam*. E. E. Smith's "Tennyson Criticism 1923–1996: From Fragmentation to Tension in Polarity" (1967) and Kerry McSweeney's "The State of Tennyson Criticism" (1974) attempt in a more limited way the approach I apply in this volume. Both offer some judgment on the way scholars have viewed Tennyson and on ways shifts in critical approaches to literature have affected Tennyson's reputation.

Although the principal focus of *Alfred Tennyson: The Critical Legacy* is on documenting critical responses to Tennyson's poetry, this book is also intended to explain something about the premises from which these critics have worked. My approach has been historical and chronological, rather than topical. It would be fair to say that I have produced what Lee Patterson would call "an immanent or intrinsic history" of Tennyson criticism (*Critical Terms for Literary Study*, 250). My analyses of critics' arguments do not stray far from *their* texts to examine larger social, cultural, political or religious ideologies that underlie their work. Had I done so, this would be a very different (and much longer) book. Nevertheless, I have attempted, where appropriate, to offer suggestions regarding the external factors, both literary and cultural, that motivated critics to interpret Tennyson as they did.

Indeed, the vacillations in critical methodology, as well as in the tastes of the period, can tell readers something not only about Tennyson but also about the men and women who have chosen to write about him. I have divided the study into segments that seem to me to reflect major shifts in attitude toward Tennyson, although one might argue that since the 1960s his reputation has remained relatively stable. But the shift in emphasis in critical approaches to literature reflected in the work of poststructuralists has shed new light on the poet, his poems, and the period in which he lived and worked. In keeping with the guidelines of the Literary Criticism in Perspective Series, I have included a list of Tennyson's publications and a "Works Cited" list, both arranged chronologically to assist others who might wish to read for themselves the record of scholarship as it emerged during the past century.

Critics began writing about Tennyson long before the poet died, and the volume of criticism has grown steadily for more than a century. By the time Robert Horton published *Tennyson: A Saintly Life* in 1900, the British Museum had already catalogued fifty-two books on Tennyson (Horton 1). Beetz's bibliography contains approximately forty-five hundred entries, and does not cover the last two decades of the century. Therefore, in writing a book such as *Alfred Tennyson: The Critical Legacy*, I found myself thinking of the advice the philosopher Imlac gives to the young prince in Samuel Johnson's *Rasselas:* like the poet, my function has been "to examine, not the individual, but the species; to remark general properties and large appearances" (Johnson 628). It has not been possible for me to "number the streaks of the tulip" (628): hence, quite a few excellent studies of individual works, or of Tennyson's technical merit, are not mentioned. There is little room for explications of individual poems, unless those reflect something about the larger trends in criticism or are the work of a notable and influential critic. Instead, my hope is that the readers of *Alfred Tennyson: The Critical Legacy* will come away with a sense of how Tennyson has mattered to readers for more than a century, and how readers' and critics' reaction to his poetry reveals something about the shifts in literary criticism during a period of intense, diverse study that has shaped the modern profession of letters.

Notes

[1] A concordance based on the first edition of Ricks's *Poems of Tennyson* was begun in 1980 with the permission of the editor and the publisher, Longman's. The project moved from the U.S. Naval Academy to the University of Western Ontario in 1989, where a machine-readable tape was completed. But the appearance of Ricks's second edition makes that work, too, of limited value.

Richardson, Joanna. *The Pre-eminent Victorian: A Study of Tennyson*. London: Jonathan Cape, 1962.

Ricks, Christopher, ed. *The Poems of Tennyson*. London: Longmans, 1969. *The Poems of Tennyson, I, II, & III; Second ed. Incorporating the Trinity Coll. MSS*. Berkeley: U of California P, 1987.

———. *Tennyson*. New York: Macmillan, 1972.

Ricks, Christopher, and Aidan Day, eds. *The Tennyson Archives*. 30 vols. New York: Garland, 1986–.

Ryals, Clyde de L. "Tennyson: The Poet as Critic." *Tennessee Studies in Literature* 7 (1972): 113–25.

Shannon, Edgar F. *Tennyson and the Reviewers: A Study of His Literary Reputation and of the Influence of the Critics upon His Poetry, 1827–1851*. Cambridge, MA: Harvard UP, 1952.

———. "Tennyson and the Reviewers, 1830–1842." *PMLA* 58 (1943): 181–94.

Shatto, Susan, ed. *Tennyson's "Maud": A Definitive Edition*. Norman: U of Oklahoma P, 1986.

Shatto, Susan, and Marian Shaw, eds. *In Memoriam*. Oxford: Oxford UP, 1982.

Shaw, Marion. *An Annotated Critical Bibliography of Alfred, Lord Tennyson*. London: Harvester Wheatsheaf; New York: St. Martin's Press, 1989.

Sherbo, Arthur. "Additions to the Beetz Tennyson Bibliography." *Notes and Queries* (England) 40 (December 1993): 482–84.

Smith, Elton E. "Tennyson Criticism 1923–1966: From Fragmentation to Tension in Polarity." *Victorian Newsletter* 31 (Spring 1967): 1–4.

Tennyson, Hallam. *Alfred Lord Tennyson: A Memoir*. 2 vols. London: Macmillan, 1897.

———, ed. *The Works of Alfred, Lord Tennyson*. 9 vols. London and New York: Macmillan, 1907–8.

Tennyson, Sir Charles, and Christine Fall. *Alfred Tennyson: An Annotated Bibliography*. Athens: U of Georgia P, 1967.

Tennyson, Sir Charles, Christine Fall, and Hope Dyson. *The Tennysons: Background to Genius*. London: Macmillan, 1974.

tude toward Tennyson, although one might argue that since the 1960s his reputation has remained relatively stable. But the shift in emphasis in critical approaches to literature reflected in the work of poststructuralists has shed new light on the poet, his poems, and the period in which he lived and worked. In keeping with the guidelines of the Literary Criticism in Perspective Series, I have included a list of Tennyson's publications and a "Works Cited" list, both arranged chronologically to assist others who might wish to read for themselves the record of scholarship as it emerged during the past century.

Critics began writing about Tennyson long before the poet died, and the volume of criticism has grown steadily for more than a century. By the time Robert Horton published *Tennyson: A Saintly Life* in 1900, the British Museum had already catalogued fifty-two books on Tennyson (Horton 1). Beetz's bibliography contains approximately forty-five hundred entries, and does not cover the last two decades of the century. Therefore, in writing a book such as *Alfred Tennyson: The Critical Legacy*, I found myself thinking of the advice the philosopher Imlac gives to the young prince in Samuel Johnson's *Rasselas:* like the poet, my function has been "to examine, not the individual, but the species; to remark general properties and large appearances" (Johnson 628). It has not been possible for me to "number the streaks of the tulip" (628): hence, quite a few excellent studies of individual works, or of Tennyson's technical merit, are not mentioned. There is little room for explications of individual poems, unless those reflect something about the larger trends in criticism or are the work of a notable and influential critic. Instead, my hope is that the readers of *Alfred Tennyson: The Critical Legacy* will come away with a sense of how Tennyson has mattered to readers for more than a century, and how readers' and critics' reaction to his poetry reveals something about the shifts in literary criticism during a period of intense, diverse study that has shaped the modern profession of letters.

Notes

[1] A concordance based on the first edition of Ricks's *Poems of Tennyson* was begun in 1980 with the permission of the editor and the publisher, Longman's. The project moved from the U.S. Naval Academy to the University of Western Ontario in 1989, where a machine-readable tape was completed. But the appearance of Ricks's second edition makes that work, too, of limited value.

Works Cited

Andrew, Aletha. *An Annotated Bibliography and Study of the Contemporary Criticism of Tennyson's "Idylls of the King," 1859–1886.* New York: Peter Lang, 1993.

Armstrong, Isobel. *Victorian Scrutinies: Reviews of Poetry 1830–1870.* London: Athlone, 1972.

Baker, Arthur E. *A Concordance to the Poetical and Dramatic Works of Alfred, Lord Tennyson.* London: Kegan Paul, Trench, Trubner, 1914. Reprint, New York: Barnes & Noble, 1966.

Baum, Paull F. "Alfred Lord Tennyson." *The Victorian Poets: A Guide to Research*, ed. Frederick E. Faverty. Cambridge, MA: Harvard UP, 1956.

Beetz, Kirk H. *Tennyson: A Bibliography, 1827–1982.* Metuchen, NJ: Scarecrow Press, 1984.

Bibliographies of Studies in Victorian Literature. 5 vols. Urbana: U of Illinois P, 1945–1985.

Bowden, Marjorie. *Tennyson in France.* Manchester, UK: Manchester UP, 1930.

Brightwell, Daniel B. *A Concordance to the Entire Works of Alfred Tennyson.* London: Moxon, 1869.

Campbell, Nancie, comp. *Tennyson In Lincoln: A Catalogue of the Collections in the Research Centre.* 2 vols. Lincoln, England: Tennyson Society, 1971.

Clark, Barbara R. "Tennyson across the Atlantic." *Tennyson Research Bulletin* 5:1 (November 1987): 1–8.

Cook, E. T. "The Second Thoughts of Poets." *Literary Recreations.* London: Macmillan, 1918. 246–317. Reprint, Freeport, NY: Books for Libraries Press, 1968.

Cruse, Amy. *The Victorians and Their Reading.* London: Allen & Unwin; Boston: Houghton Mifflin, 1935.

Eidson, John O. *Tennyson in America: His Reputation and Influence from 1827 to 1858.* Athens: U of Georgia P, 1943.

Ehrsam, Theodore G., Robert H. Deily, and Robert M. Smith. "Alfred Lord Tennyson." *Bibliographies of Twelve Victorian Authors.* New York: Wilson, 1936. 299–362.

Hoge, James O., ed. *Lady Tennyson's Journal.* Charlottesville: UP of Virginia, 1981.

———, ed. *The Letters of Emily Lady Tennyson.* University Park: Pennsylvania State UP, 1974.

Horton, Robert F. *Alfred Tennyson: A Saintly Life*. London: Dent, 1900. Reprint, New York: Haskell House, 1973.

Hunt, John D. "Tennyson, 1809–1832." In *English Poetry: Select Bibliographical Guides*. Ed. A. E. Dyson. London: Oxford UP, 1971. 265–83.

Johnson, E. D. H. "Alfred, Lord Tennyson." In *The Victorian Poets: A Guide to Research*. Ed. Frederic E. Faverty. Cambridge, MA: Harvard UP, 1968. 33–80.

Johnson, Samuel. "Rasselas." *Samuel Johnson: Rasselas, Selected Poems, and Selected Prose*. Ed. Bertrand Bronson. San Francisco: Rinehart, 1971.

Lang, Cecil Y., and Edgar F. Shannon, Jr., eds. *The Letters of Alfred Lord Tennyson*. 3 vols. Oxford: Clarendon Press; Cambridge, MA: Harvard UP, 1981–1990.

Lounsbury, Thomas R. *The Life and Times of Tennyson: From 1809 to 1850*. London: Oxford UP; New Haven: Yale UP, 1915.

Mabie, Hamilton W. "The Influence of Tennyson in America: Its Sources and Extent." *Review of Reviews* (6 December 1892): 553–56.

Marchand, Leslie A. "Tennyson." *The Athenaeum: A Mirror of Victorian Culture*. Chapel Hill: U of North Carolina P, 1941. Reprint, New York: Octagon, 1971. 267–82.

Marshall, George O. *A Tennyson Handbook*. New York: Twayne Publishers, 1963.

McSweeney, Kerry. "The State of Tennyson Criticism." *Papers on Language and Literature* 10 (1974): 433–46.

Moulton, Charles W., ed. "Alfred, Lord Tennyson." *The Library of Literary Criticism of English and American Authors*. Vol. 8. Buffalo: Moulton, 1904–5. 64–111.

Ormond, Leonée. *Alfred Tennyson: A Literary Life*. New York: St. Martin's, 1993.

Paden, W. D. "Tennyson and the Reviewers (1829–1835)." *Studies in English in Honor of Raphael Dorman O'Leary and Selden Lincoln Whitcomb*. Lawrence: U of Kansas P, 1940. 15–39.

Page, Norman, ed. *Tennyson, Interviews and Recollections*. Totowa, NJ: Barnes & Noble Books, 1983.

Patterson, Lee. "Literary History." In *Critical Terms for Literary Study*. Ed. Frank Lentricchia and Thomas McLaughlin. 2nd ed. Chicago: U of Chicago P, 1995.

Revel, Peter, and Sian Allsobrook. *A Catalogue of the Tennyson Collection in the Library of University College, Cardiff*. Cardiff, Wales: University College, 1972.

Richardson, Joanna. *The Pre-eminent Victorian: A Study of Tennyson*. London: Jonathan Cape, 1962.

Ricks, Christopher, ed. *The Poems of Tennyson*. London: Longmans, 1969. *The Poems of Tennyson, I, II, & III; Second ed. Incorporating the Trinity Coll. MSS.* Berkeley: U of California P, 1987.

———. *Tennyson*. New York: Macmillan, 1972.

Ricks, Christopher, and Aidan Day, eds. *The Tennyson Archives*. 30 vols. New York: Garland, 1986–.

Ryals, Clyde de L. "Tennyson: The Poet as Critic." *Tennessee Studies in Literature* 7 (1972): 113–25.

Shannon, Edgar F. *Tennyson and the Reviewers: A Study of His Literary Reputation and of the Influence of the Critics upon His Poetry, 1827–1851*. Cambridge, MA: Harvard UP, 1952.

———. "Tennyson and the Reviewers, 1830–1842." *PMLA* 58 (1943): 181–94.

Shatto, Susan, ed. *Tennyson's "Maud": A Definitive Edition*. Norman: U of Oklahoma P, 1986.

Shatto, Susan, and Marian Shaw, eds. *In Memoriam*. Oxford: Oxford UP, 1982.

Shaw, Marion. *An Annotated Critical Bibliography of Alfred, Lord Tennyson*. London: Harvester Wheatsheaf; New York: St. Martin's Press, 1989.

Sherbo, Arthur. "Additions to the Beetz Tennyson Bibliography." *Notes and Queries* (England) 40 (December 1993): 482–84.

Smith, Elton E. "Tennyson Criticism 1923–1966: From Fragmentation to Tension in Polarity." *Victorian Newsletter* 31 (Spring 1967): 1–4.

Tennyson, Hallam. *Alfred Lord Tennyson: A Memoir*. 2 vols. London: Macmillan, 1897.

———, ed. *The Works of Alfred, Lord Tennyson*. 9 vols. London and New York: Macmillan, 1907–8.

Tennyson, Sir Charles, and Christine Fall. *Alfred Tennyson: An Annotated Bibliography*. Athens: U of Georgia P, 1967.

Tennyson, Sir Charles, Christine Fall, and Hope Dyson. *The Tennysons: Background to Genius*. London: Macmillan, 1974.

1: Tennyson Among His Contemporaries: 1827–1892

TO APPRECIATE THE VICISSITUDES OF Tennyson criticism in the twentieth century, it is necessary to understand how his reputation first developed among his contemporaries in the nineteenth. Of course, any assessment of the early critical reception of Tennyson's poems must be undertaken with a certain degree of wariness. Tennyson often encouraged his friends to write reviews of his work, so his first readers would have been encouraged to buy his books by someone who had a vested interest in seeing Tennyson's career advanced. The most famous, and in some ways most biased, was written by the poet's bosom friend and fellow Cambridge Apostle Arthur Henry Hallam. His essay on Tennyson's 1830 volume, *Poems, Chiefly Lyrical* in the *Englishman's Magazine* (1831), bore the pretentious title "On the Genius of Alfred Tennyson."[1] Another close friend, James Spedding, provided a similar encomium of the 1842 *Poems* in the *Edinburgh Review*. He praises Tennyson for his "sound view of human life and the condition of man in the world," for his "healthy, manly, and simple" moral views (Jump 146), and for his exceptional ability at versification. His only reservation: these poems cannot be accepted "as a satisfactory account of the gifts which they show" Tennyson possesses (151). Carefully avoiding any mention that Tennyson is also his good friend, Spedding argues that the poet can, and will, do even more spectacular work in the future. Suffice it to say that one needs to be cautious of such special pleading.

Nevertheless, many of the poet's earliest critics were men from a generation raised to appreciate the work of Dryden, Pope, Gray, and their neoclassical contemporaries. These critics had given only grudging acceptance to Wordsworth and Coleridge, considerably less credit to Shelley and Keats. Byron had won their admiration, and Scott had given them a new standard for contemporary poetry in his ballads and chivalric narratives. It is little wonder that the first volumes of a young poet with a penchant for introspection and unusual metrics were met with patronizing skepticism.

Among these first critics, only W. J. Fox had excessive praise for the 1830 volume. Whether Thomas Lounsbury is right to call Fox a "crazy panegyrist" (211) may be debatable, but there is no denying his enthusiasm for the new poet. After a lengthy introduction in which he expresses his belief that poetry is but one of many vehicles for universal human improvement, Fox informs readers that many of Tennyson's works offer excellent character studies. A man of his times, Fox chides the young poet for his propensity to use irregular meter and his occasional inclusion of words that "young ladies of the present day" might not "be accustomed to read or sing in the parlour." Though the "very originality" of these poems might "prevent their being generally appreciated for a time," Fox is convinced that Tennyson might mend his idiosyncratic ways and begin to write poetry that would serve a better public service. Speaking as one who measured the temper of the times, Fox observes that "a genuine poet has deep responsibilities for his country and the world, to the present and future generations, to earth and heaven"; he must, therefore "consecrate himself to their promotion" (Jump 32–33).

By contrast, John Wilson, the infamous "Christopher North," attacked Tennyson's 1830 volume with gusto. The subjects are often silly, he says, the versification rough, the poet's knowledge of the world and human nature incomplete. The worst offense, however, is that he seems to have become the darling of the Cockney School, a group including William Hazlitt, Leigh Hunt, Keats, and Shelley, which had drawn ridicule from *Blackwood's* reviewers in the past. Their own writing flaunted accepted — that is, neoclassic — poetic norms, especially with regard to rhyme and meter. That men like Hunt would find Tennyson a poet of promise immediately made him anathema to critics such as Wilson. Worse still, Wilson goes on to say, Tennyson has been over praised by contemporaries who are either too blind to his faults or too ignorant themselves to offer seasoned criticism. Not content simply to excoriate Tennyson's work, Wilson savages the reviewers who have been so wrongheaded in celebrating the new poet. He even attributes the demise of the *Englishman's Magazine* to its publication of Hallam's 1831 review, which raised such a "general guffaw" that the journal "expired in convulsions" (Jump 51).

Unfortunately, Tennyson did not have the good sense to refrain from retaliating publicly against Wilson. He dashed off a nine-line satire, "To Christopher North," which he included in his next volume of poems. This puerile response to a respected critic did little to enamor Tennyson with the sages of the day. There is little wonder, then, that the 1833 volume evoked vitriolic response from established reviewers.

Another critic writing for the *Quarterly Review,* John Wilson Croker, typifies this reaction. His disparaging critique of Tennyson's *Poems* (1833) bears overtones of his damaging review of Keats's work in 1818; in fact, Croker goes out of his way to make the comparison explicit, ironically calling Tennyson "another and a brighter star of that galaxy or *milky way* of poetry of which the lamented Keats was the harbinger" (Jump 66; Croker's italics). In prose dripping with irony, Croker appears to praise while damning the young poet for his excesses. Near the end of the review, he takes pains to castigate Tennyson for the satire on Christopher North, using it as the springboard to attack him for his inability to accept what Croker considers honest criticism intended simply to help him improve in his craft. The viciousness of his remark prompted Tennyson's most distinguished modern editor, Christopher Ricks, to describe Croker's review as "venomous" (Ricks 1969, xxx).

Whether Croker, Wilson, and other early reviewers were aiming principally at Tennyson or the associates who held him in high esteem may be debated. Twentieth-century scholar Edgar Shannon believes that "nothing more than the association of Tennyson with radicalism and the Cockney poets was needed to incite Croker" to write severely. In the view of many early reviewers, Shannon says, Tennyson was part of the radical crowd that was thought to be headquartered at Cambridge (*Tennyson,* 25, 22).

In 1835, Tennyson found a champion against Croker. The young John Stuart Mill, writing in an early issue of the *London Review* (July 1835), accuses the *Quarterly Review* of practicing needless antagonism toward new voices. Meeting the work of emerging writers "with a curl of the lip," the critic for the *Quarterly* gains pleasure not from the work being reviewed, but from "his own cleverness in making it contemptible" (Jump 85). Having put Croker in his place, Mill enumerates the good qualities he finds in Tennyson's poems, claiming they display beyond question that Tennyson has a "poetic temperament"; the volumes of 1830 and 1833 show that he is mastering his craft (92). He is not without faults, Mill says, but his natural gift for versification indicates that, if he works diligently, these can be turned to strengths and future poems may indeed be great.

American readers were less critical. Largely due to the influence of Ralph Waldo Emerson and James Russell Lowell, a coterie at Harvard and throughout the Boston area read Tennyson's works enthusiastically. By 1840, he was being linked with Spenser as "the greatest of poets" (Eidson 9). The early volumes were reviewed favorably in several journals, including the *Western Messenger* in Louisville, Kentucky. The admiring commentary written by Margaret Fuller for the *Dial* in 1841 indicates the high favor in which Tennyson was held by his American cousins.[2]

Reviewers in France also took notice of Tennyson's 1830 and 1833 volumes, and while most simply acknowledged him as one of the emerging new voices, several wrote longer analyses. The writers for *L'Europe Littéraire* (1834) and the influential *Revue des Deux Mondes* (1833) cited his originality and predicted great things for this new poetic voice from England. However, a later critique in the *Revue* by E. D. Forgues (*Revue,* 1847), while more detailed, is less laudatory. Forgues acknowledges Tennyson's mastery of style and technique, but believes his thought is "hazy" and his philosophy "null." He is unlikely, Forgues says, to have lasting influence in France (Bowden 17).[3]

Many twentieth-century critics have pointed out Tennyson's sensitivity to adverse criticism, and there is certainly evidence that the sting of Croker's bite was not fully soothed by the balm of Mill's more balanced assessment. At the same time, Tennyson suffered a series of personal setbacks. In 1831, his father died. In 1833, Arthur Henry Hallam died. In 1836, Rosa Baring rejected Alfred's suit (and perhaps a marriage proposal as well). In 1837, the Tennyson family was forced to move from Somersby Rectory to Epping Forest. Whether negative criticism or the series of personal tragedies that brought significant change to his life affected him more may be open to question; what is certain is that Tennyson waited a decade to publish another volume of poetry. In 1842, he brought out two volumes. The first contained selections of earlier works, many revised; the second consisted of previously unpublished poems. This time, the reviewers reacted more kindly.

John Sterling, like Tennyson an Apostle at Cambridge, wrote a balanced review that appeared in what might seem a most unlikely place: the *Quarterly Review* (September 1842), which had published Croker's hostile attack a decade earlier. After a lengthy introduction in which he bemoans the absence of any great poets in his own time — the influence of his mentor Thomas Carlyle is most evident at this point — Sterling praises Tennyson for producing verse that is fit to its station and worthy of readers' attention. He is especially enthusiastic about the English idylls, which he calls "a real addition to our literature" (Jump 122). Leigh Hunt, still active in literary circles long after his early friends Keats and Shelley had died, seconds Sterling in praising Tennyson's work (*Church of England Quarterly Review*, October 1842), calling him "a kind of philosophical Keats" (Jump 136). Having expressed confidence in Tennyson's poetic powers more than a decade earlier (*Tatler*, February 1831), he encourages Tennyson to outgrow his boyish desire for unqualified praise (128). Hunt's balanced critique indicates that the tide was turning in the poet's favor. R. H. Horne acknowledges this explicitly in *A New Spirit of the Age* (1844) when he awards Tennyson "the title of a true poet of the highest class of genius" (153). Horne is among the earliest to notice a characteristic that later critics, including T. S. Eliot, would highlight in describing Tennyson's limitations: while he can be "intensely tragic" and display "great power of concentration," he "is not at all dramatic" (Jump 160). Horne is perceptive, too, in recognizing that, although little acknowledged in earlier reviews, "Ulysses" is "one of the most exquisite . . . poems in the language" (Jump 163).

Fox, Mill, Hunt, Sterling, and certainly Hallam and Spedding all express their belief that Tennyson's early efforts would not be his best. They predicted that, once he turned to loftier subjects, he would produce works that would rank with the greatest in the language.[4] In fact, many of these reviewers challenged the poet to become more of a teacher and less a melancholy lyricist. John Forster, writing in the *Examiner* in 1842, expresses these thoughts succinctly: "we think that he would find himself able to fly a higher flight than lyric, idyl, or eclogue, and we counsel him to try it" (Shannon, *Tennyson*, 62).

Unfortunately, the first of Tennyson's long poems did not produce the reaction his champions had predicted. *The Princess* (1847, 1850), a medley told by several contemporary young men and women about a medieval prince's conquest of a proto-feminist princess, met with what can best be described as mixed reviews. While some early commentaries were decidedly favorable (cf. Shannon, *Tennyson*, 98–100), strong criticisms by writers in influential periodicals such as the *Spectator*, *Athenaeum*, and *Atlas* gave the public a negative impression of the poem. Dramatist J. W. Marston sums up critical opinion quite succinctly in the opening sentence of his *Athenaeum* review in 1848: "There is so much to admire in this volume that we cannot wish it unwritten," he says, but "so much also to censure that, while we could recognize the whole if tendered as a pledge of genius, we cannot accept it as a due consummation of that faculty" (Jump 166).

On the other side of the ocean, however, the young poet was faring much better. Edgar Allan Poe, long a champion of Tennyson, delivered a lecture in 1848 that was subsequently printed in *Home Journal* and *Sartain's Union Magazine* in 1850. In what is certainly Poe's most influential critical statement, "The Poetic Principle," the American poet offered his British counterpart the highest praise to date: "I call him, and *think* him the noblest of poets — *not* because the impressions he produces are at *all* times, the most profound — *not* because the poetical excitement which he induces is at all times the most intense — but because it *is,* at all times, the most ethereal — in other words, the most elevating and most pure. No poet is so little of the earth" (Eidson 61). As Gerhard Joseph demonstrates in "Poe and Tennyson" (1973), the admiration was mutual.

Though *The Princess* may not have been the blockbuster Tennyson had hoped it would be, he did not have to wait long to come into his own as the undisputed major poet of his age. During the "ten years' silence" from 1833–1842, and all the while he was working on *The Princess,* Tennyson was also writing and revising dozens of short lyrics inspired by the death of his friend Arthur Henry Hallam. The poet claimed that many of the poems in the 1842 volumes were inspired by his thoughts of Hallam; "Ulysses," for example, "was written soon after Arthur Hallam's death, and gave my feeling about the need for going forward and braving the struggle of life" (Hallam Tennyson 1:196). For nearly two decades Tennyson collected these lyrics, working them over and trying to decide how he might use them. The result was the publication, in 1850, of *In Memoriam, A. H. H.,* one of the great English elegies.[5]

The poem appeared anonymously, and some reviewers immediately began speculating about its authorship. One went so far as to surmise that it was written by a widow as a tribute to her late husband. Not all were in the dark, however. Novelist Charles Kingsley, writing in *Fraser's Magazine* (September 1850), expressed what many thought: "All the world, somehow, knows the author" (Jump 173). Reaction to the poem was almost universally favorable. Writing in the *Leader,* philosopher and editor George Henry Lewes called the poem superior to Milton's *Lycidas,* and predicted it would become "the solace and delight of every house where poetry is loved" (Shannon, *Tennyson,* 142). The reviewer for the *Guardian* thought that "judged even by the standard of Shakespeare and Spenser, Mr. Tennyson will not be found wanting" (142–43). Its appeal to the idealism and faith Victorians sought in literature was a special strength, according to J. W. Marston of the *Athenaeum,* who claimed that "in its moral scope the book will endear itself to all who suffer" (143).

Kingsley's review is especially noteworthy because it represents a new turn in Tennyson criticism: the age of unqualified, perhaps even hyperbolic, praise for anything the poet published. *In Memoriam,* he states without hesitation, is "the noblest Christian poem which England has produced for two centuries" (Jump 173). Kingsley looks back at Tennyson's earlier work to demonstrate how the seeds of this great elegy were planted in the lyrics and narrative poems of the 1830, 1833, and 1842 volumes. "This latest and highest volume," he remarks, brings together "all the poet's peculiar excellencies . . . fused down in a perfect unity to bear on his subject with that care and finish which only a labour of love can inspire" (182). For his readers Kingsley provides lengthy quotations — without comment. Like so many Victorians who stood in awe of Tennyson's masterpiece, Kingsley felt it would be "an injustice to the poet to think they needed any" (184).

In similar fashion, Coventry Patmore, reviewing the book in *Palladium,* declared it "the best religious poetry that has ever been written in our language," in large part because "secular knowledge is humbled before loving faith" (Shannon, *Tennyson,* 145, 149). The French critic Joseph Milsand shared these sentiments, concluding his article in the *Revue Britannique* (1850) with the observation that "One could make this book one's Bible" (Bowden 19).

It would be disingenuous, however, to suggest that there were no negative reactions. Perversely, American critics, who had been high on Tennyson's earlier work, were critical of *In Memoriam.* Some, like the reviewer for *Brownson's Quarterly Review,* thought it "feeble, diffuse, and tiresome," and the critic writing for the *Southern Literary Messenger* considered it "monotonous," and lacking in "varying rhythm" (Eidson 78–79). Some who had embraced the 1842 volumes found *In Memoriam* tedious, overdone, and too long.

Nevertheless, the poem touched the Victorian reading public like nothing else published before it. As his son Hallam observed a half-century later, "members of the scientific community "cheered him with words of genuine admiration for his love of nature" and for "the eagerness with which he welcomed all the latest scientific discourses" (Hallam Tennyson 1:299). William Gladstone, who had known Hallam at Eton before the latter had met Tennyson at Cambridge, said *In Memoriam* was "perhaps the richest oblation ever offered by the affection of friendship at the tomb of the departed" (Hallam Tennyson 1:299). In retrospect, the most important reader turned out to be Prince Albert. He found the poem comforting and illuminating. Certainly that had great influence when, in 1850, the Royal Family received news of the death of the poet laureate, William Wordsworth. Although the Queen was advised to consider some other, more established poets to succeed him, Albert set to work helping to direct the Queen's favor in another direction. In October 1850 she authorized her ministers to write to Tennyson and offer the laureateship to him (Charles Tennyson 254).

If Tennyson thought that the favor of the Queen would assure him popular success in any endeavor, he was soon proven wrong. While some of his occasional work met with acclaim — his 1852 "Ode on the Death of the Duke of Wellington" was considered by many a fine tribute to Britain's savior during the Napoleonic Wars — he was soon to find that the Victorian reading public was not ready for a long, experimental poem, no matter how he tried to give it a patriotic twist. *Maud* (1854) had many more detractors than supporters. Among the most vicious and most oft-cited detractors was the poet W. E. Aytoun, whose review in *Blackwood's* in 1855 castigates Tennyson for a litany of faults that extend back to his early career, and laments the "chirping of numerous indiscreet admirers who are incapable of distinguishing one note from another" (quoted in Mordell 141). "We could never join in the admiration which we have heard expressed for *In Memoriam*," he says; it is "simply a dirge . . . conveying no impression of reality or truthfulness to the mind." Certainly poets are given "voices" for "something better than to keep wheezing all day long like a chorus of consumptive sextons" (141–42). Rising from his "perusal" of *Maud* "dispirited and sorrowful" (143), Aytoun proceeds to catalogue the poem's weaknesses: it is ill-conceived, poorly organized, needlessly vague, and hopelessly patriotic at its conclusion. Dubbing the hero "Misanthropos," Aytoun criticizes Tennyson for weak characterization and an unmanly attachment to sentimentality. The simple verses that may be understood by the common reader are "nothing but namby-pamby" (157). The passages in which the speaker raves madly are simply gibberish. Aytoun concludes with an apology for having to present such an unfavorable review, but, he observes, "we have performed our duty" (161) in alerting readers less sophisticated than he to the many foibles of a poetaster passing off as great art a poem "ill considered, crude, tawdry, and objectionable" (160). The venom seems to drip from his pen as he concludes what he professes to be an impartial judgment.

Nevertheless, a sympathetic critic, George Brimley (*Cambridge Essays,* 1855), performed the role taken by John Stuart Mill in 1835. The "loudest professional critics" may find delight in tracing the "gradual degradation" of Tennyson's talent, Brimley says, but the public will have nothing of that attitude (Jump 191–92). Brimley finds *Maud* excellent in both theme and execution. To call for a happy ending is to miss the point; the poem is "a tragedy," and a first-rate one (196).

Ironically, it was in a favorable criticism of *Maud* that a science writer made a significant advancement in Tennyson criticism. R. J. Mann, a fan of the poem, took time to produce what may be considered the first monograph about Tennyson's poetry. *Maud Vindicated* (1856) is an "earnest appeal" (Jump 198) to the general readership for the merits of the poem. Knowing that the "guild of critics" that are forever hobbled by the "trammels of contradictory casuistry and shallow pretence" (197–98) will never approve of the poem, Mann offers a detailed critique of *Maud*'s dramatic structure and analyzes with sympathy the poem's main character. His attention to detail should make proponents of New Criticism take note; what these scholars purport to have invented, Mann was practicing with uncommon skill nearly fifty years before "close reading" became *de rigueur* among academics.

Despite the negative criticism directed at *Maud*, there was no question that by the end of the 1850s Tennyson had achieved a level of popularity shared by few poets before or after him. Only the Brownings seemed to rival him, and for many readers Robert Browning, at least, was an acquired taste. When in 1859 the poet laureate brought out a new volume, *Idylls of the King,* many Victorians thought they were witnessing the emergence of a modern Milton; perhaps the members of the Union Club who debated the merits of the two poets more than twenty years earlier had not been far from right. *Idylls of the King* had the marks of an epic, even though Tennyson had produced only four stories, adapted from medieval stories of King Arthur but given a decidedly Victorian moral slant. The majority view was decidedly positive. The novelist Charles Dickens wrote fulsomely to a friend: "Lord! What a blessed thing it is to read a man who can really write; I thought nothing could be finer than the first poem till I came to the third; but when I had read the last, it seemed to me to be absolutely unapproachable" (quoted in Waugh 67).

Tennyson was particularly pleased with the review written by Gladstone. The politician who was to be helpful to Tennyson in later years frequently wrote on literary topics; his *Quarterly Review* essay (October 1859) on the *Idylls* is actually a retrospective on Tennyson's career to date. As Kingsley does in reviewing *In Memoriam,* Gladstone mines earlier works to discover the sources for poetic expression and morality that would make the *Idylls* at once a "national" and a "Christian" epic, both "highly national" and "universal," resting "upon those depths and breadths of our nature to which all its truly great developments in all nations are alike essentially and closely related" (Jump 250). Gladstone is a typical Victorian reviewer. He balances comments on technical matters (applauding Tennyson's skillful use of repetition, for example), including long quotations so readers could get a sense of the work unencumbered by commentary, and reserving the highest praise for passages that promote accepted moral standards.

Representative of the impact of the *Idylls* on sympathetic readers are the comments of Walter Bagehot, who was emerging as an influential voice among Victorian critics. Bagehot was an editor at *The National Review* beginning in 1855, and edited *The Economist* from 1860 until his death in 1877. His 1859 review of Tennyson's Arthurian poem gives insight into the growing general assessment of the poet's place not only in his own age, but also in the canon of English poets. Bagehot acknowledges that, for the first two decades, people who admired Tennyson were often referred to disparagingly as "Tennysonians." That term was no longer in use by 1859. Instead, Victorian readers had come to believe that Tennyson knew how to pick his subject, and how to present it in an interesting way. Citing examples from the *Idylls*, Bagehot demonstrates how medieval characters are appropriately transformed into mouthpieces for modern concerns. Avoiding the excesses and the questionable morality of his sources, Tennyson manages to raise the Arthurian story to a fable of modern life and a treatise on modern values — two qualities most admired by Bagehot and his contemporaries.

Most notably, at the end of the review Bagehot shifts his focus from a discussion of the poem to a discussion of "Mr. Tennyson's position in the hierarchy of our poets" (Jump 238). Through careful comparison, he manages to place Tennyson just below Shelley, ahead of Wordsworth, Coleridge, and Keats, but still below those pole stars of English letters, Shakespeare and Milton. The coming decades would prove that even this rather grandiose judgment would be less flattering than that afforded to Tennyson by Victorians who sought from his poetry not only literary pleasure but moral counsel and spiritual comfort. Five years later, however, Bagehot wrote a *National Review* article, "Wordsworth, Tennyson, and Browning: or, Pure, Ornate, and Grotesque Art in English Poetry." In this review of *Enoch Arden* and Browning's *Dramatis Personae,* he uses the title poem to show how "ornate" art is created by elevating simple subjects to grand importance through language that subtly overdignifies both character and action.

Other important Victorians, however, were not as pleased with the *Idylls* as Gladstone and Bagehot. Thomas Carlyle observed that "we read" the *Idylls* "with considerable impatience at being treated so very like infants, though the lollipops were so superlative" (Ricks 273). Elizabeth Barrett Browning thought "the work, as a whole, produced a feeling of disappointment" (268). Gerard Manley Hopkins begrudgingly admitted that *In Mem-*

oriam was a great poem, but he thought *Idylls* should be called "Charades from the Middle Ages" (Jump 334). In 1872 Lafcadio Hearn, then a young reporter and critic, wrote admiringly of the *Idylls* in a review for the Cincinnati *Enquirer* but had little good to say about "Gareth and Lynette," which he found "thinner and weaker, and more fantastic, and has less point or design, and fewer good features" than any of the other idylls written to that date (1:23).

At this point in his career, Tennyson also found qualified support among the French. Three important critics writing in the middle decades of the century saw in his poetry a genuine mastery of poetic technique coupled with a perceptive critique of the human condition. In the 1860s Hippolyte Taine expressed qualified admiration, citing the felicities of works such as "Locksley Hall," *Idylls of the King,* and *Maud,* but dismissing *In Memoriam* as "stiff, dull, and too skillfully arranged," a poem in which the mourner wears his grief "like a well-bred gentleman" (Bowden 28). Although Taine's ultimate judgment is that Tennyson is something of a dilettante, his purity of style and moral grandeur are important contributions to poetry (29). Writing at the same time, Émile Montegut offered balanced critiques, especially of Tennyson's later work, as did Edmund Sherer, whose otherwise favorable judgment (except for *Maud*) is tempered with an admonition made by critics both before and after him: "There is a heat of passion, a tumult of the mind, a ruin of life's ideals, that Tennyson's verse is powerless to express. His poetry, whether deliberately or by reason of his inspiration I know not, keeps itself too strictly within the realm of what is seemly and conventional" (Bowden 41). The symbolists of the 1880s and 1890s, however, were fulsome in their praise. Charles Baudelaire, Paul Verlaine, and Stéphane Mallarmé acknowledged Tennyson's influence, citing *Idylls of the King* as a source of inspiration for much of their work (Bowden 119 and *passim*). French critics writing in the decades between the poet's death in 1892 and the centenary of his birth in 1909 spared him the harsh attacks that were to characterize English criticism during the same period (145–48).

Among his own generation, and among many in the succeeding one, Tennyson rose in stature with every work he published. From the mid-1850s until the last quarter of the century, detractors were few, and negative comments generally limited to commentary on individual works. What was written, however, is worth noting, because the seeds for what has come to be known as "The Reaction Against Tennyson" were being sown while the laureate was at the height of his popularity. The first notable attack was made by Alfred Austin in an 1869 essay in the *Temple Bar*. Austin begins by acknowledging that it had become commonplace to consider Tennyson the poet of the age. The problem, he observes, is that "the conventional sense of the majority so overpowers the critical sense of the discriminating minority" that it is almost impossible to challenge this opinion (Jump 294). Nevertheless, Austin does so in a lengthy diatribe, launching his negative assessment with the bald statement that "Mr. Tennyson is not a great poet" (295). He is not even a poet of the second rank, Austin says, but decidedly minor in technical competence and guilty of the most grievous fault in a poet who ascribes to greatness: timidity. With irony bordering on disdain, Austin proceeds to analyze selected lyrics and some of the major narrative poems, including *Idylls of the King,* citing Tennyson's penchant for perfecting scenes and sentimentalizing at the expense of dealing honestly with subjects important to his readers.

Austin concludes his assessment by comparing Tennyson unfavorably with two English writers whom he considers among the first rank, Wordsworth and Shakespeare. Unlike either of them, Tennyson "never soars" (Jump 308). His unpoetic nature makes him poor company for either. The problem lies not simply with Tennyson, however; Austin disparages his Victorian contemporaries for elevating a poet such as Tennyson for qualities that Shakespeare would have disdained. Undoubtedly, Austin speculates, if Shakespeare had lived in Victorian England, he would not be accorded the status of greatness, because Victorians would not recognize his strengths. Conversely, had Tennyson lived during the Renaissance, he would certainly have been no more than "the author of some courtly masques" (309). Setting himself above the common reader, Austin asserts that the discriminating critic "is not bound by the average tastes of his time" (310), and can therefore pronounce adverse judgment on figures who are no more than poetasters. His final appeal is posed as a sarcastic question, to which he provides a quick answer: "Can anybody in his senses imagine posterity speaking of our age as the age of Tennyson? Posterity will be too kind to do anything so sardonic . . . the age of Tennyson! The notion is, of course, preposterous" (310). To accord Tennyson the mantle of greatness simply assures the Victorians that they will be "scoffed at in less partial times as a parcel of indiscriminating dunces" (311). Austin was the first of a group that would come to be known as "Reactionaries," critics who argued that Tennyson did not deserve the accolades of great poet, teacher, and sage that many Victorians had bestowed on him. Over the next century, many would follow Austin's lead, but none would be more strident.[6]

Some were quick to follow suit, and their criticisms stung Tennyson personally, such as the one by J. H. Friswell in his 1870 volume *Modern Writers Honestly Criticized.* Friswell attacked not only his poetry but Tennyson's character (Charles Tennyson 390). Taking a tack similar to Austin's in denigrating works that others considered among Tennyson's greatest achievements, A. C. Swinburne singles out *Idylls of the King* for special opprobrium. His insightful volume *Under the Microscope* (1872) contains brief comments that reveal his distaste for the laureate's overt moralism. Calling the poem the "Morte d'Albert," Swinburne asserts that Tennyson "lowered and deformed the outline of the Arthurian story" (Jump 318–19). Swinburne's criticism of Tennyson was not all one-sided, however. Although he continues his attack on the *Idylls* in "Tennyson and Musset" in 1886, he lavishes praise on "Rizpah," a shorter narrative in which Tennyson blends the elements of poetry masterfully. Whether modern critics would agree completely with Swinburne is open to question; in the twentieth century, *Idylls of the King* has enjoyed a critical resurgence, while "Rizpah" has remained a much-appreciated minor work.

The attacks by Austin and Swinburne met with quick response from Tennyson's friends and supporters. One principal champion during the later years of his life was James T. Knowles. He became friends with Tennyson in 1866, and spent the next four decades raising a strident voice against the younger generation of detractors. In 1870, Knowles wrote a lengthy letter to the editor of the *Spectator* to supplement that paper's 1869 review of the expanded version of *Idylls of the King*, which included four new Arthurian tales. He also wrote an article in the 1873 *Contemporary Review* responding to charges leveled at Tennyson by Swinburne in *Under the Microscope*. Knowles argues that the *Idylls* is a symbolic tale in which Arthur stands for "'the King within us' — our highest nature . . . conscience; spirit; the moral soul; the religious sense; the noble resolve." Tennyson's Arthurian epic is the story of "the perpetual warfare between the spirit and the flesh" (Jump 313). Knowles continued to support Tennyson by using the publication he founded in 1877, *The Nineteenth Century*, as a platform for promoting the poet and his works.

The adulation Knowles expresses was certainly the majority view throughout the 1870s until the poet's death. Each year there seemed to emerge some greater effusion of praise, until Tennyson achieved the dual status of sage and saint. Writing with the advantage of hindsight in 1923, Sir Harold Nicolson explains the reaction against Tennyson that crystallized in the decades following his death as an attempt by moderns to demythologize "the Victorian idols," of which Tennyson was most representative. "For over fifty years his votaries prostrated themselves before the shrine they had built for him" (Nicolson 5).

Foremost among the idolaters Nicolson had in mind is historian and literary critic Peter Bayne. In *Lessons from My Masters* (1879), Bayne adds new material to articles on Tennyson published during the 1850s and 1860s, revising his judgments when necessary to demonstrate Tennyson's greatness not only as a poet but as a teacher of "principal truths" about life (5). In almost reverential tones, Bayne describes the "quality of charm" (204) that characterizes Tennyson's best work. Comparing him to Keats and Scott, he sees Tennyson as a leader in the "triumphant reaction against the spirit and influence of Byron" (223) — an influence Victorians found deleterious. Bayne celebrates Tennyson for promoting "responsibility to God," "constancy in the marriage relationship," "mutual affection" rather than "worldly advantage" as motive for marriage, and "love of mankind, love of country, enthusiasm for knowledge, faith in freedom, hope of immortality." In his meandering and eclectic critique Bayne is interested principally in explaining why the "Poet of the People" (273) appealed to contemporaries. "Take him for all in all," Bayne concludes, "Tennyson must, I think, be pronounced the greatest poet of his time" (364).

With such sentiments running high, it is no wonder that the publishing house of Chatto & Windus would bring out a full-length biography of the poet in 1884. Written by Henry J. Jennings, author of biographies of contemporary figures, *Lord Tennyson: A Biographical Sketch,* is typical of the genre in Victorian England. Focusing more on reminiscences by Tennyson's friends — the enlarged edition of 1892, published shortly after Tennyson's death, is even more generous in offering such personal recollections — Jennings is high on praise and only grudgingly willing to acknowledge criticism. Some of Jennings's mistakes can be attributed to his lack of information — Tennyson worked hard to keep his private life private. Nevertheless, it seems willfully deceptive to call his boyhood under the mentally unstable and stern father who tyrannized the family at Somersby a time when "the refining quality" of good taste and culture shed "warm and mellowing rays over that tranquil Somersby home" (5).

Though half a century had passed since these early criticisms had appeared, Jennings seems compelled to attack John Wilson for publishing such "very vulgar stuff" in 1830 (30), and John Wilson Croker for having the audacity to print his "insulting review" in 1833 (38). Jennings comes close to deifying Tennyson on more than one occasion. He praises the 1842 volume for its "exquisite portraiture of women" (52). He says *In Memoriam* "gives to the language of Faith an utterance as noble and as elevating" as one by any clergy (75). He dismisses the "savage" criticism of *Maud* as wrongheaded (93–95). Like many of his Victorian contemporaries, he believes that in *Idylls of the King* Tennyson has transformed the "rude and uncultured manners" and "barbarous morals" of medieval Arthurian tales by giving them a "halo of romantic grace" (104–5). He exalts Tennyson as "preeminently a master of narrative" (138) — a claim hotly disputed by some Victorians and many in succeeding generations. He is careful, too, to note that Tennyson and his wife "kept their union free from those deplorable discords which too often cast a shadow over the marriages of literary men" (72–73). If one wishes to read only one brief book that captures virtually every aspect of High Victorianism, Jennings's biography of Tennyson would serve as a sound model.

Another strong but more balanced supporter of Tennyson, the theologian and critic R. H. Hutton, published a lengthy, favorable essay on the poet in his *Literary Essays* (1888). Hutton provides a strong defense of the

Idylls, despite what he calls some significant defects, unequivocally acknowledges *In Memoriam* as the laureate's greatest poem, and offers shrewd observations on some of the shorter poems. His assessment that "Tithonus" and "Ulysses" are among Tennyson's superior productions, and "Lucretius" a better poem than the more popular "Enoch Arden," have been supported by critics for more than a century. Hutton's greatest contribution to the history of Tennyson's criticism, however, is his clear description of Victorian values that led contemporary readers to adopt Tennyson as the literary spokesperson of their age. Directly attacking Swinburne's claim that the artist has no obligation to be moral, Hutton celebrates Tennyson's ability to promote right thinking and correct behavior without compromising his art.

F. W. H. Myers carries this theme even farther in his essay "Tennyson as Prophet" (1889). Acknowledging that Tennyson's exceptional craftsmanship has obscured his prophetic message, Myers demonstrates ways Christian readers can have their faith strengthened by carefully reading the laureate's work. Tennyson and Browning are the "veritable fountain-heads of the spiritual energy of our time" (Jump 412). More than any other poet, Tennyson is the prophet of "a Spiritual Universe," the "proclaimer of man's spirit as part and parcel of that Universe, and indestructible as the very root of things" (411).

While he was being celebrated for his accomplishments as a lyricist, narrative poet, and spiritual guide, Tennyson was turning his attention to the genre that had intrigued him since his teenage years: the drama. Beginning in the 1870s, perhaps because he was secure in his fame in other forms of poetry, he took up writing plays. As a later biographer notes, "As the foremost poet of [his] day he was inevitably compared to Shakespeare, and it was natural for him to begin equating the talents of the greatest Elizabethan dramatist with his own and to consider the possibility of his being Shakespeare's successor" (Martin 511). The experiment did not produce the results Tennyson had sought. He found his subjects in English history, but the plays he wrote were too long and lacked dramatic quality. Many praised his writing, but few were willing to produce his works on stage. The young Henry James observed of *Queen Mary,* presented in London in 1876, that the play was simply "a dramatised chronicle, without an internal structure. . . . It has no shape; it is cast in no mould; it has neither beginning, middle, nor end, save the chronological ones" (Martin 512). Only *Becket,* written in 1879 but not brought to the stage until 1893, proved a critical success, and that may have had more to do with the actor/producer Henry Irving's savvy handling of both the text and the production than to Tennyson's skill as a dramatist. Even Irving questioned his ability in the genre: "Tennyson is a great poet," he told Wilfrid Ward, "but he cannot write plays; what a pity he tries, they are the greatest rubbish!" (Martin 523).

Although his plays did not receive wide acclaim, Tennyson's individual works continued to generate exceptional praise from his contemporaries. For example, Alfred Gatty, a clergyman in York, found solace in writing *A Key to Tennyson's "In Memoriam"* (1881) so he could be certain that the indisputable "earnestness and piety" of the work and its "deep thought and reverent speculation" on death would not be misinterpreted by readers (vi). Elizabeth Chapman offers a prose redaction of the work for much the same reason in *A Companion to "In Memoriam"* (1888). In what could be called the standard Victorian interpretation of Tennyson's elegy, John F. Genung's *Tennyson's "In Memoriam"* (1884) begins with the assertion that the poem "stands inseparably related to what is deepest and most vital in the thought of its time" (9). Tennyson did not lead his age, Genung says; rather, he "*found* his age, giving voice to the religious thought of his time" (14). In elevated language that reads at times like a Victorian sermon, Genung explains how *In Memoriam* is a poem of its time, intensely linked with the hopes and fears of Tennyson's contemporaries. Readers can appreciate the work only by "surrendering" themselves "obediently" to the poet's "thought and spirit" (26). "To the spirit of its time," Genung concludes, the poem gives "the ideal interpretation" (57). Such sentiments would be welcome to the ears of mid-Victorian devotees of their laureate, but they would become weapons in the hands of modern revisionists who would wish to dismiss Tennyson's work as irrelevant.

American critics writing toward the end of the nineteenth century were more balanced in assessing Tennyson's work. In *Victorian Poets* (1875), E. C. Stedman, the foremost American scholar of his day, says that, "The influence of Alfred Tennyson has been almost unprecedentedly dominant, fascinating, extended, yet of late has somewhat vexed the public mind" (151). After providing extensive commentary on dozens of the poems to assess the "inherent quality" (153) of Tennyson's poems, Stedman proclaims that the laureate has greater breadth of interest and mental ability than his rivals Arnold and Browning. Conventionally, Stedman judges *Idylls of the King* to be Tennyson's "master-work," calling it the "greatest narrative poem since *Paradise Lost*" (175). Like most mainstream British critics, Stedman concludes that Tennyson is "certainly to be regarded, in time to come, as, all in all, the fullest representative of the refined, speculative, complex Victorian age" (200).

Near the end of the nineteenth century, the function of Tennyson's poetry in America was outlined by the man who would later come to be recognized as that country's greatest poet of the century. In a January 1887 review of Tennyson's *Locksley Hall Sixty Years After,* Walt Whitman links Tennyson with Carlyle as the "deep-sounding and high-soaring voices" that have issued "warning calls, threats, checks, [and] neutralizings" about the "blindness, excesses, of the prevailing tendency" toward democracy. The poet's strengths, Whitman says, are admired in America. If he has faults, the "doubts, swervings, doublings upon himself, have been typical of our age" (*Rivulets of Prose*, 97). The poet has served America through "his character," his "moral line," and his fine "verbalism," best exemplified in *Idylls of the King*. Tennyson's works, Whitman says, have helped form the American character from the Atlantic to the Pacific. Even when one acknowledges Whitman's tendency toward hyperbole, the high praise in this essay carries a note of authenticity that signals the American poet's genuine respect for the work of his British counterpart. Just how much Tennyson influenced Whitman is ably discussed by David Daiches in "Imagery and Mood in Tennyson and Whitman" (1961).

Long before he became known as one of America's first great philosophers, Josiah Royce published a review of *Locksley Hall Sixty Years After* in the *Harvard Monthly*, later reprinted in *Studies of Good and Evil* (1898). Written while he was still a student, Royce's essay displays some of the insight that would make him one of the distinguished American minds of the century. Focusing not on poetic technique but on the ethical dimension of the poetry, Royce questions the judgment of many who found that, in his later years, Tennyson was simply a failed Romantic. In Royce's view, rather than being a pessimist, Tennyson is actually motivated by a desire to promote "courage" and "faith in the real world" (87).

Studies published in the last year of Tennyson's life make it clear the public was aware that the poet's career was drawing to a close. John Vance Cheney, an admirer of Stedman's work on Tennyson, follows a line similar to that of his mentor and of Josiah Royce in promoting Tennyson as a deep religious thinker. Attacking the claims of Edmund Gosse and William C. Dowden that Tennyson did not possess a first-rate intellect, Cheney advances in *The Golden Guess* (1892) the theory that he stands above his peers Browning and Swinburne because he sees more clearly than they the hand of God behind the workings of nature. Cheney is especially enthusiastic about what he calls the practical advice Tennyson offers through his poetry. Writing almost rhapsodically, Cheney claims the poet's "uniformity of great excellence" (192) makes anything he has written "at once a guaranty for pure song" and a "sovereign rebuke to the effrontery of rattling, brassy poetastry and husky mongrelism" (189). Like Cheney, Eugene Parsons offers in his slim monograph *Tennyson's Life and Poetry and Mistakes Concerning Tennyson* (1892) a somewhat varnished review of the poet's career, stressing Tennyson's harmony with his family, his readers, and the world around him. There is some value in Parsons's introductory bibliographic review, and his notes on mistakes made by earlier critics no doubt had positive influence on subsequent writers.

Despite these outbursts of high praise, the dark clouds that had begun to gather as early as the 1850s were beginning to swell, signaling the impending thunderstorm that would come to be known as the Reaction Against Tennyson. An early detractor, Henry S. Salt, issued his critique of Tennyson's intellectual acumen amid the voices celebrating the laureate's preeminence not only as a poet but as a seer and sage. *Tennyson as a Thinker* appeared originally in 1889, and was revised and reissued twenty years later in a brief monograph that takes on the prevailing opinion about Tennyson's role as a philosopher. Directly attacking the enthusiastic commentary of F. W. H. Myers, Salt says Myers's claim that Tennyson was "a great thinker" is a "preposterous statement" (8). When he moves away from lyric poetry, his true strength, "his work becomes weaker" and his genius is "trammeled by discussions in which . . . he was by no means called upon to interfere" (9).

Salt attacks Tennyson's views on immortality as shallow, then accuses him of being both a religious bigot and a political reactionary. Further, he had an "innate distrust of the people" (17). *Maud*, Salt says, is "one of the most signal instances of how a good poet may be a bad philosopher" (19). *Idylls of the King* is even worse, as it presents a hero who is destroyed by "his own smug sanctity, with its blind self-complacent conceit" (23). He may be representative, as some critics claim, but what he represents is what is at best a self-satisfied acceptance of conventional morality and British imperial dominance. In a century, Salt concludes, critics will smile in looking back on the "ecstatic tributes" paid by contemporaries to Tennyson's genius (29). Few critics before or since have crowded so much invective into so little space.

There would continue to be critics who would praise Tennyson without reserve, but Salt's attack reflected a growing acceptance of the attitude expressed by Alfred Austin in 1869: the poet was not without his faults. The problem lay not in Tennyson's craftsmanship, however, but in his moral stance; a new generation did not care to be preached at in verse. The dangers of "return[ing] to the way of our fathers" were alluded to by the young W. B. Yeats, who warned fellow poets in 1892 that a "a casting out of descriptions of nature for the sake of nature, of the moral law for the sake of the moral law, a casting out of all anecdotes and of that brooding over scientific opinion" had "so often extinguished the central flame in Tennyson" (163). For Yeats and the new generation of poets, the poetry of symbolism was superior to the poetry of statement.

Notes

[1] The citations from many of the reviews quoted in this chapter are taken from John D. Jump's excellent collection, *Tennyson: The Critical Heritage* (1967). Although Jump is highly selective, the reviews he includes give a remarkably accurate portrait of

the reaction of Tennyson's contemporaries to his work. For a detailed analysis of Hallam's review, see Eileen T. Johnston, "Hallam's Review of Tennyson: Its Contexts and Significance," *Texas Studies in Literature and Language* (1981).

[2] Tennyson's reception in America from his earliest publications through the appearance of *Maud* has been analyzed with exceptional thoroughness and insight by John O. Eidson, *Tennyson in America* (1943). His careful examination of primary sources and his scholarly discussion of the controversies surrounding the poet's works remains definitive. Further, his work contains a comprehensive bibliography of reviews and notices, making it an indispensable source for those interested in tracing Tennyson's reputation during the nineteenth century.

[3] The history of Tennyson's reception in France is chronicled with great care by Marjorie Bowden, *Tennyson in France* (1930); citations of French criticism are taken from Bowden's study.

[4] In 1833, the Union Club at Cambridge took up for debate the rather startling topic "Tennyson or Milton: Which the Greater Poet?" (Charles Tennyson, *Alfred Tennyson*, 141). For a thorough account of the activities of this debating and social club, see Peter Allen, *The Cambridge Apostles: The Early Years* (1978) and John Coyle and Richard Cronin, "Tennyson and the Apostles" (2000).

[5] The best accounts of the composition and organization of *In Memoriam* are those by Eleanor Mattes, *In Memoriam: The Way of a Soul*, 1951, and Susan Shatto and Marian Shaw, Introduction, *In Memoriam*, 1982. Both Shannon, *Tennyson and the Reviewers*, and Eidson discuss the ten-years' silence at length, as does Joyce Green, "Tennyson's Development during the Ten-Years' Silence (1832–42)" (1951).

[6] Austin wrote a guarded recantation of his extremist position in 1885, publishing a highly critical review of Swinburne's strictures against Tennyson ("A Vindication of Tennyson," reprinted in *The Bridling of Pegasus*, 1910). In this article, Austin admits that his classification of Tennyson as too "feminine" was an opinion "advanced with exaggeration" (209). Ironically, in 1896 Austin became Poet Laureate, a position Tennyson had held for forty-two years. A cursory glance at a twentieth-century anthology of Victorian poetry gives testimony to the judgment of posterity regarding these two poets.

Works Cited

Allen, Peter. *The Cambridge Apostles: The Early Years.* Cambridge: Cambridge UP, 1978.

Austin, Alfred. "A Vindication of Tennyson." *The Bridling of Pegasus: Prose Papers on Poetry.* London: Macmillan, 1910. 197–217.

Aytoun, W. E. Review of *Maud. Blackwood's Edinburgh Magazine* 78 (September 1855): 311–21. Reprinted in *Notorious Literary Attacks.* Ed. Albert Mordell. New York: Boni & Liveright, 1926; Freeport, NY: Books for Libraries Press, 1969. 138–61.

Bagehot, Walter. "Wordsworth, Tennyson, and Browning; or Pure, Ornate, and Grotesque Art in English Poetry." *National Review* n.s. 1 (November 1864): 27–66. Reprinted in *Literary Studies, II*. London: Longmans Green, 1905; London: J. M. Dent, 1911. 305–52.

Bayne, Peter. *Lessons from My Masters: Carlyle, Tennyson, and Ruskin*. London: J. Clark, 1879.

Bowden, Marjorie. *Tennyson in France*. Manchester, UK: Manchester UP, 1930.

Chapman, Elizabeth R. *A Companion to "In Memoriam."* London: Macmillan, 1888. 2nd ed. London: Macmillan, 1901.

Cheney, John V. *The Golden Guess: Essays on Poetry and the Poets*. Boston: Lee and Shepard, 1892. 161–201.

Coyle, John, and Richard Cronin. "Tennyson and the Apostles." In *Rethinking Victorian Culture*. Ed. Juliet John and Alice Jenkins. London: Macmillan, 2000.

Daiches, David. "Imagery and Mood in Tennyson and Whitman." *English Studies Today* 11 (1961): 217–32.

Eidson, John O. *Tennyson in America: His Reputation and Influence from 1827 to 1858*. Athens: U of Georgia P, 1943.

Gatty, Alfred. *A Key to Tennyson's "In Memoriam."* London: D. Bogue, 1881. Reprint, New York: Haskell House, 1972.

Genung, John F. *Tennyson's "In Memoriam": Its Purpose and Its Structure: A Study*. Boston: Houghton Mifflin, 1884. Reprint, New York: Haskell House, 1970.

Green, Joyce. "Tennyson's Development During the 'Ten Years' Silence' (1932–1842)." *PMLA* 66 (September 1951): 662–97.

Hearn, Lafcadio. "Idylls of the King." *Occidental Gleanings*. Vol. 1. New York: Dodd, Mead, 1925. 1–25.

Hutton, R. H. *Literary Essays*. London: Macmillan, 1888.

Jennings, Henry J. *Lord Tennyson: A Biographical Sketch*. London: Chatto & Windus, 1884. Rev. and enlarged ed. 1892. Reprint, Folcroft, PA: Folcroft Press, 1972.

Johnston, Eileen T. "Hallam's Review of Tennyson: Its Contexts and Significance." *Texas Studies in Literature and Language* 23 (Spring 1981): 1–26.

Joseph, Gerhard. "Poe and Tennyson." *PMLA* 88 (1973): 418–28.

Jump, John D., ed. *Tennyson: The Critical Heritage*. London: Routledge & Kegan Paul; New York: Barnes & Noble, 1967.

Lounsbury, Thomas R. *The Life and Times of Tennyson: From 1809 to 1850*. London: Oxford UP; New Haven: Yale UP, 1915.

Martin, Robert Bernard. *Tennyson: The Unquiet Heart.* London: Faber; Oxford: Clarendon Press; New York: Oxford UP, 1980.

Mattes, Eleanor B. *In Memoriam: The Way of a Soul.* New York: Exposition, 1951.

Myers, F. W. H. "Tennyson as Prophet." *Science and a Future Life.* London: Macmillan, 1893. 27–65.

Nicolson, Sir Harold. *Tennyson: Aspects of His Life, Character and Poetry.* London: Constable, 1923; 2nd ed., 1925. Reprint, London: Arrow Books, 1960; Garden City, NY: Anchor Books, 1962.

Parsons, Eugene. *Tennyson's Life and Poetry: And Mistakes Concerning Tennyson.* Chicago: Craig, 1892.

Ricks, Christopher, ed. *The Poems of Tennyson.* London: Longmans, 1969; 2nd rev. ed., 3 vols. Berkeley: U of California P, 1987.

Royce, Josiah. "Tennyson and Pessimism." *Studies of Good and Evil.* New York: Appleton, 1898. Reprint, Hamden, CT: Archon Books, 1964. 76–88.

Salt, Henry S. *Tennyson as a Thinker.* London: Reeves, 1889. Reprint, 1893, 1909.

Shannon, Edgar F. "The Critical Reception of Tennyson's *Maud.*" *PMLA* 68 (June 1953): 397–417.

———. *Tennyson and the Reviewers; A Study of His Literary Reputation and of the Influence of the Critics upon His Poetry, 1827–1851.* Cambridge, MA: Harvard UP, 1952.

Shatto, Susan, and Marion Shaw, eds. *In Memoriam.* Oxford: Oxford UP, 1982.

Stedman, E. C. *Victorian Poets.* Boston: Osgood, 1875; Boston: Houghton Mifflin, 1887. 150–233.

Swinburne, Algernon Charles. *Miscellanies.* London: Chatto & Windus, 1886. Reprint, 1895.

———. *Under the Microscope.* London: White, 1872. 36–45.

Tennyson, Charles. *Alfred Tennyson.* New York: Macmillan, 1949.

Tennyson, Hallam. *Alfred Lord Tennyson: A Memoir.* 2 vols. London: Macmillan, 1897.

Waugh, Arthur. *Alfred Lord Tennyson, a Study of His Life and Work.* New York: United States Book Co., 1892. London: Heinemann, 1902.

Whitman, Walt. "A Word About Tennyson." *Critic* 10 (1 January 1887): 1–2. Reprinted in *November Boughs.* Philadelphia: McKay, 1888. 65–67; *Democratic Vistas.* London: Scott, 1888. 125–29; *Rivulets of Prose.* New York: Greenberg, 1928. 92–98.

Yeats, W. B. "The Symbolism of Poetry," *The Dome,* 1900. Reprinted in *Essays and Introductions.* London: Macmillan, 1961. 153–64.

2: A Mixed Legacy: 1892–1916

TENNYSON'S DEATH BROUGHT FORTH dozens of personal recollections and reminiscences by friends, family, and acquaintances. The month after his funeral, a reviewer for *Blackwood's* (November 1892) provided a review of his career, commenting that "minor voices chirp on" (748) but the country's greatest poetic voice has gone silent. The scholar Herbert Paul offered a more detailed retrospective for *The New Review* (November 1892), outlining the major events of Tennyson's life and commenting on his many achievements. *The Nineteenth Century* ran articles in December 1892 and January 1893, each titled "Aspects of Tennyson." In the first, H. D. Traill celebrates Tennyson's accomplishments but warns prophetically that dissenting voices have already begun to cast doubt on his greatness. Traill, of course, believes that "considered as the artist" Tennyson's "rank in the corps [of great poets] is fixed, unchangeable" (953). In the second essay, Tennyson's personal friend James Knowles writes about his relationship with the poet, providing insight into his character.

Many of these early eulogists, like William Boyd Carpenter, the Bishop of Ripon, sought to elevate Tennyson's life and work as exemplary models for those wishing to better themselves (*The Message and Meaning of Tennyson*, 1893). In an 1893 essay in the *Church Quarterly Review* (reprinted in *Modern Poets of Faith, Doubt, and Other Essays*, 1904) Arthur Lyttleton, Bishop of Southampton, writes about the nation's loss, noting that "in an age of great ethical uncertainty" it was comforting to know that "the acknowledged leader of English literature should have consistently upheld a lofty ideal of purity" (3). Others, including Frederick Farrar, the Dean of Canterbury, simply recorded impressions of the poet's life and summarized Tennyson's comments on art and life (*Men I Have Known*, 1897).

If there is anything that links the late Victorian critics, it is their penchant to provide comparative assessments of literary figures. Spurred by the work of Matthew Arnold and academic critics such as George Saintsbury, the quest to determine who holds the higher place among writers was considered part of a critic's role. While the standards for such judgments might vary, one could be almost certain to find in any commentary longer than a few hundred words some attempt to "place" a poet and rank his or her achievement against others who practiced the craft.

Among the earliest summary judgments of the recently deceased laureate was that published by Edmund Gosse, longtime admirer of Tennyson but not universally laudatory in his commentary. His enigmatic essay on Tennyson was written, he says, the day after the funeral, published in the *New Review* (1892), and reprinted the next year in *Questions at Issue*. Gosse begins by asking two important questions: Does Tennyson's death signal the death of poetry in England? And if it does, will the general public really care? Reviewing the history of English poetry with an Olympian perspective that would have made Matthew Arnold proud, Gosse expresses concern that, as great as Tennyson's poetry is, the English speaking public had become more taken with the man than his work. Linking the quality of the poetry with the morality of its author is inherently dangerous. Tennyson, Gosse says, would be horrified to find that succeeding generations would value his life and career more than they would cherish his verses. Gosse expresses confidence, however — whether truthfully or ironically is open to interpretation — that "this remarkable phenomenon of the popularity of Tennyson . . . is but transitory and accidental" (193). In these months immediately following his death, admirers are simply giving in to an idolatry that cannot last; "I shall not be accused of anything like disrespect," Gosse says, "when I say that his reputation at this moment is largely mirage" (197). Gosse ends by reminding readers that poetry will survive Tennyson's death, as it has the deaths of other great writers.

Even before Tennyson died, Arthur Waugh was working on a biographical and critical study to provide late Victorian readers insight into the man who had dominated the literary world for nearly half a century. *Alfred Lord Tennyson: A Study of his Life and Work* (1892) was ready for press when news of the laureate's death reached Waugh. There is little evidence, other than his brief eulogy in the introduction, that Waugh made any serious changes to his manuscript before publishing it. *Alfred Lord Tennyson* deserves attention largely because it is the first attempt at a systematic life study. Like most biographies written during the nineteenth century, it relies heavily on published sources and reminiscences of those who knew the poet. Acknowledging that his is not to be construed as a definitive or comprehensive biography, Waugh alternates between critical analysis of Tennyson's major poems and commentary on his career, family, and friendships.

One of the more remarkable aspects of Waugh's book is its admission that the quality of Tennyson's work varies. No hagiographer, Waugh is quick to note when earlier critics have gone too far in praising Tennyson — though he also takes issue with reviewers he believes were too harsh. He dismisses most of the 1830 volume as good preparatory work, but does not believe it deserved the excessive praise Arthur Henry Hallam lavished on it in his 1831 review. Waugh does find value in most poems of the 1833 volume, putting him at odds with those hostile reviewers who were, in his view, largely responsible for Tennyson's ten-year silence. Though he engages in some special pleading for the value of *The Princess*, he is willing to acknowledge that, despite its many memorable passages, *In Memoriam* "is much too long for its subject" (104). He refuses to attack *Maud* as many of his contemporaries did, but he believes critics who find the poem one of Tennyson's best are misguided. Nevertheless, the bias of his age is reflected in his judgment of *Idylls of the King*: it is "the most characteristic" and "the most permanent of Tennyson's contributions to English literature" (127). A man of his own times, Waugh concludes that Tennyson is the great seer and prophet of his day, taking his place among the great poets of England by "preserv[ing] to us the spirit of our song" and providing for "the continuity and perfection of the national literature" (249).

Most of Waugh's judgments parallel those of other judicious Victorians, believing that Tennyson's most enduring quality is his ability to maintain an "attitude of hope." The poet's penchant for the "arguing down of doubt" gives his best work their "power and permanence" (69). Tennyson achieved greatness because he "caught the spirit of the people and crystallized it into literature" (251), reflecting in his work "an age which, with all its troubles, its doubts, and its possibilities, found for consolation one only faith, for assurance one only God" (252).

Waugh's volume was soon joined on bookshelves by another lengthy biographical and critical study, J. Cuming Walters's *Tennyson: Poet, Philosopher, Idealist* (1893). Considerably more enthusiastic about Tennyson's accomplishments than Waugh, Walters asserts at the outset that "never had poet loftier conception of his duty, never did poet live up to a higher ideal, than Alfred, Lord Tennyson" (13). In Walters's view, Tennyson is a great philosopher who possesses exceptional understanding of and insight into human nature. Given this stance, it is not surprising that Walters has little trouble defending Tennyson's treatment of women in *The Princess* or finding great merit in the "Ode on the Death of the Duke of Wellington," a poem contemporaries found wanting in many respects. Walters does not share Waugh's belief that *In Memoriam* is too long; rather, he believes its great statement of faith ranks ahead of Milton's *Paradise Lost* in justifying God's ways to humankind. "No one can rise from the study" of this elegy "without feeling strengthened, cheered, and refreshed" (120). Others may have shared this opinion, but by the end of the nineteenth century, questioning voices had begun to challenge such mid-Victorian views.

Walters is even more emphatic in his judgment of *Maud*. Refuting both supporters and detractors alike, he claims others have simply misunderstood Tennyson's intention. "In *Maud*," Walters says, "Tennyson showed that the temper of men unfitted them for peace," and though the poet himself was "an advocate for peace," he "demonstrated that war was unavoidable while every instinct of mankind drove them to rapacity" (131). He seems to have a sound grasp of the strengths and weaknesses of "Enoch Arden," Tennyson's most popular poem among Victorians, but agrees with conventional opinion that *Idylls of the King* ranks as Tennyson's greatest achievement because of the poet's ability to present King Arthur as "epochal," the model of human behavior whose career stands as "a path towards that fair ideal we strive to attain" (165).

Both of these biographies contain errors about Tennyson's life that were not to be corrected until family papers were made available to scholars. Nevertheless, reading the criticism of Waugh and Walter, one can begin to see how critical judgments first proposed in early reviews began to shape subsequent opinion about Tennyson's work.

Following Tennyson's death, it became customary for authors who had written about him to collect their previously published work and compose summative judgments on the late laureate's career. For example, Joseph Jacobs's *Tennyson and "In Memoriam"* (1892), a slim volume that appeared almost immediately after the laureate's death, contains a lengthy appreciation of Tennyson's career and a detailed analysis of *In Memoriam* to help readers interpret the poem correctly — that is, as a religious guide for those confronting the complexities of the modern world and the uncertainties of life after death. Morton Luce was quick to bring together his disparate work in a collection titled *New Studies in Tennyson, Including a Commentary on "Maud"* (1893). Luce argues that his countrymen should be "deeply thankful" Tennyson "dwelt so long among us," and grateful that his "benign influences of wisdom, grace, and beauty" remain for future generations to appreciate. Two years later Luce issued *A Handbook to the Works of Alfred, Lord Tennyson* (1895) to ensure that the next generation of readers would understand both the stylistic felicities and the moral lessons of the departed laureate. In 1901, Luce published *Tennyson* in the Temple Primers series to further expand his commentary on the poems and give an assessment of the poet's life and career.

Like Luce's work, William M. Dixon's *A Tennyson Primer* (1896) surveys the poet's career and provides critical commentary on dozens of works. Dixon offers Victorian judgments on the major poems. He acknowledges an affinity for *The Princess* and professes his admiration for *In Memoriam* as being both a personal elegy and representative of the age. Though he acknowledges the weakness of structure and characterization in *Idylls of the King*, Dixon praises the poem nevertheless for its presentation of the conflict of sense at war with soul. He expresses what so many of his Victorian colleagues felt: "The death of Alfred Tennyson seemed almost in a sense to bring the history of English poetry to a close" (125).

Throughout the 1890s, sketches of the poet's life and career appeared in books and periodicals. William Canton's "Tennyson" in David Masson's *In the Footsteps of the Poets* (1893) is representative of such essays, which were often intended to explain the poet's popularity. Joseph Jacobs's chapter on Tennyson in *Literary Studies* (1895) does much the same thing, but with an important caveat. While Tennyson deserves the mantle of seer and sage, Jacobs says, his work displays certain limitations that indicate limited vision. Though he is a master at observing and recording the natural world, Tennyson's poetry sometimes lacks passion and shows unusual reserve in discussing ideas. Furthermore, Jacobs offers an assessment of Tennyson's skills that would, in thirty years, become the dominant view: "He was not an epic poet, he was not a dramatic poet" (162). His strength lies in the lyric. Such views had been hinted at by others, such as the author of "Reputations Reconsidered: Tennyson" (1898), who, while claiming for Tennyson a "conspicuous place" among nineteenth-century writers (35), argues that his best works are his lyric poems. This would become the generally accepted view when Harold Nicolson and T. S. Eliot make the same argument in the 1920s and 1930s. Nevertheless, Jacobs ends his essay by claiming for Tennyson the primacy of place among English poets as one who most consistently and accurately reflected the character of his homeland.

Unquestionably the most important book published during the decade after Tennyson's death was the two-volume biography by his son Hallam. Typical of nineteenth-century biographies, *Alfred Tennyson: A Memoir* (1897) consists largely of excerpts from letters, memoirs, diaries, and recorded conversations. Although she did not have quite as much direct involvement as Frances Lucy Arnold had over production of G. W. E. Russell's edition of Matthew Arnold's letters, Emily Sellwood Tennyson was certainly influential in assuring that the *Memoir* would only enhance the reputation of her husband. Both mother and son wanted the Victorian laureate to be memorialized as one of England's greatest poets, most loyal citizens, and thoughtful philosophers. The ways Hallam's relationship with his father shaped the creation of the *Memoir* are documented carefully and analyzed with exceptional skill by Michael Millgate in *Testamentary Acts: Browning, Tennyson, Hardy, James* (1992).

Tennyson's friends and dozens of others who had had dealings with the poet were quick to respond to Hallam's call for materials, so much so that he was able to publish much that was not used in the *Memoir* in a companion volume, *Tennyson and His Friends,* in 1911. From the mass of materials, from his own notes of conversations with his father, and from the family archives (from which he ruthlessly purged items he judged detrimental to his father's reputation) Hallam Tennyson constructed a life story and a critical commentary that served for more than half a century as the principal source of information about the poet's life, personal relationships, and opinions about poetry and many other subjects. The two volumes also contain dozens of poems that did not appear in Tennyson's lifetime, as well as alternative versions and rejected stanzas of published works.

Universally praised by Victorian reviewers, the *Memoir* became the source for a half-dozen biographies and dozens of literary studies. Reviewing

Hallam's work in *The North American Review* (1897), Edmund Gosse praises Tennyson's son for "enabl[ing] us to look behind the curtain, to see the artist at work" (515). The main value of the *Memoir,* Gosse says, lies in "the extraordinary light" which it throws "upon the nature of [Tennyson's] intellect and temperament" (519–20). The work has exhibited remarkable staying power, too. Examining its history and influence in 1995, Philip Elliott says that the *Memoir* "shaped our concept of the poet for almost a hundred years" and "it will not likely be superseded" as a source of information about Tennyson; "we will return to it again and again as a source for materials, particularly letters, recollections, and anecdotes by those who had intimate knowledge of the poet" (Elliot 2–3).

The works that follow the publication of Hallam's *Memoir* frequently display their debt to this work not only for biographical information but also for commentary on individual poems. For example, in *Tennyson: A Critical Study* (1899) Steven Gwynn openly acknowledges his reliance on Hallam Tennyson's work in forming his assessment of Tennyson's views on love, religion, politics, and nature. While Gwynn examines the lyrics and most of the narratives as examples of Tennyson's growing interest in certain subjects, he dedicates a separate chapter to *Idylls of the King,* which he asserts is Tennyson's greatest accomplishment, fit to stand beside Spenser's *Faerie Queene.* The poet himself deserves to be thought of, Gwynn says, in the same circle as Spenser, Milton, Pope, Dryden — and even Shakespeare. Like Gwynn, Evan Cuthbertson offers a favorable assessment of both the poet's life and works in *Tennyson: The Story of his Life* (1898), a brief sketch based on Hallam Tennyson's *Memoir,* intended to highlight the poet's legacy to succeeding generations. Though "the days to come" will be the "wisest witness" to the question of Tennyson's "rank in the hierarchy of Parnassus" (127), Cuthbertson has no doubt about what ought to happen over the next century. "As he has been to our own century," he says, "surely Tennyson will be also to those to follow — one of the light-bearers of the world" (128).

The same favorable bias is evident in the work of John Murray Moore, whose 1897–98 lectures were collected in *Three Aspects of Tennyson* (1901). Writing about Tennyson first as a poet of Nature, then as a National Poet, Moore builds to a crescendo in his chapter on "Tennyson as a Poet of Humanity." In his final summing-up, Moore says Tennyson's works "teach the Great Truth that Progress is the Law of Man's being, and Faith, Hope, and Love its triple inspiration." From Tennyson readers learn that God's gift of free will is granted so people "may conform" their own wills "to the Will of [their] Maker." "The whole spirit and tone of his best poems," Moore says with assurance, "are calculated to help men to carry into their lives the sublime ethical and spiritual teachings of Jesus" (143–44).

Though written by one who had known and admired Tennyson during the later years of the poet's life, Alfred Lyall's *Tennyson,* written for the English Men of Letters Series (1902), fulfills the promise of the series by taking a critical look at Tennyson's work. Writing what may appropriately be called a literary biography, Lyall intersperses his account of the poet's life with critical analysis of individual poems. Considering Tennyson representative of the "prevailing spirit" and "national character" of his age (2), Lyall demonstrates how poems such as *The Princess* and *In Memoriam* vivify and comment on issues important to Victorians. While admitting that he likes both poems, and that he finds *Maud* and *Idylls of the King* works of exceptional merit as well, Lyall is not shy about pointing out defects of style or technique that weaken each of these works. He is careful to include not only the praise heaped on Tennyson by contemporaries, but also the criticism of men such as John Ruskin, who said that Tennyson had wasted his talents on the *Idylls* by creating "visions of things past" rather than concentrating on "the living present" (99). Lyall even has the courage to admit that Tennyson is not a deep thinker. Even "when he is dropping his plummet into the abyss of the mysteries that encompass human existence and destiny," Lyall says, Tennyson "rarely carries abstract thought to any depth" (124).

In his concluding chapters, Lyall attempts to define Tennyson's philosophy of life and identify issues that occupied him throughout his career. His list — human immortality, the existence of God, the idea of progress, the advance of science, the growing influence of democracy on England — may not seem particularly startling to critics of the twenty-first century, but Lyall's succinct summation provides a representative view of what the later Victorians thought of their recently deceased laureate. Though he relies heavily on Hallam Tennyson's *Memoir* for details about the poet's life, Lyall's assessment of Tennyson's accomplishments and defects, and his keen analysis of the ways Tennyson's work mirrors the concerns of the Victorians, provides a sound platform for further studies. With foresight he may not have intended, Lyall admits that "it will be right for the future historian to treat Tennyson as a representative of the Victorian period"; later ages, Lyall says, will "draw inferences from his work as to the general intellectual and political tendencies of the nineteenth century" (186). That work was being done already, and would occupy critics for the next half century.

Less scholarly than Lyall's work but revealing in its assessment of the poet, A. C. Benson's *Alfred Tennyson* (1904) covers much of the same ground. Like Lyall, Benson was an admirer of Tennyson, and he relies on the poet's own words for much of his commentary on individual works. As biography, Benson's work is highly derivative, relying on Hallam Tennyson's *Memoir* and other contemporary records. His judgment of the poems, however, differs from Lyall in one critical aspect. Benson believes, as did Tennyson's lifelong friend Edward FitzGerald, that "Tennyson's real gift was the lyric gift" (214) and that his best work is in his early lyrics and *In Memoriam*. Further, Benson claims that those who give primacy of place to Tennyson's work as a public poet are wrong. Rather, he says, Tennyson is "the lonely dreamer, lingering in the still and secret places, listening to the music of the woods . . . he stands on the edge of the abyss" and looks "with faltering eyes into the dark" to find some hope that "there is something beyond and above and around all" (215–16). It is not too far a leap from this assessment to that of Harold Nicolson, who in 1923 damned Tennyson by declaring him a brooding, melancholy hysteric.

In the last decade of the nineteenth century, American eulogists abounded as well. Hamilton W. Mabie says in his 1892 essay "The Influence of Tennyson in America" that "As a force in the popular culture of the country Tennyson's influence has been greater than that of any other English poet" (Eidson 148). Like Joseph Jacobs in England, American critic Thomas Davidson examines Tennyson's great elegy in *A Prolegomena to "In Memoriam"* (1897) to demonstrate Tennyson's efficacy as a religious teacher. The distinguished California jurist Timothy Rearden writes affectionately about Tennyson in *Petrarch and Other Essays* (1897), surveying the poet's life and offering brief assessments of major poems. Prophetically, however, Rearden asserts that "Tennyson closes a generation of poets" (95). The next generation, he predicts, will not consider Tennyson representative; instead, they will look to new models for creating their art.

Scholarly studies by Americans joined those by British critics on library shelves. For example, *The Growth of the "Idylls of the King"* (1895) by the German-trained American scholar Richard Jones contains a highly technical analysis of the poem along with commentary on sources. Jones's attempt to provide variant readings reflects more on his scholarly bias than on his desire to promote wide readership, but his work shows how seriously the academic community at the close of the century treated the Arthurian epic. Henry Van Dyke, who had written frequently and not always supportively about Tennyson in periodicals during the latter half of the century, collected his work in *The Poetry of Tennyson* (1898, revised and reissued as *Studies in Tennyson*, 1920) to demonstrate his superiority to all others of his age.

Not all were so laudatory, however. Arthur Innes writes in *Seers and Singers* (1893) that Tennyson has consistently been praised when he should have been condemned — that though an excellent craftsman, he lacks vigor and tends to be overrefined. Rather than examining his work from the perspective of contemporary standards, Innes tries to see what might be appealing to succeeding generations. Viewed in this light, much of what Victorians admired will not, in Innes's view, stand the test of time. He is especially critical of *Idylls of the King*, where he finds Tennyson to be out of touch with the world in which he lived and the world to come, because he offers no sense of realism to underpin his critique of modern society.

Stephen V. Gurteen, a scholar at Cambridge, offers similar cautionary notes on *Idylls of the King* in his extensive review of Arthurian materials, *The*

Arthurian Epic (1895). Claiming that Tennyson violated the spirit of Arthurian epic in his poem, Gurteen goes on for more than four hundred pages to demonstrate how the best parts of *Idylls* are derived directly from Malory and other medieval sources, while the weakest sections are pure inventions by Tennyson. He savages "The Holy Grail" as a perversion of the legend. Having before him "in this allegorical romance one of the most exquisite conceptions and most artistic productions in literature," Tennyson proceeded to "miss the allegory and has produced the tale, shorn of its unique fascination and bereft of its deep spiritual meaning" (260). Modern critics might offer the rejoinder that, far from missing the allegory, Tennyson turns the traditional tale on its head to show how the pursuit of ideals can lead to anarchy. But in 1895, Gurteen's assessment would have been either vilified as wrongheaded or accepted as proof that the laureate simply was not smart enough to understand his sources. Such was the state of Tennyson's reputation at the time.

Other studies of *Idylls of the King* were more supportive. Mungo MacCallum's *Tennyson's "Idylls" and Arthurian Story from the XVIth Century* (1894) begins with the premise that Tennyson's story is a misunderstood epic. Attacking contemporaries who had disparaged the poem, MacCallum asserts that most readers have misunderstood its "allegoric character" or adopted "a false allegoric clue" (viii). His detailed and somewhat derivative history of the Arthurian legend precedes four substantial chapters on *Idylls of the King* in which he demonstrates how Tennyson vivifies the age-old conflict of sense at war with soul (phrases actually found in the poem's "envoy" to the Queen). Harold Littledale's *Essays on Lord Tennyson's "Idylls of the King"* (1893), written as a commentary for undergraduates wishing to understand the Arthurian tale, offers readings of each idyll, noting parallels to earlier Arthurian works and to other important literature that influenced Tennyson's choice of metaphor, simile, and other devices. Morley Stevenson's *The Spiritual Teaching of the Holy Grail* (1903) is actually a series of sermons based on Tennyson's version of the Grail legend. Ignoring the literary qualities of the work, Stevenson examines the poem "chiefly to draw from it the teaching which it has for our spiritual good" (1). Stevenson reprises his approach in *The Spiritual Teaching of Tennyson's "In Memoriam"* (1904), using the poem as a touchstone for discussing sorrow, suffering, death, faith, doubt, and the Supreme Deity. In the same fashion Henry Jones transformed a lecture given at the University of Glasgow into *The Immortality of the Soul in Tennyson and Browning* (1907) to reach a wider audience with his ideas about the value of Tennyson's poetry as a tool for understanding the concept of immortality.

The most extensive critical commentary on Tennyson's poetry written in the late nineteenth century is Stopford Brooke's *Tennyson, His Art and Relation to Modern Life* (1894). Brooke had known Tennyson, and the poet had approved Brooke's assessments of individual poems. Brooke's Victorian prejudices are apparent in the opening pages of his study, where he praises Tennyson for his simplicity by comparing him favorably not only to his successors (Swinburne, Morris, Meredith, and Symonds, for example) but also to those "later Elizabethans" — the Metaphysical poets such as Donne — who often drifted into "obscurity of thought or obscurity of expression" (5). Further, Brooke says, not only the art but also the character of a poet must be exemplary, and Tennyson measures up to these high standards. Brooke finds Tennyson a Christian poet without a definite creed, one who held no definite opinions about infinite truths. In this, Brooke said Tennyson was like "Christ Himself" (21).

Although he does not acknowledge it directly, Brooke is heavily influenced by the critical method of Matthew Arnold, whose concepts of objectivity and high seriousness gave later Victorians a moral standard by which to evaluate literature. Hence, it is not surprising to find Brooke dismissing "The Two Voices" because "the self-involution of the poem places it on a lower level than poetry which loses self-thought in the creation of a being beyond the self of the poet" (106). Brooke organizes his study chronologically to demonstrate how Tennyson's concept of his role as a poet developed over time. With surprising insight, however, he notes that for the first half of his career Tennyson seemed to be in harmony with the spirit of his age, while in the last forty years of his life he seemed to stop developing and to stand in opposition to growing intellectual, social, religious, and cultural changes taking place around him.[1]

Brooke's interpretations of individual poems are representative of Victorian approaches to Tennyson's work. He devotes two chapters to *The Princess*, one of them on the "woman question." While praising Tennyson for taking up the issue, he acknowledges that by the end of the century, his idea that men and women share separate, complementary, but unequal talents is outdated. His two chapters on *In Memoriam* offer enlightening commentary on the structure of the poem, and certainly form the basis for A. C. Bradley's later, more extensive study. He devotes more than a quarter of his book to *Idylls of the King*, offering sensible analysis that runs counter to the detailed studies of the allegory that Victorians found so inspiring. "No one, a hundred years hence," Brooke says, "will care a straw about the allegory; but men will always care for the story, and how the poet has made the persons in it set forth their human nature on the stage of life." For this reason, *Idylls of the King* is actually inferior to its source, Sir Thomas Malory's *Morte D'Arthur*, because "the humanity, not the metaphysics, is the interesting thing," and Malory's "far-off mythic Arthur is more at home with us than the Arthur of the *Idylls*" (265).

Brooke also includes a groundbreaking analysis of a group of poems he calls Tennyson's "dramatic monologues," providing a critical vocabulary for assessing the differences between both drama and narrative poetry and works such as "Locksley Hall Sixty Years After," "Rizpah," or "Northern Farmer." He devotes a chapter to examining Tennyson's speculative theology, and another to his "nature-poetry." Throughout, Brooke maintains a sense of critical distance from his subject, and though his presuppositions may exhibit Victorian tendencies, his method is a precursor to twentieth-century critical analysis. His conclusion about Tennyson's staying power, however, seems out of place in his own day, when books and articles attacking the laureate's work were already in great supply. "The permanence of the work of Tennyson is secure," he asserts at the end of his study (509). From the perspective of another century he may have been right, but it would be a half-century before all of Tennyson's major works received the acclaim implied in Brooke's sweeping judgment.

Another influential critic of the late century, Andrew Lang, is even more fulsome in his praise for the poet. *Alfred Tennyson* (1901) is more an appreciation than a true scholarly analysis; in fact, Lang says in his preface that he relies on Hallam Tennyson's *Memoir* for details about the poet's life, and that he deliberately avoids the critical judgments of others so he can provide readers with a personal reaction to Tennyson's poems. Lang is clearly devoted to his subject, and finds Tennyson a man of sound mind and sage opinions. With some prescience, he refutes a judgment not to be made for twenty years when he observes that "if ever the term 'morbid' could have been applied to Tennyson, it would have been in the years immediately following the death of Arthur Hallam. But the application would have been unjust" (31). Despite Lang's warnings, however, the portrait of the poet as a morbid, introspective lyricist, popularized in the 1920s by Harold Nicolson, would become the dominant view among critics for nearly half a century.

Lang's enduring value as a critic is compromised by many of his opinions and prejudices that color his view of Tennyson's greatness. For example, he finds greatest merit in works that celebrate Victorian values; hence it is no surprise that he has high praise for *In Memoriam* and *Idylls of the King*, but finds fault with *Maud*. He is critical of Tennyson for his portrait of women in *The Princess* not because the poet finds women different from men, but because Tennyson ascribes too much hope for their ascendancy as men's equals. "Probably the 'educational movement' will not make much difference to womankind on the whole," Lang observes, except in rare cases of genius. There is nothing remarkable, therefore, in his assessment that "Guinevere" is "the greatest of the *Idylls*," and that this poem is Tennyson's crowning achievement. For Lang, Tennyson's rank among poets is secure, somewhere in the pantheon just below Shakespeare, Homer, and Dante; and no one will ever surpass him "for exquisite variety and varied exquisiteness" (225).

Unfortunately, the most distinguished critic of the late nineteenth century, George Saintsbury, may have unintentionally contributed to the diminution of the poet's stature in three important works published between 1895 and 1910. Two short chapters in *Corrected Impressions* (1895) record Saintsbury's lifelong love of Tennyson's poetry; but Saintsbury insists that Tennyson "does his best in lyric" (35), and that his special faculty as an artist lies in his ability to combine "poetical music" with "poetical picture drawing" (38). In *A History of Nineteenth-Century Literature* (1896) Saintsbury hails Tennyson as "the very greatest genius" of his age, but claims the poet "dared not attempt work on the grand scale"; instead, he "put in short pieces . . . what his forerunners would have spun into long poems" (259). He seems to want to give Tennyson due credit for all his work. He takes exception to Edward FitzGerald's claim that Tennyson's best work was written by 1842, and asserts that charges of "excessive prettiness" and "want of profundity" are unfair (267). In *A History of English Prosody, from the Twelfth Century to the Present Day* (1910), Saintsbury praises the poet for his technical prowess, claiming his early volumes "founded the last new dynasty (up to the present moment) of English prosody" (185). Because the academic world respected Saintsbury's opinion, there can be little doubt that even those who found much to praise in Tennyson could not overcome the limitations on his greatness expressed obliquely by the greatest critic of the age.

Late-century assessments critical of Tennyson often followed the path taken by Hiram Stanley in "Tennyson's Rank as a Poet," an essay originally published in the *Dial* in Chicago and reprinted in his *Essays on Literary Art* (1897). Applying what he calls "scientific criticism" (13) to Tennyson's poetry, Hiram looks to discern what is of permanent value. What he discovers is that, while Tennyson has "superior talent" and "at times genius," he lacks the "consummate insight and frank fervid creativeness of the great masters" (15). Hiram denies him the first rank even in his lyrical work; and in epic and dramatic poetry — the "higher arts" — Tennyson "rarely rises above third rate" (18). He is good at the picturesque, Stanley says, and fine in literary technique. But on the whole, he belongs in the "third order" of poets (24), joining such diverse artists as Cowper, Pope, and Keats. Fortunately for Tennyson — and for Keats — the principles of scientific criticism were to change over the next half-century, allowing them to move up the ladder to join poets such as Wordsworth and Shelley. Nevertheless, even W. J. Dawson, whose adulatory assessment of Tennyson's poetry covers eight chapters in all the editions of *Makers of Modern Poetry*, says in the preface to the seventh edition (1899) that it now "seems likely that Tennyson will live for further generations" only through their reading of *In Memoriam* and selected lyrics. The "laborious fruit of his genius, 'The Idylls of the King' is already half dead" (vi).

Dawson had evidence on which to base this sobering judgment, as detractors were becoming more common. Nevertheless, there remained at the end of the century a formidable number of supporters who believed Tennyson had something to say to succeeding generations about moral, social, and religious issues. Several late-century writers on both sides of the Atlantic set out to demonstrate the presence of theological principles underlying Tennyson's art, among them John Oates in *The Teaching of Tennyson* (1895), a lengthy philosophical analysis of the poet's ethical and religious ideas. He begins with the premise that Tennyson was a great teacher, and that his works can help readers deal with important questions about this life and the next: "We shall find" in Tennyson's poetry "that he not only gives an ethical law for the guidance of life, but an answer to those deeper questions that utter their tremulous voices in the shrine of the soul" (7). Dividing Tennyson's work into three broad categories — ethical poems, emotional poems, and religious poems — Oates presents a *schema* for reading the poems as guides to a happy life.

Richard Armstrong's chapter on Tennyson in *Faith and Doubt in the Century's Poets* (1898), describes Tennyson as a poet of faith, which Armstrong considers a higher passion than hope, a characteristic of so many English writers of the nineteenth century. Tennyson's "mastery of Lucretian and Darwinian philosophies" made his faith distinguishable from "mediocre orthodoxies" of the period (75). The "brave Doubter" (78) gave fullest expression to his ideals in *Idylls of the King*, Armstrong says; his King Arthur is an exemplar in poetry, as Tennyson was in his life, of what is best in humankind. Armstrong's summary of Tennyson's creed, stressing the importance of living rightly and trusting one's instincts in matters of faith, suggests how deeply the poet was able to impress some members of the clergy that he was a valuable moral teacher.

Similarly, the American writer Augustus Strong, president of New York's Rochester Theological Seminary, closes his study *The Great Poets and Their Theology* (1897) with a lengthy chapter on Tennyson. Asserting at the outset that great poets "give united and harmonious testimony to the fundamental concepts of natural religion, if not to those of the specifically Christian theme" (vii), Strong links Tennyson with Homer, Virgil, Dante, Milton, Wordsworth, and Browning as an artist who "deals with truth" — not abstractly, but "in its power to move and sway the soul" (455). Predictably, he concentrates on the theology behind *In Memoriam*, "the greatest poem of our century," in which Tennyson demonstrates "faith triumphant over doubt" (475). He also offers an unusual interpretation of *Idylls of the King*, which he calls Tennyson's *Paradise Lost*. The crowning glory of Tennyson's third period of development, one characterized by "broad humanity" (477), the poem contains in Arthur "no mere allegorical phantom" but "a living, breathing human being instead" (479).

Unfortunately, Strong finds the later period of Tennyson's career characterized by "growing despondency" (515); the poet was still besieged by doubts about God and the afterlife. When he speaks of God, Tennyson resorts to "methods of expression derived from the agnostic school of modern thinkers" (483). Although he celebrates Christ as humankind's savior, he cannot escape the gloomy atmosphere cast by modern society over the natural world and human relationships. Nevertheless, he is a poet whose works generally celebrate a God who has made the world and who cares for His creation.

E. H. Sneath looks at the major philosophical theories that underlie Tennyson's poetry and demonstrates the poet's lifelong interest in philosophy. *The Mind of Tennyson* (1900) treats the poet as a genuine philosopher, well versed in the work of such diverse figures as Kant, Locke, Hobbes, Spinoza, Berkeley, and others. The product of an Age of Doubt, Tennyson would have naturally found the subjects of philosophy attractive, Sneath says. He was "profoundly in touch with his age" (21) — a claim that critics such as Francis Adams would find outrageous — and his poetry demonstrates his lifelong struggle to come to grips with the concepts of God, freedom, and immortality. Ever quick to praise the poet and condemn his detractors, Sneath demonstrates that he is a devotee of the laureate and an enthusiastic disciple of his teaching. Like Sneath, J. W. Hayes says in *Tennyson and Scientific Theology* (1909) that those who "regard him merely as a noble and pure Poet" have done a disservice to Tennyson, who ranks "as a Scientist and Metaphysician" among the best minds of his age (2). "It is a libel on our Poet," Hayes continues "to insinuate that his scientific knowledge spoiled either his verse, his imagination, or his deep religious feelings" (5). Hayes's careful yet highly selective reading of Tennyson's poetry is aimed at demonstrating the poet's status as a mystic whose "life of purity and patient research" in the sciences "made him "pre-eminently fitted to receive higher truths from Nature Study" (35). The fault for the succeeding generation's failure to appreciate him lies not in Tennyson but in "the mass of humanity" who "has not yet risen" to understand the "sublime concept" of progressive evolution (40–41).

Another study of the poet's religious views, Charles F. G. Masterman's *Tennyson as a Religious Teacher* (1900), asserts at the outset that "Tennyson's poetry is the perfect reflection" of an age of "bewildering complexity." Masterman posits that religious problems "occupy a larger place in [Tennyson's] writings than in those of almost any other English poet" (2). Although as a progressive Tennyson was often "waging open warfare" on the "popular philosophies" of the Victorians (5), he was intensely committed to exploring religious topics as a means of teaching his readers how to live. Masterman mines the Tennyson canon to see how the poet dealt with subjects such as the vastness of the universe and the insignificance of humankind, questions about the "apprehension of God, the existence of Self, the hope of Immortality" (7), and issues of evolution, natural theology, ethics, and theology. His aim, he says, is to "yield a clear outline of the teaching of perhaps the most widely influential thinker among all the poets of the century which is now at its close" (8).

Although he is not universally complimentary, there is never a question in Masterman's mind that Tennyson deserves the status of sage and seer. His attitude is expressed clearly in his assertion that Tennyson, like other great poets, must have been "compelled, whether he would or no, to become a teacher" (234). Masterman is so imbued with Victorian principles of criticism that he adopts unquestioningly Matthew Arnold's dictum that poetry is a "criticism of life" (236). Because Tennyson gives readers reason for hope and action, and energy and purpose for living, he is a great religious teacher (237). Comparing him with Walt Whitman and Robert Browning, Masterman elevates Tennyson to the pinnacle of Victorian poet-teachers: "it cannot be doubted," he concludes, "that he possesses a real, and even an increasing, importance as a religious teacher" (239).

In a similar study, *Modern Poets and Christian Teaching: Tennyson* (1907), American scholar William Emory Smyser attempts to present "as simply and directly as possible those poems of Tennyson in which he has given expression to the fundamental principles of his faith" (7). Predictably, he provides an extensive critique of *In Memoriam*, but also examines both earlier and later poems to demonstrate Tennyson's commitment to faith in the concept of immortality and his rejection of materialism. Smyser claims that the "ethical influence of Tennyson's poetry" has been "immense," and the "spiritual philosophy from which it derives is profound" (133). There is no question in Smyser's mind that Tennyson believed "the meaning of the universe is moral," that "virtue and truth are a part of the essential order of things established from the very foundation of the world" (134). Those assertions underlie Smyser's examination of *Idylls of the King*, a poem in which he holds that Tennyson best demonstrates his moral code.

Frank C. Gunsaulus, another American theologian, approaches Tennyson with similar purpose in *The Higher Ministries of English Poetry* (1907). Asserting that the major Victorian poets had trained themselves to expose wrongs in human nature and society, Gunsaulus concludes that Tennyson's work is an excellent source for ministers to mine for examples to explain concepts such as morality and immortality. Tennyson's "priestly function," he says, lies principally in "welcoming to the finer consciousness and aspiration of man" the "Immanent God" whom all people seek (112).

Perhaps the most excessive claims for Tennyson, however, are made by Robert F. Horton in *Tennyson: A Saintly Life* (1900). Wishing to correct the "criticisms and detractions" that had gained "dubious currency" since the poet's death, Horton offers his study of Tennyson "from a particular point of view, an ethical, or I may even say a religious, point of view" (viii–ix). He is not particularly interested in Tennyson's poetry, though, unless it helps illuminate the character of its composer. Deriving information about the life from Hallam Tennyson's *Memoir*, and relying on Stopford Brooke and Frederic Harrison for critical opinion, Horton focuses on the personal qualities that, in his view, make Tennyson one of the contemporary "saints of humanity" (8). Thus, the departed laureate is a shining example of manly, virtuous living. He found his calling as a poet and devoted his life to producing works that celebrate Victorian virtues: fidelity in marriage, faith in God, selfless service to others. In a particularly rhapsodic passage, Horton compares Tennyson to his fictional King Arthur, the perfect gentleman and blameless ruler — a judgment that sat well with many in the 1860s and 1870s, but less so with turn-of-the-century readers. In Horton's view, Tennyson never fell below the highest standards of conduct, and he influenced others through his writings to lead a better life. Though he is hesitant to "estimate Tennyson as a poet," Horton is certain that "his work did what hymns and sermons ought to do, only much more effectually," namely, to serve as "the medium of instruction to the spirit of man, the medium of praise to God" (302).

Not only was Tennyson exploited to prop up the study of religion and ethics, but some used his poetry as a means of exploring important social issues. William C. Gordon's *The Social Ideals of Alfred Tennyson* (1906) is an extended attempt to combine literary study with the new branch of social science, sociology. Highly selective in his use of texts, Gordon examines ways Tennyson uses individual poems to comment on matters such as the roles of men and women in Victorian society, the concept and importance of family, and the function of social institutions, democracy, and the idea of progress.

While some scholars were willing to grant works such as Gordon's some leeway in testing the limits of Tennyson's usefulness, it should not be surprising that others would meet the more extreme flights of fancy such as Horton's study with skepticism. Following the lead of Alfred Austin and others, children of the Victorians often vilified their parents' literary favorites, and they found a ready target in Tennyson's verse. Among the most vitriolic, and most systematic, was Francis Adams, whose attack appears as the first entry in his *Essays on Modernity: Criticisms and Dialogues* (1899). His judgment of Tennyson is "hopelessly irreconcilable with that which we" — presumably he means previous critics — "held once, if judgment it could be called, and not the blind acceptance of the enthusiasm of the generation that immediately preceded us" (4). Adams sets out to correct the judgment of his predecessors by attacking Tennyson for his artistry, his ideas, and his morality.

Had early critics been perceptive, Adams says, Tennyson would never even have been noticed. Citing a review of Tennyson's early work, he observes that no less a critic than Samuel Taylor Coleridge believed "nothing could show us more clearly the dearth of all excellence" than attempts to "treat with anything approaching seriousness such a book as *Poems, Chiefly Lyrical*" (7). Tennyson's early work demonstrates the poet's inability to face life squarely and his tendency to "make of life a pretty play" (8). Nothing he published for the next ten years showed improvement; the accomplishments of a decade include only "a few snatches of fine verse" and "nothing of any permanent interest. It is a notable record," Adams continues sardonically, "even for a popular poet" (13). Far from being a thoughtful analysis of immortality or the conflict of science and faith, *In Memoriam* simply reveals Tennyson's "childlike, commercial egotism with a perfect simplicity of primal shamelessness" (15). The elegy for Hallam demonstrates "how shockingly wanting in knowledge as a thinker" Tennyson really is (17). The poem would be "one of the most dishonest works ever written by a man of ability," Adams continues, "were it not for a dozen snatches of sweet and true affection which he had in his heart of hearts for his friend" (20).

Adams believes the "myopic stumblings" of mid-century poems give way to later poems that are even worse (25). The "negative criticism of his age" that appear in Tennyson's late poetry "cannot be taken seriously for one moment. It is childish" (27). The worst of the production of his later years, Adams asserts, is *Idylls of the King*. In that poem "we are never once allowed to approach reality except with a thousand polite precautions" (29). Arthur is hardly ideal, nor is he really a modern gentleman; he is simply unreasonably priggish. His treatment of the fallen queen in "Guinevere" — one of the idylls most beloved by Victorian readers — is a "hateful scene, the most revolting exhibition of false sentiment and fiendish cruelty in all literature" (33).

Fortunately, Adams says, the critical mood is changing. "At this hour one is at least spared the trouble of wasting time on any such vain proposition" as one that ascribes Tennyson a place beside Shakespeare, Milton, and Chaucer as one of the great poets of England (23). Yet, like other critics who get beyond the aura of the Victorian laureate to assess the value of his contributions to literature, Adams concludes with a prediction that subsequently proved to be true. Referring to the excellent volume of Wordsworth's poetry selected and edited by Matthew Arnold, Adams observes that "thirty or forty years hence the Matthew Arnold of the day will present to his public a similar volume of Tennyson, but it will be a slim one" that will "cut out nine-tenths of that portion of the poet's work on which perchance he most prided himself when alive" (36). In Adams's view, there is simply not much in the Tennyson canon that could survive the test of time.

An even more prestigious critic who had once praised Tennyson now aligned himself among the Reactionaries. J. M. Robertson, free-thinker and philosopher, had written in *Essays Toward a Critical Method* (1889) that Tennyson was both a master of verse forms and a spirited seer who gave hope to his age through his poetry. In that volume, "the singer of our youth" had become "the Virgil of our time" (282). But Robertson leads off his new study, *Browning and Tennyson as Teachers* (1903), with the charge that "not merely has [Tennyson] obtruded his theology on his readers a hundred times, vacillating and inconsistent as it is," but he has "again and again attacked men of another way of thinking, not only with arrogance but with fanaticism" (7). Robertson may be the first to suggest in print that Tennyson suffered from "a psychosis which kept him for a time at odds with his contemporaries" (11), although the allusion is to his practice during the 1830s and 1840s. Robertson finds Tennyson a strong artist but a weak thinker: his "philosophy is only his egoism, his affirmation of how the world suits him" (44).

Tennyson's chief fault, Robertson asserts, is that he universalizes his own beliefs about religion and morality. This habit is sorrowfully displayed in many works, but especially in *Maud* (56). Robertson is especially harsh on Tennyson's religious pronouncements: "his utterances are either platitudes or fallacies; he is always either begging the question or ignoring the *elenchus;* a curate could be more plausible" (73). In the end, Robertson concludes, Tennyson's ability as an artist helps him transcend his limitations as a thinker — but not without great cost to the poetry. Most tellingly, Robertson offers a condemnatory judgment that precedes Harold Nicolson's by two decades when he declares that Tennyson was "a man helplessly possessed alternately by two spirits. . . . The moral and intellectual rifts run through his whole life: the double nature asserts itself at every turn" (69).

Comparing the work of Masterman and Smyser with that of Robertson and Adams makes it clear that general critical opinion regarding Tennyson's achievement began to diverge during the decade after the poet's death. Frederic Harrison's various assessments illustrate this trend. Harrison, long-time literary and social critic, had written occasionally about Tennyson during the last decades of the nineteenth century, but in 1900 he codified his judgment of the poet's status in *Tennyson, Ruskin, Mill and Other Literary Estimates* (1900). Harrison respects Tennyson as the finest poet of his time and has praise for *In Memoriam,* but admits he is not swept away by the elegy. Similarly, he offers limited praise for *Idylls of the King,* but faults the poet for not fully mastering his materials. Like many early detractors of the poem, Harrison believes Tennyson did not do justice to Malory. After dismissing the other longer works, Harrison speaks lovingly about Tennyson's lyrics. It is not surprising that he believes the poet reached his zenith in

1859, because in his view, Tennyson was always "more the artist than the thinker" (41).

Continuing his revisionist role in a review of Alfred Lyall's critical biography of Tennyson (*North American Review* 1903), Harrison notes that the poet falls short as a philosopher. His habit of working up a "recondite thesis by piecing together a *sorites* of ingenious arguments" might be "a mode of art singularly popular, but it is not the art of the greatest masters of song" (860). Harrison concludes that "the future will no doubt be content to remember little more than a half, or even a third, of his immense output" (867). Similar thoughts run through his 1909 essay "The Centenary of Tennyson," in which he once again tries to establish Tennyson's place among the English poets. Somewhat precociously, he claims that, a century after the poet's birth and less than twenty years after his death, critics can now "judge his place without favor, partisanship, or fear of offence" (226). A visionary and iconoclast throughout his life, Harrison demonstrates his personal prejudices in his final judgment of the poet: Tennyson ranks among England's greatest poets — but not at the top of the list.

Among Tennyson's supporters, William M. Dixon, who had written more extensively about Tennyson in 1896, devoted space in *English Epic and Heroic Poetry* (1912) to a defense of the poet's narrative work. Acknowledging that the ongoing reaction against Tennyson was fueled in part by the adulation of mid-Victorian critics — "criticism of Tennyson was praise of Tennyson" for them, he admits (309) — Dixon attempts to rescue *Idylls of the King* from the vilification of his own contemporaries. The problem with the poem is not in the poetry, he concludes, but in modern readers: the allegory so important to Tennyson's contemporaries was simply not accepted by succeeding generations.

The dawn of the new century saw little abatement in the publication of monographs on Tennyson's major works. Condé Pallen, an American critic whose 1885 work had elicited a kind note of support from the poet, published *The Meaning of "The Idylls of the King": An Essay in Interpretation* in 1904 to demonstrate the poem's unity and to argue that Tennyson intended *Idylls* to be "the poetic setting of a great truth to be uttered to the world" (13). This modern Arthurian epic is an answer to a growing movement, Pallen says, against which Tennyson fought during the last half of his life: "the fetich [*sic*] worship of the ugly by the school of Naturalism" (18). Reading the poem as allegory, he argues that its main purpose is "to show forth the kingship of the soul" (19). Another reader sympathetic to the *Idylls*, John F. Genung, author of an 1884 study of *In Memoriam*, published in 1907 *The "Idylls" and the Ages*, a lecture given to the Browning Society in Boston in 1906. Genung examines the continuing relevance of Tennyson's Arthurian tale, comparing it to works by Browning to illustrate the spiritual dimension present in the work of both poets.

Certainly the most influential monograph to appear at this time was A. C. Bradley's *A Commentary on Tennyson's "In Memoriam"* (1901), a work intended to "be of use" to readers in dealing with "many of the difficulties of interpretation" that Bradley encountered "in my own reading of the poem, in conversation, in teaching, and in books on the subject" (x). Like John Genung before him, Bradley gives readers a detailed, almost stanza-by-stanza prose summary of the poem, supplementing his explication with background information on sources and occasionally pointing out how individual stanzas further the poet's principal themes. The value of Bradley's study, however, lies in the introductory chapters. In these he deals with the background to the poem, principally Tennyson's relationship with Arthur Henry Hallam; the structure, rhyme, and meter; and the ideas that inform the poem. While recognizing that the ideas in the poem cannot really be separated from the poetry, Bradley discusses Tennyson's handling of concepts of immortality and death, and his struggle with faith and doubt. The chapter on the structure was quickly recognized as a valuable explanation of the artistry of the poem, and continues to be cited, if sometimes refuted, as a demonstration of the way Tennyson brought order to the disparate lyrics that make up *In Memoriam*.

Bradley's was not the only study of *In Memoriam* to appear in the first decade of the new century. In contrast to his *Commentary*, however, William Rader's *The Elegy of Faith* (1902) loses its effectiveness as a study of the poem as a representative elegy because the author is too frequently given to hyperbole. The fact is nowhere more evident than in his summation that *In Memoriam* is "the poem of the eternal love and the mercy that endureth forever; a rebuke to agnosticism, an answer to pessimism, a philosophy of sorrow, a panacea for bereavement, an expression of faith, a confidence in human destiny, a definition of death, a triumphant wrestling with doubts . . . the best and completest statement of faith in the century" (56). The American scholar Henry Shepherd's *A Commentary on Tennyson's "In Memoriam"* (1908), remarkably similar to Bradley's work, provides a section-by-section gloss, sometimes simply summarizing the action or mood of individual lyrics, at other times offering extensive critical analysis. T. Herbert Warren's 1906 *Edinburgh Review* essay "*In Memoriam* After Fifty Years" also covers much of the same ground as Bradley. Though Warren offers little new critical commentary, he does acknowledge that around the poem "there was a growth of a whole literature of elucidation, illustration, and commentary" (308).

Tennyson's place among his Victorian contemporaries is made clear in several representative studies of Victorian literature: William M. Payne's *The Greater English Poets of the Nineteenth Century* (1907), Arnold Smith's *The Main Tendencies of Victorian Poetry* (1907), Arthur Francis Bell's *Leaders of English Literature* (1915), Laurie Magnus's *English Literature in the Nine-*

teenth Century (1909), Hugh Walker's *Literature of the Victorian* Era (1910), and G. K. Chesterton's *The Victorian Age in Literature* (1913). The contrasts among them are noteworthy. Payne examines not aesthetic merit, but the role of poets "in their relations to the world of thought and action" (v). Viewed in this light, Tennyson is the beneficiary of the confluence of events in English history, literature, and social thought: his poetry is inspired by a need to entertain and inspire. By the end of his career he had become a sage counselor and a trustworthy spiritual guide useful in resolving social and religious perplexities. Through his poetry, Tennyson "earned, beyond any other poet of his time, the love, the gratitude, and the reverence of his fellow men" (245). In Payne's view, Tennyson is almost a candidate for sainthood.

Arthur Francis Bell is less fulsome than Payne but equally convinced that Tennyson is the major poet of the age and worthy of continuing study. However, his brief summary of the laureate's career shows signs that even Tennyson's supporters were coming to accept post-Victorian judgments about his work. Bell agrees that the *Idylls,* once considered Tennyson's greatest achievement, are really flawed by lack of coherence and an unrealistically drawn portrait of King Arthur. Acknowledging that it is hard to judge the merits of a poet "so near to ourselves" (192), he suggests that it is better "to approach Tennyson rather as a poet pure and simple rather than as the possessor of any given set of ideas or preacher of any definite gospel" (193).

The views of Laurie Magnus are quite different from Payne's. Magnus begins her examination of Tennyson's poems with a caution: "Those who look, as contemporaries did, for a complete answer in Tennyson" to life's most compelling questions "are likely to be disappointed" (224). Many of his poems are wonderful works of art, but the philosophy he espouses is sometimes ephemeral, sometimes wrongheaded. Magnus's conclusions look forward to Harold Nicolson and Paull Baum rather than back toward the Victorian critics. It may be "too sweeping" to say that Tennyson's continuing fame "will stand" on a few lyrics (240), she says, yet the poet's "inspiration was hardly strong enough" to carry off the larger themes he set out to examine in his longer works. Linked so closely to his own times, he "missed the permanent aspect and the reconciling power of vision" (241).

The second section of Arnold Smith's *The Main Tendencies of Victorian Poetry* is devoted to a discussion of Tennyson's work as "The Poetry of Hope," contrasted with the work of Browning ("The Poetry of Optimism") and that of Matthew Arnold and Arthur Hugh Clough ("The Poetry of Intellectual Doubt"). While Smith offers a balanced assessment of Tennyson's accomplishments, he is more interested in demonstrating how the poet influenced readers. Considering his focus, it is not surprising that he devotes considerable attention to *In Memoriam,* but has mixed feelings about *Idylls of the King,* a work he considers too overtly didactic.

Hugh Walker wrote about Tennyson early and late in his career, and in his books one can see a gradual shift in opinion. In his 1895 study *The Greater English Poets,* Walker had classified Tennyson with Arnold and Browning as the three greatest poets of their age. Though initially a mere dilettante, Walker says, Tennyson grew in strength of conviction and willingness to confront contemporary problems. In his chapters on Tennyson in *The Age of Tennyson* (1897), a summary assessment of Victorian poetry and prose done for the Handbooks of English Literature series, Walker reiterates his views. In fact, his choice of title suggests the preeminence he accords to Tennyson among his contemporaries. By 1910, however, Walker has come to different conclusions. Again he praises Tennyson's growth in the characteristic Matthew Arnold would call "high seriousness." Nevertheless, the "day" of Tennyson and Browning is "past, and in the younger poets we detect the struggle after ideals which are not the ideals of the older men" (288). Though he still admires much of the poetry, Walker believes the characteristics that make Tennyson representative of his age now make him largely irrelevant. He is especially critical of the poet's son Hallam for "smooth[ing] away" the rough edges that so many of the poet's contemporaries found worthy of remark.

G. K. Chesterton comes to the same conclusion. Ten years before *The Victorian Age in Literature* appeared, Chesterton had coauthored with Richard Garnett a brief, illustrated life of Tennyson (*Tennyson,* 1903) in which he had acknowledged the poet's limitations but suggested that his work was worthy of continuing study. Writing a decade later at a time when the reaction against the Victorians was high, Chesterton tries to explain the reasons for such negativity. He attributes his own contemporaries' disdain for the Victorians, and especially Tennyson, to the moral smugness Victorians were so prone to display, and to their "odd provincialism" (81). Tennyson is vilified by the Moderns because he held the mainstream views of his age. "He was a Victorian in the bad as well as the good sense; he could not keep priggishness out of long poems" (85). Nevertheless, Chesterton still admires Tennyson's artistry. "He was a great poet," and "to discredit him in that respect is contemptible" (84). His greatness, however, lies principally in his lyric poetry — a view gaining ascendancy among critics of Chesterton's time. Chesterton makes the same argument for Tennyson's limitation in a brief piece written at the time of the centenary of Tennyson's birth, and included in *The Uses of Diversity* (1920): Although Tennyson is a fine poet, he was relatively uneducated in science and too willing to accept the facile compromises regarding evolution that helped his Victorian contemporaries reconcile scientific discovery with religious belief.

Some critics refused to be seduced by modernist arguments. Solomon Gingerich demonstrates his resistance in *Wordsworth, Tennyson, and Browning: A Study in Human Freedom* (1911), a work intended to determine the poet's attitudes toward the concept of free will. Citing the struggle "between fact and faith" (116) as the principal conflict of the age during which Tennyson wrote, Gingerich illustrates the poet's relationship to the times, noting how ideas such as evolution, democracy, determinism, and mysticism affected him and how he, in turn, affected readers' perceptions of these topics. Gingerich devotes separate chapters to Tennyson's writings about the conflicts between freedom and law, and between art and law.

Two other powerful academic voices who lectured against the Reactionaries were Sir Henry Jones and William P. Ker. Jones, professor of Moral Philosophy at the University of Glasgow, took Tennyson's detractors to task in his 1909 speech before the British Academy (reprinted in *Essays on Literature and Education*, 1924), arguing that academic critics who vilify Tennyson are out of step with the general public, who find great beauty and great solace in his work. He goes so far as to say that the "defects or limitations" ascribed to Tennyson's poetry "are in great part our own" (72). Because "detachment from the poetry of Tennyson has not yet come," estimates of his place among English poets "are not safe" (75–76). What can be asserted without question, Jones says, are two signs of Tennyson's greatness: the "absolute originality" of his "artistic touch," and the "absolute fidelity of his rendering of his age" (77).

Ker's 1909 Leslie Stephen Lecture celebrates Tennyson's career, concentrating on his technical and stylistic achievements and praising his abilities as a visionary poet. Ker speaks as though Tennyson were still universally acknowledged as a great poet. He cautions readers not to let Tennyson's lesser works diminish his stature: "a good poem," he says "has a value of its own which nothing can spoil" (261). Ironically, however, Ker finds Tennyson's best poetry to be his lyric work. He finds difficulties with much of his didactic poetry, because it is tied too closely to the age in which it was written. For this reason, Ker finds *Idylls of the King* especially problematic, exhibiting faults in construction, imagination, and characterization. Clearly, critical opinion was shifting toward a very different view of the laureate than that held by Tennyson's contemporaries.

Like Ker and Frederic Harrison, other writers in 1909 took advantage of the year to write centenary tributes to Tennyson. W. F. Rawnsley, son of the poet's friend Drummond Rawnsley (who officiated at Tennyson's marriage in 1850), does little more than chronicle Tennyson's life and weave together a narrative of his career from materials written by Tennyson's friends and contemporaries. In "Tennyson Centenary" (1912) he makes a case that *In Memoriam* is valuable as a poem of faith, and he demonstrates Tennyson's use of science, but seems more intent on celebrating the poet's life than criticizing his works. T. Herbert Warren's 1909 lecture at Oxford (*The Centenary of Tennyson*, 1909) provides a similar overview. On the other hand, Paul Elmer More's Shelburne Lecture in the same year is a more studied analysis of what made Tennyson the representative poet of his age. More finds the secret to Tennyson's success among his contemporaries in his ability to compromise between the conclusions to which his insight into human nature and the natural world had led him, and the demands that he offer comfort to his readers. This "spirit of compromise," More says, "rests on a denial of religious dualism" (221) that led to a pronouncement that the material world was steadily evolving toward the spiritual.

That Tennyson's reputation was on the wane is no better illustrated than in retorts to the Reactionaries published in the centenary year. E. W. Cook argues in "Appreciations and Depreciations of Tennyson" (1909) that the practice of literary criticism "has never fallen to such abysmal depths of vulgarity and insanity" as it has in vilifying Tennyson (473). He urges his contemporaries to "have done with the blight of carping criticism which seeks to belittle Tennyson's magnificent output" (474). The same point is made by the author of "Our Debt to Tennyson" in the *Spectator* (1909): "There are too many critics, destructive and skeptical in character, who suppose that nothing good can come out of a mind not in revolt" against social and moral norms (231).

Surprisingly, it seems that not everyone writing in the first decades of the new century realized a shift in critical opinion regarding Tennyson was taking place. Edward H. Griggs's *The Poetry and Philosophy of Tennyson* (1906) is actually an outline for lectures to be delivered in classes for students wanting to learn more about the "two widely different elements of Tennyson's contribution to the modern spirit" (7). Using *In Memoriam* and *Idylls of the King* as his base texts, Griggs sketches the growth of Tennyson's spiritual philosophy and his prescription for restoring character and meaning to modern life. In 1911, the Merrill Company in New York brought out an edition of *Idylls of the King* for use in the high-school classroom. The introduction by W. D. Lewis, filled with factual inaccuracies and unfounded speculations, presents the poet as a kind of seer and saint. Lewis encourages teachers to use this volume to "lessen the number of young people who pass through the great awakening period of adolescence without apparently seeing any of the deeper problems of life, or coming to a fuller appreciation of their own personality and its responsibilities" (17). Because *Idylls* displays "the effect upon society of sin in high place" (16), students should find its lessons illuminating. This annotated edition with copious notes, study questions, and a guide for teachers gives clear proof that, no matter what academic critics were saying, Tennyson's poetry still held a place of honor among the general public.

R. Brimley Johnson's *Tennyson and His Poetry* (1913) is another laudatory review of Tennyson's life and career. Intended as a combination biography and critical introduction, Johnson's book contains large selections of Tennyson's poetry — half a dozen works are quoted in full, and nearly forty others are excerpted. Johnson's aim is to use Tennyson's biography as an introduction to his poetry. A Victorian by temperament, Johnson finds *In Memoriam* great because in it Tennyson answers "the riddle of the universe" (63). Tennyson is particularly good, Johnson says, at "finding new links between past and present, and discovering the common humanity in all ages" (143). Johnson is disappointed that the generation writing after Tennyson's death has expressed "so much mistaken enthusiasm" for early works at the expense of poems in which he "attempted the expression of thought or feeling" (156). Because of this bias, Tennyson's message of faith and hope has not reached modern readers.

One writer who had high praise for Tennyson's later work was W. Forbes Gray. In *The Poets Laureate of England* (1915) Gray celebrates Tennyson's career as laureate, saying Tennyson deserves credit for "having seen that the time had arrived for a broader and more dignified interpretation" of his official duties than had most of his predecessors, and for "giving brilliant and memorable effect to his conception" (257–58). Gray cites examples from poems such as "Ode on the Death of the Duke of Wellington," "Charge of the Light Brigade," "Hands All Round," and "Riflemen, Form!" to demonstrate the quality of Tennyson's official verse. Gray's unequivocal praise is best summed up in his conclusion: Tennyson, he says, "conferred far more honour on the Laureateship than the Laureateship could confer on him" (273).

In the same year, two biographies appeared by writers who also thought highly of Tennyson. The first, by Arthur Turnbull, is both highly derivative from earlier sources and professedly laudatory. Turnbull begins *Life and Writings of Alfred, Lord Tennyson* (1915) by claiming Tennyson is one of those writers "who are shaping the time to come," and therefore worthy of a new life study so future generations may "re-assess our indebtedness" to him (2). Like so many authors influenced by Victorian values, Turnbull sanctifies Tennyson's life as a means of elevating his poetry. His enthusiastic praise for *In Memoriam* as a poem of faith and *Idylls of the King* as a great work of morality is predictable. His observations on *The Princess*, however, are worth noting. Calling it "one of the last great works of art of the Romantic Movement" (105), Turnbull provides an excellent analysis of the blending of feudal social ideals and modern science that often characterizes the best of Tennyson's work. Likening him to Alexander Pope in his ability to influence his age, Turnbull claims for Tennyson the mantle of the last and best of England's epic poets.

Turnbull's work is overshadowed, however, by the work of the American scholar Thomas Lounsbury, whose lifelong devotion to Tennyson became legendary among generations of students at Yale. Lounsbury, a fan of Tennyson's poetry from childhood, began lecturing and writing about Tennyson in the 1870s, and simultaneously began collecting materials about the poet's reception in England and America. His *Life and Times of Tennyson, 1809–1850* (1915) would seem at first glance to be the first of a two-part study that would rival, or perhaps even surpass, Hallam Tennyson's *Memoir*. Lounsbury does not intend to compete with the poet's son, however; acknowledging the primacy of place to Hallam's book, he sets out to write "an account of how Tennyson impressed his contemporaries" (xi). In more than five hundred pages he traces carefully the reception of each of Tennyson's volumes up to the publication of *In Memoriam*, which established once and for all the poet's status as the spokesperson for his age. What strikes most readers about Lounsbury's study is that, despite his professed admiration for Tennyson, he is capable of acknowledging the work of critics who sometimes judged the youthful poet's work harshly. No one interested in understanding the way Tennyson established his reputation among contemporaries can ignore Lounsbury's monumental study.

Between 1896 and 1902, the American writer and teacher Lafcadio Hearn delivered a series of lectures on English and American writers to students in Tokyo, Japan. (In 1916, notes from Hearn's students were used by Columbia University professor John D. Erskine to produce a volume titled *Appreciations of Poetry*.) Speaking about Tennyson, Hearn repeated to students many of the conclusions reached by Victorian writers regarding the poet's value to the literary tradition. "No other English poet, except perhaps Poe, has ever given so many familiar quotations to the English language," he says, and none "has influenced and enriched the English language so much as Tennyson" (32). For these qualities, Hearn says, he is worthy of continuing study.[2]

Critics like Turnbull, Lounsbury, and Hearn were swimming against the tide. Despite the publications of dozens of works celebrating the poet's merits, those by detractors continued to attract attention. Henry Salt's 1889 monograph was reissued in 1909, the centenary of Tennyson's birth, and the editors of *Current Literature* thought enough of it to publish a review ominously titled "Is Tennyson's Influence on the Wane?" The status of Tennyson's reputation — and the prevailing critical opinion — comes through clearly in a massive work intended to be an official assessment of English literature. The thirteen-volume *Cambridge History of English Literature*, edited A. W. Ward and A. R. Waller (1916), contains lengthy chapters on virtually every poet, novelist, essayist, and dramatist from the Anglo-Saxon period through the turn of the twentieth century. In the essay on Tennyson, Sir Herbert Grierson begins by citing the poet's close affiliation with and sympathy for the middle classes — a position that signaled for twentieth-century intellectuals some inherent fault that would prohibit any writer from achieving true greatness. Grierson asserts that, throughout his career, Tennyson sought a *via media* in dealing with theological and philosophical issues. The internal tensions produced by the conflicts between "the advances of physical sciences" and the poet's "sensitive and conservative temperament" were the crucible in which was forged "some of the most haunting notes of Tennyson's poetry" (27). The early works display a certain natural felicity because Tennyson was most at home when writing about the natural world or the world of fantasy; these subjects could serve easily as vehicles for creating poetry in which mood dominates. The long poems of his later years were doomed to failure from the start, Grierson says, because Tennyson was simply "not a great dramatist" and "not a great narrative poet" (49). Additionally, the poet's attempt at allegory was woefully inadequate. Hence, in 1916, Grierson asserts that *Idylls of the King* is "probably the chief stumbling block to a young student of Tennyson" (42). Incapable of living up to the role of seer thrust on him by his contemporaries, Tennyson is destined to be remembered "not as a thinker" but "as one of the most gifted and . . . conscientious workmen among English poets" (49). Clearly, for students who relied on *The Cambridge History* the judgment of Tennyson was surely to be modestly disdainful.[3]

In some ways, though, Grierson was merely echoing the judgment of the writer for the *Nation,* who calls Tennyson "one of the most splendid of minor poets." Such assessments may have shocked Tennyson's contemporaries, says the writer for the *Literary Digest,* whose commentary on the *Nation*'s review is ominously titled "Tennyson as a Minor Poet" (1914). Yet as this critic notes with a certain tinge of sadness, to say that "Tennyson's muse wore a crinoline is to make him rather ridiculous to a generation that wears its tango skirts" (619).

The extent to which Tennyson's reputation had sunk by the beginning of the First World War is made clear in A. C. Bradley's celebrated lecture "The Reaction Against Tennyson," delivered in 1914 and published in 1917. It remains a key document for those wishing to judge critical opinion of the poet — and concurrently gain some idea of what British critics valued at the beginning of the war years. Even Bradley, a longtime supporter of Tennyson, seems unable to offer unqualified praise. In 1914 he says, "the nadir of [Tennyson's] fame may not quite be reached, but it can hardly be far off" (92). He laments the fact that the uniform derision of the Victorians has blinded the public to some fine poems written by a sensitive poet who understood the crises of his time. Nevertheless, Bradley says, the reaction has not been without value, since it is hastening "that sifting process to which the works of all poets have to submit" (4). The chief cause of most negative criticism has been due to the rejection of Tennyson's ideas by a generation that does not find them appealing. For this reason, Bradley observes, "the whole collection of the *Idylls,* his most ambitious work, is probably the most obnoxious" (17). Bradley argues that it is unfair to ask a poet to be simultaneously a philosopher. Those who reject a poet for unfashionable ideas simply do not know how to read poetry. He uses *In Memoriam* as a test case to prove his thesis, relying on his own seminal study of the poem to prove its inherent aesthetic value.

Unfortunately, despite his vehement denial of their principal tenets, Bradley reveals himself to side with those he calls Reactionaries in several ways. First, he acknowledges that none of Tennyson's long poems is truly his best work. The *Idylls,* for example, "swarm with beautiful passages" but "the whole, beyond doubt, fails to satisfy" (18–19). *Maud* and *In Memoriam* are better because they take advantage of Tennyson's exceptional ability as a lyric poet. In this genre he is "unsurpassed" because he possesses two qualities: "accuracy and delicacy" of perception, and "felicity" in "translat[ing] into language that which he perceives" (27).

Though written with obvious admiration for Tennyson and thorough knowledge of his work, Bradley's essay has all the earmarks of a salvage operation. He seems sincere when, at the beginning of his essay, he says, "I will hazard a prophecy. I believe [Tennyson] will be considered the best poet of his age" (4). That bold assertion undergoes significant qualification throughout the remainder of Bradley's commentary, and leaves one wondering if it were ever going to be possible for Tennyson to emerge from the obscurity toward which the general tone of condescension and castigation was leading.

Notes

[1] Brooke's claim that Tennyson became increasingly frustrated and demoralized by advances in science is challenged by J. W. Hayes (*Tennyson and Scientific Theology,* 1909), who declares Brooke wrong, then goes on to point out how Tennyson revels in scientific advancements even in his old age. Hayes believes, however, that Tennyson found in science a confirmation of his faith in immortality and in a benevolent deity.

[2] Hearn offers similar positive observations in a lecture on Tennyson that became part of the two-volume *History of English Literature* published in 1927. Hearn's views are somewhat iconoclastic, however. While others may have agreed with him that Tennyson is an inheritor of the Romantic tradition, few would concur that *The Princess* was "Tennyson's supremely perfect creation" (644). In 1940 one of Hearn's students, Shigetsugu Kishi, issued his notes on Hearn's lectures at the Imperial University under the title *Lafcadio Hearn's Lectures on Tennyson*; Kishi's notes indicate the level of specificity Hearn employed in explicating Tennyson's works for a Japanese audience.

[3] More than two decades later, Grierson maintained his position that Tennyson was limited in ability. Writing with J. C. Smith in a single-volume, *A Critical History of English Poetry* (1944), he explains how Tennyson was shaped by his age and in turn helped to shape it. The best he can say about Tennyson is that he is representative of his age. Some of his lyrics are masterful, but his long poems are found wanting. Further, Grierson promotes the notion popularized by Harold Nicolson in 1923 and W. H. Auden in 1940 that Tennyson had no intellectual depth.

Works Cited

Adams, Francis. "Tennyson." *Essays in Modernity: Criticism and Dialogues.* London: Lane, 1899. 3–39.

Armstrong, Richard A. "Alfred Tennyson." *Faith and Doubt in the Century's Poets.* New York: Whitman, 1898. 67–90.

Bell, A. F. "Tennyson and Browning." *Leaders of English Literature.* London: Bell, 1915. 182–94.

Benson, Arthur C. *Alfred Tennyson.* New York: Dutton, 1904. Reprint, New York: Greenwood Press, 1969.

Bradley, A. C. *A Commentary on Tennyson's "In Memoriam,"* New York: Macmillan, 1901. 3rd ed., rev. London: Macmillan, 1915.

———. *The Reaction Against Tennyson.* London: Oxford UP, 1917. Reprinted in *A Miscellany.* London: Macmillan, 1929. 1–31; *English Critical Essays.* Ed. P. M. Jones. New York: Oxford UP, 1933. 59–87.

Brooke, Stopford A. *Tennyson: His Art and Relation to Modern Life.* London: Isbister, 1894. New York: G. P. Putnam's Sons, 1894. 5th ed.: London: Isbister; New York: Putnam, 1902. Reprint, New York: AMS Press, 1970.

Canton, William. "Tennyson." In *In the Footsteps of the Poets.* Ed. David Masson. London: Isbister, 1893.

Carpenter, William Boyd. *The Message of Tennyson.* London: Macmillan, 1893.

Chesterton, G. K. "Great Victorian Poets." *The Victorian Age in Literature.* New York: Holt, 1913; London: Williams & Norgate, 1914. 160–69. Reprint, South Bend, IN: U of Notre Dame P, 1963. 79–103.

———. "Tennyson." *The Uses of Diversity.* New York: Dodd, Mead, 1921. 18–23.

Chesterton, G. K., and Richard Garnett. *Tennyson.* London: Hodder and Stoughton, 1903.

Cook, E. W. "Appreciations and Depreciations of Tennyson." *Academy* 77 (28 August 1909): 473–74.

Cuthbertson, Evan J. *Tennyson: The Story of His Life.* London: Chambers, 1898. Reprint, Folcroft, PA: Folcroft Press, 1973.

Davidson, Thomas. *A Prolegomena to "In Memoriam."* Boston: Houghton Mifflin, 1897.

Dawson, W. J. *Makers of Modern Poetry.* 7th ed. London: Hodder and Stoughton. 1899. 169–269.

Dixon, W. M. "Narrative Poetry in the Nineteenth Century — Tennyson, Morris, Arnold." *English Epic and Heroic Poetry.* London: Dent, 1912. Reprint, New York: Haskell House, 1964. 302–29.

———. *A Tennyson Primer: With a Critical Essay.* London: Methuen, 1896. Reprint, New York: Haskell House, 1971.

Eidson, John O. *Tennyson in America: His Reputation and Influence from 1827 to 1858.* Athens: U of Georgia P, 1943.

Elliott, Philip Lovin. *The Making of the Memoir.* Lincoln, England: Tennyson Society, 1995.

Farrar, Frederick W. "Lord Tennyson." *Men I Have Known.* New York: Crowell, 1897. 1–41.

Genung, John F. *The "Idylls" and the Ages: A Valuation of Tennyson's "Idylls of the King," Elucidated in Part by Comparisons between Tennyson and Browning.* New York: Crowell, 1907.

Gingerich, Solomon F. *Wordsworth, Tennyson, and Browning: A Study in Human Freedom.* Ann Arbor, MI: Wahr, 1911. 113–75. Reprint, New York, Gordian Press, 1968.

Gordon, William C. *The Social Ideals of Alfred Tennyson as Related to His Time.* London: Unwin, 1906. Chicago: U of Chicago P, 1906. Reprint, New York: Haskell House, 1966.

Gosse, Edmund. "Life of Tennyson." *North American Review* 165 (November 1897): 513–26.

———. "Tennyson — and After." *Questions at Issue.* London: Heinemann, 1893. 175–98.

Gray, W. F. "Alfred, Lord Tennyson." *The Poets Laureate of England.* New York: Dutton, 1915. 252–73.

Grierson, Herbert J. C. "The Tennysons." In *Cambridge History of English Literature.* Vol. 13. Ed. A. W. Ward and A. R. Waller. Cambridge: Cambridge UP, 1916. 13:25–53.

Grierson, Herbert J. C., and J. C. Smith. *A Critical History of English Poetry.* London: Chatto & Windus, 1944; New York: Oxford UP, 1944.

Griggs, Edward H. *The Poetry and Philosophy of Tennyson.* New York: Huebsch, 1906.

Gunsaulus, Frank W. "Alfred Tennyson." *The Higher Ministries of Recent English Poetry.* New York: Revell, 1907. 107–17.

Gurteen, Stephen H. V. *The Arthurian Epic: A Comparative Study of the Cambrian, Breton, and Anglo-Norman Versions of the Story and Tennyson's "Idylls of the King."* New York: Putnam, 1895. Reprint, New York: Haskell House, 1965.

Gwynn, Steven L. *Tennyson: A Critical Study.* London: Blackie, 1899. Reprint, New York: Haskell House, 1974.

Harrison, Frederic. "The Centenary of Tennyson." *Nineteenth Century and After* 66 (August 1909): 226–33. Reprinted in *Among My Books*. New York: Macmillan, 1912. 284–96.

———. "Tennyson." *Tennyson, Ruskin, Mill and Other Literary Estimates.* New York: Macmillan, 1900. 1–47.

———. "Tennyson: A New Estimate." *North American Review* 176 (June 1903): 856–67.

Hayes, J. W. *Tennyson and Scientific Theology.* London: Stock, 1909. Reprint, Brooklyn, NY: Haskell, 1977.

Hearn, Lafcadio. *Hearn's Lectures on Tennyson.* Ed. Shigetsugu Kishi. Tokyo: Hokuseido; Pasadena, CA: Perking, 1941. Reprint, Norwood, PA: Norwood Editions, 1978.

———. "Studies in Tennyson." In *Appreciations of Poetry.* Ed. J. Erskine. New York: Dodd, Mead, 1916. 30–36.

———. "Tennyson and the Great Poetry." *A History of English Literature: A Series of Lectures.* Vol. 2. Tokyo: Hokuseido, 1927. 637–46.

Horton, Robert F. *Alfred Tennyson: A Saintly Life.* London: Dent, 1900. Reprint, New York: Haskell House, 1973.

Innes, Arthur D. *Seers And Singers: A Study of Five English Poets.* London: A. D. Innes, 1893.

"Is Tennyson's Influence on the Wane?" *Current Literature* 47 (September 1909): 275–78.

Jacobs, Joseph. "Alfred Tennyson." *Literary Studies.* London: Nutt, 1895. 155–71.

———. *Tennyson and "In Memoriam": An Appreciation and a Study.* London: Nutt, 1892. Reprint, Folcroft, PA: Folcroft Press, 1974.

Johnson, R. Brimley. *Tennyson and His Poetry.* London: Harrap, 1913. Reprint, Port Washington, NY: Kennikat Press, 1970.

Jones, Henry. *The Immortality of the Soul in the Poems of Tennyson and Browning.* Boston: American Unitarian Association, 1907.

———. "Tennyson." *British Academy Proceedings* 4 (1909): 131–45.

Jones, Richard D. *The Growth of the "Idylls of the King."* Philadelphia: J. B. Lippincott, 1895.

Ker, William P. *Tennyson: The Leslie Stephen Lecture.* Cambridge: Cambridge UP, 1909. Reprinted in *Collected Essays of W. P. Ker.* Vol. 1. London: Macmillan, 1925. 258–76.

Knowles, James T. "Aspects of Tennyson." *Nineteenth Century* 33 (January 1893): 164–88.

Lang, Andrew. *Alfred Tennyson.* New York: Dodd, Mead, 1901.

Lewis, W. D. "Introduction." *Tennyson's "Idylls of the King."* New York: Merrill, 1911.

Littledale, Harold. *Essays on Lord Tennyson's "Idylls of the King."* London: Macmillan, 1893.

Lounsbury, Thomas R. *The Life and Times of Tennyson: From 1809 to 1850.* London: Oxford UP; New Haven: Yale UP, 1915.

Luce, Morton. *A Handbook to the Works of Alfred, Lord Tennyson.* London: Bell, 1895. Rev. ed., 1914. Reprint, New York: Burton Franklin, 1970.

———. *New Studies in Tennyson, Including a Commentary on "Maud."* London: Baker, 1893. Reprint, Folcroft, PA: Folcroft Press, 1973.

———. *Tennyson.* London: Dent, 1901.

Lyall, Sir Alfred. *Tennyson.* London: Macmillan, 1902. Reprint, New York: Haskell House, 1977.

Lyttleton, Arthur T. "Tennyson." *Modern Poets of Faith, Doubt, and Other Essays.* London: Murray, 1904. 1–32.

Mabie, Hamilton W. "The Influence of Tennyson in America: Its Sources and Extent." *Review of Reviews* (6 December 1892): 553–56.

MacCallum, M. W. *Tennyson's "Idylls of the King" and Arthurian Story from the XVIth Century.* Glasgow: MacLehose, 1894.

Magnus, Laurie. *English Literature in the Nineteenth Century.* New York: Putnam, 1909. 224–42, 280–86.

Masterman, C. F. G. *Tennyson as a Religious Teacher.* London: Methuen, 1900.

Millgate, Michael. *Testamentary Acts: Browning, Tennyson, James, Hardy.* Oxford: Clarendon Press; New York: Oxford UP, 1992.

Moore, John M. *Three Aspects of the Late Alfred Lord Tennyson.* Manchester: Marsden, 1901. Reprint, New York: Haskell House, 1972.

More, Paul Elmer. "Tennyson." *Shelburne Essays.* 7th Series. New York: Putnam, 1910. 64–94. Reprinted in *Modern Essays.* Ed. J. M. Berdan. New York: Macmillan, 1916. 204–28.

Oates, John. *The Teaching of Tennyson.* London: J. Bowden, 1895. 2nd ed. 1898. Reprint, New York: Haskell House, 1973.

"Our Debt to Tennyson." *Spectator* 103 (14 August 1909): 230–31.

Pallen, Condé B. *The Meaning of "The Idylls of the King": An Essay in Interpretation.* New York: American Book Co., 1904.

Paul, Herbert W. "Tennyson." *New Review* 7 (November 1892): 513–32.

Payne, William M. "Alfred Tennyson." *The Greater English Poets of the Nineteenth Century.* New York: Holt, 1907. 221–50.

Rader, William. *The Elegy of Faith: A Study of "In Memoriam."* New York: Crowell, 1902.

Rawnsley, William F. "Tennyson Centenary." *Introduction to the Poets.* London: Routledge, 1912. 243–313.

Rearden, Timothy H. "Alfred Tennyson, Poet Laureate." *Petrarch and Other Essays.* San Francisco: Doxey, 1897. 43–96.

"Reputations Reconsidered: III. Lord Tennyson." *Academy* 53 (8 January 1898): 34–36.

Robertson, J. M. "The Art of Tennyson." *Essays Towards a Critical Method.* London: Unwin, 1889.

———. "Tennyson." *Browning and Tennyson as Teachers.* London: Brown, 1903. 1–83.

Saintsbury, George. "Tennyson." *Corrected Impressions: Essays on Victorian Writers.* London: Heinemann; New York: Dodd, 1895. 21–40.

———. "Tennyson." *A History of Nineteenth-Century Literature.* London: Macmillan, 1896. 253–68.

———. "Tennyson and Browning." *A History of English Prosody, from the Twelfth Century to the Present Day.* Vol. 3. London: Macmillan, 1910. 183–217.

Salt, Henry S. *Tennyson as a Thinker.* London: Reeves, 1893. Reprint, 1909.

Shepherd, Henry E. *A Commentary on Tennyson's "In Memoriam."* New York: Neale, 1908.

Smith, Arnold. "Tennyson." *The Main Tendencies of Victorian Poetry.* London: Simkin, Marshall, Hamilton, Kent, 1907. 59–104.

Smyser, William E. *Tennyson.* Cincinnati: Eaton and Mains, 1907.

Sneath, Elias H. *The Mind of Tennyson: His Thoughts on God, Freedom, and Immortality.* Westminster: Constable, 1900. Reprint, New York: Gordian Press, 1970.

Stanley, Hiram M. "Tennyson's Rank as a Poet." *Essays on Literary Art.* London: Swan Sonnenschein, 1897. 13–24.

Stevenson, Morley. *Spiritual Teaching of the Holy Grail.* London: Wells, Gardner, and Darton, 1903.

———. *Spiritual Teaching of Tennyson's "In Memoriam": Six Lenten Addresses.* London: Gardner, Darton, 1904.

Strong, Augustus Hopkins. "Tennyson." *The Great Poets and Their Theology.* Philadelphia: Griffith and Rowland, 1897. 449–524.

"Tennyson." *Blackwood's Edinburgh Magazine* 152 (November 1892): 748–66.

"Tennyson as a Minor Poet." *Literary Digest* 48 (21 March 1914): 619–20.

Tennyson, Hallam, ed. *Alfred Lord Tennyson: A Memoir*. 2 vols. London: Macmillan, 1897.

———. *Tennyson and His Friends*. London: Macmillan, 1911.

Traill, H. D. "Aspects of Tennyson." *Nineteenth Century* 32 (December 1892): 952–66. Reprint, *Living Age* 196 (11 February 1893): 415–25.

Turnbull, Arthur. *Life and Writings of Alfred, Lord Tennyson*. New York: Scribner, 1915.

Van Dyke, Henry. *The Poetry of Tennyson*. Cambridge: Cambridge UP, 1898; New York: Charles Scribner's Sons, 1902. Rev. and reissued as *Studies in Tennyson*. New York: Scribner, 1920. Reprint, Port Washington, NY: Kennikat Press, 1966.

Walker, Hugh. *Age of Tennyson*. London: Bell, 1897.

———. *The Greater Victorian Poets: Tennyson, Browning, and Arnold*. London: Swan Sonnenschein, 1895.

———. *The Literature of the Victorian Era*. Cambridge: Cambridge UP, 1910. 2nd ed., 1921. 287–309, 374–410.

Walters, J. C. *Tennyson: Poet, Philosopher, Idealist: Studies of the Life, Work, and Teaching of the Poet Laureate*. London: Kegan Paul, Trench, Trubner, 1893. Reprint, New York: Haskell House, 1971.

Warren, T. Herbert. *The Centenary of Tennyson, 1809–1909*. Oxford: Clarendon Press, 1909.

———. "*In Memoriam* after Fifty Years." *Edinburgh Review* 203 (April 1906): 297–318.

Waugh, Arthur. *Alfred Lord Tennyson, a Study of His Life and Work*. New York: United States Book Co., 1892. London: Heinemann, 1902.

Yeats, W. B. "The Symbolism of Poetry." *The Dome*, 1900. Reprint, *Essays and Introductions*. London: Macmillan, 1961. 153–64.

3: Criticism Pro and Con: 1916–1959

HOW SERIOUS THE REACTION AGAINST Tennyson had become by the First World War may be seen in a brief essay by Alice Meynell. Writing in 1917 Meynell, herself a poet, displays the conflicted views so typical of her generation. Fearing that less judicious readers might dismiss all of Tennyson because of "the peculiar Tennyson trick" of appealing to sentimentalism and bourgeois taste (80), Meynell attempts to salvage what she can of the poet's reputation by proposing the idea of The Two Tennysons. "If ever there was a poet who needed to be parted from himself," she argues, it is Tennyson (79). His "weakest kind of work" was blank verse (81) and he was indeed sentimental, even maudlin on occasion. He is "hardly a great master of imagery" (83) — but he is a master of scene-painting, and for this alone Meynell wishes to save him from those who would toss all his work on the ash heap of history. Although given to "excessive ease" (81) in his style, Meynell says he is a poet who can capture the imagination through his vivid descriptions, providing "a new apprehension of nature" (88). The Tennyson Meynell admires is England's "wild poet" (89), not the laureate suitable for drawing rooms.

Similar sentiments are echoed by F. J. C. Hearnshaw, who asks in "Tennyson Twenty-Five Years After" (1917): "Will [Tennyson] live; or will the comparative neglect and indifference with which he has been regarded during the past quarter of a century continue to be his lot during the present and subsequent generations?" (353) Hearnshaw believes that, although the passing of the Victorian era "with its transitional doubts and ephemeral perplexities" has "rendered much of his didactic poetry obsolete," Tennyson will survive "as a permanent memorial" of that age and "as the writer of some of the most exquisite lyrics in the language" (353).

At the same time Harvard philosopher George Herbert Palmer was expressing his admiration for Tennyson in *Formative Types of English Poetry* (1918), a collection of lectures given at Pacific Theological Seminary. Dealing with the philosophical underpinnings of the poet's art, Palmer discusses the qualities that make him distinctive among English poets: his focus on England as both subject and theme; his treatment of marriage "as the source of the deepest and most constant happiness in life" (242); his appreciation and understanding of nature; and his ability to make sense of the problems of his age. Palmer believes Tennyson "enlarge[d] the bounds of English poetry by introducing something which it had not known before" (246–47), namely, a "reconstitution of our verse" and a marked advance in the "handling of character" (247). Tennyson "introduced into English poetry a new kind of portrait-painting, the portraiture not of any man as a whole but of some single mood, into which for the moment all the man's character and all his surroundings are absorbed" (256). Palmer's assessment serves as a thoughtful counterclaim to that of many late Victorian and Edwardian critics — and others throughout the first half of the twentieth century, who, enamored of the tools of Freudian analysis, find Tennyson's portraits unconvincing.

Raymond M. Alden's *Alfred Tennyson: How to Know Him* (1917), a book written for college students and the general public, perpetuates Victorian myths about the laureate. Alden examines the poetry by genre, examining Tennyson's character and his influence on contemporaries. In Alden's view, Tennyson was a strong anti-materialist who supported the importance of religious belief. The poet was not afraid to take up the controversies of his day, introducing new ways to understand the traditional tenets of Christianity. His conservatism, Alden says, is a special strength.

Alden's bias comes through from beginning to end in his study. He opens by asserting that "The life which [Tennyson] lived, might be called the most typical and most happy poet's life of any of the great English men of letters" (1). The early reviewers who took Tennyson to task for his 1830 and 1833 volumes did so because "it was an age of much bitterness in reviewing" (14). He asserts that the poet has fallen out of favor during the early years of the twentieth century because of "our dislike for the didactic" (355). He even goes so far as to take on critics who devalue *Idylls of the King*. The reaction against Tennyson is, in his view, a sign of modern humanity's misguided sense of values. "It would seem then, that the matters which have led the present generation to lose touch with Tennyson as a representative poet of our race are not altogether to our credit" (363). When the blindness that affects critics of the early twentieth century is lifted, Alden says, Tennyson's reputation will rise again.

Despite the general tenor among academic critics that Tennyson had little to say to the modern world, quite a few supporters still took time to defend him, especially after the First World War ended. Geraldine Hodgson's article "The Legacy of Tennyson" in her book *Criticism at a Venture* (1919) attacks Tennyson's detractors, claiming for him a revered place in literature as a "consummate craftsman" (10). No poet in English, she says, has ever been so successful at blending "accurate observation, intense appreciation of Nature, and perfect imagination" (14). The only disquieting element of her otherwise supportive analysis is her insistence that Tennyson's best works are his lyrics — a position soon to be championed by the most influential critic of the postwar decade, Sir Harold Nicolson. Little of that sense of frustration is present in Jean Pauline Smith's *The Aesthetic Nature of Tennyson* (1920).

Smith finds that, in short or long works, the poet's keen appreciation for sensory experience led him to create masterpieces that touch his readers both emotionally and intellectually.

Others agreed. In fact, in 1920 G. H. Blore had great praise for Tennyson in *Victorian Worthies* (1920), a book intended to help shape the character of schoolboys. The previous year the American geologist William North Rice had written in *The Poet of Science and Other Addresses* (1919) that Tennyson was the most adroit of all the English poets in adapting the materials of science to his art. Finding Tennyson a keen observer of nature who "draws his material in large degree from recondite facts of science and scientific theories" (17), Rice argues persuasively that the poet "gave early acceptance to the views of Darwin" and "recognized the role of evolution, even in the ethical development of humanity" (28). For Rice, there is no doubt that Tennyson is a poet of faith rather than a harbinger of doubt.

Still others were even more appreciative of Tennyson's role as a spokesperson for the vocation of the poet. In *The Laureateship* (1921), Edmund Broadus praises Tennyson for resurrecting the position of poet laureate, which had become almost irrelevant by 1850. Broadus has no qualms about calling him the greatest poet of his generation: "when men called Tennyson 'the laureate,' they thought of him as . . . the poet-interpreter of the thought of his time, and the poet-sage" (190). Broadus believes Tennyson kept sufficient distance from both Court and Parliament to function effectively in his office.

Another supporter, J. F. A. Pyre, saw Tennyson as a voice of hope in a world recently driven to despair. Though he did not publish *The Formation of Tennyson's Style* until 1921, Pyre had completed his work initially as a dissertation years before the outbreak of hostilities in Europe. While the revision for the press contains more than one allusion to the importance of Tennyson's ability to provide hope for those devastated by the war, much of Pyre's work is organized along the lines of the kind of Germanic scholarship practiced in American graduate schools at the turn of the twentieth century. Pyre concentrates on the early works, tracing Tennyson's development from his early imitative efforts to his development of an independent style that echoes earlier models while adding a strain of originality that has since come to be known as Tennysonian. Filling his work with charts that categorize meter, rhyme scheme, stress, and repetitive images, Pyre demonstrates ways Tennyson revised early poems carefully to produce, by 1842, a collection of first-rate work that has earned him a place among England's greatest poets. As he grew older, Pyre says, Tennyson moved toward a simplicity that modified his tendency toward ornate expression.

Another work appearing in 1921 suggests that, whatever his reputation, Tennyson continued to be a subject worthy of study by academics. In "The Influence of Carlyle on Tennyson," DeWitt T. Starnes identifies parallel passages that demonstrate how much the poet looked to Carlyle's writing for ideas and inspiration. Following the method of German rather than British or American critics, Starnes concludes only that the parallels prove Tennyson's debt to Carlyle; he says nothing about the value of the poetry or the importance of the poet as a spokesperson for his age. Starnes's work would be extended three decades later by W. D. Templeman in "Tennyson's 'Locksley Hall' and Thomas Carlyle" (1950), an article that does more than its title suggests by reviewing similarities between Tennyson and other Victorians who suffered a crisis of faith.

Yet even an admirer like Oliver Elton could not be immune to the growing trend in delimiting Tennyson's accomplishments. Elton claims in *A Survey of English Literature, 1830–1880* (1920) that Tennyson was the greatest of the Victorians, but he follows the growing tendency to value Tennyson's lyrics over his long poems. "We think too much of Tennyson as imperiously respectable, as the voice of Victorian England, and as somehow breaking with the freer traditions of romance" (330). Actually, Elton says, Tennyson's "character is at times in conflict with his heart" (332). In his view, Tennyson is a Romantic manqué. While Elton acknowledges *In Memoriam* as a work of intellectual and spiritual significance, his greatest praise is for *Maud*, which he says "is really Tennyson's greatest and most genuine production of any length" (350). *Idylls of the King* is a failure except in its splendid parts. The equivocation of Elton's opinion is nowhere better present than in his final assessment: "Tennyson commanded a style and a music . . . adequate, we may think, for the great poems which he never wrote" (361).

Two others sympathetic toward Tennyson but uncomfortable in promoting him wholeheartedly amid such a groundswell of negative commentary were J. C. Squire and Robert Lynd. Both were frequent contributors to literary periodicals, and Squire's 1921 article on Tennyson (reprinted in *Essays on Poetry*, 1923) illustrates the dilemma in which postwar critics found themselves. Squire consistently pleads the case for Tennyson as a great poet, but his essay is devoted to finding fault with his work. Squire believes "there is more" in the reaction against Tennyson than "a mere automatic revulsion against idolatry" (64). The "permanence of his achievement," Squire says, and "the poetic quality of his work was certainly adversely affected by his conception of his function" (69). Squire says Tennyson "faked; he is not all of a piece; much of his writing did not really come from himself" (71). Then, having exhausted his criticisms, Squire concludes that Tennyson "remains," and that "too much of his good poetry" has "been too much questioned and too much ignored" (81).

This curious vacillation can be seen in Lynd's work as well. Lynd argues in "Tennyson: A Contemporary Criticism" (1921) that Tennyson's diminished reputation is due less to hostile critics than to the passing of time. But his fall is directly associated with his tendency to promote Victorian values which have been discredited. Further, he believes "Tennyson was by no means the complete artist that for years he was generally accepted as being" (135). From this premise, Lynd proceeds to demonstrate that Tennyson's best work were his shorter, lyrical poems that emphasize keen descriptions of the natural world and strong moods of melancholy.

In 1923, the English philosopher J. W. Mackail defended Tennyson, but seemed to recognize that in praising him he was working against the grain. In his lecture on Tennyson, printed in *Studies of English Poets* (1926), Mackail proclaims Tennyson's greatness, but finds himself forced to acknowledge that he "had not the dramatic, any more than he had the narrative, gift" (245–46). What is left, of course, are those qualities as a lyricist which will allow Tennyson to live on among the English poets — among the second rank. Clearly the stage was set for the major critical works that would assign Tennyson a place among the lesser English poets.

Despite the impassioned complaints of Tennyson's supporters during the first decades of the twentieth century, the great debunking of the Tennyson myth reached its zenith not in these early years, but a bit later. Unquestionably, 1923 marks a watershed in Tennyson criticism. In that year, two biographical and critical studies, one actually presenting itself as a defense of the poet, condemned him to the ranks of the ephemeral, neurotic, and hardly important literary versifiers from an age when priggish morality and smug hypocrisy were ascendant. Much of subsequent criticism on Tennyson for the next forty years was shaped by the work of Sir Harold Nicolson and Hugh Fausset, whose assessments differ only in the level of sarcasm and vitriol that distinguishes the latter's work from the castigations and expressed frustrations of the former's.

Ironically, Nicolson claims that he was interested primarily in rescuing Tennyson from oblivion and restoring him to appropriate status within the pantheon of English poets. Writing thirty years after the poet's death, Nicolson would no doubt claim to be providing a much needed corrective to the diatribes of detractors who had led the famous reaction against the Victorian laureate. This is precisely the kind of special pleading he makes throughout *Tennyson: Aspects of His Life, Character, and Poetry* (1923), one of the most influential studies published during the years immediately following the First World War.

The careful reader of Nicolson's study soon learns, however, that the author does not mean to restore Tennyson's reputation. Rather, he intends to expose the Victorian poet, seer, and moral arbiter of his age for what he really was: a morbid, self-absorbed introvert whose best poetry was written before he was thirty, and whose excessive concern for popular opinion robbed him of the chance to be a truly competent Romantic poet. Instead, Nicolson says, Tennyson bowed to the desires of his Cambridge colleagues, especially Arthur Henry Hallam, who lavished excessive and undeserved praise on his juvenile efforts and encouraged him to use his talents for instruction, not merely self-expression. In Nicolson's view, early critics had less influence on Tennyson than his circle of friends, who kept insisting he had the talent to write something bigger — meaning, of course, more prophetic and educational. Nicolson believes Tennyson simply was not up to the task. Instead, "the great lyric poet" of Lincolnshire "had already been tamed," the "wild animal that lurked within him had been caged" (25). The demand for producing something grand and educational was taken up by critics sympathetic to Tennyson in the years before he published *In Memoriam*, further driving him to stultify his Romantic tendencies. The poetry Nicolson finds simpering was produced, he says, due to "the influence of that peculiar condition of public taste" that promoted production of Keepsake volumes — that is, the tastes of the Victorians, for whom Nicolson has little use (103). Even his marriage turned into a form of imprisonment for Tennyson: "the wistful lady who became his wife was able, with little worsted strands, to bind what was most wild in him and most original" by convincing him that he was, indeed, the prophet of his age (157–58).

Unfortunately, Nicolson is eclectic in his selection of poems for analysis — a fault he shares with many of his contemporaries and critics of the preceding generation. Wherever possible, he offers biographical readings to give further emphasis to his theory that Tennyson was a frustrated Romantic. In attempting to salvage what he considers the best of Tennyson's work, Nicolson ends up savaging the poet's character and mental stability. It should not be surprising to find him taking this approach in an age when psychological criticism was coming of age, however. He does justice to *In Memoriam*, and seems to like some aspects of *Maud*, but in his 1923 edition he dismisses *Idylls of the King* as unworthy of attention. His attempt to correct this impression by including a discussion of the poem in his 1962 revision of his biography is even-handed, but it had little effect on critical trends, since his omission in the first edition became a tacit judgment that the poem did not merit critical attention.

To see how strongly Nicolson held these views, one need only compare his chapter on "Love, Politics and Religion" with the one on "Lyrical Inspiration." The former presents Tennyson as a tentative, not-too-intelligent versifier struggling to explain the workings of society and the cosmos; the latter celebrates the poet with great affection (and considerable skill) as a truly remarkable lyricist able to capture emotions and the natural world in his poetry. Nicolson seems to revel in his conclusion that "the age of Tennyson is past" (306) — never, he suggests, to return.

Nicolson's deprecating view of Tennyson pales, however, beside the sometimes vicious and almost always derogatory assessment of Hugh I'Anson Fausset. His *Tennyson: A Modern Portrait* (1923) begins by defending modern — that is, post-Victorian — critics: "We have read so often of late that the young criticize Tennyson merely out of a rather dissolute caprice"; such an accusation is "a libel . . . upon their sincerity" (vii). Fausset defends his own contemporaries, arguing that the "self-absorption" Tennyson developed as a child and the "perpetual gratification of easy experiences" (13) remained with him throughout his life and led him to create secondrate poetry that simply pandered to the Victorian public's penchant for avoiding harsh truths about society, politics, or religion. Tracing Tennyson's career from his sheltered existence at Somersby to his years at Cambridge, Fausset reveals how the influence of his friends among the Apostles was disastrous to his growth as a poet. Though he "was always to prove most at home with the unreal," Fausset claims, Tennyson responded to the criticism of his friends that his poetry had no moral purpose by "seek[ing] to acquit himself with more manly, serious verse" (31). Early criticism simply made Tennyson more petulant and secretive. Instead of taking the advice of sage reviewers like Christopher North, Fausset says, Tennyson and his friends "retired to their dainty garden of Hesperidean fancy to worship graven images and the featureless wraith of 'progress.' And thither many followed them in meek submission for fifty years" (38). It is hard to believe that, after reaching such a judgment, Fausset found it worthwhile to continue his study, since he was obviously out of sympathy with his subject.

Parting company with Nicolson, who found merit in Tennyson's early lyrics, Fausset judges almost all of the early poetry puerile; even the revised poems in the 1842 volume and the new ones that brought Tennyson public acclaim as the successor to the Romantics leave him cold. What others have described as a difficult decade for the poet (1831–1842) Fausset characterizes as a period in which Tennyson led an "extraordinarily privileged" life, "praised, petted, and revered by family and friends" (60). Being neither "creative nor imaginative" (71), Tennyson wrote poem after poem that was merely picturesque or sentimental. Fausset is willing to admit, albeit grudgingly, that the poet genuinely grieved over the loss of his friend Arthur Henry Hallam, and that the memory of his friend "inspired all the truest and deepest poetry that he ever wrote" (76).[1]

Which among the poems are true and deep Fausset does not always clearly identify. He believes that the poems of the 1842 volume demonstrate "that conflict between genius and commonplace" in Tennyson's work "which was to end in so overwhelming victory for the latter" (99). *The Princess* "lacks emotional intensity" (135), demonstrates Tennyson's willingness to "accept contemporary standards" of morality and social values (136), and stands as "the first clear announcement of a contented compromise with life" (137). While *In Memoriam* may highlight the struggles the Victorians faced between faith and doubt, Fausset believes Tennyson's "synthesis" was "too easy and superficial to excite in him either profound emotion or passionate thought, the two forces out of which poetry is born" (152). *Idylls of the King* and the later poetry, especially the occasional poems Tennyson produced as poet laureate, fare no better under Fausset's critical attack. The "critics' instinctive dislike" of *Maud*, Fausset says, "we can see now to have been justified" (190). The poem may have "great beauty" as some post-Victorian critics have acknowledged, but Fausset finds "organically it is false and characterless" (193).

Fausset seems to resent the fact that, later in his life, Tennyson became a kind of cult figure. This was especially destructive, because Tennyson fed public prejudices about the Idea of Progress and the smug moral hypocrisy that post-Victorian England found so reprehensible. Only in his later years, when he finally discovered that his naïve view of society was simply untenable, did he write with a sincerity that "wakes our hearts to sympathy" (269). For most of his career, however, Tennyson seldom "spent himself upon the hazard of thought, or brooded over mysteries too deep or painful to plumb" (249).

Only in his descriptions of Tennyson's family life does Fausset deign to say something complimentary. In his view, Tennyson was a devoted family man, a fine host (although he disliked being interrupted by strangers), and a concerned property owner. Ironically, Fausset's portrait of the Tennysons' home life at Farringford and Aldworth approaches the level of a Victorian domestic set piece such as one finds at the end of "The Two Voices," when Tennyson's speaker is saved from suicide by seeing a family on its way to church. Nevertheless, while Fausset may admire Tennyson for his behavior as husband and father, he makes it clear throughout that the poet has been overvalued as an artist and thinker. Fausset saves his most stinging criticism for his final paragraph. "The result" of Tennyson's "high-mindedness," he says, "was the catastrophe of savagery and folly which we have known, and the decimating of a generation" who had gone off to die for the false ideals bequeathed to them by Tennyson and their other grandfathers (302).[2]

One problem in showing the depths to which Tennyson's reputation sunk in the 1920s and 1930s is that one is frequently looking for negative evidence; the proof, as poststructuralists might say, is in the gaps, in what is not said. One has to infer from the absence of book-length studies and the paucity of articles that treat his work seriously that critics thought Tennyson's work unworthy of study. The few books published during the period between Nicolson and Fausset's studies and the resurrection of his reputation by Jerome Buckley in 1960 were either minority reports or addendums to Nicolson and Fausset.

The disdain in which academic critics held Tennyson is noted succinctly by Albert Mordell in a note to his 1926 collection *Notorious Literary Attacks:* "Today there is a reaction against Tennyson and he ranks as the author of a few good poems and lyrics and some fine stanzas in *In Memoriam*" (xxxiv). The title of Henry Ten Eck Perry's 1927 essay aptly expresses the new majority opinion: "The Tennyson Tragedy." Had Tennyson not insisted that "the world should put into practice the truths which he enumerates," he may have produced poetry that would have stood the test of time, Perry says (99). Unfortunately, Tennyson was limited by his "divided personality," alternatively "half escaping from the present into the past and half escaping from himself among the people about him" (106). "Baffled by the present," Perry says, Tennyson was forever looking "yearningly backward and expectantly forward" (111), missing the chance to speak to his contemporaries and to all ages. Perry acknowledges that his summary is based largely on the work of Nicolson, whose "devastating analysis" of the poet is "by far the most penetrating and stimulating study of Tennyson's personality that has yet been made" (100).

Despite the finality of such judgments, a few Tennyson lovers continued to express their views publicly, though they constituted a distinct minority. In *The Nineteenth Century and After* (1923), a publication founded by Tennyson's friend James Knowles, T. Herbert Warren wrote a lengthy defense of Tennyson against the revisionists, arguing that interest in Tennyson "never really died," but seemingly suffered "some partial eclipse and diminution, though far less than 'the critics' believed" (509). The problem with Nicolson and Fausset, he says, is that they both make "the same general mistake. They start with a preconception of the Victorian Age" — and with a prejudice against it. Further, "they treat it too much as a homogeneous whole," and assert that Tennyson was "its slave or lackey" (511). Warren, who knew Tennyson and had written about him frequently, claims that in neither book is there "a great deal" that is "new." Instead, both Nicolson and Fausset "repeat the old, old criticisms" (514) and substitute modern psychological analysis for literary criticism — a practice Warren finds wrongheaded.

In some cases, the defenders' claims for Tennyson's greatness were made with outright disregard for hostile criticism. For example, Arthur Hoyt argues in *The Spiritual Message of English Poetry* (1924) that "the worth of Tennyson lies not in his music" but in "the mass, variety, and elevation of his thought" (69). Acknowledging in his preface that his work is not literary criticism but an attempt to demonstrate "the relation of modern English poetry to the higher thought and impulse of the race" (ix), Hoyt follows the lead of Matthew Arnold in defining poetry as a criticism of life, then proceeds to explain how Tennyson helps readers discern what is important in living a good life. For Hoyt, works such as *Idylls of the King* and especially *In Memoriam* are guidebooks for living. He writes as if he were completely unaware of, or unconcerned with, critical developments during the three decades since Tennyson's death.

A stronger and more studied defense was offered by the poet Alfred Noyes in *Some Aspects of Modern Poetry* (1924). His essay on Tennyson, based on his Lowell Lectures, provides a thoughtful analysis of the qualities of Tennyson's poetry that mark him as a giant among English writers. The chief reason for vilifying Tennyson in the early years of the twentieth century — his ability to "completely sum up and express the great Victorian era in which he lived" (156) — will one day be recognized, Noyes says, as his principal strength. Further, his detractors have failed to notice that "Tennyson himself is by far the most savage satirist of what was false in his own age" (157). Noyes finds Tennyson a "clear-sighted critic" (159) who "stood like a rock for certain great fundamental faiths" (161). Recent deprecations are based on a misapprehension of the poet's powers of thought and insight. Noyes compares Tennyson with Shakespeare, finding similarities in their insight and lyrical powers. He defends *Idylls of the King* for its moral qualities — a strong stance and one surely unpopular with academic critics of the 1920s. Noyes argues that contemporary critics are wrong — not only about Tennyson, but about what is valuable in life.

Detractors outweighed defenders, however, as Edward Shanks's *London Mercury* essay on Tennyson (1927) demonstrates. Although he thinks Tennyson's "second appearance in the sunshine" is "a good thing" (163), Shanks agrees with Nicolson and Fausset that Tennyson can be interesting only if read in limited selections. Tennyson was "genuinely feminine" (167) — a term Shanks uses with disparaging overtones. A willing "slave of his age," he "wore his fetters as though they were garlands" (169). Suffering from "an inferiority complex" (170), Tennyson wrote for his audience, who wanted to think little about difficult matters. Further, Shanks says, he was "incapable of handling the major forms" (171) — although, unlike Nicolson, and T. S. Eliot later, Shanks thinks Tennyson "could tell a story in verse" (173). Surprisingly, though he does not call it great, Shanks has some kind words for *Idylls of the King*. Finally, he acknowledges that Tennyson's "second trip into the sunlight has been marked by a general and determined effort to find weaknesses in him" (175–76). This is necessary, however, because in Shanks's view, that is the only way the little good that exists in the Tennyson canon can be extracted from the mass of doggerel that Victorian readers found so comforting.

For the lectures he eventually published as *Reinspecting Victorian Religion* (1928), G. G. Atkins focuses on *Idylls of the King* and *In Memoriam* to demonstrate how "deeply saturated" Tennyson was "with a feeling for the religious side of life" (7), a feeling he shares with Browning. While his assessment of Tennyson's religious views adds little to the work of earlier critics, his comment that "Tennyson's slow, brooding way of composition implies some excess of critical faculty" (46) is a valuable insight. Unfortunately, Atkins's laudatory judgment of both poems is marred by his apparent lack of knowledge of literary tradition or critical opinion. For example, his observation that "the *Idylls* are themselves but the retelling of Malory's *Morte D'Arthur*" (59) is at odds with the fine body of late Victorian scholarship on the poem. His claim that in *In Memoriam* "Tennyson carried the heart of the nineteenth century to the great world's altar stairs, and his seeking hands, uplifted, are the hands of three generations" (59) displays more of Atkins's predilection for the Victorians than it reveals about Tennyson's poem.

More balanced, perhaps, is Laurie Magnus's assessment of Tennyson's reputation in her 1929 essay "Tennyson a Hundred Years After." Choosing her title to signal the fact that a century had passed since Tennyson won the Chancellor's Prize at Cambridge for "Timbuctoo," Magnus notes that his Francophobia, his attempts to reconcile science and religion, and his celebration of King Arthur as both national and moral hero have been the principal causes for Tennyson's failing out of favor with the modern generation. Magnus believes, however, that much of what he wrote is both first-rate poetry and sound philosophy. Not only is his "place secure among the masters of English literature," but "his gift as interpreter and seer" has been overlooked by a generation that "has worshipped strange gods of beauty and formulated unaccustomed truths" (670).

John Macy offers a divided judgment in "Tennyson: The Perfect Laureate" (1929), lamenting that "the indifference to Tennyson" by the generation that came of age at the turn of the twentieth century "was a mistake and a loss, for we missed a great poet" (376). Tennyson's reputation among his contemporaries had actually gotten in the way of modern readers' ability to appreciate his work. Nevertheless, Macy criticizes Tennyson's lack of narrative skill which led to "the whole tedious *Princess*" (379); his heavy moralizing in *Idylls of the King*, which led to his penchant to "Albertize the captain of the Round Table" (382); and his "unfortunate wooing of the dramatic muse" (385). "What remains imperishable," Macy says, "is the true Tennyson, a lyric poet" whose gifts in the genre are "high and rare" (380). The lyric Tennyson is exactly what Nicolson was trying to save.

Christopher Scaife, a lecturer in Egypt whose remarks on Tennyson appeared under the title *The Poetry of Alfred Tennyson: An Appreciation* (1930), seems confused about the poet's achievements. There is no doubt that he admires the Victorian laureate; he writes effusively about *In Memoriam* and *Maud*, and praises Tennyson for trying to adapt older forms of poetry to meet the needs of a new industrial society. When Tennyson failed, as he does in *The Princess* or in both versions of "Locksley Hall," Scaife believes the failure is due "largely" to "the incompatibility" between the poet's "literary equipment and his material" (39). In the end, however, Scaife admits that Tennyson must be read "in drastic selection" (96). He reached that conclusion, perhaps, because he had been influenced by Nicolson and Fausset, whom he cites specifically in his Foreword as having begun "in so distinguished a manner" to establish Tennyson's compositions "in a just relation to the corpus of English poetry" (96).

The direction of Tennyson criticism in the 1930s is evident in the observation of Marjorie Bowden, whose *Tennyson in France* (1930), discussed in the introduction to this volume, was a major contribution to the history of Tennyson criticism: "The giant of Victorian days has now dwindled. . . . Tennyson has passed into history. His philosophy, his modes of thought, were perishable; his art may be well enduring. It is useless to rail at the idol, now that the idol has fallen. The Poet Laureate is dead; what remains is to judge the poet" (1). The problem with Tennyson, lamented Cornelius Weygandt in 1936, is that the ideas with which he grappled — religious crises, treatment of women, acceptance of science and especially evolution — are "worn or ordinary today" (*The Time of Tennyson*, 101). Certainly, there were still some who thought the fault lay not in Tennyson but in his critics. Ernest Harstock muses sadly in "Poor Old Tennyson!" (1930) that "it is the style today for everyone who prides himself on intellectual emancipation to sneer casually and contemptuously if any indiscreet person admits such a terrible lapse of gustatory etiquette as to champion poor old Tennyson" (28).

Bowden's assessment is echoed by A. C. Ward in the introduction to *Revaluations: Studies in Biography* (1931): "The Victorians are near enough to us to be astonishing because they are still near enough to be 'old-fashioned,' and therefore seemingly dowdy inside and out. The wicked we may condone, even applaud, the dowdy never." Nevertheless, he observes, "the shadow of a first 'dating' is lifting from the Victorians" (vii–viii). The criticism of the decade bears out his assessment.

Lascelles Abercrombie's essay in *Revaluations* is representative of critical commentary in the decade. He defends Tennyson from his most vitriolic detractors, even going so far as to find merit in "Enoch Arden," the poem most savaged at the turn of the century. Nevertheless, the shadow of Harold Nicolson's judgment looms over Abercrombie's reading of the Tennyson canon. Tennyson fails as a narrative poet, Abercrombie says, because he has no ability to structure his works. Hence, *Idylls of the King* and even *In Memoriam* are not great poems; rather "*Maud* is his supreme achievement" (72). Tennyson is, however, a master "of moods, of fantasies, of reveries, above all of imaginative perception" (67). Abercrombie gives Tennyson credit for having intellectual appeal (a claim to be challenged a decade later by W. H. Auden); he continues with his qualified praise by noting that the poet can "give his readers moments of phrase, of music, of imagery, not to be equaled elsewhere" (76). But Tennyson's place is becoming fixed — and fixed much lower than his Victorian contemporaries would have accorded him. "It seems pretty certain," Abercrombie concludes, "that he will never again rank with Chaucer and Wordsworth — let alone, as he did once, above them beside Milton" (64).

In similar fashion, John Collier laments the failure of Tennyson to realize his potential as an artist. Collier's essay on Tennyson in *Harold and*

Hugh Massingham's *The Great Victorians* (1932) criticizes the poet's ability to create realistic characters and his penchant for moralizing. By nature a picturesque poet and a born lyricist, Tennyson "so much desired the acclamations of the many" (461) that he refused to refrain from writing in genres for which he was ill-equipped by talent and temperament. Though he was among the first to "absorb the modern consciousness" (463–64), he failed to act upon the instincts that would have made him a superb poet — and a rebel in his own time. "No failure," Collier concludes, "has been so tragic and so absurd as his" (469).

While not saying so directly, the poet Walter De La Mare demonstrates his agreement with Abercrombie and Collier in his essay on Tennyson originally printed in the *Times Literary Supplement* (1930) and reprinted in *Pleasures and Speculations* (1940). While he chides critics for devaluing Tennyson and notes that "the fact that a writer is no longer written about" does not mean "he is no longer read" (25), De La Mare seems unable to offer a judgment of the poet much different from the majority opinion of his day. Tennyson chose to "write for that rather nebulous norm, the general reader" (33) and hence limited his own value for future generations. With sadness, De La Mare concludes that what Tennyson seemed to value most highly, his character portraits, were quaint rather than realistic. "Purely as a poet" he may be "justly compared with Coventry Patmore and Christina Rossetti" (46). In the 1930s, the praise rings faint.

The title of Humbert Wolfe's slim volume *Tennyson* (1930), actually a study of *Maud*, perpetuates the view that Tennyson is at his best when writing lyric poetry. Though he is willing to concede that the Victorians were no less deluded by their optimism than their grandchildren are by cynicism, Wolfe finds Tennyson a man of his age — an age that had fallen into disrepute by the third decade of the twentieth century. Wolfe's claims to be attempting a restoration of Tennyson's reputation, proving "by a single example" that the negative criticism of three decades is more the result of a "reaction against Victorianism than of reading the poet" (55). *Maud* is great, Wolfe intimates, because it is counter-cultural; in it Tennyson was not afraid to experiment, and in doing so he created his real legacy. The "new method of narrative in verse" has "passed into general use." Tennyson was the first to see that "it was enough for the poet to do a series of apparently disconnected pastels and to leave the silences between to weave the complete tapestry in the reader's mind" (32). Metrical innovations and "passion" set him apart from his contemporaries (48–49). The pleading seems both contrived, and weak. Certainly, the quality of "passion" is subject to varying interpretation, and one wonders why Wolfe should choose to celebrate it in Tennyson, unless it was all he could find to praise in a poet he otherwise finds distasteful for his overt moralizing.

In 1930 F. L. Lucas, a Cambridge scholar clearly influenced by the First World War, published *Eight Victorian Poets*, a collection of essays based on radio talks delivered on the British Broadcasting Company system. Acknowledging that "a hundred people will finish a new book on Tennyson for one who explores *In Memoriam*" (xx), in this sympathetic essay Lucas attempts to interest readers in returning to the poetry by sketching Tennyson's career and accomplishments. He admits that though Tennyson's "resurrection has often been prophesied," it "has hardly come" (10). Lucas himself seems tentative in awarding Tennyson the status of first-rate poet, preferring instead to follow Nicolson's lead in praising the lyric at the expense of narrative and dramatic work. While "Tennyson remains a great poet" he is neither a great thinker nor skilled in developing character (13).

Despite the relatively low status in which Tennyson was held by formalist critics, two studies of the relationship between poetry and science contain significant discussion of Tennyson's work. In *Scientific Thought in Poetry* (1931) Ralph B. Crum gives Tennyson a prominent place among poets dealing with problems of science. Crum sees Tennyson accepting the importance of science and willing to "modify his ideas in relation to the latest scientific findings" (159). Contradicting those who believe Tennyson struggled to stem the loss of religious faith brought on by scientific advance, Crum argues that Tennyson "advanced an explanation of evolution which is perfectly in harmony with the Darwinian theory of natural selection" (159). While he may have had "shortcomings" as a religious or philosophic thinker, Crum says Tennyson "was evidently thoroughly alert scientifically," bearing favorable comparison with Goethe (170–71). Crum believes Tennyson's career demonstrates a healthy movement away from an overbearing concern for aesthetic issues to engagement with human problems. Crum, for one, finds this a genuine artistic accomplishment.

So does Lionel Stevenson in his oft-cited 1932 study *Darwin Among the Poets*. In a book examining the impact of evolutionary thought on nineteenth- and twentieth-century poetry, Stevenson traces Tennyson's interest in science from childhood through old age. He demonstrates how that predilection colors all of Tennyson's poetry, providing not only apt metaphors but also subject matter for some of his most memorable work. For Tennyson, the idea of scientific evolution "inevitably became merged with that of progress" (67) — something he celebrated when young and decried when older. Tennyson's specific break with Darwinian theory came when he found it promoted a form of materialism that denied the existence of the deity; reacting to this trend, Tennyson drifted "toward a more explicit pantheism" (95). While the poet's "natural interest in science" prompted him toward rational analysis of matters involving humankind's past and future, Stevenson notes that Tennyson "always desisted" from relying too much on reason "whenever his cherished faith was endangered" (114). Tennyson eventually found it necessary to "oppose the organized evidence of the physical scientists with an equally systematic creed," supplementing ideas of evolution with "a spiritual counterpart" (115).

What is notable about both Crum and Stevenson is their underlying assumption that Tennyson was both well-read in the sciences and measured in his responses to them. Far from being the deranged melancholic that Nicolson and Fausset declare him to have been, the poet believed deeply in the concept of immortality and in the idea that humankind was evolving progressively toward some higher — if indefinable — end. Both offer extended critiques of *In Memoriam,* and commentary on poems such as *Lucretius,* to demonstrate that Tennyson was in command not only of his artistic skills but also of his subject when it came to writing about the science of his day.

Often, the judgment of great poets who are also great critics is apt to shape critical opinion for decades. One need only recall the effect of Dr. Samuel Johnson's disparagement of the Metaphysicals or Matthew Arnold's insistence that the lack of "high seriousness" disqualifies Chaucer from wearing the mantle of greatness. In the twentieth century, T. S. Eliot and W. H. Auden perpetuated the negative view of Tennyson that dominated the half-century following his death. While neither had excessive praise for Tennyson's work, both admired him and both, either directly or indirectly, were influenced by him.[3] Nevertheless, their summary judgments of Tennyson's artistic merit damned him with faint praise, further delaying the restoration of his reputation by at least two decades.

Eliot's study of *In Memoriam* in *Essays Ancient and Modern* (1936), an expanded version of his introduction to the Wilson Classics edition of *Poems of Tennyson,* begins with an assertion that "Tennyson is a great poet." Like all great poets, his work possesses "abundance, variety, and complete competence" (175). Had he stopped there, Eliot might have hastened the rehabilitation of Tennyson's reputation and spurred critical analysis of the poetry to discern how these three qualities combine to create great literature. Almost immediately, however, he begins to explain why Tennyson is not viewed highly by the postwar generation. Following the lead of Harold Nicolson, whose study he finds "admirable" (187), Eliot reinforces the notion that there were two Tennysons, the public figure whose didactic works leave modern readers cold, and the moody lyricist whose best work is intensely emotional, tending "towards the blackest of melancholies" (181). Eliot first attributes the shift in appreciation of Tennyson's poetry to a change in taste: "The reading of long poems is not nowadays much practiced; in the age of Tennyson it appears to have been easier" (178). Even if this taste were recaptured, however, Tennyson might not fare well because his long poems are not like others', but are "always descriptive, and always picturesque; they are never really narrative" (179). In fact, Eliot concludes, "for narrative Tennyson had no gift at all" (180); he simply "could not tell a story at all" (181).

In his best long poems, *In Memoriam* and *Maud*, Tennyson manages to "turn his limitations to good purpose" (180). Though he is not as enthusiastic about *Maud* as Humbert Wolfe, Eliot finds merit in the work, but believes *In Memoriam* is Tennyson's greatest achievement, which must be read in its entirety to appreciate the great irony that lies within it. Tennyson intended the poem on the conscious level to express hope to his contemporaries. Eliot notes, however, that beneath the surface — here Eliot means in the clues that reveal Tennyson's unconscious mind — the poet exposes himself as an honest doubter. *In Memoriam* is "not religious because of the quality of its faith, but because of the quality of its doubt. Its faith is a poor thing, but its doubt is a very intense experience." The poem is "a poem of despair, but of despair of a religious kind" (187).

Though he had the finest "ear for vowel sound" of any English poet, Tennyson's "subtler feeling for some moods of anguish" makes him "the saddest of all English poets" (188–89). When he tries to write didactically, he goes away from his strength. In fact, Eliot thinks Tennyson's growth as a poet stopped with *In Memoriam*. Upon completing his elegy for Hallam, Tennyson "turned aside from the journey through the dark night" and became "the surface flatterer of his own time." For this reason he has been "rewarded with the despite of an age that succeeds his own in shallowness" (190).

Auden may have had an even greater impact than Eliot in reducing Tennyson's reputation among literary critics. His twelve-page introduction to *A Selection From the Poems of Alfred Tennyson* (1944) contains a brief summary of the Victorian poet's life, comments from Nicolson's study, and a comparative analysis of the work of Tennyson and the French poet Charles Baudelaire, with whom Auden thinks Tennyson had much in common — but who was different, and better, in key ways. Interspersed in this narrative is a single paragraph, however, in which Auden renders his own assessment of Tennyson's poetic sensibility, intellectual capacity, and psychological temperament: "[Tennyson] had the finest ear, perhaps, of any English poet; he was also undoubtedly the stupidest; there was little about melancholia that he didn't know; there was little else that he did" (x). What young academic critic would be willing to risk his reputation defending Tennyson as a great poet in the face of such damning commentary? It is a wonder that even the few who did write appreciatively would have had the fortitude to risk ridicule for their opinion after Auden had been so definitive in his.

Other major critics helped perpetuate the view that Tennyson was worth reading only selectively. In his influential study *Mythology and the Romantic Tradition in English Poetry* (1937), Douglas Bush follows Nicolson's lead in concluding that Tennyson lives on into the twentieth century "as a poet of lyrical, especially elegiac, moments, and within limits, as a superb artist in words" (197). While Tennyson was able to make exceptionally good use of classical sources, Bush concludes that he is, ultimately, "an artist who had consummate powers of expression and not very much, except as an emotional poet, to say" (199). Samuel Chew, well known to decades of English graduate students for his work with Richard Altick on *The Nineteenth Century and After* in the four-volume *A Literary History of England* (1948), writes more kindly about Tennyson in his introduction to his edition of Tennyson's poems for Odyssey Press (1941). Chew also follows received opinion that the lyric temperament infused all of Tennyson's best work, and that the poet "was seldom" able to "venture with success into the field of social criticism" (xxv). All of Tennyson's longer works, including *In Memoriam*, suffer from Tennyson's insufficiently developed "architectonic skill" (xxviii).

However, in his influential study *The Concept of Nature in Nineteenth-Century English Poetry* (1936), Joseph Warren Beach takes Tennyson seriously as a poet and thinker. Calling him "the most clear-headed of poets" (406), he does great justice to Tennyson's ideas about the contrast between the material and spiritual world. Claiming Tennyson possessed a healthy, "unromantic common sense" (406) in portraying nature, Beach says the poet understood the advances taking place in science, adopting ideas of evolution because they fit his notion that the material world — including humankind — was making steady progress toward union with its Creator. Beach warns readers, however, that Tennyson "did not wish to see this materialistic theory [Darwinism] applied to the genesis of man's mind and spirit" (432).

R. V. Routh was less sanguine about Tennyson's accomplishments, and his chapter on Tennyson in *Towards the Twentieth Century* (1937) demonstrates how the poet began as an inheritor of Romanticism but, through a series of self-motivated conversions, ended up becoming the spokesperson for an age of compromise and denial. Throughout his career, Routh says, Tennyson attacked the growing ascendancy of materialism, celebrating in his poetry the idea that humankind possessed a spiritual dimension that set them apart from other created beings and guaranteed immortality. According to Routh the poet's real failing is that he "did not face the spiritual problem of the nineteenth century," but instead attacked the concept of materialism made popular a century earlier (86). Even younger contemporaries realized the poet laureate was not addressing the real religious and philosophical issues facing the Victorians, so "they began to resent his authority and to discard his teaching" (88). In Routh's view, Tennyson was passé long before he was laid to rest in Westminster Abbey.

Some evidence that critical opinion was starting to change as war erupted in Europe is hinted at in remarks made by Ifor B. Evans in *Tradition and Romanticism* (1940): "When criticism detaches commentary on the nineteenth century from perspective it may appear Tennyson is its most enduring poet" (159). But then Evans follows the lead of Eliot and Nicolson in assessing the poet's real genius. The talented lyric poet found himself too frequently succumbing to the "dim and sentimental demands of a vast audience for easy narrative" (158). While *In Memoriam* is a poem of great merit, having "no parallel in the nineteenth century" as a philosophical poem (163), Tennyson's work as the poet laureate is generally little more than an attempt to pander to public taste. In the final analysis, Evans mimics his critical predecessors in asserting that the "self-tortured mystic" of *In Memoriam* is the poet who will be revered in future generations.[4]

An even more curious judgment is offered by Bernard Groom in his brief monograph *On the Diction of Tennyson, Browning, and Arnold* (1939). Groom repeatedly stresses the strength of Tennyson's artistry, noting his ability to create verse that was strong, colorful, descriptive, and composed in meter appropriate to his subject. In Tennyson, "language is inseparably blended with thought and sensation" (17). Ironically, however, Groom says that Tennyson may have achieved success as a poet precisely because he was not an original thinker. Rather, he "kept well abreast of the new movements in thought during his century" (13).

Though negative reaction had begun when Tennyson was in his fading years, some of Tennyson's late-Victorian contemporaries were still alive and writing well into the twentieth century, and George M. Young's 1939 Warton Lecture indicates that for many who were weaned on the Victorian laureate's verse, admiration still ran strong. Young combines personal reminiscence with brief critical analysis to reiterate claims that, despite modern criticisms, Tennyson is a consummate craftsman, able to create vivid images of the natural world and express his personal emotions in verse that has universal applicability.

The fiftieth anniversary of Tennyson's death occurred while Britain was engaged in a fight for national survival. It is easy to look back and note with irony the critical commentary that emerged during the Second World War. Some of the negativism gave way to a new round of approbation for Tennyson's patriotic spirit. In "Tennyson (After Fifty Years)" (1942), Arthur Quiller Couch noted that, since the First World War "scarcely a single young man of letters had a good word to say of Tennyson" (269), but the events of worldwide conflagration were beginning to make Tennyson's work more palatable. Among those finding revisionism necessary was none other than Sir Harold Nicolson, whose brief review of "the fluctuations in Tennyson's reputation" in "Tennyson: Fifty Years After" (1942) begins with the assertion that Tennyson was "a great poet" (333). Still convinced, however, that the measure of greatness was a poet's ability to write "pure poetry," Nicolson argues that Tennyson was great despite his many efforts at didacticism. He wrote many poems, Nicolson says, that have "nothing whatever to do either with his age or with the rather self-conscious attitude which he adopted toward his own poetic mission" (336). For this reason, there is much to admire in the Tennyson canon, and Nicolson claims to "look forward with confidence to a Tennyson revival" (336).

During the War, the *Times Literary Supplement* ran an article by the distinguished British critic G. Wilson Knight that resurrected Victorian notions of Tennyson as a patriotic poet. Reprinted in Knight's *Neglected Powers* (1971), the original carried a title that would surely appeal to a public embroiled in a struggle for national survival: "Excalibur: An Essay on Tennyson." Knight takes issue with critics who read piecemeal among Tennyson's works. Taking his corpus as a whole, Knight argues that Tennyson is "a great national poet" (419) who promotes British imperialism because the British have a duty to improve other nations. While such chauvinistic arguments would fall out of favor within two decades, the point was certainly not lost on readers who had only recently experienced the wrath of Nazi air attacks.

W. D. Paden's interesting if somewhat limited study *Tennyson in Egypt* (1942) displays the same high regard for Tennyson as his earlier article "Tennyson and the Reviewers" (1940). Concentrating on the poet's first publication, *Poems by Two Brothers,* Paden follows the critical method popularized among scholars by John Livingston Lowes in his book about Coleridge's "Kubla Khan," *The Road to Xanadu* (1927), that is, by searching among Tennyson's earliest poems for evidence of his readings about the Middle East. Applying terms from psychology to the poems, Paden demonstrates how Tennyson's reading unconsciously directs and supports the imagery in his poetry.

In 1944, Roy Basler published an essay that can be classified as one of the most important challenges to the detractors of Tennyson. Principally an analysis of *Maud,* "Tennyson, The Psychologist" begins with the assertion that those who have "cast aspersions" on Tennyson's "intellectual capacity" reveal in their critiques "the critics' rather than the poet's deficiency" (143). Basler reveals Tennyson's exceptionally sophisticated understanding of nineteenth-century concepts of psychology and his ability to use these in creating a masterful work of psychological analysis in *Maud.* After offering a detailed reading of the poem, Basler takes on earlier critics who frequently dismissed Tennyson purely because his poetry was didactic. Such an approach has blinded them to the poet's artistic merits. In Basler's view, Tennyson managed to dramatize complex psychological concepts that would not be fully explained until the next century.

Another new critical voice that would influence attitudes toward the Victorians made its appearance near the end of the war. George Ford devotes two chapters to Tennyson's poetry in *Keats and the Victorians* (1944). With a bit of wry irony, Ford titles the first chapter "Keats's Debt to Tennyson." His point is that Tennyson and his Cambridge companions were responsible for Keats's obtaining the posthumous fame that led to his enshrinement as one of the great Romantic poets. Ford's second chapter, "Tennyson's Debt to Keats," offers a conventional but persuasive assessment of the Romantic poet's influence on the future laureate.

Graham Hough is also among the minority who were not influenced too heavily by negative criticism. His essay "The Natural Theology of *In Memoriam*" (1947) is intended to demonstrate that the "philosophy" of the poem, discredited by many including Eliot, is of value. Believing "Tennyson's aim was to make an emotionally satisfying synthesis of current scientific and religious thought" (110), Hough traces the origins of the argument to the many sources in eighteenth- and nineteenth-century religious and scientific writings with which Tennyson was familiar. His reading restores a dimension of the work overlooked for nearly three decades by those who had argued that the only real value of *In Memoriam* lay in its ability to reveal the emotional state of the speaker.

By contrast, F. L. Lucas stresses the limitations of Tennyson's achievement in his introduction to *Tennyson, Poetry and Prose* in 1947. Following the lead of Nicolson, Fausset, and Auden, Lucas tries to salvage what is still useful or pleasing among the poet's works. He acknowledges that the reaction following the 1890s may have gone too far, but he finds some justice in the claims that Tennyson was simply too detached from the world to be a great poet. Further, he asserts that Tennyson's best poetry was written prior to 1850 — before he became moralistic and judgmental. The situation is really worse than it appears, Lucas says. "Apart from accidental prejudices of periods, this sense of morality in Tennyson's work, which remains probably the most serious hindrance to its enjoyment, is due also, I think, to a real weakness in Tennyson himself" (ix–x). Because he "never learnt really to know men and women" (x), he had to resort to his own feelings and impressions of human behavior. As a result, despite his technical mastery, "he tends to fade into a lovely voice with little to say" (xi). Further, Lucas asserts, Tennyson's "genius was not epic" (xv), and he lacked "the intellectual courage of Ibsen or Hardy" in confronting social problems (xv–xvi). He is not passionate, he cannot draw characters, and he could not tell stories (xvi). One wonders what Lucas found worth including in a new anthology of Tennyson's verse. The answer is predictable: some of the perennially respected lyrics, including those interwoven into *The Princess* and *Maud*, but nothing from the narrative verse, and certainly nothing from *Idylls of the King*.[5]

Less damning than Lucas, but also deprecatory in assessing Tennyson's achievement, is the commentary of one of the founders of the New Criticism, Cleanth Brooks. Brooks introduces his fine analysis of "Tears, Idle Tears" in *The Well Wrought Urn* with the observation that "Tennyson is perhaps the last English poet one would think of associating with the subtleties of paradox and ambiguity" (167). To Brooks, Tennyson is so clearly a poet of direct statement — and therefore hardly a poet at all — that when these qualities creep into his work, it is a happy accident. Acknowledging that "Tears, Idle Tears" is an exceptionally good poem, Brooks concludes simply that Tennyson "blundered into" success in writing this lyric.

The last strong argument against Tennyson is Paull F. Baum's *Tennyson Sixty Years After* (1948). Playing off the title of Tennyson's revisionist view of the world in "Locksley Hall Sixty Years After," Baum presents what he believes to be a revisionist view of the poet, aimed at salvaging what little good there might be from a welter of poems whose appeal died when the Victorian age passed away. Presuming to "apply the aesthetic rather than the moral test" to Tennyson's verse (v), Baum determines that much of the work does not measure up to accepted standards of great poetry. Baum's critical biography is an attempt to separate legend from fact, to dissociate "Tennyson the interpreter of his age" from Tennyson the poet (21). The result, in his opinion, is that what the Victorians considered Tennyson's best work is often wanting in poetic power, and instead is simply a collection of moral platitudes that appealed to his audience's wrongheaded notion of their moral superiority.

Throughout his study Baum reveals himself the intellectual descendant of Nicolson and Fausset, arguing that there were two Tennysons, and claiming that only the morbid lyricist produced great poetry. That is why, he says at the beginning of his discussion of the 1842 volume, he devotes so much space to them, because "they represent Tennyson still largely untouched by external influences — what is sometimes called the essential Tennyson." After 1842, "Tennyson's work changed — changed for the worse, in the opinion of many critics." In Baum's view, however, "Tennyson became not a better or a worse poet, but a different man, practicing his art, exercising his gifts on alien material" (66). Not surprisingly, Baum has high praise for "Ulysses" and "The Lady of Shalott," a poem "as near perfect as the work of mortals ever gets to be" (74). But he has little use for the poetry of the later years; not only *Idylls of the King*, but even *In Memoriam* comes under attack. In Baum's view, when Tennyson realized that a large reading public could be garnered by writing poems such as his English idylls — and longer ones like *In Memoriam, Idylls of the King*, and "Enoch Arden," which all share similarities with these examples of domestic bathos — Tennyson "bartered half his artistic soul" to achieve fame among his contemporaries (73).

The summary judgments of Tennyson's most important works reveal both Baum's reliance on what he calls aesthetic criteria and his biases in favor of the Romantic qualities of poetry in general. *The Princess*, Baum says, showed promise, because in it Tennyson displays "poetic wit" and "a delicate sense of human comedy" (103), but he abandoned this form of writing to please his contemporaries who wanted poetry to be serious. *In Memoriam* is deficient not for its theology but for its lack of "form and coherence," its excess of variety in both style and content (124). Though it contains some of Tennyson's "best poetry," *Maud* is "Tennyson's worst poem" (139). His classical poems contain "very little of the Greek spirit" (155). Baum is especially harsh on the *Idylls*. King Arthur he declares a "failure as a human being," a "failure as a leader," and "most clearly" a "failure as the hero of a story" (184). Individual idylls demonstrate the poet's lack of judgment or artistic skill. "The poem seems to me," Baum concludes, "utterly wanting in unity and coherence of structure," "utterly wanting also in unity and coherence of meaning" (213).

Because "it never seems to have occurred" to Tennyson "to inquire into aesthetic principles," Baum concludes, and because he was too willing to compromise with his readers' tastes, he failed to produce much good poetry (174). Baum believes he is helping his readers "to recognize and appreciate the genuine poetry work" and "separate it from the inferior work" because it is necessary "to save [Tennyson] from unjust praise" (234–35). Baum's own prejudices come through in judgments such as these: "It is impossible not to recognize that Tennyson's muse was not prolific" (236). "In a word, Tennyson had not much to say, not very much that demanded utterance" (237). Tennyson may have had a "rich and soaring" imagination, but "it was limited in its sources" (277). He is "greatest by *moments*" — always provided that "the moments are not too long" (285). Although there had been many other low points in Tennyson's reputation, it would be hard not to say that with the publication of Baum's book it had reached its nadir among academic critics. Within a year, however, the tide would start to turn.

Two works that appeared in 1949 were notable in affecting a shift in critical opinion, although neither made an immediate impact. The first, Sir Charles Tennyson's biography of his grandfather, made the world aware of the person behind the poems, expanding and correcting impressions of the poet as saint, a fiction created by Sir Charles's uncle Hallam Tennyson in the two-volume *Memoir*. The second was an essay that appeared in the *University of Toronto Quarterly* by F. E. L. Priestley, which treated with respect Tennyson's *Idylls of the King*. The impact these studies had on the reputation of the poet and one of his major works would grow steadily during the next two decades.

Sir Charles Tennyson was an unlikely leader of this revolution. Though not an academic critic, he undertook a new biography of his grandfather because he had access to family papers that had not been used before to provide an assessment of the poet and his work. In his introduction Sir Charles says that he writes with some trepidation because of his family connections and because others with greater scholarly training have already covered many of the issues with which he deals. Unlike his Uncle Hallam, however,

Charles Tennyson deals with the poet as if he were simply another subject for a life study. The grandson's access to private family papers gives him an advantage over earlier biographers (perhaps even over his uncle) in trying to explain his grandfather's complex character and account for the biographical genesis of many of his poems.

In some ways, *Alfred Tennyson* (1949) is like many Victorian biographies: extensive quotations and dozens of personal reminiscences fill its pages, and individual poems receive little attention except to show how the poet transformed his experiences or his reading into art.[6] Unlike Hallam Tennyson's hagiographic *Memoir,* however, or Harold Nicolson's condescending monograph, Charles Tennyson wishes to help scholars and other readers understand his grandfather's genius rather than simply asserting it in the face of half-a-century of criticism that would have suggested the contrary.

The accounts of Tennyson's early years are fleshed out in greater detail than one finds in most earlier biographies. Charles Tennyson is especially good — perhaps because he is painstakingly honest — in examining the relationship between the poet and his irascible father, who terrorized the family from the time Alfred was a small child. The love-hate relationship between father and son, coupled with the genetic tendency toward depression that afflicted many in the Tennyson line, were responsible in part for the impression that Alfred was a moody, morbid youth who had a "tormented adolescence" (52) and whose moods of depression as a young man were "almost pathological" (82). While freely acknowledging these traits, Charles Tennyson make it clear these were not the only reasons for Tennyson's poetic gift. Throughout his narrative, he attempts to humanize his grandfather. He praises the poet for his concern for family, especially his mother, wife, and children, and celebrates his love for Arthur Henry Hallam. However, he cites with equal candor Tennyson's aversion to crowds, his intense need for privacy, his concurrent but seemingly contradictory desire to be the center of attention (especially when he could read his own poetry to groups in his house or elsewhere), and his continuing penchant for dressing and behaving eccentrically.

At times, though, one must wonder if Charles Tennyson is naïve or merely disingenuous in some of his assessments. For example, he claims that Tennyson and Hallam had intended to bring out a joint volume of poetry in 1833, but that Hallam withdrew "partly on his father's instigation," "having come to feel his own work was still too crude" (87). Anyone familiar with Henry Hallam's grand designs for his son's future would assume (rightly, I believe) that the "instigation" was more likely prompted by the father's concern that his son may be too closely associated with such a radical or commoner as Alfred Tennyson. What Nicolson describes as a fault, the poet's inability to focus on art for its own sake rather than succumb to the calls for didacticism by his Cambridge colleagues, Charles Tennyson calls simply a "conflict" (131). He tries to explain away criticisms of *The Princess* by Tennyson's contemporaries by saying that, because his grandfather had to approach his subject "as a poet," he was not able to deal with the complex issues of women's rights "on the economic or sociological plane" (219).

When Charles Tennyson speculates on the poet's motives, he is almost always conservative. His most significant contribution, no doubt, is his rather understated but firm conviction that the work of Tennyson's later life was as important as, and in poetic terms frequently as good as, the lyric poems of the poet's younger years. His account of *Maud* is remarkably balanced, noting how the form seemed to suit Tennyson quite well, but acknowledging that readers found it difficult to understand — sometimes with good reason. His comments on *Idylls of the King* are also reasoned, but he makes it clear that he believes these deserve to rank among Tennyson's greater achievements, not shunned as didactic set pieces. However, he seems to go out of his way to say of the four *Idylls* published in 1869 that "each of the episodes is eminently readable" and "there is practically no directly didactic writing," but rather, "the symbolic character of the whole series is unmistakable." Echoing the remarks the poet had made to Hallam Tennyson and that are quoted in the *Memoir,* Charles Tennyson believes the poem allows every reader to "find his own interpretation according to his ability" (384). Readers at the end of the twentieth century would consider such remarks a belaboring of the obvious, but those in 1949 would have found Charles Tennyson's assessment either a throwback to Victorian days or a radical revisioning of the Arthurian epic. The depths to which the *Idylls* had sunk in popular and critical estimation can be seen in the evidence Charles Tennyson marshals to support his judgment: Mungo MacCallum's *Tennyson's "Idylls of the King" and Arthurian Story from the XVIth Century,* a study published in 1894.

Charles Tennyson's final judgment of his grandfather's career and accomplishments is worth noting because it is one of the most balanced assessments written either during the poet's lifetime or after it. The poet's "life of pleasant wonders was checkered by shadows of misery and heartbreak" throughout his years of adolescence and young adulthood, and the scandals of family life "produced in Alfred's sensitive spirit some unfortunate reactions which he never wholly overcame" (537–38). Nevertheless, Charles Tennyson says, his grandfather made great use of his intense interest in the world around him — both the natural world and the world of humankind. "No impartial student can fail to realize his grasp of scientific and philosophic principles," even though modern critics recoil at Tennyson's insistence on relying on his "intuitive assumptions" about the world and its Creator (539). His grasp of matters so vital to men and women of his time, and his ability to write a variety of poetry that had wide appeal, made him not only much respected in his own time, but deserving attention from succeeding generations.

Noting that, by 1949, interest in Tennyson was on the upswing, Charles Tennyson closes his work by quoting from a critic of the "generation which is leading the return to Tennyson" that Tennyson was not only a master of technique but "the most human" of poets (541). Not all would come to accept the grandson's portrait of Tennyson unequivocally. As University of Virginia scholar Arthur K. Davis notes in his review of Sir Charles Tennyson's book, "it will scarcely appeal either to the devotees of popular biography or to the ultra-modern critics" (308). Nevertheless, it is certainly true that Charles Tennyson's biography became for half a century the standard to which critics referred when seeking information about the poet's life. Hence, his assessment lies at the source of many subsequent commentaries on Tennyson and his work.

While not as sweeping in scope as Sir Charles Tennyson's biography, F. E. L. Priestley's "Tennyson's *Idylls*" (1949) was a watershed in criticism of Tennyson's Arthurian poem, the work that had been almost universally savaged, even by many of Tennyson's admirers, since the turn of the twentieth century. In his opening paragraphs, Priestley dismisses the notion that the *Idylls* are escapist; instead, he claims "they represent one of Tennyson's most earnest and important efforts to deal with major problems of his time" (35). He insists that, to appreciate Tennyson's achievement, one must read the *Idylls* in final form, ignoring the piecemeal composition of the individual poems. By doing so one can see that "the tragic collapse of Arthur's work in the *Idylls* is an allegory of the collapse of society, of nation, and of individual, which must follow the rejection of spiritual values" (37). Priestley's careful explication of the poem demonstrates how the failure of Christian values leads to tragedy; in this way the poem serves as a warning not only for Tennyson's contemporaries but for any society that abandons spiritual values. While Priestley's reading is fairly traditional in many regards, his insistence that the *Idylls* deserves serious attention marks a major turn in critical commentary on the poem.

Though not as immediately influential as Charles Tennyson's biography, Arthur Carr's essay "Tennyson as a Modern Poet" (1950) is no less perceptive in responding to prevailing critical attitudes of the 1930s and 1940s. Carr argues that critics such as T. S. Eliot and W. H. Auden have trouble with Tennyson because they see in him a "covert capitulation" to conformity (311). Carr, on the other hand, sees Tennyson as a precursor to several important writers: Joyce, whose work is characterized by a moody self-consciousness, Yeats, who invented mythic systems, and Huxley, who found "mysticism" an effective strategy to "castigate a materialistic culture" (312). Throughout his career Tennyson strove to make poetry both a vehicle of personal expression and a means of dealing with issues confronting his readers. Like modern poets, Tennyson constantly dealt with the competing demands of private and public worlds. The central theme of Tennyson's work, Carr says, is seen in "The Ancient Sage": "If there is a definitive Tennysonian theme, this is it — a reiterated and dreamlike sense of loss that becomes idyllic self-assurance" (323).

Carr believes that Tennyson's subjective crisis over the death of Arthur Henry Hallam was a kind of gateway to understanding major public crises. Though "the materialistic world must be, at length, defeated," the poet thought "the way to transcendental values lies through loss, death, and defeat" (328). Tennyson is modern, Carr says, especially in *In Memoriam,* "in his attempt to provide the personal themes" of the poem with a "formal structure responsive to both private instinct and the elegiac traditions. His attempt embodies in practical form the question of the artist's involvement or non-involvement in the life of his culture" (329). However, Carr sees the poem as the apogee of Tennyson's achievement; from 1850 until his death his career is "basically a recapitulation of his earlier development" (330). Far from being a victim of the Victorians' willingness to compromise between idealistic values and the evidence of the real world about human behavior and human destiny, Tennyson "works out remorselessly the fatal consequences of the romantic tradition. . . . After him, the deluge, the spreading chaos of 'modern art'" becomes the main business of the artist. Tennyson, Carr asserts, "is one of its makers" (332).

The centenary of the publication of *In Memoriam* brought forth a number of essays, but not every critic had praise for Tennyson's elegy. D. G. James argues in his 1950 Warton Lecture "Wordsworth and Tennyson" that *In Memoriam* is less compelling as autobiography than *The Prelude*. Tennyson's elegy, James says, demonstrates that "he is less a poet than Wordsworth" (124), largely because he is less confident in his poetic powers than his Romantic predecessors. While there is "much in *In Memoriam* for which we have good reason to be grateful," the poem "falls short of the weak hold it has upon the truth" that "the highest beauty and love we can aspire to has terror in it" (128). Tennyson tried too hard, James says, to allay humankind's fears, and in the process he made them seem inordinately unimportant. By contrast, Bella Milmed's "*In Memoriam* a Century Later" (1950) celebrates the enduring qualities of the elegy. Noting how different the poem may appear to readers who had witnessed two world wars, she claims the questions Tennyson asks about the conflicts between science and religion have perpetual relevance.

In the same year, two essays on Tennyson by Humphry House appeared in his volume *All in Due Time* (1950). In the first, House tries to capture the essence of Tennyson's vision of himself as a poet and explain how Tennyson understood the use of poetry both as an instrument for social change and as a means of self-preservation. Like many of his own contemporaries,

House argues that Tennyson is a poet of doubt. Focusing on *In Memoriam,* he explains how, despite the pattern that leads from despair to hope, the real strength of the work depends on Tennyson's ability to represent his emotional states, especially the equivocation he feels about the "larger hope" of which he speaks. What makes House's judgments somewhat different from that of critics writing earlier in the century, though, is that they stem from a genuine appreciation for the Victorians' accomplishments — an appreciation not necessarily shared by Nicolson, Fausset, Eliot, or Auden. In another essay in the volume, "Are the Victorians Coming Back?," House argues there is much to admire among the Victorians once prejudices about their sentimentality and moral earnestness are overcome. It is from a perspective of admiration that he explores Tennyson as a representative of an age that is not simply sentimental but also exceptionally self-critical and genuinely concerned with issues of importance to humankind.

Comments by the distinguished British critic F. W. Bateson in *Romantic Schizophrenia: English Poetry: A Critical Introduction* (1950) are similar to those of House in that his ambivalence about Tennyson's achievement is presented in a study that acknowledges the complexity of the Victorian age. Bateson's brief comments on "Tears, Idle Tears" demonstrate how Tennyson was a victim of a form of schizophrenia that gives the best Victorian poetry a disturbing resonance. While Tennyson could sympathize with the plight of the poor or with other social, religious, and political dilemmas, there existed "between his conscience and his imagination" a "hiatus, a total lack of connection" that, in Bateson's view, is evidenced by a "psychic division" in his poetry (225). Ironically, his assessment is reminiscent of the observation made by one of Tennyson's contemporaries, Matthew Arnold, who wrote poignantly about the "buried life" that existed in Victorian men and women.

In 1951, Eleanor Mattes published a brief volume that was to have profound influence on Tennyson scholarship. *In Memoriam: The Way of A Soul* is an assessment of the major influences that shaped Tennyson's religious beliefs as evidenced in his elegy for Hallam. She provides a sound discussion of the way Arthur Henry Hallam's essay "Theodicaea Novissima" influenced Tennyson's idea that there was reason to trust his intuition about the doctrine of immortality, or the way scientific controversy gave rise to doubts about the validity of his belief. The real significance of Mattes's work, however, lies in her painstaking reconstruction of the chronological order in which the individual lyrics of *In Memoriam* were written. Using the order of composition, she then demonstrates how the poem grew as a response not only to Tennyson's personal grief but also to the major challenges to religious belief in the first half of the nineteenth century. The appendix in which she justifies the order of composition has proven to be a most valuable resource to scholars wishing to explore both the poet's work habits and his interests during the crucial years between Hallam's death and the publication of the poem that established Tennyson's reputation among his Victorian contemporaries.

By the early 1950s the mainstream scholarly community was beginning to treat the Victorians with greater respect. Lionel Stevenson observed in his 1952 article "The Pertinacious Victorian Poets" that the Victorians seemed "to be emerging at last from the cloud of contempt that had overshadowed [them] for the past generation" (232). Jerome H. Buckley's *The Victorian Temper* (1951) is an excellent example of the change in attitude. After noting in an introductory chapter how complex the term "Victorian" had become in the half-century since the Queen's death, he explores the careers of several key figures to unravel the various strands of thought and action that characterized the age. In treating Tennyson's works, Buckley makes clear his admiration for the poet, calling him an artist of the first rank and an exemplar of Victorian values. Always caught between his call to art for art's sake and his need to influence society through his poetry, Tennyson gradually moved away from pleasing a small group of admirers to find a larger audience. Breaking from previous critical opinion on the wisdom of such a move, Buckley calls Tennyson admirable for adopting the mantle of prophet and sage. Buckley's observation that Tennyson, "more than any other Victorian poet," was "sensitive to the spiritual temper of the time" (84) is delivered as a compliment; and his observation that Tennyson became the "true interpreter" (84) of his age is made to elevate the poet's reputation, not damn him as a hypocritical moralist.

In the same year, another major twentieth-century critic wrote perceptively about Tennyson's artistic merits. Marshall McLuhan's "Tennyson and Picturesque Poetry" (1951) is an extensive examination of the poet's use of landscape. McLuhan argues that Tennyson's best poetry requires "patient and alert attention," and that he "deserves to be re-read and revalued with the aid of recovered reading ability" (278). Further, McLuhan claims that "if anybody ever had and consciously cultivated a movie-camera eye it was Tennyson" (280). As a result, he predicts that "it will be the Tennyson of the precise ear and eye who will provide the most unexpected and persistent enjoyment" (278). Subsequent works by critics such as Carol Christ (*The Finer Optic*, 1975) and other poststructuralists have demonstrated the wisdom of McLuhan's observation.

One of the most significant works published in the wake of Sir Charles Tennyson's biography of his grandfather was E. D. H. Johnson's *The Alien Vision in Victorian Poetry* (1952). Beginning from the premise that modern critics have created inadequate portraits of the major Victorian poets, Johnson sets out to show how Tennyson, Browning, and Arnold managed to write poetry for "a modern reading public little sensitive to the life of the imagination" (v). Johnson breaks with the traditional modern view by asserting that all three wrote poetry with multiple levels of meaning that Victorian readers often missed in their zeal to find moral lessons or religious solace in these poets' works.

Johnson's reading of Tennyson's poetry is simultaneously sympathetic and modernist. He posits that Tennyson did not sell out to his Victorian readers, as Nicolson and Fausset had argued. Instead, recognizing the need to conform to public taste if he wished to reach a wide audience, Tennyson increasingly chose "to disguise his private thoughts under extrinsic layers of meaning" (13). Like an early deconstructionist, Johnson notes how "the recurrence of certain themes and an habitual reliance on certain formal devices at variance with the expressed content of the material" frequently characterize the work of Tennyson's later period, when he was Queen Victoria's laureate. The key to understanding the double meaning of much of Tennyson's work lies, Johnson says, in the poet's use of dream, madness, and vision, devices that let him say things through characters or situations sufficiently outside the mainstream that he would not be held accountable for these alien opinions by his adoring Victorian readers.

In a sense Johnson is writing a revisionist history of Tennyson criticism, arguing especially that *Idylls of the King* is indeed the major work that Victorian readers believed it was — but for reasons different from those ascribed to it by Tennyson's contemporaries. The poem operates on two levels — one the moralistic, almost allegorical story of "sense at war with soul" that Tennyson acknowledged in the epilogue he added in 1873, the other an attempt to deal with the poet's lifelong concern with the struggle to discriminate between appearance and reality. "Every action has its imaginative counterpart through the instrumentality of dream madness, vision, and the quest," Johnson says, linking the work to others generally considered among Tennyson's finest. The "central emphasis" of *Idylls of the King* develops, as does all of Tennyson's best poetry, "from an inner rather than an outer awareness, from the life of the imagination rather than from a sense of responsibility to society" (63). Johnson's assessment, along with those of F. E. L. Priestley before him and Jerome Buckley, who would follow in less than a decade, restored *Idylls of the King* to a place of prominence beside *In Memoriam* in the Tennyson canon, a place it held for the remainder of the century.

Not all important critics were swayed by these arguments for revaluation. The noted scholar Douglas Bush, whose monumental works on the influence of the classics on English literature had won him accolades in the 1930s, found it necessary to assign Tennyson a secondary place in his survey *English Poetry: The Main Currents from Chaucer to the Present* (1952). Bush believes Tennyson was a frustrated Romantic who wanted to believe in the progress of the human spirit, but who found that the advances of science and the experiences of tragedy in his personal life kept him from adopting this outlook unequivocally. Predictably, Bush praises the early poetry and

In Memoriam, but dismisses *Idylls of the King* with the observation that the poem "is not much read in our time" (161). Bush seems to be glad that it is not.

On the other hand, Charles Tennyson continued to insist that the *Idylls* was worth reading. In his *Six Tennyson Essays* (1954), which contains criticism not included in his biography of his grandfather, Sir Charles aims to demonstrate "the range, depth and complexity of the creative work of a great poet" (vii). He explores such topics as Tennyson's humor, his attitude toward politics and religion, and his techniques of versification. Perhaps the most important contribution, however, is an essay on *Idylls of the King,* in which Charles Tennyson takes on the criticisms of T. S. Eliot and others who assert that Tennyson was not a good narrative poet. Charles Tennyson claims that "a careful consideration" of his grandfather's work clearly demonstrates "that he was a brilliant and singularly versatile story-teller" (179). Ranging widely among the poet's works but concentrating on the "Lancelot and Elaine" idyll, Charles Tennyson makes a strong argument to support what was starting to be the majority opinion about the *Idylls* and about Tennyson's gifts as a narrative poet.

That the tide of criticism was finally turning in Tennyson's favor was noted by Viscount Esher, who begins his essay "Tennyson's Influence on his Times" (1954) by remarking that "we are told that at last the Reaction in favour of Tennyson has arrived" (35). While the claim may be a bit premature, it was not far from being accurate. For example, the respected English scholar Aubrey de Selincourt's brief biographical sketch of Tennyson in his *Six Great Poets* (1956) is aimed at giving general readers a sense of the influence of the poet's life on his work. De Selincourt is curiously cheerful in handling biographical details, and he seems convinced that the innate greatness of Tennyson's craftsmanship will allow his work to survive the vagaries of criticism that have caused a temporary decline in his reputation. In fact, De Selincourt is distressed by what was then the current trend in literary criticism, the reliance on Freudian psychology as the basis for literary analysis. He recognizes that Tennyson was by temperament conservative and patriotic, but he does not believe these attributes detract from his capabilities as a poet.

Another of the great English critics of the mid-century, Basil Willey, devotes a chapter to Tennyson in *More Nineteenth-Century Studies: A Group of Honest Doubters* (1956), an exploration of the phenomenon of the loss of faith suffered by so many nineteenth-century figures. Combining biography with brief critical analysis, Willey defends Tennyson against charges that he was overly sentimental, too vague, and unconvincing in his defense of the concept of immortality. Willey praises Tennyson's style, citing examples from early poetry and *The Princess.* Predictably, the bulk of his study is devoted to examining *In Memoriam,* the poem that best demonstrates Tennyson's struggle with faith and doubt. Willey provides an excellent synopsis of Tennyson's understanding of nineteenth-century science, citing parallels between the writings of scientists such as Robert Chambers and Charles Lyell and passages in the poem. Unfortunately, Willey does not address any of the poetry of Tennyson's later career.

Warren Beck, however, does look at Tennyson's later work, specifically *Idylls of the King*. In "Clouds Upon Camelot" (1956) he laments that, while university critics had long ago relegated the poem to obscurity, it was still a staple of high-school classrooms. Beck points out what he believes are the essential artistic and ideological deficiencies of the *Idylls*, and promotes the now-familiar view that Tennyson is best appreciated through a study of his shorter works.

Tennyson's limitations are also noted by Hoxie Fairchild, whose extensive work examining the influence of religion on English poetry has long been recognized by scholars from several fields. Hence, while her method of reading poetry may be questionable, her judgment of Tennyson's rightful claim to be thought of as a Victorian sage and seer is worth noting. In the fourth volume of *Religious Trends in English Poetry* (1957), she takes issue with critics who try to divide Tennyson's works into "early" and "late" or "private" and "laureate" periods. Even in "his querulous and disappointed old age," she says, "his fundamental beliefs and aspirations were those of his youth" (102). Fairchild analyzes the body of Tennyson's work to extract his religious premises and concerns. Generally following the same tack as G. M. Masterson in *Tennyson as a Religious Teacher* (1900), she acknowledges the inconsistencies in Tennyson's logic, considering them the inevitable results of an attempt to give poetic expression to complex ideas. Not surprisingly, she concludes that his poetry offers a "slender basis" for his reputation among his contemporaries as "a great philosophical poet" (127). Closing with an anecdote about the clergyman who visited Tennyson on his deathbed, she says, "The Vicar probably thought with the majority of cultivated Victorians, that the Lord of Language who now lay so silent had been the century's supreme singer of Christian faith and wisdom" (131). Fairchild argues that he did not deserve such accolades; her assessment is closer to that of T. S. Eliot, who valued Tennyson not for his convictions, but for his doubt.

Like many critics during this period, R. A. Foakes links Tennyson with his Romantic predecessors and stresses the continuity of tradition between the Victorians and their immediate literary predecessors. In *The Romantic Assertion* (1958) Foakes concentrates on *In Memoriam* to demonstrate how the Romantics' conception of poetry influences Tennyson, not only in his decision to link shorter "fragments" into a long poem, but in his development of a "vision of love" (116) as the means for human salvation in a world where belief in God is increasingly called into question.

How Tennyson was perceived by a majority of critics as the decade of the 1950s came to a close might be illustrated by W. W. Robson's article "The Dilemma of Tennyson," originally published in 1957 and reprinted in *Critical Essays* (1967). Focusing principally on "Ulysses," Robson demonstrates how the strident action called for in the poem is negated by the languid rhythms and sonorous language used by the speaker to encourage action. This "radical discrepancy between the strenuousness aspired to, and the medium in which the aspiration is expressed" (194) highlights for Robson the problem with Tennyson: though he was a man of notable "intellectual and moral preoccupations," he seems to be "content with the style of a minor poet" (195). As Tennyson moved more and more into the public sphere, his poetic powers diminished. "The decline of Tennyson," Robson concludes, "is to me a much more painful spectacle than the decline of Wordsworth" (196). The major poems such as *The Princess* and *Maud* exhibit a "peculiar sadness" that "seems tacitly to acknowledge the inability of their author to confront the world as a poet" (199).

But there were dissenting voices, the best evidence of which was the publication of one of the most influential studies focusing on an individual Tennyson poem: John Killham's *Tennyson and "The Princess": Reflections of an Age* (1958). Exhibiting the same level of wide-ranging scholarship that had made John Livingston Lowes's *The Road To Xanadu* (1927) a classic study of the creative imagination, *Tennyson and "The Princess"* argues forcefully and persuasively that Tennyson's "medley" is no mere appeal for popular acclaim. On the contrary, Killham believes it is "a perfect example of an encounter between a man of marked talents and a moment which was inimical to their expression" (vii). The poet's triumph comes because he is able to forge contemporary concerns with feminism, sociology, and science into a creative work that, while "not an overlooked masterpiece," is still "when properly understood" a "great deal more valuable than some estimates have allowed" (2). In lengthy, well-researched chapters Killham examines what he calls the feminist controversy in England, ideas about university education and the appropriateness of educating women, the growing interest in science, the literary sources for Tennyson's story, and the ways Tennyson weaves together these themes into a modern fairy tale that would have appealed to his first readers, who would have recognized how much of their concerns and interests were being addressed. Throughout his study, Killham makes no apologies for Tennyson's intellect or his craft. To him, Tennyson is a major poet and *The Princess* a major work — one that ranks, in his estimation, "as part of the canon of great art" (278).

An article arguing for a change in the critical appraisal of "Ulysses," Edgar Hill Duncan's "Tennyson: A Modern Appraisal" (1959), offers a succinct summary of the Reactionaries' major arguments before launching into a highly favorable reading of the poem. Duncan reviews trends in Tennyson criticism since H. J. C. Grierson's influential article in the *Cambridge History of English Literature* (1916). He argues that the penchant for trying to separate the "real" Tennyson from the Victorian laureate had become a kind of "critical game" (14), a trend that concerns him because such prejudices have damaged the reputation of some of Tennyson's best poetry. Duncan hopes to correct this trend at least for one poem, his personal favorite.

The possibility of a sea change in the critical view of Tennyson was hinted at also by a critic better known for his work on Carlyle. Early in his career, Charles Richard Sanders published two essays on Tennyson, collected later in his *Carlyle's Friendships and Other Studies* (1977), that point the way toward a new assessment of the poet's stature. Sanders may be better known by Tennyson scholars for his 1961 *PMLA* article "Carlyle and Tennyson," the best source for understanding the friendship between these two men and the influence Carlyle had on Tennyson's poetry. But in "Tennyson and the Human Hand," an essay published in the *Victorian Newsletter* four years earlier (1957), Sanders concludes his examination of the poet's use of this important image with observations that point toward the work soon to be undertaken first by Jerome Buckley and then by a host of scholars who could finally put the ghosts of Nicolson and Auden behind them. "Tennyson was an artist," Sanders says, more deserving of serious study than some of his successors whose works had displaced his among English and American readers. He was "a master spirit, if not a respectable philosopher" who should not be rejected because he wrote melodiously or occasionally "lapsed into sentimentalism." At the time he is writing, Sanders believes critics "are giving too little consideration to the remarkable quality of Tennyson' imagination and to the artistic gifts and insight into life that are related to it" (303–4). Fortunately, this lacuna in critical appreciation was soon to be filled.

Notes

[1] Even in his assessment of this significant relationship Fausset seems dismissive. His disdain may be subtly reflected in the glaring error that appears as the caption to the photo opposite page 24. A portrait of Hallam is identified as "Arthur Hugh Hallam" rather than "Arthur Henry Hallam."

[2] Fausset is a bit more reserved in his critique of the poet in "The Hidden Tennyson," an essay he included in his 1947 collection *Poets and Pundits*. In that work he praises *In Memoriam* as the best example of Tennyson's ability to combine personal experience with skilled craftsmanship. Yet Fausset cannot resist the temptation to criticize the qualities for which Tennyson's Victorian contemporaries admired the Laureate. What makes Tennyson palatable to the modernists, Fausset says, is the discovery that "beneath the recoiling sensibility, fastidiousness and moral dignity" he displayed in his public persona there lay "a more primitive and healthy strain" (189).

³ Eliot's opinion of Tennyson and Tennyson's influence on Eliot's poetry have been the subjects of several critical studies. Among the more illuminating are Denis Donoghoe, "From Tennyson to Eliot," *The Ordinary Universe: Soundings in Modern Literature* (1968); Linda Rae Pratt, "The Holy Grail: Subversion and Revival of a Tradition in Tennyson and T. S. Eliot" (1973); Nancy D. Hargrove, "Landscape as Symbol in Tennyson and T. S. Eliot" (1974); Carol T. Christ, "T. S. Eliot and the Victorians" (1981); and Jack Kolb, "Laureate Envy: T. S. Eliot on Tennyson" (1998). For Auden's own assessment of his relationship to Tennyson, see his remarks in "The Poet of No More — W. H. Auden Offers Some Personal Reflections on Tennyson"(1972).

⁴ Evans also makes brief comments about Tennyson in *Literature and Science* (1954), noting what he considers the poet's fears concerning the advancement of science, expressed in *In Memoriam,* and his avoidance of contemporary issues in *Idylls of the King.*

⁵ One might also wonder why the editor of the Longmans series of booklets on British poets would have chosen Lucas to compose the one on the Victorian laureate (*Tennyson,* 1957), since he seems so dismissive of Tennyson's accomplishments.

⁶ Later in life, Sir Charles Tennyson proved he could be both a good scholar and a perceptive critic. His contributions to the *Tennyson Research Bulletin* in the 1960s and 1970s demonstrate his interest in both the details of Tennyson's life and in the aesthetic dimensions of his poetry. Perhaps the best example of the grandson's ability to interpret his grandfather's work is contained in "The Dream in Tennyson's Poetry," an essay Charles Tennyson contributed to the *Virginia Quarterly Review* in 1964.

Works Cited

Abercrombie, Lascelles. "Tennyson." In Lascelles Abercrombie, Lord David Cecil, G. K. Chesterton, et al. *Revaluations: Studies in Biography.* London: Oxford UP, 1931. 60–76.

Alden, Raymond M. *Alfred Tennyson: How to Know Him.* Indianapolis: Bobbs-Merrill, 1917. Reprint, Norwood, PA: Norwood Editions, 1977.

Altick, Richard, and Samuel Chew. *The Nineteenth Century and After: A Literary History of England.* Vol. 4. New York: Appleton Century Crofts, 1948.

Atkins, Gaius Glenn. *Reinspecting Victorian Religion.* New York: Macmillan, 1928.

Auden W. H. "Introduction." *A Selection from the Poems of Tennyson.* New York: Doubleday, 1944.

Basler, Roy P. "Tennyson the Psychologist." *South Atlantic Quarterly* 43 (April 1944): 143–59.

Bateson, Frederick W. *Romantic Schizophrenia: English Poetry: A Critical Introduction.* New York: Longmans, 1950.

Baum, Paull F. *Tennyson Sixty Years After*. Chapel Hill: U of North Carolina P, 1948.

Beach, Joseph Warren. "Tennyson." *The Concept of Nature in Nineteenth-Century English Poetry*. New York: Macmillan, 1936. Reprint, New York: Russell & Russell, 1966. 406–34.

Beck, Warren. "Clouds Upon Camelot." *English Journal* 45 (1956): 447–54.

Blore, George H. "Alfred Tennyson." *Victorian Worthies*. London: Milford, 1920. 150–75.

Bowden, Marjorie. *Tennyson in France*. Manchester, UK: Manchester UP, 1930.

Broadus, Edmund K. *The Laureateship*. Oxford: Clarendon Press, 1921. Reprint, Freeport, NY: Books for Libraries Press, 1966. 184–96.

Brooks, Cleanth. *The Well Wrought Urn: Studies in the Structure of Poetry*. New York: Harcourt Brace, 1947.

Buckley, Jerome H. "Tennyson — The Two Voices." *The Victorian Temper: A Study in Literary Culture*. Cambridge, MA: Harvard UP, 1951. 66–86.

Bush, Douglas. *English Poetry: The Main Currents from Chaucer to the Present*. New York: Oxford UP, 1952.

———. "Tennyson." *Mythology and the Romantic Tradition in English Poetry*. Cambridge, MA: Harvard UP, 1937. 197–228.

Carr, Arthur J. "Tennyson as a Modern Poet." *University of Toronto Quarterly* 19 (1950): 361–82. Reprinted in *Victorian Literature: Modern Essays in Criticism*. Ed. Austin Wright. New York: Oxford UP, 1961. 311–33.

Chew, Samuel C. "Introduction." *Tennyson: Representative Poems*. New York: Odyssey, 1941: xi–xlii.

Christ, Carol T. "T. S. Eliot and the Victorians." *Modern Philology* 79:2 (1981): 157–65.

Collier, John. "Lord Tennyson." In *The Great Victorians*. Ed. H. J. Massingham and H. Massingham. London: Nicholson & Watson, 1932. 503–16.

Crum, Ralph B. "Nature Red in Tooth and Claw: Tennyson's Problem." *Scientific Thought in Poetry*. New York: Columbia UP, 1931. 157–90.

Davis, Arthur K. Jr. "Mid-Century Tennyson." *Virginia Quarterly Review* 26 (1950): 307–11.

De La Mare, Walter. *Pleasures and Speculations*. London: Faber & Faber, 1940.

de Selincourt, Aubrey. "Alfred, Lord Tennyson." *Six Great Poets*. London: Hamilton, 1956.

Donoghoe, Denis. "From Tennyson to Eliot." *The Ordinary Universe: Soundings in Modern Literature*. New York: Macmillan; London: Faber & Faber, 1968. 90–107.

Duncan, Edgar H. "Tennyson: A Modern Appraisal." *Tennessee Studies in Literature* 4 (1959): 13–30.

Eliot, T. S. *"In Memoriam."* *Essays Ancient and Modern.* London: Faber & Faber; New York: Harcourt, 1936. 175–90.

Elton, Oliver. "Tennyson." *A Survey of English Literature, 1830–1880.* Vol. 3. London: Arnold, 1920. 330–61. Rev. and reprinted in *Tennyson and Matthew Arnold.* London: Arnold, 1924. Reprint, New York: Haskell House, 1971.

Esher, Viscount. "Tennyson's Influence on His Times." In *Essays by Divers Hands: Being the Transactions of the Royal Society of Literature* n.s. 28 (1954): 35–47.

Evans, B. Ifor. *Literature and Science.* London: Allen & Unwin, 1954. 72–78.

———. *Tradition and Romanticism.* London: Methuen, 1940. Reprint, Hamden, CT: Archon Books, 1964.

Fairchild, Hoxie N. *Religious Trends in English Poetry.* Vol. 4: *1830–1880: Christianity and Romanticism in the Victorian Era.* New York: Columbia UP, 1957. 102–31.

Fausset, Hugh I'Anson. "The Hidden Tennyson." *Poets and Pundits: Essays and Addresses.* New Haven: Yale UP, 1947. 187–91.

———. *Tennyson, A Modern Portrait.* London: Selwyn & Blount; New York: Appleton, 1923.

Foakes, Reginald A. "The Rhetoric of Faith." *The Romantic Assertion: A Study in the Language of Nineteenth-Century Poetry.* New Haven: Yale UP, 1958. 111–38.

Ford, George H. *Keats and the Victorians: A Study of His Influence and Rise to Fame, 1821–1895.* New Haven: Yale UP, 1944. Reprint, Hamden, CT: Archon Books, 1962. 17–48.

Grierson, Herbert J. C. "The Tennysons." In *Cambridge History of English Literature.* Ed. A. W. Ward and A. R. Waller. Vol. 13. Cambridge: Cambridge UP, 1916. 25–53.

Groom, Bernard. *On the Diction of Tennyson, Browning, and Arnold.* Oxford: Clarendon Press, 1939. Reprint, Hamden, CT: Archon, 1970.

Hargrove, Nancy D. "Landscape as Symbol in Tennyson and T. S. Eliot." *Victorians Institute Journal* 3 (1974): 73–83.

Harstock, Ernest. "Poor Tennyson." *Personalist* 11 (1930): 28–31.

Hearnshaw, Fossey J. C. "Tennyson Twenty-Five Years After." *Spectator* 119 (6 October 1917): 352–53.

———. "Tennyson Twenty-Five Years After." *Spectator* 119 (10 November 1917): 522.

Hodgson, Geraldine E. "The Legacy of Tennyson." *Criticism at a Venture.* London: Macdonald, 1919. 167–72.

Hough, Graham. "The Natural Theology of *In Memoriam.*" *Selected Essays.* London: Cambridge UP, 1978. 110–25.

House, Humphry. "Tennyson and the Spirit of the Age." *All in Due Time.* London: Rupert Hart-Davis, 1955. 121–29.

Hoyt, Arthur S. *The Spiritual Message of Modern English Poetry.* New York: Macmillan, 1924. 67–85, 89–112.

James, David G. "Wordsworth and Tennyson." *British Academy* 36 (1950): 113–20.

Johnson, E. D. H. "Tennyson." *The Alien Vision of Victorian Poetry.* Princeton: Princeton UP, 1952. 3–68.

Killham, John. *Tennyson and "The Princess": Reflections of an Age.* London: Athlone Press, 1958.

Knight, G. Wilson. *Neglected Powers: Essays on Nineteenth and Twentieth Century Literature.* London: Routledge & Kegan Paul; New York: Barnes & Noble, 1971.

Kolb, Jack. "Laureate Envy: T. S. Eliot on Tennyson." *ANQ: A Quarterly Journal of Short Articles, Notes, and Reviews* 11:3 (Summer 1998): 29–37.

Lowes, John Livingston. *The Road to Xanadu: A Study in the Creative Imagination.* Boston: Houghton Mifflin, 1927.

Lucas, F. L. "Introduction." *Tennyson, Poetry and Prose.* Oxford: Clarendon Press, 1947.

———. "Tennyson." *Eight Victorian Poets.* New York: Macmillan, 1930. 3–19. Subsequent editions published as *Ten Victorian Poets.*

———. *Tennyson.* London: Longmans, Green, 1957. Reprint, 1961.

Lynd, Robert. "Tennyson: A Contemporary Criticism." *Art of Letters.* New York: Scribner, 1921. 134–38.

Mackail, John W. "Tennyson." *Studies of English Poets.* London: Longmans, Green, 1926. 227–51.

Macy, John. "Tennyson, the Perfect Laureate." *Bookman* (NY) 69 (June 1929): 375–86.

Magnus, Laurie. "Tennyson a Hundred Years After." *Cornhill Magazine* n.s. 68 (May 1929): 660–70.

Mattes, Eleanor B. *"In Memoriam": The Way of a Soul.* New York: Exposition, 1951.

McLuhan, H. Marshall. "Tennyson and Picturesque Poetry." *Essays in Criticism* 1 (July 1951): 262–82.

Meynell, Alice. "Some Thoughts of a Reader of Tennyson." *Hearts of Controversy*. London: Burns & Oates, 1917. 1–22. Reprinted in *Alice Meynell: Prose & Poetry*. London: Jonathan Cape, 1947. 79–89.

Milmed, Bella K. "*In Memoriam* a Century Later." *Antioch Review* 10 (1950): 471–92.

Nicolson, Sir Harold. *Tennyson; Aspects of His Life, Character and Poetry*. London: Constable, 1923; 2nd ed., Boston: Houghton Mifflin, 1925. Reprint, London: Arrow Books, 1960; Garden City, NY: Anchor Books, 1962.

———. "Tennyson: Fifty Years After." *Poetry Review* 33 (November 1942): 333–36.

Noyes, Alfred. "Tennyson and Some Recent Critics." *Some Aspects of Modern Poetry*. London: Hodder & Stoughton; New York: Stokes, 1924. Reprinted as *Tennyson*. Edinburgh: Blackie, 1932. 153–99.

Paden, W. D. "Tennyson and the Reviewers (1829–1835)." *Studies in English in Honor of Raphael Dorman O'Leary and Selden Lincoln Whitcomb*. Lawrence: U of Kansas P, 1940. Reprint, Freeport, NY: Books for Libraries Press, 1968. 15–39.

———. *Tennyson in Egypt: A Study of the Imagery in His Earlier Work*. Lawrence: U of Kansas P, 1942.

Palmer, George H. "Alfred Tennyson." *Formative Types in English Poetry*. Boston: Houghton Mifflin, 1918. 233–69.

Perry, Henry Ten Eyck. "The Tennyson Tragedy." *Southwest Review* 12 (January 1927): 97–112.

Pratt, Linda R. "The Holy Grail: Subversion and Revival of a Tradition in Tennyson and T. S. Eliot." *Victorian Poetry* 11 (1973): 307–21.

Priestley, F. E. L. "Tennyson's *Idylls*." *University of Toronto Quarterly* 19 (October 1949): 35–49.

Pyre, James F. A. *The Formation of Tennyson's Style; A Study, Primarily, of the Versification of the Early Poems*. Madison: U of Wisconsin P, 1920. Reprint, New York: Phaeton Press, 1968.

Quiller-Couch, Arthur. "Tennyson After Fifty Years." *Poetry Review* 33 (1942): 269–71.

Rice, William North. "The Poet of Science." *The Poet of Science and Other Addresses*. New York: Abingdon, 1919. 11–45.

Robson, W. W. "The Dilemma of Tennyson." *Critical Essays*. New York: Barnes & Noble, 1967. 191–99.

Routh, H. V. *Towards the Twentieth Century*. New York: Macmillan, 1937.

Scaife, Christopher H. *Poetry of Alfred Tennyson: An Essay in Appreciation*. London: Cobden-Sanderson, 1930.

Shanks, Edward B. "The Return of Tennyson." *Second Essays on Literature.* London: Collins, 1927. Reprint, Freeport, NY: Books for Libraries Press, 1968. 163–76.

Smith, Jean Pauline. *The Aesthetic Nature of Tennyson.* New York: White, 1920. Reprint, New York: Haskell House, 1971.

Squire, John C. "Tennyson." *London Mercury* 2 (August 1920): 443–55. Reprinted in *Essays on Poetry.* London: Hodder & Stoughton, 1923. 63–87.

Starnes, De Witt T. "The Influence of Carlyle on Tennyson." *Texas Review* 6 (July 1921): 316–36.

Stevenson, Lionel. "Alfred Tennyson." *Darwin Among the Poets.* Chicago: U of Chicago P, 1932; Reprint, New York: Russell & Russell, 1963. 55–116.

———. "The Pertinacious Victorian Poets." *University of Toronto Quarterly* 21 (April 1952): 237–45.

Templeman, W. D. "Tennyson's 'Locksley Hall' and Thomas Carlyle." *Booker Memorial Studies.* New York: Russell & Russell, 1950. 34–58.

Tennyson, Charles, Sir. *Alfred Tennyson.* New York: Macmillan, 1949.

———. "The Dream in Tennyson's Poetry." *Virginia Quarterly Review* 40 (Spring 1964): 228–48.

———. *Six Tennyson Essays.* London: Cassell, 1954. Reprint, Wakefield: S. R. Publishers, 1971.

Ward, A. C. "Introduction." In Lascelles Abercrombie, Lord David Cecil, G. K. Chesterton, et al. *Revaluations: Studies in Biography.* London: Oxford UP, 1931.

Warren, T. Herbert. "The Real Tennyson." *Nineteenth Century and After* 94 (October 1923): 507–19.

Weygandt, Cornelius. *The Times of Tennyson: English Victorian Poetry as It Affected America.* New York: Appleton, Century, 1936.

Willey, Basil. "Tennyson." *More Nineteenth-Century Studies: A Group of Honest Doubters.* London: Chatto & Windus, 1956. 53–105.

Wolfe, Humbert. *Tennyson.* London: Faber & Faber, 1930. Reprint, Freeport, NY: Books for Libraries Press, 1969.

Young, G. M. *The Age of Tennyson.* London: Oxford UP, 1939.

4: The Tennyson Revival: 1960–1969

IT IS ALWAYS DANGEROUS TO CITE a single book as the source of a change in attitudes toward any writer. With that caveat in mind, it may not be too farfetched to say that Jerome Buckley's *Tennyson: The Growth of a Poet* (1960) was a watershed in Tennyson criticism. Virtually everyone writing about Tennyson after the publication of Buckley's study has found it necessary to cite this work, either to expand on Buckley's suggestions on to refute his claims for Tennyson's greatness.

Buckley had already written approvingly of Tennyson in *The Victorian Temper* (1951) and had edited Tennyson's poems for the Riverside Press (1958). In the introduction to that edition, Buckley reveals his prejudice against Nicolson's view of the two Tennysons. Calling Nicolson's study "brilliant though incomplete," he argues that "the distinction" between the morbid lyricist and the compromising laureate is "essentially false and misleading" (ix). Buckley claims Tennyson is a worthy successor to the Romantics, a poet who revels in the kind of work that Matthew Arnold was to disparage in the preface to his own 1853 volume of poetry. Tennyson's poetry, Buckley says, "deals typically not with the great action seen as an object in itself but with the search through situation and symbol for meaning and the sudden illuminating discovery of purpose" (xxi).

This judgment is carried forward, expanded, and defended brilliantly in the new book. Setting out to "study Tennyson's developing sensibility as a guide to critical evaluation" (*Tennyson,* vii), Buckley writes a critical biography that emphasizes the influence of Tennyson's experience on his work. More sympathetic than Nicolson's "biased" study or Baum's "scholarly but hostile" volume, Buckley assumes that "Tennyson by endowment and attainment was a major poet" (viii). Like his predecessors, Buckley finds that Tennyson struggled early and throughout his life with the problem of reconciling the desire to produce great art with the competing need to serve society. But time after time, Buckley says, the poet managed to do both.

Given these introductory salvos, it is not surprising that much of Buckley's study is intended as a corrective to earlier criticism. Buckley argues that the young Tennyson learned from his life in the country and from his experiences at Cambridge, but that these shaping influences were tempered by an innate genius. Hence, the specific influence of the Apostles "has frequently been overestimated"; Tennyson was better able than his friends to distinguish between the poet's role as teacher and mere "didacticism in verse" (34). In the years before he published *In Memoriam,* Tennyson wrestled with the problem of the poet's role in society, and much of his work reflects the influence of his Romantic predecessors who grappled with the same issue. Thus "The Palace of Art," for instance, assumes a major role in the Tennyson canon because "no other poem" among his early work "registers so directly or didactically the poet's reluctant sense of social responsibility" (53). The appearance of his elegy for Arthur Henry Hallam was a turning point in Tennyson's career because it allowed him to teach a larger public through reflections on his personal experience of grief, loss, doubt, and faith.

Buckley's readings of individual poems suggest his belief that Tennyson was in command of his material and had the ability to transform his personal experiences (including his doubts about the afterlife) into great art. Contrary to received wisdom that Tennyson was blind to his limitations and overly sensitive to criticism, Buckley claims the poet "was quite conscious of his own defects and fully aware of the aesthetic directions that his verse ideally should follow" (71). During the famous ten-years' silence, Tennyson "grew steadily in the power of detachment" (77). Many of the new poems in the 1842 volume, and many of those revised for reissue, were more objective in tone than earlier works because Tennyson wanted "to convince his new public and perhaps himself that he was at one with his age, capable of popular speech, and by no means willfully eccentric" (80). While early twentieth-century critics — many of whom took modernism and its celebration of alienation as standards of poetic excellence — would criticize Tennyson for this movement toward popularity, Buckley sees it as a strength.

Buckley's chapters on the major poems have been particularly influential in shaping critical opinion of scholars in the last half of the twentieth century. *The Princess,* he says, is not a "mere burlesque of the feminist cause" (99); rather, its "deepest theme" is "the clash between shadow and substance, illusion and truth, the ultimate relation between art and life" (101). *In Memoriam,* a superb accomplishment blending personal experience with issues of public concern, achieves artistic unity and rises to greatness because of Tennyson's ability to build on recurring symbols that suggest many of the same themes as *The Princess. Maud* is infused with Tennyson's "distaste for all false convention," and is "at once the most dissonant of all his major works and the most varied in its rich operatic harmonies" (140). It is, in Buckley's view, "the most carefully constructed of Tennyson's longer poems," in which the verse "is calculated and controlled with great discretion" (144).

The major contribution Buckley makes to the restoration of Tennyson's reputation occurs in his chapter on *Idylls of the King.* Buckley laments the fact that "The *Idylls* have too frequently been dismissed . . . as an elaborate exercise in rhetoric," and "the relevance of their central themes both to Victorian England and to the modern world has been accordingly for the most part ignored" (191). Taking the chapter title from the "Gareth and Lynette" idyll, Buckley demonstrates how the poem is like Camelot, a "city built to music." The *Idylls* has a unity that parallels the symphony. "The unity of the sequence," Buckley argues, "lies not in action or plot but in theme, imagery, and atmosphere" (173). Tennyson's skillful weaving of recurring symbols and his use of parallel scenes among early and late idylls give the poem cohesion and reveal the poet's concerns for modern social and moral problems. Buckley acknowledges that the figure of the king is not realistic, but in his view that is precisely what Tennyson intended. The interest in the poem lies in the action of those who try to conform or willfully rebel against what is clearly recognized as the highest ideals for human behavior and social decorum. The poem is the poet's "somber vision" of the fate of modern society wherein ideals have been sacrificed to personal pleasures.

With few exceptions, Buckley finds Tennyson's later work strong, filled with social criticism and concerns about immortality that preoccupied the poet throughout his life. The later poems express their themes in polished, controlled language that at once appeals to a popular audience yet retains a sense of serious inquiry that challenges readers to think deeply about the human condition. In Buckley's opinion, the poetry of Tennyson's old age is of a piece with his younger efforts. Throughout his life the poet remained "obedient to the one clear call of his own imagination," developing his best poetry from "the constant interaction between public knowledge and private feeling." Reversing the judgment of earlier critics, Buckley concludes that Tennyson's work will "endure, even apart from its aesthetic worth, as a mirror of his civilization" (255).

Buckley's laudatory assessment did not catch on immediately. Donald Smalley, a highly respected critic who reviewed *Tennyson: The Growth of a Poet* for the *Journal of English and Germanic Philology* (1962), cautioned against accepting Buckley's praise for the unity of *Idylls of the King* and his judgment that it ranks with *In Memoriam* as Tennyson's greatest accomplishment. Even more critical is the judgment of James Reeves. Surveying the progress and development of English verse in *A Short History of English Poetry 1340–1940* (1962), Reeves concludes his historical review of Tennyson's work with this rather enigmatic observation: "It is difficult to sum up his achievement. His poems are not particularly attractive to the present generation, but they have in them qualities which may well recommend them to future readers" (182). Like reviewers for more than sixty years, Reeves finds that "Tennyson never surprises us" (183) in his work; he may be a master of language, but he seems to have little to say about the human condition. Hugh Sykes Davies makes similar comments in *The Poets and Their Critics* (1962), grudgingly admitting that Tennyson "deserves preserving" only because "his personal predicament illustrates so fully the predicament of poetry in his time" (244). Attempts to restore "a reputation that is plainly drowning" are doomed, however. James Benziger is not quite as harsh, but he asserts in *Images of Eternity* (1962), a study of the vestiges of Romantic idealism in Victorian poetry, that despite the many insights about human nature found in *In Memoriam* and the general mastery of style that Tennyson exhibits in much of his poetry, he failed to create in any of his work "a great masterpiece of the moral imagination" (158).

John Killham, who had already made his mark as a proponent of Tennyson's excellence with his well-researched and thoughtful study *Tennyson and "The Princess": Reflections of an Age* (1958), took advantage of renewed interest in the poet's work to bring to a larger audience some of the fine criticism published earlier in the century. *Critical Essays on the Poetry of Tennyson* (1960) reprints G. M. Young's "The Age of Tennyson" and Arthur Carr's "Tennyson as a Modern Poet" to establish the Victorian context of Tennyson's work and demonstrate the modern qualities of his poetry. The volume also includes essays by Marshall McLuhan on Tennyson and the picturesque and on the Romantic epic, by distinguished Victorian scholars G. Robert Stange and Lionel Stevenson on Tennyson's use of myth and symbol, and by New Critics Cleanth Brooks, Graham Hough, Leo Spitzer, and others on such poems as "Ulysses" and "Tears, Idle Tears." T. S. Eliot's influential 1936 essay on *In Memoriam* and F. E. L. Priestley's groundbreaking study of *Idylls of the King* conclude the volume. Killham's contribution is a fine introduction that traces the major movements in Tennyson criticism from the poet's death to the mid-twentieth century. Given the high quality of scholarship and critical analysis, it is understandable that *Critical Essays on the Poetry of Tennyson* became a handy text containing opinion about the poet and his work, cited with great regularity by scholars for the next half-century.

The second major groundbreaking reassessment of Tennyson appeared two years after Buckley's book. Valerie Pitt's *Tennyson Laureate* (1962) takes on Harold Nicolson, T. S. Eliot, and others who find Tennyson a morbid, nearly psychotic character whose best work consists of technically polished Romantic lyrics. In an introduction that provides a fine, succinct summary of Tennyson criticism during the first half of the twentieth century, Pitt outlines the arguments made by those who dismissed Tennyson's later poetry as needlessly didactic and offensively moralistic. Pitt finds even Buckley to be too tied to the idea of "the two Tennysons" to be totally objective in his assessment. Pitt acknowledges that, after he became poet laureate, Tennyson worked with a decided interest in public poetry; yet his later poetry was not, as earlier critics suggest, accepted blindly by an adoring public. Moreover, Pitt says, "The really interesting problem in the study of Tennyson" is not "Why did his poetic power flag and fail after he became Laureate," but rather "How did the poet of a purely private emotion become the poet of a public order?" (15).

Pitt answers the question confidently and competently, and in the process develops a balanced portrait of Tennyson that explains his concern for craftsmanship, his focus on personal matters, and his desire to address some of the evils he saw in Victorian society. The title is somewhat misleading; much more than a study of Tennyson's later works, *Tennyson Laureate* explains how Tennyson's early efforts set the stage for his career as Victoria's laureate. Pitt sees the young Tennyson struggling, as so many Romantic poets did, with the conflicting desires to produce art for art's sake versus the need to do something useful for society. The early poems are Tennyson's repeated attempts to answer the question, "How is the poet to find and establish himself?" (65). As he mastered his craft, Pitt says, Tennyson found that he was developing techniques that would allow him to use his personal experiences to address issues of larger concern.

In a fine chapter on *In Memoriam,* Pitt demonstrates how the poet managed to combine his personal grief with the struggles of his countrymen to find meaning in a world that seemed to be governed by no universal laws. The death of Hallam drove Tennyson to wrestle with the issues that all society found problematic: "death, endurance, time and the nobility of man." Tennyson's elegy for Hallam addresses and expands these themes, "gathers and orders the moral experience of [his early] years, and neither Tennyson's later life, nor his later work, can be understood without this record" (85). Working carefully with various manuscripts of individual lyrics, Pitt demonstrates how Tennyson shaped the work to bring order to his rambling thoughts on the topics that concerned him and his countrymen. Unlike Tennyson's Victorian contemporaries, Pitt sees less concern with conventional religious faith in the elegy; there is "no suggestion that" the love Tennyson seems to associate with God is "anything other than friendship" (115). Nevertheless, by "particularising common symbol or common idiom" Tennyson makes of *In Memoriam* "less a great emotional than a great reflective poem," discovering through it "the theme of change in permanence" (119). This theme, developed through years in much of his early poetry, became Tennyson's subject during his years as poet laureate.

For Tennyson, Pitt claims, the laureateship was "not so much an honour as a function, and a function which gave direction as well as public recognition to his inner sense of his own gifts and his own vocation" (148–49). Poems written after 1850 frequently deal with the evils of materialism and the values of imperialism because Tennyson felt passionately about both topics. Although not a strong original thinker, Tennyson leaned on the theories of close friends Thomas Carlyle and Frederick Denison Maurice as philosophical underpinnings for his poetry. The laureate was an imperialist partly because he assumed (wrongly) that all colonials shared English values, partly because he felt deeply that the British could bring order to a world in great need of it. Pitt offers sympathetic readings of *Maud* and *Idylls of the King,* describing both as poems in which Tennyson deals with social rather than moral issues. She also provides sensible, sympathetic readings of many of Tennyson's occasional poems, judging them better than earlier critics have believed, because many of them use the occasion of a funeral, marriage, or public event as a reason to examine again the growing tendency toward disorder in society. Pitt finds irony in the fact that Yeats and Eliot took such pains to distance their works from Tennyson; in doing so, she says, they assert his power to create a tradition. More than any other poet of his century, Tennyson "expanded the possibilities of the language" while "creating and maintaining a poetic tradition which the first mass audience in the world could accept." This, Pitt says, "was in itself, a considerable achievement," suggesting "unusual greatness" (269–70).

In the same year, Joanna Richardson issued *The Pre-Eminent Victorian* (1962), a full-scale biography modeled on Sir Charles Tennyson's 1949 life of his grandfather. Providing less critical commentary than Pitt, Richardson instead concentrates on the many friendships and acquaintances Tennyson developed during his career. Consequently, she pays less attention to the poet's early life, opting instead to detail his activities during the years after he became poet laureate. Like Victorian biographers, Richardson quotes extensively from letters, diaries, and memoirs to give readers a sense of what Tennyson's contemporaries said about him. She skirts around the issue of Tennyson's relationship with his wife, one that subsequent biographers have dealt with more frankly; her discussion of the poet's friendship with the flamboyant and domineering photographer Julia Cameron might be described as chaste. Although she comments only briefly on individual poems, Richardson does try to show how contemporary events spurred Tennyson's imagination and led him to choose appropriate subjects — even his Arthurian stories.

When Richardson writes about Tennyson's Victorian qualities, she does so without prejudice. Her assessment of his strengths and flaws — as a poet and as husband, father, friend, and businessman — are provided without the mocking or condescending tones of those who had written about the Victorian laureate from the 1920s to the 1950s. She makes few apologies for either the man or his times; instead, she writes with both understanding and deference to an age in which people lived with the pressures of constant change and significant challenges to their deepest beliefs about human nature and the material world. She is not blind to the fact that Tennyson became kind of a cult figure, but she resists the temptation to moralize about some of the Victorians' misguided notions regarding social, religious, or aesthetic matters. Her concluding judgment of Tennyson as a poet and Victorian figure seems measured and sensible: He was "Victorian" in his interest in science, his need for reassurance about immortality, his attitude toward women ("an attitude of worship, puritanism, and condescension"), his class-consciousness, and his intense political chauvinism. What makes Tennyson the preeminent Victorian is that his life and work were one: "Tennyson's sense of mission embraced more than poetry: it included every action of his life" (292). This statement Richardson offers not by way of excuse, but by way of summation; for her there is no stigma in having been "Victorian."

The following year saw the publication of another seminal work in Tennyson studies, Ralph Rader's *Tennyson's "Maud": The Biographical Genesis* (1963). Combining the best methods of scholarship with a keen critical sense, Rader demonstrates how Tennyson's infatuation with Rosa Baring, a neighbor in Somersby, influenced more than a dozen important poems, most notably "Locksley Hall" and *Maud*. Taking his cue from Sir Charles Tennyson's writings about his grandfather's relationship with Baring, Rader mines Tennyson family papers, diaries, and letters from the poet's neighbors and friends, and other primary and secondary sources from the Victorian era to construct his case for the influence Rosa exerted on Tennyson during the years after Arthur Henry Hallam's death. His conclusions regarding Tennyson's passion for Rosa affected future biographers and critics for the remainder of the century.

Elton Edward Smith's *The Two Voices: A Tennyson Study* (1964) is one of the studies published after 1960 that assumes it is not necessary to defend Tennyson's rightful place as a major poet. Taking issue with Buckley, whom he finds still too immersed in the controversy over "two Tennysons" — the private poet who wrote great lyrics, the laureate who wrote almost nothing of lasting value — Smith argues instead for one poet with two distinct voices. He believes Tennyson struggled all his life with important "tensions" (21) that are exhibited throughout his work: art versus society, sense versus soul, doubt versus faith, past versus present, and delicacy versus strength. For this reason, much of Tennyson's poetry shows a tendency toward one extreme followed by a correction toward a more centrist position on these issues. For this reason, too, Smith argues, Tennyson often made use of fragments to construct works he considered whole and complete, *In Memoriam* being the most sustained example.

Although there is little startling in Smith's thesis, his observations on the effect of these tensions is often enlightening. For example, he notes that in *Idylls of the King,* Tennyson makes Guinevere and Lancelot the "malefactors of Sense" — a position easily accepted by his Victorian contemporaries. However, the poet makes the Holy Grail, long a symbol of the highest form of purity, the "malefactor of Soul." Smith believes this unusual diversion from received symbolic significance is due to Tennyson's "underlying ambivalence and his own most trenchant criticism of the retreat into asceticism" (67–68). Similarly, in *In Memoriam* Tennyson displays both faith and doubt, never settling on either side of the deep religious questions that lie beneath the surface of his elegy for the departed Hallam. Though Tennyson wants to believe in a "God Whose purposes are regnant in the universe," Smith says, he sees all around him "that universe dying everywhere," seemingly "empty of the presence of God" (113–14). Citing both early poems and ones written at the mid-point and end of his career, Smith notes how Tennyson was always genuinely ambivalent about science, recognizing its importance and the "inevitability of its advance," but at the same time deploring its effect on the "cultural treasures of the past," on art, on the imagination, and on "the validity of faith" (113). In the chapter titled "Delicacy versus Strength," Smith anticipates critics of the 1980s and 1990s in discussing "the 'Apollo-Hercules' combination of [Tennyson's] personality, the 'Camilla-Ajax' combination of his style, and the feminine-masculine *personae* of his poems" (143). R. A. Forsyth echoes Smith's views about Tennyson's ambivalence toward science in "The Myth of Nature and the Victorian Compromise of the Imagination" (1964). In fact, Forsyth believes Tennyson harbored an "incipient hostility to Science" because he dreaded "its exclusive veracity" (222).

Throughout his career, Smith says, Tennyson consistently "presents a view of life" in his poetry, "then proceeds to argue against his own presentation, by word, by tone, by choice of topic, or through the concealing play of masks" (170). Because they have not understood his method, Smith says, "critics past and present tend to see different Tennysons" (181). This "natural tendency" toward a reductionist interpretation of the poet's character has simply blinded them to Tennyson's ability to deal with a multitude of controversies while maintaining a consistent view of himself and the world. In Smith's view, critics "seem to miss" in Tennyson "his extraordinarily explicit honesty" about his inability to resolve unequivocally the complex issues he faces. "The Tennyson poem tends to become a kind of dialogue, a juxtaposition" of opposites that do not always resolve themselves, as Hegelians might wish, in a new synthesis. Nevertheless, Smith says, "the agony with which he cries from the toils of opposing tendencies proclaims his magnificent honesty and his kinship with the torn and divided men of all ages" (195).

An interesting and frequently neglected study of *In Memoriam* appeared in the same year as Smith's longer work. K. W. Gransden's *Tennyson: "In Memoriam"* (1964) is intended as a guide for students, but its argument for Tennyson's classical and neoclassical roots is a persuasive antidote to the growing tendency among critics to view Tennyson as an inheritor of the Romantic tradition. Though he focuses principally on Tennyson's elegy for Hallam, Gransden makes a strong case for the laureate's intellectual prowess. His comparison of Tennyson and Wordsworth in their use of nature makes it clear how different these poets were. In *In Memoriam*, Gransden argues, the "natural descriptions" serve a "structural function," tracing the "changing state of the poet's mind" (30). He emphasizes the unity of the poem, claiming it depicts the "journey from doubt and despair to acceptance" (51). In this he disagrees with T. S. Eliot and other modern critics who focus on the quality of Tennyson's doubt. These "modern critics have tended to see in the poem a reflection of our modern static mental condition," he says (60). Gransden believes the poem's concluding sections and its epilogue are essential for explaining "Tennyson's faith in the moral evolution of man" (63).

Another detailed and illuminating study appearing in 1964 was George W. Whiting's *The Artist and Tennyson*. Issued as a special number of *Rice University Studies,* Whiting's monograph describes the influence Tennyson's poetry had as an inspiration for nineteenth-century painters and sculptors. A result of a lifetime of careful study — the volume was issued posthumously as a tribute to Whiting by his colleagues at Rice — *The Artist and Tennyson* is an intriguing look at the synergies that existed among the arts in Victorian England. It is also a reminder of the extent of Tennyson's influence during his lifetime.

Among the new wave of critics following Buckley in seeing Tennyson as a major figure of great accomplishment was Clyde Ryals, who published two important studies of Tennyson in the 1960s. The first, *Theme and Symbol in Tennyson's Poems to 1850* (1964), traces Tennyson's debt to the Romantics through the poems published before he assumed the laureateship. Ryals's thesis is that "the conflict in Tennyson's early poems revolves around an epistemological problem: the divergence between objective reality and the subjective realm of the mind" (25), and that the tensions apparent in so many of the poems in the 1830, 1833, and 1842 volumes stem from this central issue. Carefully tracing the poet's use of imagery, Ryals shows how Tennyson's concern for the nature of reality leads him to deal with certain themes recurrently. The importance of myth and the use of the past become characteristics of the poetry during this period, and remain so for virtually all of the poet's life.

Ryals is generally sympathetic to the early poetry, though he acknowledges weaknesses in some works that he believes Tennyson should never have published. His curious comment regarding the 1842 volume says as much about Ryals as it does about Tennyson: "To my mind, the collection is one of the strangest publications ever to come from the mind of man. There is much that is fine, but almost as much that is dross" (161). That judgment seems based on Ryals's prejudice in favor of the introspective poems dealing with loss, grief, and the role of the poet — the characteristics that link Tennyson with his Romantic predecessors. Ryals has little use for many of the poems now known as the English idylls, domestic sketches that appealed to Tennyson's Victorian readers.

The chapter on *In Memoriam* is an exceptionally fine close reading of the poem, demonstrating not only the poet's skill but the critic's ability to discern patterns and sense the emotional undertones at play in this complex study of personal grief, universal love, and scientific debate. Expanding the arguments he had made in his earlier article "The 'Heavenly Friend': The New Mythus of *In Memoriam*" (1962), Ryals points out the significance of repeated images and the symbolic use Tennyson frequently makes of nature. Though he acknowledges that Tennyson's elegy is both a personal statement and a study of larger issues involving all of humankind, Ryals aligns himself with the critical tradition of Sir Harold Nicolson and against that of the Victorians — and Valerie Pitt — in asserting that "Tennyson was most himself when his melancholic sensibility was activated by loss." He was then "liberated from a concern with his mission as an oracular poet, which role he often assumed with a certain half-hidden misgiving" (210). On the other hand, Ryals does not follow Nicolson in relegating Tennyson to the second rank among poets. He dismisses the notion that Tennyson simply compromised with the mainstream thinking of his age by refusing to let his imagination take him to conclusions that might have been unpopular with readers. Instead, "Tennyson is a great poet," Ryals asserts in his Afterword, "mainly because he was able to combine the creative freedom of a dream with truth to human experience" (272). Turning upside down the notion that Tennyson is most representative of the Victorian age, Ryals boldly asserts instead that he "is like a man of the mid-twentieth century in the dress of a century earlier.... His art is melancholy because it looks backward and forward, with regret for a vanished past and often with apprehension to a fearful future" (274).

Ryals second major publication, *From the Great Deep* (1967), continues his close analysis of Tennyson's imagery and symbolism, focusing on the work published serially during Tennyson's laureate years. *From the Great Deep* has an added distinction: it is the first book-length study of Tennyson's Arthurian poem to appear in more than half a century. It should be pointed out, however, that F. E. L. Priestley's 1949 article on the *Idylls* had already begun the process of restoration, and that, two years before Ryals's book appeared, renowned Victorian scholar Kathleen Tillotson offered a laudatory assessment of *Idylls of the King* in her essay "Tennyson's Serial Poem," included in her *Mid-Victorian Studies* (1965). Nevertheless, *From the Great Deep* is the first of four important studies of the *Idylls* that, collectively, demonstrate the prominence of the poem not only during the Victorian era, but within the canon of English literature.

Relying little on the half-dozen earlier studies done by Tennyson's contemporaries, Ryals instead examines the poem to illuminate the principal themes that took shape as Tennyson composed individual idylls over a period of forty years. Rather than decrying Tennyson's use of the idyll as he did in his previous study, Ryals finds the form appropriate and masterfully handled in a work he considers "a philosophical poem" (vii). Acknowledging that the *Idylls* was crafted into a single, unified poem by the time Tennyson completed his final revisions shortly before his death, Ryals moves back and forth in his discussion, sometimes examining individual idylls in the order of composition, sometimes looking at them as they were finally linked together to achieve a coherent portrait of individual heroism, social discord, and moral commentary. In *Idylls of the King*, Ryals says, Tennyson shows how the power of love — true love for that which is best in humanity (Tennyson's substitute for God) and not simply erotic passion — has the ability to redeem individuals and perhaps, one day, redeem society as well.

Ryals's most significant contribution to appreciating the *Idylls*, and ultimately to our understanding of Tennyson as a student of human nature, is his analysis of King Arthur. For Ryals, Arthur is both hero and villain. The king establishes ideals and promotes freedom, but in binding his knights to follow impossible standards he robs them of freedom and makes them dependent on him. The kingdom decays and collapses because no one is able to live up to Arthur's high calling. In Ryals's view, Lancelot and Guinevere's adulterous relationship is not a cause for the fall of Camelot; rather, it is symptomatic of the many ways in which humans fail to live up to ideals. His reading of "The Holy Grail" demonstrates that, for Tennyson, asceticism is no answer to the demands that one live by high moral standards. The quest for this unattainable object leaves the kingdom near ruin. Ryals believes the poet's sympathies are made clear by Arthur's admonition at the end of the idyll that the right way to achieve the vision of the ideal is by successfully carrying out one's duty.

Ryals's assessment of the *Idylls* demonstrates that Tennyson could be Victorian and modern simultaneously. In presenting Arthur as a tragic figure — he cannot establish a perfect society, but he is rewarded for his efforts when he is apotheosized upon his death bed — Tennyson follows a belief shared with his contemporaries in the cyclical, evolutionary nature of history: humankind is evolving gradually toward a higher end, and King Arthur (like Arthur Henry Hallam in *In Memoriam*) is a sign of what humankind might eventually become. At the same time, Ryals contends that "with the possible exception of Wagner no one in the nineteenth century, I believe, explored so thoroughly or so well as Tennyson the psychology of erotic love" (143). Ryals's assessment overturns the judgments of many Modernist critics, including T. S. Eliot, who complained of Tennyson's inability to create complex characters. Building on F. E. L. Priestley's 1949 article and Jerome Buckley's chapter on the poem, *From the Great Deep* prepared the way for significant studies of *Idylls of the King* that subsequently restored it to a place of prominence in the Tennyson canon.

J. B. Steane's *Tennyson*, originally published in London by Evans in 1966, became part of the ARCO Literary Critiques Series in 1969, volumes designed to give "the ordinary man who reads for pleasure [a] straightforward account of literature and writers" (3). Steane begins by acknowledging that in the mid-1960s "'Tennyson' is still an emotionally-toned word," requiring readers to "clear the mind of associations and attitudes formed there by habit rather than judgment" (4). He then provides a detailed, chronologically organized assessment of the poet's career, acknowledging the critical controversies of the past century without dwelling on them. His readings of *In Memoriam* and *Maud* are tempered, concentrating on poetic technique. *Idylls of the King* he finds "quite enjoyable" if read in their entirety (113). On occasion, Steane is critical, as his remarks on the early volumes demonstrate: some of the poems are "irritating," others "sentimental"; "most readers would probably be happy with an anthology of about twenty-five" (34).

Lurking in the background of Steane's rather gentlemanly approach, however, is his constant awareness that he is writing against a strong reactive tradition. This he sees as ironic: "While criticism of Tennyson in this century has argued that he is limited and regrettable" because he was, in the view of the twentieth century, an "escapist," his contemporaries thought of him "as a modernist," "one who specifically brought modern life into poetry" (150). Although Steane's book is not groundbreaking scholarship, it does fulfill its purpose of introducing readers to a poet who is, in Steane's view, well worth reading.

Another 1966 study that adds significantly to understanding something of Tennyson and his critics is Robert Preyer's "Alfred Tennyson: The Poetry and Politics of Conservative Vision." Preyer is direct and unapologetic in branding Tennyson a conservative, bent on upholding the old order against the encroachments of modernism. His best poetry, Preyer says, deals lovingly with the values of an England that had passed away by the nineteenth century. Tennyson writes of contemporary issues because he was expected to do so, not because he believed in the value of progress. And yet, Preyer notes, his contemporaries loved him. The secret to his success lay in his ability to "redirect" his readers' attention "from a particularized human situation to an absorbing and mysterious cosmic display" (339). The importance of Preyer's observations lies in his careful articulation of a thesis that was already being challenged: That Tennyson was a spokesperson for his age. Ironically, Preyer expresses what was becoming a minority opinion among twentieth-century critics when he sees Tennyson as a champion of the past; by the 1960s the trend was to see him as a subversive undermining the values he appeared to uphold. The tug-of-war among critics on this issue would continue until the end of the century.

Three studies of *Idylls of the King* followed Ryals's work in short order. Examining the three as a group offers some sense of the extent to which Tennyson's Arthurian poem had risen in stature since Jerome Buckley resurrected interest in it. In *Perception and Design in Tennyson's Idylls of the King* (1969), John R. Reed is interested in the "moral design" of Tennyson's poetry (3), arguing that the poet's concern in the body of his work "is not really with theology and philosophy, but with the individual's examination of his own powers" (9). By way of introduction, he traces the moral design he finds in poems such as "The Two Voices" and *Maud*, but the greater part of his monograph concentrates on Tennyson's Arthurian epic.

Like Buckley, Reed finds the *Idylls* to be a unified poem rather than a collection of fragments on a common subject. In fact, he argues that the moral design is what gives the poem its unity. In some ways, Reed's study is a throwback to the work of Mungo MacCallum and other turn-of-the-century critics who praised Tennyson for the moral dimension of his Arthurian work. Reed's two-part analysis is curiously organized. To demonstrate the moral design he considers individual idylls in their order of composition, but when he discusses themes of identity and authority or freedom vs. confinement he treats the poem as a completed unit, reading the work as it appeared in final form in 1885. To his credit, Reed offers one of the most sustained thematic interpretations of the *Idylls*, exploring the development of what he calls the realized ideal in the character of Arthur and the (mostly failed) attempts of others to realize the ideal in themselves. Reed sees Arthur as a hero and other characters as imperfect humans trying to emulate the blameless king. Such strident conservatism stands at one end of a spectrum of interpretative statements about what certainly was for twentieth-century critics the most controversial of all of Tennyson's major poems.

While not as detailed in its analysis of *Idylls of the King* as Reed's work, J. Philip Eggers's *King Arthur's Laureate* (1971) examines the poem from various perspectives to "capture" its "social meaning" (xii). Beginning with the assumption that the *Idylls* is a major Victorian work of art, Eggers reviews its serial composition, examines other nineteenth-century Arthurian works, and discusses the critical reception of the *Idylls* among Tennyson's contemporaries. His assessment of the completed poem, in which he finds unity achieved through recurring patterns of imagery, is less compelling than Reed's, but his study is a good introduction for those wishing to learn about the impact the poem made on the Victorians.

The third book on *Idylls of the King* to appear within less than a decade after Ryals's study was John D. Rosenberg's *The Fall of Camelot* (1973). Rosenberg's judgment of the poem is unequivocal: "The *Idylls of the King*," he says in his opening sentence, "is one of the four or five indisputably great long poems in our language" (1). After demonstrating that, despite their protestations, modern poets such as Yeats, Eliot, and even Wallace Stevens owe a debt to Tennyson, Rosenberg explains why *Idylls of the King* is not escapist literature but a penetrating analysis of modern society. He argues that the poem is unified not simply by its story but by an interweaving of themes (reality vs. allusion, identity vs. disintegration of personality), repetition of leitmotifs and key imagery, and a sophisticated use of scene-painting in which character and landscape are inextricably interwoven.

In a chapter titled "Timescape" Rosenberg argues that details within individual idylls create a realistic chronology for Arthur's reign that exists in parallel with the atemporal atmosphere created by the elements of Romance within the story. His chapter on "Landscape" demonstrates how Tennyson is able to evoke aspects of character by placing individuals within settings that suggest their emotional states. With exceptional understanding of details, he explains how Tennyson operates as a symbolist poet before the term became fashionable among literary artists. Rosenberg is especially good at analyzing Tennyson's complex characters, particularly Arthur, Lancelot, and Guinevere, to show that they are far from the caricatures that other critics have labeled them to be. He is unwavering in his belief that Tennyson has created a poem of exceptional unity on every level: "The deeper one penetrates the *Idylls*," he says, "the more one perceives that its interrelations are inexhaustible, that each of its parts reflects the infinite complexity of the whole" (134). Fifteen years later, In "Tennyson and the Passing of Arthur" (1987) Rosenberg would return to his subject to write a more extensive argument on the importance of the poem as a recreation of the Arthurian legend.

Further evidence of the revival of interest in Tennyson's Arthurian poem can be found in John Pfordresher's *A Variorum Edition of Tennyson's Idylls of the King* (1973). This work of meticulous scholarship catalogues the many changes Tennyson made to the poem as it grew incrementally over the thirty-year span. Like others writing on the *Idylls* in the 1960s and 1970s, Pfordresher operates from the assumption that the poem is one of the greatest in the language and deserves the attention he has given it.

During the 1960s, the number of articles and notes on Tennyson's poems expanded exponentially. Tennyson criticism became almost a cottage industry in academe; scholars seem to have rediscovered both major and minor works. A sampling among these offers some example of the variety of approaches taken toward the Victorian laureate and his work: Howard Fulweiler's "Tennyson and the 'Summons from the Sea'" (1965) explores Tennyson's use of sea imagery throughout his career. Marvel Shmiefsky's "*In Memoriam:* Its Seasonal Imagery Reconsidered" (1967) takes a similar approach in re-examining Tennyson's elegy. In "On the Major Poems of Tennyson's *Enoch Arden* Volume" (1965) Thomas Assad explicates poems that had been immensely popular among Victorians but dismissed as sentimental claptrap by later generations. Joseph Sendry's "'The Palace of Art' Revisited" (1966) is one of nearly forty detailed examinations of one of Tennyson's earliest works of distinction. Alicia Ostriker's 1967 *PMLA* article "The Three Modes of Tennyson's Prosody" updates and expands the work of James Pyre, who had done groundbreaking analysis of prosody in *The Formation of Tennyson's Style* (1921). Joseph Solimine explores Tennyson's political attitudes in "The Burkean Idea of the State in Tennyson's Poetry: The Vision in Crisis" (1967). Eugene August takes another look at Tennyson's religious beliefs in "Tennyson and Teilhard: The Faith of *In Memoriam*" (1969), while Fred Kaplan examines his attitude toward the artist in "Woven Paces and Waving Hands: Tennyson's Merlin and the Fallen Artist" (1969). While many are indeed revisionist in their assessment of the poet's achievements, it is not uncommon to find received opinion being recycled, as it is in the introduction of James Walton's "Tennyson's Patrimony: From 'The Outcast' to 'Maud'" (1969). In explaining how Tennyson dealt with "the problem of how one is to develop his poetic gift without endangering his moral and psychic life," Walton asserts that "Amphion," a poem appearing in 1842, "illustrates the poet's growing tendency to suppress the complexity of his vision in an effort to establish his moral solidarity with the common man" (733). The ghosts of Nicolson and Fausset live on.

In the closing years of this decade, several scholars writing about common themes among poets and novelists offered judgments about Tennyson's work. Warren Anderson's "Types of the Classical in Arnold, Tennyson, and Browning," included in a collection titled *Victorian Essays: A Symposium* (1967) covers well-trodden ground, but his observations on the stature of the three poets is worth noting: "In that notable age of poetry which gained its first mature powers at the nineteenth-century's mid-point Arnold, Tennyson, and Browning rule their several provinces of the sensibilities like medieval barons" (60). There seems no hint of apology in calling the Victorians notable for their achievement, nor in citing Tennyson as one of the pantheon who dominated the practice of poetry during the age.

In *The Victorian Debate* (1968), Raymond Chapman attempts to reverse a tendency he finds in critics of the preceding two decades to idealize the Victorians. In reaction to those of the first half-century who rejected the Victorians and their work, Chapman finds that scholars of the 1950s and 1960s tend to "envy the Victorians for their stability" (1). His aim is to "find a way between the extremes," to pay our Victorian forebears "the ultimate tribute of trying to understand" them (2). Chapman's judgment of Tennyson and his contemporaries is not, however, particularly laudatory. Writing comparatively about Tennyson and Browning, he asserts that the Victorians had "no poetic movement comparable to Romanticism" (194). These two giants of the age, Chapman says, were too willing to compromise poetic integrity to public taste. In tones generally condescending, he offers a rather harsh judgment of Tennyson's contributions to the advance of poetry. Coming as it does, however, in the midst of a general wave of positive criticism, Chapman's view did not seem to affect his contemporaries or diminish their zeal to investigate the intellectual background of Tennyson's major poetry.

Patricia Ball has a much more balanced view of Tennyson. In *The Central Self* (1968), a work that expands the case she initially put forward in "Tennyson and the Romantics" (1963), she argues that the Victorians were worthy inheritors of the Romantic mantle, concerned with maintaining the high calling of the poet. For them, however, the concept of self was something more complex, and at times more frightening, than it had appeared to their forebears. Like the Romantics, Tennyson and his contemporaries explored the concept of self through "two kinds of imaginative expression": the "dramatized utterance" and the more directly "personal voice" (2). Ball considers Tennyson a major poetic voice in the Romantic tradition; it is unfortunate, she observes, that "to many he remains a poet of his time in a restrictive sense" (167). By carefully examining selected poems, most especially *In Memoriam* and *Maud,* she demonstrates that Tennyson was capable of being the kind of chameleon poet Keats has spoken of: he could write directly of his personal experience, or he could disguise himself in dramatic forms, using a variety of poetic genres to examine the problems of the self in conflict with the experience of the world.

Typical of the monographs published after Buckley's groundbreaking study, William Brashear's *The Living Will* (1969) assumes the poet's greatness not only as an artist but also as a thinker. He is interested in demonstrating how, in his most serious poetry, Tennyson "evidences to an extreme degree [a] subjective psychology" that fails to exhibit confidence in the external world, opting instead for "a reliance on the 'living will' to sustain a world of illusion above the chaos of conscious fact" (12). Brashear's reading of the poems demonstrates that this "living will" is Tennyson's way of combating the "vision of futility" that he experiences from contact with the external world. Read in this light, poems such as *In Memoriam* and especially *Idylls of the King* take on new meaning, the latter becoming a grand tragedy in which the king emerges as the hero even though the society he attempts to create is a failure.

In the course of explicating individual poems, Brashear demonstrates the exceptional depth of Tennyson's understanding of human nature, placing him in a category of thinkers that includes Kant, Carlyle, Schopenhauer, and even Nietzsche (to whom Tennyson is precursor). Far from being simply the representative of a self-serving and self-gratifying Victorian age, Tennyson exhibits in his work "the genius of a subjective poet concerned with the cosmic isolation of self and a primal and tragic struggle" (173). Perhaps, Brashear admits, Tennyson may not be Shakespeare's equal, but he certainly comes close. Brashear also includes a chapter on Tennyson in a later book, *The Gorgon's Head* (1977), a study of the concept of tragedy in nineteenth- and twentieth-century poetry. In that study, using the works of Schopenhauer and Spengler, Brashear explores Tennyson's fascination with the concept of the infinite, highlighting the poet's willingness to confront the tragic possibilities of human existence in light of the information being revealed by Victorian scientists.

Like Brashear in *The Living Will,* Gerhard Joseph concentrates on a single aspect of Tennyson's work in *Tennysonian Love: The Strange Diagonal*

(1969). Returning to a subject discussed extensively by the Victorians, Joseph acknowledges that the divided view of love shared by Tennyson and his contemporaries creates tensions that give life to his best work. The Victorians seem repulsed by the sensual form of love, yet recognized that a higher form of love was not only permissible but desired. How Tennyson dealt with both forms of love is Joseph's subject, and he examines both major and minor works to reveal the poet's complex and changing attitudes toward this concept. Joseph believes that the poet's "best work mourns a lost or unrealized love in a personal or legendary past" (191). His analysis of *The Princess* and *Idylls of the King* is especially influential in continuing the growing critical tradition that elevates both works in the Tennyson canon. He even suggests that *The Princess* is an indirect precursor of the aesthetic movement. Of particular interest is Joseph's examination of the women in Tennyson's poetry, especially the "fatal woman" who appears with great regularity in both early and later works. Joseph's assertion that "no other Victorian poet possessed of a major talent exhibits quite his representative blending of romantic eroticism and sentimental pietism" (191) makes it clear that he believes Tennyson is unequivocally deserving of the newly rediscovered respect he received during the decade of the 1960s.

Masao Miyoshi's *The Divided Self: A Perspective on the Victorians* (1969) is a similar book, "concerned with the ways in which Victorian men of letters experienced the self-division endemic to their times" (ix). Predictably, Miyoshi sees Tennyson as just such a divided self, and the early poetry shows his efforts to "cement the disparate parts of his life by moral commitment" (107). Tennyson moved away from writing pure poetry, Miyoshi says, toward more didactic work not simply because his Cambridge college mates encouraged him to do so. Rather, "the gradual ascendancy of the moral perspective in his poetry is generated from his own paramount need for a new vision of life" (114). Although Miyoshi seems to be commending the poet for his change of focus, there is little substantive difference from this assessment and those of the 1920s vintage critics who saw the same division but opted to lament the move away from pure poetry toward moralistic verse.

Both Shiv Kumar (*British Victorian Literature: Recent Revaluations*, 1969) and Isobel Armstrong (*The Major Victorian Poets: Reconsiderations*, 1969) include scholarship on Tennyson in their collections of essays that ostensibly offer new views of the Victorians. Kumar includes previously published work by Milton Millhauser, "Tennyson: Artifice and Language," originally a 1956 article in the *Journal of Aesthetics and Art Criticism*, and Allen Danzig's fine 1962 *PMLA* article "The Contraries: A Central Concept in Tennyson's Poetry." Both assume at the outset that Tennyson is a major figure, fully resurrected from the depths to which he had sunk in the first half of the century. Millhauser is critical of Tennyson's ornate style, accusing him of using artifice rather than dealing directly with human emotions — a charge leveled at the poet by Bagehot in his 1864 article "Wordsworth, Tennyson, and Browning; or Pure, Ornate, and Grotesque Art in English Poetry." Danzig's work is more useful in helping readers understand how Tennyson created his art: the poet's concept of a "dualistic universe" (113), Danzig says, shaped his best work. Armstrong's collection includes three essays that focus on individual works (*The Princess, Maud,* and *In Memoriam*) and one exploring Tennyson's use of repetition as a symbolic device. Distinguished British critics Martin Dodsworth, Bernard Bergonzi, Alan Sinfield, and A. S. Byatt operate from the premise that they are evaluating important poems by a major Victorian writer; none sees the need to justify their choice of subject.

Arthur Pollard's collection of essays, *The New History of Literature: The Victorians* (1969), has a similar aim as those by Armstrong and Kumar. John Killham, already noted for his work on *The Princess* and his own collection of important essays on the poet, contributes a thoughtful analysis of the way Tennyson responded to the prevailing ideas of his time. Killham provides an excellent, concise summary of the poet's career, noting how Tennyson was constantly trying to deal with an innate feeling that the modern spirit was somehow misguided. Killham suggests that throughout his career Tennyson struggled with his natural desire to be the "modern poet of sensation" while simultaneously fulfilling the didactic role set out for him by Hallam and the Apostles (365). Killham believes that Tennyson gradually became demoralized by the varying degree of success he achieved in exposing the evils of materialism and the need to follow ideals.

Two events late in the decade signaled a new impetus for further detailed study of the poet and his works. First, in 1967 the Tennyson Society began publishing the *Tennyson Research Bulletin,* a scholarly journal combining brief articles about Tennyson's work with news and notes about current scholarly and commemorative activities. Concurrently the Society began underwriting the publication of monographs by noted Tennyson scholars. The first of these, a slim volume hardly more than an article published in pamphlet form, deserves special mention. J. M. Gray's *Man and Myth in Victorian England: Tennyson's "The Coming of Arthur"* (1969) was the first of several publications by one of the most knowledgeable twentieth-century critics of *Idylls of the King.* In notes that run as long as his main text, Gray displays his exceptional understanding of Arthurian myth. This slim volume, its companion piece *Tennyson's Doppelganger: Balin and Balan* (1971), and a series of notes and brief essays published in the *Tennyson Research Bulletin* and other journals provide support to scholars disposed to read *Idylls of the King* as one of Tennyson's major accomplishments. Gray would bring his Arthurian studies to fruition in *Thro' The Vision of the Night: A Study of Source, Evolution and Structure in Tennyson's "Idylls of the King"* (1980), a work to be discussed in the next chapter.

Other monographs in the Tennyson Society series quickly followed, including Patrick Scott's *Tennyson's "Enoch Arden": A Victorian Best-Seller* (1970); Milton Millhauser's provocative look at Tennyson and Victorian scientific thought, *Fire and Ice: The Influence of Science on Tennyson's Poetry* (1971); and Sir Charles Tennyson's brief *Tennyson and his Times* (1974), a study of the poet's interest in and use of contemporary events in his work. The Society continued to publish occasional papers throughout the next three decades, adding to the wealth of scholarship on Tennyson. The Society also issued Occasional Papers beginning in 1974, often printing the texts of speeches given at the group's annual meeting. Distinguished among these papers are Cecil Y. Lang's *Tennyson's Arthurian Psycho-Drama* (1983), an analysis of the ways Tennyson transformed the spiritual qualities he found in Arthur Hallam into the heroic virtues of the mythical King Arthur in *Idylls of the King*; Barbara Hardy's examination of Tennyson's relationship with the genre of fiction in *Tennyson and the Novelists* (1993); Alan G. Hill's *Tennyson, Wordsworth and the "Forms" of Religion* (1997), an examination of Tennyson's debt to Wordsworth in shaping questions of religion in his poetry; and Michael Slater's fine study of Tennyson's ongoing love affair with drama in *Tennyson in the Theatre* (2000).

The second and perhaps most important event was the 1969 publication of Christopher Ricks's edition of *The Poems of Tennyson* (1969). More than simply a sound source for Tennyson's texts, the collection of variant readings, extensive textual notes, brief critical commentaries, and background information made the Ricks edition a sourcebook for future scholars by exposing, as best he could, the creative processes that made Tennyson the preeminent craftsman of his day, and perhaps in all of English poetry. The impact of the Ricks edition is best summarized by textual editor Philip Gaskell, who calls it "the great edition" and "an astonishing *tour de force*" (139). Armed now with a decade of favorable critical commentary initiated by Buckley, and with a reliable text and extensive notes in the Ricks edition, scholars of the next two decades were ready to make the case — once again — for Tennyson's rightful place as an English poet of the first rank.

Works Cited

Anderson, Warren D. "Types of the Classical in Arnold, Tennyson, and Browning." *Victorian Essays: A Symposium*. Ed. Warren D. Anderson and Thomas D. Clareson. Kent, OH: Kent State UP, 1967. 60–70.

Armstrong, Isobel, ed. *The Major Victorian Poets: Reconsiderations*. London: Routledge & Kegan Paul, 1969.

Assad, Thomas J. "On the Major Poems of Tennyson's *Enoch Arden* Volume." *Tulane Studies in English* 14 (1965): 29–56.

August, Eugene R. "Tennyson and Teilhard: The Faith of *In Memoriam.*" *PMLA* 84 (1969): 217–26.

Bagehot, Walter. "Wordsworth, Tennyson, and Browning; or Pure, Ornate, and Grotesque Art in English Poetry." *National Review* n.s. 1 (November 1864): 27–66. Reprinted in *Literary Studies, II.* London: Longmans Green, 1905; London: J. M. Dent, 1911. 305–52.

Ball, Patricia M. *The Central Self: A Study in Romantic and Victorian Imagination.* London: Athlone, 1968. 166–200.

———. "Tennyson and the Romantics." *Victorian Poetry* 1 (January 1963): 7–16.

Benziger, James. "Tennyson." *Images of Eternity: Studies in the Poetry of Religious Vision from Wordsworth to T. S. Eliot.* Carbondale: U of Southern Illinois P, 1962. 138–63.

Brashear, William R. "The Boundless Deep: Tennyson." *The Gorgon's Head: A Study in Tragedy and Despair.* Athens: U of Georgia P, 1977. 27–48.

———. *The Living Will: A Study of Tennyson and Nineteenth-Century Subjectivism.* The Hague: Mouton, 1969.

Buckley, Jerome H. "Introduction." *Poems of Tennyson.* Cambridge, MA: Riverside Press, 1958: ix–xxi.

———. *Tennyson: The Growth of a Poet.* Cambridge, MA: Harvard UP, 1960. Boston: Houghton Mifflin, 1965.

———. "Tennyson — The Two Voices." *The Victorian Temper: A Study in Literary Culture.* Cambridge, MA: Harvard UP, 1951. 66–86.

Chapman, Raymond. "Tennyson and Browning." *The Victorian Debate: English Literature and Society 1832–1901.* London: Weidenfeld & Nicolson; New York: Basic Books, 1968. 194–206.

Danzig, Allan. "The Contraries: A Central Concept in Tennyson's Poetry." *PMLA* 77 (December 1962): 577–85.

Davies, Hugh Sykes. "Lord Tennyson." *The Poets and Their Critics.* Vol. 2. London: Hutchinson, 1962. 243–95.

Eggers, John Philip. *King Arthur's Laureate: A Study of Tennyson's "Idylls of the King."* New York: New York UP, 1971.

Forsyth, R. A. "The Myth of Nature and the Victorian Compromise of the Imagination." *Journal of English Literary History* 31 (1964): 213–40.

Fulweiler, Howard W. "Tennyson and the 'Summons from the Sea.'" *Victorian Poetry* 3 (1965): 25–44.

Gaskell, Phillip. *From Writer to Reader: Studies in Editorial Method.* London: Oxford UP, 1978. 118–41.

Gransden, K. W. *Tennyson: "In Memoriam."* London: Edward Arnold, 1964.

Gray, J. M. *Man and Myth in Victorian England: Tennyson's "The Coming of Arthur."* Lincoln, England: Tennyson Society Research Centre, 1969.

———. *Tennyson's Doppelganger: Balin and Balan.* Lincoln, England: Tennyson Society, 1971.

———. *Thro' The Vision of the Night: A Study of Source, Evolution and Structure in Tennyson's "Idylls of the King."* Edinburgh: Edinburgh UP; Montreal: McGill-Queen's UP, 1980.

Hardy, Barbara. *Tennyson and the Novelists.* Lincoln, England: Tennyson Research Centre, 1993.

Joseph, Gerhard. *Tennysonian Love: The Strange Diagonal.* Minneapolis: U of Minnesota P, 1969.

Kaplan, Fred. "Woven Paces and Waving Hands: Tennyson's Merlin as a Fallen Artist." *Victorian Poetry* 7 (1969): 285–98.

Killham, John. "Tennyson (and FitzGerald)." In *The New History of Literature: The Victorians.* Ed. Arthur Pollard. London: Cresset; New York: Bantam, 1969. Reprint, New York: Bedrick, 1987. 361–86.

———. *Tennyson and "The Princess": Reflections of an Age.* London: Athlone Press, 1958.

———, ed. *Critical Essays on the Poetry of Tennyson.* London: Routledge & Paul; New York: Barnes & Noble, 1960.

Kumar, Shiv, ed. *British Victorian Literature: Recent Revaluations.* New York: New York UP, 1969.

Lang, Cecil Y. *Tennyson's Arthurian Psycho Drama.* Lincoln, England: Tennyson Research Centre, 1983.

Millhauser, Milton. *Fire And Ice: The Influence of Science on Tennyson's Poetry.* Lincoln, England: Tennyson Society, 1971.

———. "Tennyson: Artifice and Language." *Journal of Aesthetics and Art Criticism* 14 (1956): 333–38.

Miyoshi, Masao. *The Divided Self: A Perspective on the Victorians.* New York: New York UP, 1969. 107–23, 235–40.

Ostriker, Alicia. "The Three Modes of Tennyson's Prosody." *PMLA* 82 (1967): 273–84.

Pfordresher, John. *A Variorum Edition of Tennyson's "Idylls of the King."* New York: Columbia UP, 1973.

Pitt, Valerie. *Tennyson Laureate.* London: Barrie & Rockliff, 1962. Toronto: U of Toronto P, 1963.

Pollard, Arthur, ed. *The New History of Literature: The Victorians.* London: Cresset; New York: Bantam, 1969. Reprint, New York: Bedrick, 1987.

Preyer, Robert. "Alfred Tennyson: The Poetry and Politics of Conservative Vision." *Victorian Studies* 9:4 (1966): 325–52.

Priestley, F. E. L. "Tennyson's *Idylls.*" *University of Toronto Quarterly* 19 (October 1949): 35–49.

Pyre, James F. A. *The Formation of Tennyson's Style: A Study, Primarily, of the Versification of the Early Poems.* Madison: U of Wisconsin P, 1920. Reprint, New York: Phaeton Press, 1968.

Rader, Ralph W. *Tennyson's "Maud": The Biographical Genesis.* London: Cambridge UP; Berkeley: U of California P, 1963.

Reed, John R. *Perception and Design in Tennyson's "Idylls of the King."* Athens: Ohio UP, 1969.

Reeves, James. *A Short History of English Poetry 1340–1940.* London: Dutton, 1962.

Richardson, Joanna. *The Pre-eminent Victorian: A Study of Tennyson.* London: Jonathan Cape, 1962.

Ricks, Christopher, ed. *The Poems of Tennyson.* London: Longmans, 1969; 2nd ed., rev. 3 vols. Berkeley: U of California P., 1987.

Rosenberg, John D. *The Fall of Camelot; A Study of Tennyson's "Idylls of the King."* Cambridge, MA: Harvard UP, 1973.

———. "Tennyson and the Passing of Arthur." *Victorian Poetry* 25:3–4 (Autumn/Winter 1987): 141–50.

Ryals, Clyde de L. *From The Great Deep.* Athens: Ohio UP, 1967.

———. "The 'Heavenly Friend': The 'New Mythus' of *In Memoriam.*" *Personalist* 43 (Summer 1962): 383–402.

———. *Theme and Symbol in Tennyson's Poems to 1850.* London: Oxford UP; Philadelphia: U of Pennsylvania P, 1964.

Scott, P. G. *Tennyson's "Enoch Arden": A Victorian Best-Seller.* Lincoln, England: Tennyson Research Centre, 1970.

Sendry, Joseph. "'The Palace of Art' Revisited." *Victorian Poetry* 4 (1966): 149–62.

Shmiefsky, Marvel. "*In Memoriam:* Its Seasonal Imagery Reconsidered." *Studies in English Literature, 1500–1900* 7 (1967): 721–39.

Slater, Michael. *Tennyson in the Theater.* Lincoln, England: Tennyson Research Centre, 2000.

Smalley, Donald. "A New Look at Tennyson — and Especially the *Idylls.*" *Journal of English and Germanic Philology* 61 (April 1962): 349–57.

Smith, Elton Edward. *The Two Voices: A Tennyson Study.* Lincoln: U of Nebraska P, 1964.

Solimine, Joseph. "The Burkean Idea of the State in Tennyson's Poetry: The Vision in Crisis." *Huntington Library Quarterly* 30 (1967): 147–65.

Steane, J. B. *Tennyson.* London: Evans, 1966.

Tennyson, Sir Charles. *Tennyson and His Times.* Lincoln, England: Tennyson Research Centre, 1974.

Tennyson Research Bulletin. Lincoln, England: Tennyson Research Centre. 1967–.

Tillotson, Kathleen. "Tennyson's Serial Poem." *Mid-Victorian Studies.* London: Athlone Press, 1965. 80–109.

Walton, James. "Tennyson's Patrimony: From 'The Outcast' to 'Maud.'" *Texas Studies in Literature and Language* 11 (1969): 733–59.

Whiting, George W. "The Artist and Tennyson." *Rice University Studies* 50 (1964): 1–84.

5: The Height of Critical Acclaim: 1970–1980

DURING THE 1960S AND 1970S several British publishers created series of critical volumes designed to help students and general readers develop an appreciation for Victorian poets and novelists. John Pettigrew's contribution to the Edwin Arnold series, *Tennyson: The Early Poems* (1970), offers brief analyses of poems published in the volumes of 1827, 1830, 1833, and 1842. What is significant about this work is that Pettigrew adds his voice to the growing cadre of scholars who feel compelled to counter the "hopelessly partial" criticism of Sir Harold Nicolson (7) and demonstrate how Tennyson makes "great poetry out of his quarrels" between his tendency toward the personal, private side and his desire to please his friends by being a public poet (14). On the other hand, the Longman series volume on Tennyson written by B. C. Southam presents an enigmatic portrait of the poet. Southam's *Tennyson* (1971) seems highly eclectic in its selection of poems that merit explication. Southam believes Tennyson was a frustrated Romantic, and his interpretations bear out that conviction.

Distinguished critics Morse Peckham and Harold Bloom both wrote briefly about Tennyson, but with decidedly different points of view. Peckham's chapter on Tennyson in *Romantic Revolutionaries* (1970) ties the Victorian poet closely to his Romantic forebears, concentrating on Tennyson's early poems to demonstrate his development of a creative imagination. Peckham is decidedly laudatory in his reading of Tennyson's work. Arguing that "today we rather have a tendency to sneer at the Victorians for their facile belief in progress," he explains how Tennyson's idea of progress links him much more closely to figures such as Wordsworth and Coleridge than to many Victorian contemporaries. Peckham has much good to say not only about *In Memoriam* but also about *Idylls of the King*, a work he believes exhibits tendencies toward modernism as well as links to the Romantic tradition. By contrast, Bloom observes in *The Ringers in the Tower* (1970) that "the Tennyson who counts for most" is "certainly a Romantic poet" and not "a Victorian anti-Romantic" (146). Bloom celebrates the early poems, especially "Mariana" and "Recollections of the Arabian Nights," because these demonstrate the poet's ability to display his creative imagination before he let himself be overcome by the need to use his work for social instruction.

Derek Colville's *Victorian Poetry and the Romantic Religion* (1970) mirrors the works of Peckham and Bloom in its thesis that the Victorians were the spiritual and aesthetic descendants of the Romantics. Colville concentrates, however, on the ways Arnold, Browning, and Tennyson reformulated Romantic ideals for their Victorian audience. In his view, Tennyson found the Romantic poets attractive because in Romanticism's "persistent recreation of transcendental experience" was something he had known intuitively all his life (230). Colville's readings of several of the early poems, "The Lover's Tale," and *In Memoriam* demonstrate the strong bent toward Platonism that Tennyson shared with his Romantic forebears. The last of these poems is, in Colville's judgment, quintessentially Romantic while being decidedly Victorian. Tennyson was more significant as a Victorian poet because he was more consistent than any of the other major figures of his age in dealing with the fractious nature of modern society: the "schisms" of his age were an "impetus for almost everything significant he ever wrote" (232).

James Kissane's *Alfred Tennyson* (1970), a volume in the Twayne English Authors series, serves more as a review of received opinion about the poet than as a new analysis of his poems. Several years earlier, Kissane had written a fine essay explaining the strong points and limitations of Tennyson's achievement as an artist, "The Passion of the Past and the Curse of Time" (1965). In keeping with the format of the Twayne series, Kissane's introductory chapter reviews Tennyson's life and reputation. Surprisingly, though, the bulk of his study is organized not chronologically but by literary genre, describing Tennyson's work in lyric, dramatic, and narrative modes. It is also surprising that Kissane admits to being less than enthusiastic about Tennyson's achievement than one might expect of a critic selected to write a volume for Twayne. Somewhat apologetically, Kissane insists that "writing this book has increased my respect for and enjoyment of Tennyson's poetry by a considerable measure" (8).

In the 1970s several works published by noted Victorian scholars offer further insight into Tennyson's method and achievement in *In Memoriam*. John Dixon Hunt's *"In Memoriam": A Casebook* (1970) demonstrates the continuing interest in Tennyson's elegy. Dixon collects key essays and chapters from books to illustrate the wide range of critical assessments written by Tennyson's contemporaries and respected twentieth-century scholars. Choosing judiciously from among hundreds of previously published commentaries, Dixon includes T. S. Eliot's seminal essay, Graham Hough's "The Natural Theology of *In Memoriam,*" Jerome Buckley's chapter on the poem from *Tennyson: The Growth of a Poet,* and more than a dozen other brief, insightful critiques.

In his perceptive essay "The Dynamic Unity of *In Memoriam*" in *The Modern Spirit: Essays on the Continuity of Nineteenth and Twentieth Century Literature* (1970), Robert Langbaum attempts to rescue the poem from those who believe it presents a "compromise between science and religion" (53). Actually, Langbaum says, the poem is intended to stand against the predominant thought of the 1830s and 1840s. The poem is important because it is so topical.

Similarly, Patricia Ball's commentary on *In Memoriam* in *The Heart's Events: The Victorian Poetry of Relationships* (1976) demonstrates how Tennyson's elegy for his friend is yet another example of a peculiarly mid-Victorian phenomenon. In the poem, the loss of a loved one produces a "profound dislocation" which forces Tennyson "to search out the meaning" of this "central relationship" in his life (185). Ball claims the work is unified through the growth of the poet's self-awareness as he comes to define and understand his relationship with Hallam.

Alan Sinfield's *The Language of Tennyson's "In Memoriam"* (1971) delivers more than the title promises. He begins with a deceptively simple goal: to explain how the "key" to Tennyson's success in this "rather good poem" lies in the poet's use of language (1). Free from the political rhetoric of his later criticism, Sinfield's book is much more than a study of Tennyson's elegy, and indeed is possibly the best critique of the poem since A. C. Bradley's 1901 *Commentary*. Calling Tennyson an inheritor of the Romantic tradition, Sinfield explains how "elements of his art" are equally influenced by "impulses more often associated with the eighteenth century" (18). Sinfield demonstrates how the "form" of the poem "recreates the shapes of the life of the emotions" (29). Sinfield's study owes much to the work of philologists and practitioners of semiotics, but his focus remains on the emotional impact of language, not simply on its grammatical and syntactical aspects. His conclusion is stated early in the study, and then demonstrated in his careful investigation of diction, syntax, imagery, sound, and rhythm: "The structure and language of *In Memoriam*" are "product[s] of a desperate need for order in the absence of any clear and agreed means of establishing it" (39). Ultimately, this book is not simply about *In Memoriam*, but about Tennyson's place at the center of a continuum from the enlightenment to the modernist period, his concern for language tying him to both the ordered world of Pope and the symbolist world of Yeats and Eliot.

Three years after bringing out his edition of Tennyson's poems for the Longman's Annotated English Poets series, Christopher Ricks produced a critical biography of Tennyson for Macmillan's Masters of World Literature series. His *Tennyson* (1972) is distinguished by the insightful if sometimes opinionated assessments of individual poems. Perhaps the most informative observation Ricks makes about Tennyson's poetry is that so much of it ends before a logical conclusion is reached; the reader is often left wondering about the outcome of events. This method — the "art of the penultimate" as Ricks calls it (49) — parallels the poet's own continual questioning of endings for which he could have no certainty — specifically, about human immortality. In the course of writing about the poet's life, Ricks offers detailed explications about works that had come to be considered important in the Tennyson canon. Where he is able to do so, Ricks explains how the incidents of Tennyson's career gave life to these poems.

Though not as detailed as Sir Charles Tennyson's biography, Ricks's discussion of the poet's life is nevertheless balanced and peppered with reasoned speculations that explain the poet's propensity for dealing with certain themes, particularly suicide. Ricks is more forthcoming than previous biographers in discussing Dr. Tennyson's precarious mental state and the deleterious effect it had on his children, including Alfred. Ricks also explores the practical side of Tennyson's relationship with Arthur Henry Hallam, discusses his tenuous (but not disastrous) financial situation during the 1830s and 1840s, and recounts briefly yet clearly his on-again, off-again romance with Emily Sellwood. Like most of Tennyson's biographers, however, Ricks devotes little attention to Tennyson's personal life after he became poet laureate, opting instead to review the major poems produced after *In Memoriam* and commenting on Tennyson's growing conservative tendencies.

Because Ricks had established himself as the acknowledged twentieth-century expert on the texts of Tennyson's poems, any judgment of individual works offered in his critical biography must be taken seriously. He seems to be tied to the tradition begun by the early revisionists and made famous by Harold Nicolson and T. S. Eliot. "Tennyson is supremely a poet of doubt, of a divided mind" (138), Ricks declares. The poet's best work is that which maintains a sense of doubt, or contains beneath the surface sense of optimism a strong strain of suspension from optimistic judgment about the human condition.

Ricks is also not ready to accept the more recent assessments of *The Princess, In Memoriam, Maud,* and especially *Idylls of the King*. None of these poems, he says, is a unified whole. Unfortunately, "literary criticism since Tennyson's time" has become "more skilled at imagining some such unity where it may not exist and . . . more skilled at exculpating works of art which in fact deserve the higher compliment of not being whisked away into the irreproachable" (212–13). Ricks says that Tennyson never intended these works to be seen as unified long poems approaching the epic; rather, their individual sections are linked loosely to create, in some cases, a sense of the poet's varying responses to one of more major themes. While he is gentle in his reproofs of *In Memoriam* and *Maud,* Ricks is less considerate of Tennyson's Arthurian story. Reacting to the extended studies by John Phillip Eggers, Clyde Ryals, John Reed, and most of all Jerome Buckley, Ricks goes out of his way to point out the faults in *Idylls of the King*. These include inadequate moral vision and serious stylistic deficiencies. "A full-length critique of the *Idylls*' style would be a dispiriting matter," Ricks concludes. Such a condemnation from the poet's modern editor cannot be dismissed lightly.

Ricks is particularly well qualified to comment on Tennyson's style, of course, and to detail the poet's borrowings — not only from other poets, but from himself as well. Ricks notes how much in Tennyson's later work is actually taken from poems begun decades earlier, sometimes lifted without emendation. He believes many of the concerns the poet expresses as an old man were with him as a teenager. One such subject was the idea of Time; with consummate skill, Ricks cites passages from printed texts and manuscript sources to demonstrate how much the poet was occupied with this elusive concept. The point of this analysis is to highlight the danger in critics' talking about the "progress" of Tennyson's thought. "There is no breach between the young Tennyson and the old," Ricks asserts (307). To read him any other way is to do an injustice to his poetic ability and to misunderstand both his achievements and his failures.

Ward Hellstrom, author of *On the Poems of Tennyson* (1972), focuses on individual poems to explain why some are masterpieces, others only competent journeyman's work. The strength of his study lies in the close readings he provides of poems such as *In Memoriam, Maud,* and *Idylls of the King.* If there is an underlying thesis, it is that Tennyson was for most of his life in the debt of Liberal Anglicans whose theology and sense of history informed his best poetry. Some of Hellstrom's assessments are notably iconoclastic. For example, he claims that *In Memoriam* is not about Arthur Henry Hallam at all, but that Tennyson simply uses Hallam as a convenient tool to demonstrate the real theme of the poem, the spiritual regeneration of the "poet" who speaks throughout the individual lyrics. Similarly, he eschews the allegorical nature of *Idylls of the King* to focus on the role of women in the poem, a theme that would be taken up later — with decidedly different conclusions — by feminists.

Perhaps the most intriguing statement in Hellstrom's book appears in his conclusion. "The Victorian world is now opening to us," he says, "at a sufficient distance that a more positive and more accurate judgment can be made" about Tennyson's reputation. He is "one of many spokesmen for the age," not in a narrow sense, however, but because "he addresses the problems that were real for the Victorians and real for us" (162–63). For the student of Tennyson criticism, these remarks certainly have the ring of *déjà vu*; similar claims were made as early as the 1920s, but the fact that Hellstrom feels compelled to repeat them suggests that as late as 1970 the jury was still out about the Victorians and their laureate.

F. E. L. Priestley, whose 1949 article on *Idylls of the King* was an early attempt to restore that poem to its rightful place as a major work in the canon of English literature, turned his considerable skill as a critic of poetic language to the entire Tennyson corpus in 1973. His *Language and Structure in Tennyson's Poetry,* a part of the Language Library series by Andre Deutsch publishers, concentrates on the ways Tennyson uses words, diction, rhetoric, poetic structure, and sounds to evoke meaning. Priestley demonstrates how, throughout his career, Tennyson experimented with language and structure to accommodate his interest in dealing with issues important to his contemporaries. Though not organized on strict chronological lines, the book offers insight into the young poet's developing mastery of style in his early volumes. Among the many notable insights Priestley offers is that Tennyson, like his Romantic predecessors, was not averse to mixing traditional genres to create new forms of poetry. Priestley argues that both *In Memoriam* and *Idylls of the King* are actually new poetic genres, mixing traditional forms such as elegy, lyric, epic, and romance. The mixture of genres was, he says, a stumbling block for early critics, but became a way for Tennyson to reach wide audiences by combining comic and tragic forms.

While the majority of his examples are taken from *In Memoriam*, Priestley is particularly adept at demonstrating how Tennyson is able to use the technical tools of his trade to create a wide variety of poems that deal with an equally diverse set of themes. Priestley is particularly good at close analysis of word choice, syntax, the use of alliteration and assonance, modulation of stresses within individual lines and stanzas, and the stanzaic patterns that help create meaning. Equally important are his cautionary notes regarding Tennyson's philosophical bent. Although twentieth-century critics have been quick to dismiss the poet's depth of thought, Priestley says that it is necessary for the "careful reader" to "determine precisely" what a writer understands by the terms his uses (174). Applying that standard to Tennyson, Priestley demonstrates that the poet's insights into the key questions of his day regarding science, faith, and philosophy, as these terms were understood by his contemporaries, is much more penetrating than some have been willing to grant him.

Tennyson's relationship to his age continued to be a topic of great interest to scholars during this decade. As part of the Writers and Their Background Series, D. J. Palmer assembled a collection of essays by a group of distinguished scholars specializing in Victorian studies. Intended to provide students and scholars a context for understanding the laureate, the essays in *Tennyson* (1973) describe the social, cultural, intellectual, political, and religious milieu in which the poet lived. An excellent introduction to Tennyson's life and career, the book is further demonstration that in the 1970s his reputation had come full circle.

As it had in the prior decade, specialized study of individual poems dominated critical commentary in the 1970s. When the Victorian scholar Lionel Stevenson retired from Duke University, Clyde Ryals assembled *Nineteenth Century Literary Perspectives* (1974), a *festschrift* consisting of seventeen essays whose authors read like a Who's Who in Victorian criticism. G. Robert Stange contributed an intriguing comparative assessment of Tennyson and Baudelaire organized around the theme of the voyage. Dwight

Culler's "Tennyson We Cannot Live by Art," a study of "The Palace of Art," is written with the same insight into the poet that characterizes Culler's longer study published three years later.

Scholarly journals included scores of articles on Tennyson and his poems. Studies of *In Memoriam* and *Idylls of the King* were most prevalent, but commentary on *The Princess, Maud,* "Ulysses," "The Palace of Art," and other works made frequent appearance in scholarly publications. The majority opinion on *In Memoriam* can be seen in works such as John Boyd's "*In Memoriam* and the Logic of Feeling" (1972), which demonstrates the contrast between logic and emotional experience in the poem; Michael Y. Mason's "*In Memoriam:* The Dramatization of Sorrow" (1972), an argument demonstrating how Tennyson's use of dramatic techniques allows him to express excessive grief while maintaining some distance from this potentially destructive emotion; Kerry McSweeney's "The Natural Pattern of Consolation in *In Memoriam*" (1973), a study of the way nature serves as a healing force for grief; and Susan Gliserman's "Early Victorian Science Writers and Tennyson's *In Memoriam*" (1975), an article examining the influence of scientific writing on Tennyson's elegy. A sampling of the growing interest in specialized study of *Idylls of the King* is evidenced in, among others, the work of Jeffrey Helterman, "Narrative Modes and the Dynamics of Passion in *Idylls of the King*" (1974); Ronald Lbrach, "Myth and Romance in *Idylls of the King*" (1975); and Kerry McSweeney, "Tennyson's Quarrel with Himself: The Tristram Group of *Idylls*" (1977). Two fine articles on the dramatic qualities and heroic concepts of "Ulysses" appeared in the early years of the decade: R. F. Storch's "The Fugitive from the Ancestral Hearth: Tennyson's 'Ulysses'" (1971), and Tony Robbins's "Tennyson's 'Ulysses': The Significance of the Homeric and Dantesque Backgrounds" (1973).

Another major study of the poet appeared in 1975. James Kincaid's *Tennyson's Major Poems* (1975) posits an intriguing thesis and presents forceful arguments rooted in sound, detailed analysis of individual poems expressed in vivid, direct language. Kincaid claims that at "the center of Tennyson's major poetry" is the "interplay and conflict of the comic and ironic modes." The poet's career is most appropriately appreciated, Kincaid says, as "a strong and courageous resistance to the demands of ironic art" (3), a resistance best exhibited during mid-career when he attempted to write comic poetry on the model of Dante and others. While providing penetrating assessments of works such as "The Palace of Art," "The Two Voices," "The Lady of Shalott," and "Ulysses," which he considers masterpieces in the ironic mode, Kincaid is at his best in exploring the complexities of major works in both genres: *The Princess, In Memoriam,* and *Maud,* all sustained efforts to present a comic view of the world, and *Idylls of the King,* which he proclaims "the major ironic work of art of the century" (3).

Kincaid's views of these works is grounded in the best scholarship of the first three-quarters of the twentieth century, and serves as the basis for much of the work done by scholars in the century's last decades. His discussion of the conflict between heroic and domestic comedy in *The Princess* gives dignity to Princess Ida. His thoughtful reading of *In Memoriam* explains how the poem "goes beyond religion to the comic myth that informs and contains religion" (80). Seeing the movement of the poem from irony to comedy, Kincaid demonstrates how difficult it was for Tennyson to sustain a comic vision in a world where order seemed ready to dissolve into chaos. *Maud,* the "darkest" of all of Tennyson's comedies, follows the typical comic pattern "from isolation to social acceptance" (110), but the "comic solution" remains troubling: the "symbol of war carries such enormous weight in providing the resolution" (131). "It is hard to imagine," Kincaid says, "a conclusion that would be darker yet still remain comic" (133).

In *Idylls of the King* Tennyson returns to the ironic mode that characterized much of his earlier work, producing what is in Kincaid's view a poem "which has more and more come to be recognized as his major work and one of the two or three most important poems of the century" (150). Viewed in this light, Tennyson's dramatization of the fall of ideals at the hands of time is ironic on multiple levels: "its narrative structure parodies romance; its tone parodies comedy; its characters, particularly its central hero, parody tragedy" (151). It would be hard to find a reading of the *Idylls* more antithetical to the Victorian and post-Victorian views that celebrated the optimism of the poem. With exceptional skill and insight, Kincaid demonstrates how the poem progresses from the comic world of "Gareth and Lynette" where "there are no real problems" (165) to "the nightmare stage of irony" in the final four idylls, where "images of absolute bondage, cynicism, and utter waste dominate" (198). No reading of the poem after Kincaid's has been able to fully counter his view that the poem celebrates nothing heroic, but instead demonstrates the failure of the ideal to transform the natural trajectory of the world that is grounded not in progress but entropy.

Another of the rising Victorian scholars who found much good to write about Tennyson was Carol Christ, author of *The Finer Optic: The Aesthetic of Particularity in Victorian Poetry* (1975). Discovering "a preoccupation in Victorian poetry with the particular and the subjective," she explores the significance of this tendency in Tennyson and several contemporaries, showing how "concern with the particular" extends "from the use of detail" to the "epistemological issues it implies" (ix). Tennyson was always intensely interested in minute details; he had a habit of reversing the adage expressed by Dr. Samuel Johnson in *Rasselas* that the business of the poet is not with tracing the streaks of the tulip, but in describing general properties. For Tennyson, Christ argues, the essence of explaining the relationship between the self and the world was in discovering the universal in the particular. Such tendencies place him firmly in the Romantic tradition. Two years later, Christ shifted her focus to examine Tennyson's work from a feminist perspective as part of an important work in Victorian gender studies, Martha Vicinus's *A Widening Sphere: Changing Roles of Victorian Women* (1977). In "Victorian Masculinity and the Angel in the House," Christ looks at the Victorians' concept of the ideal woman in the work of Tennyson and Coventry Patmore, whose poem provides the title phrase of her article. Believing that the Victorians' "concept of masculinity" (147) is revealed in these poets' description of gender relationships, Christ analyzes several poems, especially *The Princess*, to demonstrate Tennyson's belief in "the redemptive power" of women to help men "regenerate" themselves through their love for the ideal maiden (153).

Wendell Stacy Johnson's *Sex and Marriage in Victorian Poetry* (1975), a book much like Christ's in its sweeping look at a particular aspect of Victorian society as reflected in the poetry of the period, includes a lengthy chapter on Tennyson in which the author makes clear his appreciation for the poet's mastery of craft and insight into contemporary issues. Johnson sees the idea of marriage playing a central role in four major poems, and deduces that Tennyson sees humankind's salvation through marriage. In some cases the act of divorce is seen as metaphor for the larger act of separating components of the human person (for example, the division of "sense" and "soul" that characterizes *Idylls of the King*). Johnson notes shrewdly that in his early poetry, Tennyson frequently presents his readers with characters who are alone and frustrated, further emphasizing the fact that the importance of marriage for social harmony and progress was a lifelong concern for the poet. Five years later, Richard McGhee expands Johnson's thesis in *Marriage, Duty and Desire in Victorian Poetry* (1980), claiming that the "dialectic of love and duty," a major informing principle in all of Tennyson's major work, "is more than a personal or ethical matter" for the poet. "It is an epistemological and metaphysical concern" (30). Love and marriage becomes for Tennyson a metaphor of the struggle the artist feels between his roles in the private and public spheres. McGhee's excellent analysis of *Idylls of the King* demonstrates his appreciation for Tennyson's ability to use the breakup of marriages as a visible parallel to the larger social issue, the dissolution of ideals.

Although it is limited in new insight, Paul Turner's *Tennyson* (1976) for the Routledge Author Guides series is nevertheless one of those valuable studies that offers a sound examination of Tennyson's life and literary career. Turner had written a thoughtful essay on Tennyson nearly three decades earlier. "The Stupidest English Poet" (1949), a call for revaluation of Tennyson's reputation, had concentrated on Tennyson's thought, specifically his speculative theology. Turner's *Tennyson*, like other books in the Routledge series, focuses on the social and historical background that shaped the poet's ideas and affected him personally and professionally. After brief chapters describing the characteristics of the Victorian age and outlining the major events in Tennyson's life, Turner examines several poems to demonstrate Tennyson's reliance on both literary tradition and contemporary events. Believing Tennyson "showed a special gift for adapting previous literature to purposes of self-expression" (35), Turner devotes considerable space to drawing parallels between individual poems and their sources in classical or Renaissance literature.

On the major poems Turner is especially good at summarizing Tennyson's use of sources and describing briefly the major themes with which the poet grappled. He admits that Tennyson's view of women's place is out of step with twentieth-century attitudes regarding liberation and equality, but nevertheless believes *The Princess* accomplishes its purpose in raising the status of women while concurrently offering readers some of the finest comic writing of its time. *In Memoriam,* he says, "might be summarized as an attempt to harmonize two slightly discordant concepts, spiritual evolution and physical evolution" (121). His analysis of Tennyson's reliance on both literary sources and contemporary scientific writing is succinct and convincing. Turner's source study of *Maud* is intriguing in that he finds the roots of some of the scenes in this monodrama in poems that appeared in the same volume in which the germ of the poem, the lyric "O, that 'twere possible" appeared in the 1830s.

Like Buckley and Kincaid, Turner believes *Idylls of the King* is a major poetic accomplishment. Interpreting the work sociologically, Turner argues that the poem is designed as a commentary on "the history of England during Tennyson's lifetime, which he saw as a period of political and scientific progress followed by one of spiritual decline" (152). Much of Turner's study is devoted to examining Tennyson's transformation of his source material, but his conclusion is that the poet used his sources to produce a poem of lasting value. Unfortunately, he concludes, "it is only because of the modern reluctance to read any long poem as a whole, and to take any ethic seriously which cannot readily be squared with the doctrines of Freudian, Jungian or Behavioural psychology, that the impressiveness of Tennyson's achievement is not yet widely recognized" (169). Turner's conclusion about the *Idylls* suggests in miniature his assessment of the poet's reputation as a whole. While Tennyson is no longer subject to significant deprecation, "two factors still prevent him from standing quite as high in public estimation as he deserves": first, the notion that "we are a superior species to the Victorians," and second, the "inadequate understanding of the literary and historical context" in which Tennyson's poems were written (184). Turner's study has been designed to rectify these problems, although the evidence of criticism written since 1976 suggests he has had only limited success.

Studies of Tennyson's style began with the first published reviews of his work, and more than a half-dozen scholars wrote monographs on the subject. Yet none have proven to be as exhaustive or as influential as W. David Shaw's *Tennyson's Style* (1976), a work incorporating the insights of previous scholars, some of Shaw's previously published work, and new materials that explore the relationship between thought and modes of expression in Tennyson's poems. By the time he published this study, Shaw had already established himself as a first-rate critic of Browning, having published *The Dialectical Temper: The Rhetorical Art of Robert Browning* in 1968. His previous work on Tennyson appeared in a half-dozen distinguished scholarly periodical: two articles on *Idylls of the King* (1967, 1969), two on *In Memoriam* (1971, 1976), one on Tennyson's "poetry of debate" (1973), one on "Lucretius" (1972). In his new book Shaw extends the work of his mentor, F. E. L. Priestley, whose *Language and Structure in Tennyson's Poetry* (1973) stands with James Pyre's *The Formation of Tennyson's Style* (1921) and Alan Sinfield's *The Language of Tennyson's "In Memoriam"* (1971) as the premier scholarly works on Tennyson's style published in the twentieth century.

Shaw begins *Tennyson's Style* by asserting that critics who have tried to catalogue Tennyson as a late Romantic have done him a disservice, as have those who have tried to use the techniques of New Criticism to sort out his best poems from those containing too little paradox or irony. Scholars who wish to understand Tennyson's achievement must "remember that the rhetoric of the best Victorian poems is essentially a means of showing how the mind is moved to make moral and intellectual distinctions" (26). When read in this light, the Tennyson canon contains myriad examples of first-rate poetry that illuminates both the mind of the poet and the central concerns of his age.

More expansive than either Sinfield or Priestley, Shaw demonstrates that Tennyson is a master of style, a poet who understood how to use the structure of language to communicate or complement the ideas and emotions expressed by the words of his poems. His concluding chapter is an especially good summary of the six qualities that distinguish Tennyson's style: "repetition," "resourceful hovering" over ideas and images, "inventive use of appositional grammar and two-way syntax," an ability to combine "clarity of sense" with "suggestion of truths that are not explicit," and a facility for combining direct and indirect statement. These qualities derive, Shaw says, from Tennyson's "view of the world," his "theory of language," and "his psychological temperament and general needs" (301). Individual chapters provide detailed analysis of lyrics and narrative poems as well as *In Memoriam, Maud,* and *Idylls of the King.*

In 1976 Tennyson scholar Alan Sinfield turned his talents to editing, producing *English Poetry,* a collection of essays redacted from lectures given by distinguished British scholars. Tennyson is the subject of a conversation between John Dixon Hunt and David Palmer, who argue that the view of "two Tennysons" is wrongheaded, and that the poet exhibits throughout his career the signs of greatness for which he has come to be recognized. To prove their point, Hunt and Palmer concentrate on explaining the merits of *Idylls of the King*.

Harold Bloom, perhaps the most prolific and controversial of the Yale school of literary theorists whose works during the 1970s and 1980s reshaped the direction of literary study in America, considers Tennyson a major figure in the development of poetic tradition. In a provocative chapter in *Poetry and Repression* (1976), Bloom uses the theoretical work of Freud, Derrida, and Lacan to explain how Tennyson's unconscious debt to Keats shaped his early work and served to underpin his career. Bloom argues that "Tennyson's transformation of Keats" was "the largest single factor in British and American poetry from about 1830 until about 1915," influencing writers as disparate as the pre-Raphaelites, Yeats, Wilfred Owen, Walt Whitman, and even Wallace Stevens (145).

Another important theorist whose work on Tennyson became a touchstone for future critical work is the Marxist scholar Terry Eagleton. Eagleton's comments on the subtext of key Tennyson poems has inspired commentary and controversy during the last decades of the century. His influential essay "Tennyson: Politics and Sexuality in *The Princess* and *In Memoriam*" (1977), first presented as a conference paper, uses Marxist theory and the work of Freud and Lacan to deconstruct these two important poems. In Eagleton's view, both address what Lacan calls the disruption of the symbolic order, specifically the displacement of the patriarchy and the elevation of the power of women in society. Eagleton sees Tennyson struggling to deal effectively with women's rights and with the love he feels for Hallam while preserving the bourgeois values to which he subscribed.

Less polemical than Eagleton, but no less critical of colonialism in all its forms, literary historian Patrick Brantlinger expresses mixed emotions about Tennyson in *The Spirit of Reform: British Literature and Politics 1832–1867* (1977). Brantlinger examines Tennyson's political poems, which reveal, he says, "the social and the religious curses of his age" (185). Despite the rhetoric in poems such as "Locksley Hall" and *Maud*, Tennyson is no better than "anticlimactic" in offering resolutions to social ills, "a mere loose bandaging up of the wounds he opens" (185). Rather than stressing the need for reform, Brantlinger says with obvious disappointment, Tennyson simply emphasized "the need for moderation" (193).

Though Tennyson's work was slowly coming under the microscope of the new breed of literary theorists, the dominant form of critical discussion of his poems during the 1970s remained what theorists would come to call orthodox criticism. In that vein, Dwight Culler's *The Poetry of Tennyson* (1977) is another work that begins with the premise that Tennyson is a great poet and then proceeds to demonstrate how the poet's exceptional skill and insight is revealed in his work. Culler's overriding questions are, What was Tennyson's concept of the poet's role, and how did that evolving concept affect the production of his poetry? In general terms, Culler answers this question by defining Tennyson as an Alexandrian poet, a literary inheritor of the tradition that deals frequently with apocalyptic subjects and reinterprets received stories rather than inventing new ones. Early in his career, Culler argues, Tennyson decided that he could best succeed by writing shorter rather than longer works. Hence, his early work exploits what are considered the minor genres, and his later, major poems, although of considerable length, are really built on the principles of shorter works. Culler demonstrates how Tennyson took advantage of his skills as a poet of shorter verses in writing works such as *The Princess, In Memoriam, Maud,* and even *Idylls of the King.*

While acknowledging that many of Tennyson's poems are open to multiple readings, Culler demonstrates that quite a few lend themselves to interpretations of the artist's role in society. Using evidence from Tennyson's life, from contemporary events, and from the texts of the poems themselves, Culler explains how works such as *The Princess* can be read as a plea for poetry to be available to the general public. He is also astute at demonstrating how Tennyson could rework poems written early in his career to serve new themes. None is more notable in this vein than "The Epic," which formed the basis for "The Passing of Arthur" in *Idylls of the King*. Originally intended to demonstrate the passing of an era — notably, the loss of Arthur Hallam — in its new setting, the poem climaxes a work that prophesies "the doom of society" (217). From Culler readers learn that Tennyson was both a master of his craft and a self-conscious poet continually concerned with reaching his readers through his art.

Philip Henderson's *Tennyson: Poet and Prophet* (1978) has a title more appropriate to scholarship written a century earlier. Yet his generally laudatory study, offering personal readings of the poems, concentrates less on the prophetic side of Tennyson's career than on the his lifelong concentration on his craft. Relying heavily on the work of previous biographers, Henderson reads Tennyson's work in biographical context, stressing the links between incidents in the poet's life and individual poems. More akin to Sir Charles Tennyson's work than to the critical studies of Buckley and Culler, *Tennyson: Poet and Prophet* gives little more than passing attention to most of the poet's work except to note how Tennyson was driven to write his poems and to explain in some detail how they were received by their first readers. Throughout, Henderson includes first-hand accounts from Tennyson's contemporaries to gives readers a sense of the poet's character and habits. While he is bold in asserting the homosexual undertones of *In Memoriam*, Henderson offers little new on other major works; his critique of *Idylls of the King* is especially disappointing, and his assessment of the poet's late career seems hurried and too heavily reliant on long quotations from the diaries and letters of Tennyson's friends and acquaintances.

Although not published until 1978, Geoffrey Tillotson's chapter on Tennyson in *A View of Victorian Literature* is more appropriately seen as an answer to the criticisms of T. S. Eliot and F. R. Leavis, who frequently found Tennyson limited as a thinker and narrative poet. Originally intended as a volume in *The Oxford History of English Literature* series, Tillotson's work defines the essential characteristics of the Victorian Age and asserts unequivocally that Tennyson was its principal interpreter. Tillotson is not surprised that succeeding generations have reacted negatively to much of Tennyson's poetry, because Tennyson "chose to offer thinking on the problems of the time (as many poets do not)" (288). He attacks Eliot's claim that Tennyson had no gift for narrative, demonstrating the poet's mastery of structure. In contrast to Leavis's dismissive judgments that Tennyson's poetry is not worth the time and effort modern criticism might expend on it, Tillotson claims that when we study Tennyson's art "we are studying one of the subtlest things in our literature" (317). It seems unfortunate, in retrospect, that Tillotson took so long to complete a work he began some two decades earlier — and which languished in manuscript until his widow Kathleen, herself a respected Victorian scholar and author of a fine article on *Idylls of the King* (1965), received a commission to publish it.

In any decade after 1960, one can find dozens of articles and chapters on Tennyson's major works. In *The Victorians* (1978), a volume intended to illustrate the ways historical events shaped Victorian literature, Laurence Lerner writes on *The Princess* as an example of a part of the feminist movement dawning in England at the time. Although in Lerner's view Tennyson was "not an original thinker," he did have "a good nose for the topical" (210). Carl Dawson's chapter on *In Memoriam* in *Victorian Noon* (1979), a study of an *annus mirabilis* of the Victorian period, offers readers a perspective on the poem in historical context. Unfortunately, Dawson's concentration on the ways Wordsworth influenced the poem makes his work of limited use in gauging Tennyson's reputation at the time the poem was published.

Perhaps because literary critics tend to shy away from the more mundane aspects of literary production in favor of aesthetic considerations, the community of Tennyson scholars had to wait until 1979 for a comprehensive study of Tennyson's relations with his publishers. June Steffensen Hagen's *Tennyson and His Publishers* is a work of careful scholarship and is, despite its prosaic subject, highly entertaining reading. Carefully mining the correspondence and records of Tennyson and the men with whom he contracted for the production of his books, Hagen demonstrates that the Victorian Laureate was a good businessman even in his youth, when he was reluctant to see his work in print. Her study gives further proof to the notion that what we read in the first and subsequent editions published during his lifetime were the versions of his poetry with which Tennyson felt comfortable, and on which he wanted his reputation to rest.

Two other books published in 1979 give clear indication as to the high status of that reputation. Henry Kozicki's *Tennyson and Clio: History in the Major Poems* brings together and extends the author's fine work that had appeared during the previous ten years in journals such as *ELH, Criticism, The Journal of English Literary History, Victorian Studies,* the *Victorian Newsletter,* and *SEL.* Arguing that the body of Tennyson's work illustrates what Lionel Trilling had called in *The Liberal Imagination* an "aesthetic effect of intellectual cogency," Kozicki demonstrates how "the intellectual order that unifies Tennyson's major poems comes out of his sense of history" (xi). Tennyson's philosophy of history, built on his notions of God, humankind, and the historical process, present in his earliest works and developed during his career, moves from an optimistic notion based on the idea of progress to a darkening vision of history as anarchic. Viewed in this light, the Tennyson corpus is clearly the work of a powerful intellect engaged in serious questions about human nature and social interaction.

Similarly, the second study, Robert Pattison's *Tennyson and Tradition,* is built on the premise that Tennyson is much more than a polished phrase-spinner able to delight readers by stringing together melodious, sentimental passages. Instead, Pattison strives to "elevate Tennyson's reputation as a craftsman consciously working within a long and complex tradition of poetic forms," illustrating along the way that "critical theory" was an "active force" in Tennyson's development of his art (1). Tennyson does not simply borrow from the poetic tradition, but instead uses it as a source out of which he "evolves new creations, creations that are demonstrably linked to tradition but surpass it" (2). Concentrating on classical and Renaissance literature, Pattison argues that Tennyson's principal creative genius is expressed in his adaptations of the idyll, a form of poetry that creates detachment in the reader and whose elasticity permits the poet to graft onto it elements of other literary genres such as drama, elegy, and epic. Pattison begins with two excellent chapters on Tennyson's development of the idyll form, then reads the major poems as variations on this technique. *The Princess,* he says, is an extended idyll; *In Memoriam* blends idyll with elegy, modifying both classical and Renaissance notions of the latter to create "a new order" constructed "of the detritus of the ancient forms" (127). Pattison's brief discussion of *Maud* demonstrates how Tennyson was able to adapt the idyll to include elements of drama and the dramatic monologue.

Pattison's discussion of *Idylls of the King* celebrates the poem as a major statement about "the theme of universal process" (135). In this poem Tennyson reaches the apex of his career in adapting the idyll to create "a poem of Homeric scope" (135) in which the "shell provided by the Arthurian material" allows him to construct "objective psychological studies" of characters "not in the process of action, but in the throes of internal debate" (137). The *Idylls* are, in his view, simultaneously idyll, epic, romance, and allegory. Combining the forms permits Tennyson to indicate the complexity of world views that permeate the poem. King Arthur is truly heroic — "the one genuinely epic character" in the work (149) — but he is limited in achieving his vision because he must work with the flawed materials that are his subjects. Similarly, Pattison argues, Tennyson as poet has to work within the poetic tradition, attempting to reshape old forms to new purposes. It is his crowning achievement as a poet that he is able to do so in works such as *Idylls of the King* and *In Memoriam*, where the thematic statement — "true vision" of "a universe shot through and sustained by a divine energy, toward which the material world evolves" — is mirrored in the formal structure of the poem (150).

In 1980, the Canadian scholar J. M. Gray published *Thro' The Vision of the Night: A Study of Source, Evolution and Structure in Tennyson's "Idylls of the King,"* a work based on his previously published studies and new research. The book may be the most exhaustive source study ever done on the *Idylls*, and Gray's insightful commentary makes it one of the best critiques of the poem published during the twentieth century. Less concerned with critical analysis than with the process of composition — "the miraculous creative synthesis," as Gray calls it (v) — that led from Tennyson's earliest uses of Arthurian material to the completed sequence in 1885, Gray discusses the serial evolution of the work and the impact of the composition process on the final version. He also provides detailed analyses of parallels between Tennyson's poem and earlier Arthurian materials. His chapter on landscape and setting ranks with Rosenberg's in *The Fall of Camelot* as the best discussions on this topic. Gray also examines Tennyson's use of metaphor and simile, and discusses the function of the songs interspersed throughout the narratives. Unfortunately, his commentary on the characters is slight by comparison with the work of critics such as Reed and Eggers; such an assessment would have been most valuable to future scholars. What cannot be disputed, however, is Gray's belief that much of the previous criticism of the *Idylls* had been misguided. "Past criticism of the *Idylls*," he says in his concluding paragraph, "has often been prejudiced and frequently irrelevant." To Gray, the poem ranks with "*Troilus and Criseyde, The Faerie Queene, Paradise Lost, The Prelude,* and *The Ring and the Book* as one of the most successfully sustained long poems in English" (137).

Elizabeth Francis's edition of *Tennyson: A Collection of Critical Essays* in the Prentice Hall Twentieth Century Views series also appeared in 1980. Francis includes in her work eleven previously published selections from the most distinguished and influential scholars of the century. T. S. Eliot's essay on *In Memoriam* is flanked by a chapter from Alan Sinfield's *The Language of "In Memoriam"* and one by James Kissane (1965) that informs his 1970 book on Tennyson. Jerome Buckley's commentary on *Maud*, Christopher Ricks's assessment of the early poems, Dwight Culler's analysis of the English idylls, John Rosenberg's study of the form of *Idylls of the King*, and F. E. L. Priestley's essay on *The Princess* give readers a good summary of the best that had been said to date on these poems. Harold Bloom and W. David Shaw represent the new generation of literary theorists. Francis's own original essay on Tennyson's later poems rounds out what is certainly one of the best single volumes students and scholars alike might use to understand critical opinion about Tennyson as it had evolved during the first eight decades of the twentieth century.

To confirm that Tennyson's reputation had been completely restored in the twenty years since the publication of Jerome Buckley's 1961 study, one need only to turn to the preface of Robert B. Martin's critically acclaimed 1980 biography of the poet, *Tennyson: The Unquiet Heart*. This detailed, penetrating psychological study certainly owes much to Martin's exceptional skills as a researcher and writer. But as he admits, "the freedom from having to defend Tennyson's poetry means that one may write far more candidly about him than could the biographers who were afraid that the mention of minor blemishes on his personality and character might result in dismissal of him as a poet." Martin's warts-and-all approach is refreshingly candid, and his revelations about the Tennyson's "difficult and prickly" nature make him interesting while helping to explain something of his genius (vii).

Martin believes Tennyson suffered from hereditary epilepsy, a disease that afflicted several members of his family, including his irascible father, and that fear of becoming like George Clayton Tennyson kept the poet from entering too much into society or from marrying until, well into his adulthood, he realized that he did not have the disease. Martin's portrait of the young Tennyson makes him out to be a martyr to his father's fits and his grandfather's meddling, a self-appointed protector of his mother and siblings. The psychological details are fascinating, but they often obscure discussion of the poetry that Tennyson wrote, Martin says, to escape from his oppressing surroundings.

Because he is interested principally in Tennyson's life, Martin pays only modest attention to the poems, writing about them in biographical context. The general problem any artist faces in choosing to produce art for its own sake or to serve larger social needs was a problem that intrigued the young Tennyson, Martin says, because "he had to face the possibility that his poetry might be only an escape from external difficulties" (67). With that in mind, Martin offers brief but insightful commentary on the 1830, 1833, and 1842 volumes that demonstrate not only the growth of Tennyson's poetic powers but also his growing reputation among the British public. His discussions of the major poems shed light on the autobiographical elements in *The Princess, In Memoriam, Maud* and even *Idylls of the King*. About the last poem, Martin observes shrewdly that the poem represents "the best example in Tennyson's career of his having writer's block" (422). At his best, Martin provides tantalizing interpretations and sound judgments about Tennyson's poetic ability. For example, he refutes directly the assertion of critics like Paull Baum, who claimed Tennyson was unconcerned about aesthetics; even in old age, Martin said, "he still thought as much as ever of poetical theory, sometimes as justification for his own practice, increasingly as it applied to all poetry" (562). At times, however, Martin takes a distinctly modernist stance in judging individual poems; his comments on "Enoch Arden" and some of the English idylls reveal Martin's distaste for works heavily laden with sentimentality.

Martin's biography is more analytical than Sir Charles Tennyson's, more focused on discovering motive for Tennyson's actions, and less given to accepting received opinion, which, in his view, was often advanced to protect the poet's reputation. His strength lies in his ability to weave a seamless narrative from multiple sources and present a balanced view of Tennyson as a human being: confused, anxious, self-centered, but on occasion exceptionally solicitous of others' well-being. Martin is good at scene-painting, bringing to life stories of Tennyson's irascible behavior, his need to be the center of attention in any crowd, his deep affection for his children. He goes against the grain of both biographers and critics in asserting that Tennyson's love for Rosa Baring, the putative subject of "Locksley Hall" and *Maud*, "appears to have been more imaginary than actual" (219). He is the first biographer to explore candidly Tennyson's relationship with his wife, noting the growing estrangement that occurred once the poet discovered that his peripatetic lifestyle was to be curtailed by family responsibilities. In *Tennyson: The Unquiet Heart* one can see the blueprint for future biographical studies of the poet.

Contemporary with the publication of Martin's new biography, the iconoclastic American scholar William E. Buckler issued *The Victorian Imagination: Essays in Aesthetic Exploration* (1980). The volume includes previously published essays on other poets as well as Tennyson, but also includes seven original essays that examine Tennyson's works. In the first, aptly titled "The Tennysonian Imagination," Buckler explains how Tennyson was able to answer both the demands of Romantic poetry and those of his Victorian contemporaries "by dealing with contemporary topics emblematically" (41). In Tennyson's work Buckler finds a "rich variety within an over-all unity of effect" (52). He explains how this works in a series of individual essays explicating "Oenone," "The Lotos Eaters," "Locksley Hall," *The Princess, In Memoriam*, and *Maud*, saving his discussion of *Idylls of the King* for a separate volume published in 1984. Buckler's major contribution is to set Tennyson's works in a wider context, calling him both a major artist and major influence on his contemporaries.

More important, perhaps, than his commentary on Tennyson is Buckler's introductory chapter, in which he chastises critics of the twentieth century for failing to deal honestly with the Victorian poets and novelists. Blaming this failure on the critical methodologies developed during the early decades of the century, Buckler claims that the New Critics and their successors in academe "diminish[ed] literature in general, but their influence on Victorian literature was singularly and subtly inimical." Buckler insists that "a critical methodology that fails to take adequate measure of the Victorian experience in literature is itself thereby indicted" (2–3). Of course, Buckler takes as his standard for critical theory the work of Romantic poet Samuel Taylor Coleridge, and his hero in practical criticism is Matthew Arnold, the critic most vocal in his own day about the inadequacies of Victorian literature and the one most reviled by the successors of the New Critics, the practitioners of poststructuralist literary theories. Nevertheless, Buckler's call for a revaluation of the Victorians using critical methodologies other than the narrowly focused analysis of the New Critics was to be heeded by a score of younger scholars — and their mentors — in the final decades of the century.

Works Cited

Ball, Patricia M. *The Heart's Events: The Victorian Poetry of Relationships*. London: Athlone; Atlantic Highlands, NJ: Humanities Press, 1976.

Bloom, Harold. "Tennyson, Hallam, and Romantic Tradition." *The Ringers in the Tower: Studies in Romantic Tradition*. Chicago: U of Chicago P, 1970. 145–54.

———. "Tennyson: In the Shadow of Keats." *Poetry and Repression*. New Haven, CT: Yale UP, 1976. 143–74.

Boyd, John D. "*In Memoriam* and the Logic of Feeling." *Victorian Poetry* 10 (1972): 95–110.

Brantlinger, Patrick. *The Spirit of Reform: British Literature and Politics 1832–1867*. Cambridge, MA: Harvard UP, 1977.

Buckler, William E. *The Victorian Imagination: Essays in Aesthetic Exploration*. New York: New York UP, 1980.

Christ, Carol T. *The Finer Optic: The Aesthetic of Particularity in Victorian Poetry*. New Haven, CT: Yale UP, 1975. 17–29 and *passim*.

———. "Victorian Masculinity and the Angel in the House." In *A Widening Sphere: Changing Roles of Victorian Women*. Ed. Martha Vicinus. Bloomington: Indiana UP, 1977. 146–62.

Colville, Derek. "Tennyson." *Victorian Poetry and the Romantic Religion.* Albany: State U of New York P, 1970. 167–238.

Culler, A. Dwight. *The Poetry of Tennyson.* New Haven, CT: Yale UP, 1977.

———. "Tennyson, We Cannot Live by Art." In *Nineteenth-Century Literary Perspectives: Essays in Honor of Lionel Stevenson.* Ed. Clyde de L. Ryals. Durham, NC: Duke UP, 1974. 77–92.

Dawson, Carl. "*In Memoriam:* The Uses of Dante and Wordsworth." *Victorian Noon: English Literature to 1850.* Baltimore, MD: Johns Hopkins UP, 1979. 36–51.

Eagleton, Terry. "Tennyson: Politics and Sexuality in *The Princess* and *In Memoriam.*" In *1848: The Sociology of Literature.* Ed. Francis Barker, et al. Colchester, England: U of Essex P, 1978. 97–106.

Francis, Elizabeth A., ed. *Tennyson: A Collection of Critical Essays.* Englewood Cliffs, NJ: Prentice-Hall, 1980.

Gliserman, Susan. "Early Victorian Science Writers and Tennyson's *In Memoriam:* A Study in Cultural Exchange." *Victorian Studies* 18:3 (1975): 277–308; 18:4: 437–59.

Gray, J. M. *Thro' The Vision of the Night: A Study of Source, Evolution and Structure in Tennyson's "Idylls of the King."* Edinburgh: Edinburgh UP; Montreal: McGill-Queen's UP, 1980.

Hagen, June Steffensen. *Tennyson and His Publishers.* London: Macmillan; University Park: Pennsylvania State UP, 1979.

Hellstrom, Ward. *On the Poems of Tennyson.* Gainesville: U of Florida P, 1972.

Helterman, Jeffrey. "Narrative Modes and the Dynamics of Passion in *The Idylls of the King.*" *Victorians Institute Journal* 3 (1974): 45–59.

Henderson, Philip. *Tennyson, Poet and Prophet.* London: Routledge & Kegan Paul, 1978.

Hunt, John D., and David Palmer. "Tennyson." In *English Poetry.* Ed. Alan Sinfield. London: Sussex, 1976. 130–47.

———, ed. *Tennyson, "In Memoriam": A Casebook.* London: Macmillan, 1970.

Johnson, Wendell Stacy. "Marriage and Divorce in Tennyson." *Sex and Marriage in Victorian Poetry.* Ithaca, NY: Cornell UP, 1975. 110–84.

Kincaid, James R. *Tennyson's Major Poems: The Comic and Ironic Patterns.* New Haven, CT: Yale UP, 1975.

Kissane, James. *Alfred Tennyson.* New York: Twayne, 1970.

———. "Tennyson: The Passion of the Past and the Curse of Time." *Journal of English Literary History* 32 (1965): 85–109.

Kozicki, Henry. "A Dialectic of History in Tennyson's *Idylls.*" *Victorian Studies* 20 (1977): 141–57.

———. "'Meaning' in Tennyson's *In Memoriam*." *Studies in English Literature 1500–1900* 17 (1977): 673–94.

———. "The 'Medieval Ideal' in Tennyson's *The Princess*." *Criticism* 17 (1975): 121–30.

———. "Philosophy of History in Tennyson's Poetry to the 1842 *Poems*." *Journal of English Literary History* 42 (1975): 88–106.

———. *Tennyson and Clio: History in the Major Poems*. Baltimore, MD: Johns Hopkins UP, 1979.

Langbaum, Robert. "The Dynamic Unity of *In Memoriam*." *The Modern Spirit: Essays on the Continuity of Nineteenth and Twentieth Century Literature*. London: Chatto & Windus; New York: Oxford UP, 1970. 51–75.

Lbrach, Ronald. "Myth and Romance in *Idylls of the King*." *Dalhousie Review* 55 (1975): 511–25.

Lerner, Laurence, ed. *The Victorians*. New York: Holmes & Meier, 1978.

Martin, Robert Bernard. *Tennyson: The Unquiet Heart*. London: Faber; Oxford: Clarendon Press; New York: Oxford UP, 1980.

Mason, Michael Y. "*In Memoriam:* The Dramatization of Sorrow." *Victorian Poetry* 10 (1972): 161–77.

McGhee, Richard D. *Marriage, Duty and Desire in Victorian Poetry and Drama*. Lawrence: U of Kansas P, 1980. 29–66.

McSweeney, Kerry. "The Pattern of Natural Consolation in *In Memoriam*." *Victorian Poetry* 11 (1973): 87–99.

———. "Tennyson's Quarrel with Himself: The Tristram Group of *Idylls*." *Victorian Poetry* 15 (1977): 49–59.

Palmer, D. J., ed. *Tennyson*. London: Bell; Athens: Ohio UP, 1973.

Pattison, Robert. *Tennyson and Tradition*. Cambridge, MA: Harvard UP, 1979.

Peckham, Morse. "Escape from Charisma." *Victorian Revolutionaries: Speculations on Some Heroes of a Cultural Crisis*. New York: Braziller, 1970. 8–43.

Pettigrew, John. *Tennyson: The Early Poems*. London: Arnold, 1970.

Priestley, F. E. L. *Language and Structure in Tennyson's Poetry*. London: Deutsch, 1973.

Pyre, James F. A. *The Formation of Tennyson's Style; A Study, Primarily, of the Versification of the Early Poems*. Madison: U of Wisconsin P, 1920. Reprint, New York: Phaeton Press, 1968.

Ricks, Christopher B. *Tennyson*. New York: Macmillan, 1972. 2nd ed., Basingstoke: Macmillan, 1989.

Robbins, Tony. "Tennyson's 'Ulysses': The Significance of the Homeric and Dantesque Backgrounds." *Victorian Poetry* 11 (1973): 171–93.

Rosenberg, John D. *The Fall of Camelot: A Study of Tennyson's "Idylls of the King."* Cambridge, MA: Harvard UP, 1973.

Shaw, W. David. "Consolation and Catharsis in *In Memoriam*." *Modern Language Quarterly* 37 (1976): 47–67.

———. *The Dialectical Temper: The Rhetorical Art of Robert Browning.* Ithaca, NY: Cornell UP, 1968.

———. "The Idealist's Dilemma in *Idylls of the King*." *Victorian Poetry* 5 (1967): 41–53.

———. "*Idylls of the King:* A Dialectical Reading." *Victorian Poetry* 7 (1969): 175–90.

———. "Imagination and Intellect in Tennyson's 'Lucretius.'" *Modern Language Quarterly* 33 (1972): 130–39.

———. "*In Memoriam* and the Rhetoric of Confession." *Journal of English Literary History* 38 (1971): 80–103.

———. *Tennyson's Style*. Ithaca, NY: Cornell UP, 1976.

———. "Tennyson's 'Tithonus' and the Problem of Mortality." *Philological Quarterly* 52 (1973): 274–85.

Sinfield, Alan. *The Language of Tennyson's "In Memoriam."* Oxford: Blackwell; New York: Barnes & Noble, 1971.

Southam, B. C. *Tennyson*. Harlow, England: Longman Group, 1971.

Stange, G. Robert. "The 'Voyages' of Tennyson and Baudelaire." *Nineteenth-Century Literary Perspectives: Essays in Honor of Lionel Stevenson.* Ed. Clyde de L. Ryals.Durham, NC: Duke UP, 1974. 93–104.

Storch, R. F. "The Fugitive from the Ancestral Hearth: Tennyson's 'Ulysses.'" *Texas Studies in Literature and Language* 13 (1971): 281–97.

Tillotson, Geoffrey A. *A View of Victorian Literature*. London: Oxford UP, 1978. 286–327.

Tillotson, Kathleen. "Tennyson's Serial Poem." *Mid-Victorian Studies.* London: Athlone Press, 1965. 80–109.

Turner, Paul. "The Stupidest English Poet." *English Studies* 30 (February 1949): 1–12.

———. *Tennyson*. London: Henley; Boston: Routledge & Kegan Paul, 1976.

6: Tennyson Among the Poststructuralists: 1981–1989

IN "TENNYSON AND THE HISTORIES OF CRITICISM" (1982), a lengthy review article surveying a half-dozen studies of Tennyson published between 1979 and 1981, the distinguished critic Jerome McGann charts a course for Tennyson studies that many would follow during the next two decades. McGann warns that "ideology is not an *aesthetic* problem for a poem, it is a *critical* problem" (231). The real danger is for critics to read poems in the way made popular by New Criticism: as if the essential elements of poetry were somehow ahistorical and not affected by the cultural, political, and aesthetic assumptions — often unspoken and assumed — that undergird the practice of such criticism. At the same time, in a strong statement of self-awareness and recognition of self-limitation, McGann challenges critics who find difficulty accepting Tennyson's works "because we are uninterested in or hostile to the ideas they express"; this attitude, McGann says, is "as much a judgment upon our own ideas and their limitations as it is upon Tennyson's" (235). McGann attacks both New Critics and new theorists alike for imposing ideologies onto texts. He insists that to fully appreciate Tennyson's poems — or anyone else's — "we must grasp them in their historical uniqueness" (251). Doing so, he implies, demands both hard work and sharp attention to the assumptions one brings to reading — especially reading Tennyson.

Essays in two volumes published in 1981 aptly illustrate the changes in reading Tennyson and the reassessment of critical perceptions of his work. In *Untying the Text: A Post-Structuralist Reader* (1981) edited by Robert Young, Ann Wordsworth offers a brief reading of *In Memoriam* using new critical theories developed in the 1960s and 1970s. The essay is less about the poem than it is about the conflicting interpretative strategies of mainstream critics such as Matthew Arnold and the "antithetical criticism" of Harold Bloom and Paul de Man. Wordsworth demonstrates the inadequacies of Arnold's approach, while crediting de Man and Bloom for developing methodologies that allow the poem to be rescued from "the biographical and cultural impediments of orthodox criticism" (220). The problem with orthodox readings of Tennyson — and others, of course — is that "in orthodox criticism" such as Arnold's and most twentieth-century critical approaches, "critical judgments are backed by a consensus of opinion whose assumptions are not necessarily declared" (216). Seeing how Bloom argues with de Man and other deconstructionists allows one to view *In Memoriam* as "an uneasy mixture of referential language and a rhetorically and psychically determined one." It thus becomes easier to explain the varied quality of individual stanzas (218).

In *The Nature of Criticism* (1981), a work better classified as a study of aesthetics than as literary criticism, Colin Radford and Sally Minogue examine a portion of a 1966 essay by Christopher Ricks on *In Memoriam*. Titling this chapter "The Logical Richness of Criticism," the authors use Ricks's discussion to demonstrate the critical and philosophical assumptions that underlie even the best orthodox critic's work. Ricks has been chosen, Radford and Minogue say, because "he is a fine critic, a good representative of the modern school of practical critics" (85). Their exceptionally detailed analysis of individual sentences and phrases from the essay demonstrate how much is assumed both about Tennyson and the social context of his poetry. For the purposes of this study, what Radford and Minogue illustrate best is the new level of self-awareness that critics brought to their discussion of individual poems and of the Tennyson canon as a whole.

The foregoing paragraphs are not intended to suggest, however, that there was a sharp break between what had been mainstream academic criticism of Tennyson's work and the newer forms of exploration that would characterize much of the work of late-twentieth-century scholars. Donald Hair's *Domestic and Heroic in Tennyson's Poetry* (1981), published in the same year as Young's poststructuralist reader, is a fine example of orthodox criticism that is both well-researched and illuminating. Noting that twentieth-century critics have shown "little sympathy" for the overwhelming domestic themes and images in Tennyson's work that reflect "popular ideals" among the poet's contemporaries, Hair offers a reading of the poetry that explores "the implications of these ideals and the various ways in which they could be treated" (4). He argues that because domestic concerns had always been closely linked to the pastoral tradition, Tennyson "replaced the pastoral with the domestic" (5) to create new forms of poetry.

The most brilliant of these new poems is *In Memoriam*, a work Hair discusses at length. He also demonstrates how Tennyson uses the forms of idyll and epyllion to give greater dignity to domestic themes, reading such works as "The Miller's Daughter," Oenone," "Sea Dreams," "The Brook," and "Enoch Arden" to prove his thesis. Noting parallels between these poems and the Romance tradition, Hair launches a discussion of *The Princess* to explain how domestic and heroic values can exist in the same poem. Nearly half of Hair's study concentrates on *Idylls of the King*, a work he claims is "an heroic treatment of domestic themes, images, and actions" (122). A major theme of the *Idylls* is "use" — the ability to put heroic action into domestic service (127). Hair's reading of Tennyson's Arthurian romance demonstrates how, as he does in *The Princess,* Tennyson blends domestic and heroic virtues to illuminate social issues which concerned him deeply.

Hair's concluding chapter offers some remarks on Tennyson's reputation that warrant notice as the last decades of the century began. Both the reaction against Tennyson and the "critical indifference" that succeeded the reaction are passed. "We have moved beyond those studies that valued only a part of Tennyson's achievement," Hair argues. "The idea of two Tennysons no longer fits either our critical preoccupations or our tastes," and both readers and critics are now ready to "value Tennyson, not in spite of the fact that he was a Victorian, but because of it" (228). Nevertheless, as several major studies of the 1980s and 1990s would demonstrate, the idea that Tennyson's Romantic nature was somehow suppressed to accommodate Victorian conventions — with disastrous results — was not yet dead.

One need only to look at a volume published in the same year as Hair's to see that the "two Tennysons" theory had not died. In *Tennyson and Swinburne as Romantic Naturalists* (1981), Kerry McSweeney argues that a revaluation of Tennyson is still necessary to separate the Victorian qualities from those Romantic principles that inform his best work. Unlike Hair, McSweeney claims that while the "trickle of writing on Victoria's Laureate has become a flood, there is nevertheless no real agreement among professional critics of English literature on Tennyson's achievement and stature" (x). McSweeney believes Tennyson's greatness is his ability to function as a Romantic naturalist, one who regards "man's intimate sympathy with the natural world and its patterns of cyclical change as wholesome and liberating" (xiii). Comparing him with Swinburne, McSweeney reads Tennyson as an inheritor of the Romantic tradition struggling to write in an age that wished to distance humanity from the natural world.

Echoes of Matthew Arnold can be heard in McSweeney's lament that Tennyson had to struggle to write in a time "unpropitious" for "poets concerned with self-expression, vision, a life of immediate sympathy with the natural world, and the apprehension of beauty." Though he struggled valiantly, McSweeney argues, Tennyson eventually underwent a "complex mutation" that transformed him from a fine Romantic poet to "a largely Victorian" one (xv). In McSweeney's view, the transformation was unfortunate. McSweeney would continue his theme nearly two decades later in *Supreme Attachments: Studies in Victorian Love* (1998), analyzing *The Princess* and *Maud* to show how Tennyson deals with romantic love. Surprisingly, this later book shows little influence of the work of literary theorists, although McSweeney displays awareness of contemporary criticism of both poems.

For Richard Levine's collection of essays *The Victorian Experience: The Poets* (1982), Jerome Buckley contributed an essay sagaciously titled "The Persistence of Tennyson." Asked by the editor to provide a summary judgment of Tennyson's career and staying power with the critics, Buckley offers a succinct yet thoughtful and generally appreciative review of the poet's reputation. He observes how Tennyson's reputation has waxed and waned according to the critical proclivities of the moment as much as they have for discoveries about his artistic merit. Buckley acknowledges that his own admiration for Tennyson when a young scholar in the 1930s was countercultural, and that his praise for *Idylls of the King* in his 1960 volume *Tennyson: The Growth of a Poet* met with mixed reviews by his own contemporaries. Supplementing his earlier readings of the major poems with new observations about their merits, Buckley displays a continuing appreciation for the poet he helped to elevate to a place of prominence among Victorian critics in the latter half of the twentieth century. He would continue providing illuminating insights into Tennyson's poetry for another decade, contributing "The Myth of the Poet" to *Nineteenth Century Studies* in 1992, and "Tennyson's Landscapes" to the *Tennyson Research Bulletin* in 1996.

Tess Coslett's 1982 examination of Victorian writers' interest in scientific controversies, *The "Scientific Movement" and Victorian Literature*, suggests that even at the end of the century, critics still found great fascination in Tennyson's struggle to reconcile the findings of science with his beliefs about human nature. Unlike R. A. Forsyth, who in 1964 had declared Tennyson to be hostile toward science, Coslett argues that the poet demonstrated an appreciation for scientific discovery — and perhaps even an affinity for the practice of scientific inquiry. He believed, however, in the principle of "gradualism," a doctrine that in Coslett's view links *In Memoriam* "most closely to the scientific world view" of his day (73). Ironically, Coslett believes that, rather than being a man of faith, Tennyson was actually a closet agnostic. The extent to which Tennyson adopted the language and inspiration of science is also explored quite ably by Howard Fulweiler in "Tennyson's *In Memoriam* and the Scientific Imagination" (1984).

A festschrift for distinguished Victorian scholar Richard Altick, *Victorian Literature and Society* (1983), includes an essay by George Ford, whose *Keats and the Victorians* (1944) had done much to establish the links between Tennyson and his Romantic predecessors. Concentrating on Tennyson's education, Ford argues in "'A Great Poetical Boa-Constrictor,' Alfred Tennyson: An Educated Victorian Mind" that Tennyson is "the archetypal figure of the Victorian Age" (148). Intended as a correction against reactionary criticism, Ford's essay seems a fainthearted attempt to argue for Tennyson's greatness — a claim well established by the time of the essay's publication.

It is no surprise that Tennyson is taken up for study by Marxist critics during this new age of theory. One of the most readable works in the genre is Victor Kiernan's "Tennyson, King Arthur, and Imperialism," an essay in *Culture, Ideology, and Politics* (1982). Interested principally in the political and sociological subtext of *Idylls of the King*, Kiernan analyzes Tennyson's conservative vision of English society. His reading of the poem as a tribute to the British imperial spirit makes it clear that Arthur's kingdom shares many affinities with the real-life Empire being created by Victoria's subjects. "Empire" for Tennyson and his contemporaries, Kiernan argues, "meant in ideal terms the bringing of order and peaceful progress to lands beyond the pale" (134). Of course, to promote the empire Tennyson was forced to overlook some of the seamier aspects of colonialism, and to turn a blind eye to the horrors of war. Ironically, however, Kiernan sees the poem as an oblique criticism of England's ruling classes; the knights who are unable to live up to Arthur's high ideals are easily identified in his mind with the ruling classes that, in Tennyson's view, had failed to carry out their responsibilities to world civilization.

While Kiernan was attacking Tennyson for promoting the notion of empire in *Idylls of the King*, David Staines was praising him for his exceptional ability to adapt medieval sources for modern uses. *Tennyson's Camelot: The Idylls of the King and Its Medieval Sources* (1982) extends the work of J. M. Gray in delineating ways Tennyson recreated Arthurian myths from sources such as Malory's *Morte d'Arthur*, Lady Charlotte Guest's translation of *The Mabinogion*, and other romances that had captured his attention early in his life. Staines discusses some of Tennyson's early experiments in transforming medieval materials to suit his Victorian audience, then examines the poem in the order of composition of individual idylls, demonstrating how Tennyson reshapes not only his sources but his own previously written work to achieve some coherence in his presentation. Although one might wonder why Staines feels compelled to designate Queen Guinevere as "the ultimate focus of the entire work" (xv), he is as thorough as Gray in noting how passages in Malory inspired Tennyson's creativity. His appendixes on the composition process and his extensive bibliography give additional value to his work, even if his scope remains somewhat limited. His insistence that Tennyson was a major instigator in the resurgence of interest in medieval materials, especially Arthurian stories, is well handled, but when examined side by side with Kiernan's more penetrating analysis of the implications of such materials for the Victorian consciousness, one has to wonder if Tennyson's accomplishments are worthy of such effusive praise.

More akin to Kiernan than Staines, Isobel Armstrong offers an assessment of *In Memoriam* in *Language as Living Form in Nineteenth Century Poetry* (1982) that relies on contemporary linguistic theory to demonstrate how Tennyson frees himself from the conventions of language in his best work. Only in this way could the poet deal adequately with his grief. The importance of language lies at the root of a fine study by Dorothy Mermin published in the same year, *The Audience in the Poem* (1983). A chapter in this study of the dramatic monologue focuses on the ways readers of Tennyson's early poems come to understand characters such as St. Simeon Stylites, Ulysses, and Tithonus. Mermin posits that Tennyson was fearful of the consequences of poetic communication in his early years, but lost that fear as he became a more public figure and assumed a public role.

That Tennyson was fascinated throughout his life with the concept of madness had been a critical commonplace for nearly a century when Ann Colley published *Tennyson and Madness* (1983). Nevertheless, her fine analysis of this topic brings together the findings of previous scholarship and extends readers' understanding of ways madness occupies Tennyson's imagination in poems not ordinarily thought of as influenced by this issue. Born into a family where mental instability was rampant, Tennyson was bound to "transpose his experiences and his knowledge of insanity into his poetry," and Colley believes a "majority of the poetry takes its shape from a creative force that is fighting to remain sane and is therefore constantly moderating its own 'wilder' impulses" (3). After examining the concept of madness as it was understood by the poet's eighteenth-century forebears and nineteenth-century contemporaries, Colley explains how mental illness affected members of Tennyson's family and the poet himself. From his earliest writings, Colley argues, Tennyson "felt compelled to step back from himself and analyze the black moods and riddle their meaning" (66–67). Acting almost as a clinician, the poet writes character sketches and lengthy narratives such as "The Lover's Tale" and *Maud* in which he offers a kind of anatomy of madness.

Colley's explanation of the importance of madness as both subject and metaphor is nowhere more convincing than in her analysis of *Idylls of the King*. In that poem, she argues, Tennyson explores "the link he sees between personal and national aberrations" (87). Madness becomes for the poet a metaphor that allows him to explain how excesses of passion can lead to both personal and national disaster. The "metaphor of madness" serves the poet as "a vivid emblem" of England's "increasing moral inadequacy" (88). Colley argues persuasively that the *Idylls* "exceeds even *Maud* in its exploration of madness" (94). By revealing the dangers of uninhibited passion, Tennyson offers a warning to contemporaries of the necessity of "the sublime nature of repression" (116), a quality of character necessary, in his view, if the English people were to remain strong and sane. Colley concludes by showing how Tennyson uses tight control over poetic form to mirror his argument for control over the passions.

Tennyson's fascination with nature and the natural landscape figures prominently in Pauline Fletcher's *Gardens and Grim Ravines: The Language of Landscape in Victorian Poetry* (1983). In two chapters on Tennyson, she explains how his attachment to eighteenth-century notions of the picturesque and the sublime initially influence his work, making him a Romantic in his appreciation for the unspoiled wilds. As he grew older, Fletcher says,

Tennyson gradually came to see the wilderness as "barbaric wastelands that a man of sense should avoid" (18). Fletcher is especially interested in ways Tennyson uses the garden in poems such as *The Princess* and *Maud*. Without moralizing, she says, Tennyson employs setting to suggest with great subtlety "much about the kind of society of which it forms a part, and embodies many of the conflicts of that society" (71). For Fletcher, Tennyson ranks with the best poets in his handling of this important image.

Gerhard Joseph, who had written an influential work on Tennyson's concept of love in 1969, remained active in writing about Tennyson during the 1980s, further solidifying his reputation as one of the premier end-of-century Tennyson scholars. Perceptive articles on *Idylls of the King* appeared in 1974 and 1981. "Tennyson's Optics," an article that would form the basis of his 1992 book *Tennyson and the Text*, appeared in 1977, and another, "Victorian Frames: The Windows and Mirrors of Browning, Arnold, and Tennyson," the following year. A study of Tennyson's relationship with his good friend the politician William Ewart Gladstone was included in the *Browning Institute Studies* volume of 1982. "Tennyson's Stupidity" (1983) — its title taken from Auden's comment on the poet's intellectual capacity — demonstrates Joseph's ability to craft close readings of key poems. And "Tennyson's Parable of the Soul: *The Princess*" (1985) offers a Jungian reading of the poem, demonstrating that it can be viewed as the struggle of the male soul to shake off its anima. Joseph notes astutely that *The Princess* is the last major poem in which Tennyson focuses on women as central characters; in all his future work he assumes the role of the male. This insight tells us something of the poet's developing awareness of his need to appear manly, a concept explored in greater detail by Marion Shaw in *Alfred Lord Tennyson* (1988).

One who would not question the poet's manliness was William E. Buckler. Like his earlier work *The Victorian Imagination* (1980), Buckler's *Man and His Myths: Tennyson's "Idylls of the King" in Critical Context* (1984) is ostensibly aimed at students but is concurrently a subtle attack on previous readings of the poem that fail to recognize its complexity and the magnitude of Tennyson's accomplishment. "Fundamental" to his approach, he argues, "is the reader's role as co-creator of the Tennysonian poetic experience" (3). Long considered an iconoclast among scholars of the Victorian era, Buckler organizes his study of the *Idylls* into segments intended first to set a critical context for reading the work, then to offer a largely original extended analysis. His detailed readings illustrate the mythic and historic dimensions of the poem, a work he believes is constructed with both consummate technical skill and exceptional insight into the human condition.

In a series of brief essays following his reading, he challenges directly critics such as John Reed, Clyde Ryals, and John D. Rosenberg, whose interpretations of character and theme he finds deficient or wrongheaded.

Buckler's ornate and at times hyperbolic style has bothered more than one critic, and *Man and His Myths* shares many of the tendencies toward obscurity that characterize Buckler's other works. Nevertheless, he demonstrates a strong sense of appreciation for *Idylls of the King* as a major poem that can touch readers in any century because of Tennyson's ability to cross generic, historical, and cultural boundaries in constructing his tale.

The title of F. B. Pinion's *A Tennyson Companion* (1984) belies the book's depth of insight and value to Tennyson scholars. Far more than a "casebook" such as George Marshall's 1963 volume, Pinion's study provides sound summaries of the major works and many minor ones, as well as a detailed chronology and bibliography. Following the Ricks edition of the poems, Pinion offers brief comments on hundreds of them, sometimes noting a source of inspiration, at other times offering a suggestion regarding theme. His final chapter is a particularly good summary of the state of Tennyson criticism, and he is not shy at challenging critics of the early twentieth century for what he calls their wrongheaded notions of Tennyson's excessive morbidity and his tendency to cater to popular taste. At the same time, Pinion is honest in pointing out what he sees as the poet's principal limitations. Unable to "overcome a feeling of disappointment" (237), Tennyson did not have the depth of vision or the qualities of inspiration that distinguish Wordsworth among the English poets. His myopic focus on his role as a poet kept him from enjoying the varieties of experience that might have improved his creative genius. "Had Tennyson been gifted with more vigorous creative originality," Pinion argues, "his variety and output would have been greater" (239). One might wonder how such a statement could be applied to a poet whose works fill three thick volumes in the 1987 Ricks edition, but Pinion's point is well argued. He writes convincingly about how this limitation affects Tennyson's long poems, which are at best assembled from smaller pieces to form amalgams not always satisfying. But the "misreadings and exaggeration" (242) practiced by the critics of the early twentieth century have obscured what is surely, in Pinion's view, a great deal of first-quality work that makes Tennyson a truly fine poet.

Thomas J. Assad's *Tennysonian Lyric* (1984), a volume in the Tulane Studies in English Monograph series, begins from the premise that Tennyson is the premier Victorian poet and one of the giants of English literature. Assad provides detailed prosodic studies of a dozen short poems that he believes demonstrate Tennyson's changing attitudes toward immortality. As he explains in his opening chapters, the poet becomes progressively more subtle in his appreciation for the fragility of human life. Predictably, Assad devotes the major portion of his study to an analysis of *In Memoriam*, Tennyson's major statement on the theme. The strength of Assad's book lies in his close analysis of prosody; his analysis of grammar, poetic stress, and musical qualities illuminate the poet's exceptional ability to handle the tools of his craft.

His discussion of *In Memoriam* follows in the tradition of A. C. Bradley and Eleanor Mattes, focusing on the structure of the elegy and explaining how Tennyson modulates the readers' emotional response by creating a rising sense of emotional attachment between the speaker and the dead Hallam, and then retreating to speculate on the process by which poetry creates this sense of bonding.

More philosophical than Assad in his approach to Tennyson's major elegy, Timothy Peltason provides a thoughtful personal analysis of the poem in *Reading "In Memoriam"* (1985). Peltason had already established himself as a philosophical critic with his essay "Tennyson's Philosophy: Some Lyric Examples" (1984), where he makes the bold assertion that, despite the criticisms of Auden and Leavis, Tennyson's poetry can be read as "philosophical exercises" (51). Peltason then proceeds to offer thoughtful explications of "Tears, Idle Tears," "Ulysses," and "Tithonus."

Peltason's methodology in discussing these lyrics is foreshadowed also in his "Tennyson, Nature, and Romantic Nature Poetry" (1984), and is mirrored in his discussion of *In Memoriam*, as he looks to the text itself, rather than critical opinion, to ground his reading. Acknowledging that disparate readings have produced insight into the many themes with which Tennyson deals in the poem, Peltason asserts that *In Memoriam* is "especially about the arranging impulse in human consciousness, about the conditions under which we find ourselves pressed into making new sense of experience" (12). Urging readers to take the poem on its own terms rather than looking to theoretical frameworks into which it can be placed, he provides a stanza-by-stanza discussion of ways individual lyrics support the underlying principle he has discovered. Since the purpose of the poem is to examine ways human consciousness organizes experience, *In Memoriam* is able to accommodate discussion of many kinds of experience; its unity depends not on the subjects discussed, but on an apprehension of the process by which one mind assimilates all experience and makes sense of the world.

In the same year, feminist critic Eve Kosofsky Sedgwick initiated what might be called a minority trend in Tennyson criticism — queer theory approaches to his poetry. From time to time, readings of poems such as *In Memoriam* had intimated that the poem contained overtones of homosexuality, but in *Between Men* (1985) Sedgwick selects as her text for study *The Princess*. This work, she asserts, demonstrates the "male homosocial desire" in Victorian society (1). While the feminism exhibited by Princess Ida may be "radical" (126), its radical nature stems from its opposition to two strong forces that bind together the society Tennyson portrays: the "stylized aristocratic family" which served as the model for the Victorian middle class (124), and the male-only society in which the prince and his companions revel. Sedgwick's combination of close textual reading with contemporary critical theory served as the model for future studies of Tennyson's poetry that focus on the tensions created by homosexual desire. Notable among these are Chris Craft's fine analysis of *In Memoriam* in "'Descend, Touch, and Enter': Tennyson's Strange Manner of Address" (1988) and Richard Dellamora's exploration of the background of the poem in "Tennyson, The Apostles, and *In Memoriam*" (1990).

Also in 1985, Chelsea House publishers brought out Harold Bloom's *Alfred Lord Tennyson* in its Modern Critical Views series, a collection of important criticism published during the century. Like his predecessors and successors in the anthologizing business, Bloom begins by including T. S. Eliot's seminal essay on *In Memoriam*, and provides a summary of the poet's relationship to his age through an excerpt from G. M. Young's *The Age of Tennyson*. Essays by Robert Penn Warren, Christopher Ricks, John Holland, Robert Langbaum, Dwight Culler, and Marshall McLuhan review Tennyson's major works (and some important minor ones) while simultaneously suggesting the poet's technical merits. Bloom's own work on Tennyson is also included, excerpts from *The Ringers in the Tower* and *Poetry and Repression* demonstrating his belief that Tennyson was a Romantic poet caught in an age antithetical to Romantic beliefs.

Although clearly influenced by developments in poststructuralism, Daniel Albright's *Tennyson: The Muses' Tug-of-War* (1986) combines close readings of individual poems with a keen sensitivity to the larger ideas that influenced Tennyson's concept of the role of the poet. The volume was the inaugural book in the Virginia Victorian Series, published by the University Press of Virginia under the direction of distinguished scholars such as Cecil Lang and Jerome McGann. In this book, Albright claims that "much of Tennyson's best poetry is a kind of contest of authorship between Tennyson and his shadow, a lurking anonymity" (5). As an inheritor of the Romantic tradition, Tennyson was naturally inclined to see the sublime in the natural world, but he was simultaneously enamored with the everyday world for its own sake. Albright describes this tension as a kind of tug-of-war between "Melpomene and Urania, the muse of the commonplace and the muse of the sublime" (12). Tennyson's career, Albright says, can be characterized by his struggle to write about the "great myth" that the soul might live outside the world and its concerns. Albright's sophisticated argument throughout the book is intended to demonstrate the ways Tennyson understood and internalized the caution offered to him by his friend R. C. Trench: "Tennyson, we cannot live by art."

Albright is exceptionally good at reading individual poems to show how Tennyson struggles to accommodate the competing forces of the sublime and the ordinary. Like Donald Hair's *Domestic and Heroic in Tennyson's Poetry* (1981), Albright's book offers close analysis of poems not frequently dealt with by other critics, such as "The Talking Oak" and "Will Waterproof's Lyrical Monologue." He also provides explications of major short works, including the great dramatic monologues "Ulysses," "Tithon," and "Tithonus," and lengthy commentary on *Maud, In Memoriam,* and *The Princess.* The curious arrangement of his argument — he concludes that *The Princess* is the best statement of Tennyson's struggle with the sublime and the ordinary — may leave Albright open to question, especially since he gives scant attention to *Idylls of the King* and offers no explanation about whether (and why) Tennyson might have moved to explore other themes later in his life. Nevertheless, his detailed examination of individual poems, offered in language free from jargon and frequently peppered with fresh metaphors and colloquialisms, makes *Tennyson: The Muses' Tug-of-War* a major contribution to mainstream criticism in the last decades of the century.

One can see the dual streams of criticism best by turning immediately from Albright to the second major study of Tennyson published by Alan Sinfield. His *Tennyson* (1986), a volume in the Rereading Literature series edited by celebrated Marxist critic Terry Eagleton, is a major shot fired at the bastion of mainstream criticism. Though he claims his new work is simply an advance over his 1971 analysis of Tennyson's language, Sinfield seems to repudiate his own work along with that of others who have, in his view, been part of a conspiracy to co-opt Tennyson and transform him into a tool of the bourgeoisie. Attacking distinguished Tennysonians such as Buckley and Ricks for their "politically regressive" (9) insistence on supporting openly or covertly the hegemony of capitalist ideology, Sinfield offers a reading of Tennyson that presents the poet in a decidedly different light. Sinfield argues that mainstream criticism has celebrated Tennyson's work as universal, but there is no work that fits that category, he says, because everything is a product of the historical, social, and political context in which it was written. Sinfield offers detailed, insightful, and frequently polemic readings of dozens of shorter poems and most of the major ones to support his claim that Tennyson was constantly torn between the desire to write revolutionary work in the line of Shelley, and the need to use poetry as a means of preserving the values of the middle class. What these interpretations show is Tennyson's consistent attempt to get beyond the politics of his age, and his continuing failure to do so.

Sinfield includes an excellent chapter on Tennyson's attempts to wrestle with the question of identity, a problem he shared with his Victorian contemporaries. His rereading of *In Memoriam* owes more to new critical theories of deconstruction than the one in his own 1971 book on the poem, focusing on the underlying issues of gender that he claims have been skirted by previous critics. His reading of *Maud* is particularly provocative, as he is unabashedly supportive of the revolutionary aspects of the work. Unfortunately, he chooses not to address *Idylls of the King* in any detail, finding the task too melancholy. Sinfield is not surprised that Tennyson was such a successful poet laureate, since many of his poems became more imbued with materialist values disguised under the pseudo-idealism of the middle class. It was for this reason, Sinfield suggests, that the new intellectuals and artists such as Alfred Austin and A. C. Swinburne rejected Tennyson.

Even if one does not agree with his Marxist readings, what Sinfield demonstrates is that the principles of criticism made popular in academic circles by Jacques Derrida, Paul de Man, Roland Barthes, and Jacques Lacan are useful in re-interpreting Tennyson, and that they shed new light on his poetic practice. Sinfield is not tied slavishly to these critics, however; some, such as Geoffrey Hartman, de Man, and Jonathan Culler come under attack for their inability to carry their arguments far enough in demonstrating the ideological struggle going on beneath the surface of Tennyson's poems. Sinfield is consistent in arguing that literary criticism should be part of a larger political critique, and that too many of his colleagues have simply "been more vulnerable than most to incorporation by the dominant" values of the bourgeois culture (182). His reading of Tennyson — and Tennyson criticism — makes this thesis eminently clear.

Interestingly, in a 1990 article Sinfield appears initially less strident and a bit less polemical than in his book. The main line of argument in "Tennyson and the Cultural Politics of Prophecy" is that Tennyson's ability to combine lyric and narrative forms allows him to write subversively, even prophetically, in major and minor works. Nevertheless, Sinfield finds it imperative to end by criticizing the work of editors who interpose themselves between an author and the author's works, writing textual marginalia that lead readers to particular interpretations that are almost always conservative and supportive of bourgeois ideology. The monumental revision by Christopher Ricks of his 1969 edition of Tennyson is seen as less laudable than most mainstream critics would like the academic world to believe, because the apparatus drives readers toward predetermined readings, masking the truly flexible, subversive nature of Tennyson's best work.

To suggest that Sinfield's views have become accepted within the academic world would be gross overstatement. In a review of Peltason, Albright, Shatto, and Sinfield, critic and novelist A. S. Byatt castigates Sinfield for "[locating] complacencies in others and ignor[ing] their intelligence," and using his study of Tennyson as an excuse to express his own needs (1986). More typical of what British critics were doing in Tennyson criticism during the 1980s is Alistair Thomson's *The Poetry of Tennyson* (1986), published in the same year as Sinfield's book. In his own words, Thomson admits that, far from being a "radical revision of generally accepted opinions" about the poet (vii), his study is intended simply to survey the poems he considers valuable. In that light, he discusses dozens of the major works (long and short), offering personal, sometimes iconoclastic readings that are often at odds with those of writers such as Buckley, Culler, Ricks, and Sinfield. Although Thomson had suggested four years earlier that Tennyson had continuing doubts about the value of his craft (1982), in this book he makes it clear that Tennyson is an inheritor and proponent of the Romantic tradition, displaying from youth to old age a penchant for experimentation and a firm belief in the poet's role as an agent for change in society. His text is peppered with summary judgments — "'The Kraken' is one of the few good sonnets Tennyson wrote" he observes in passing (27) — and he is especially harsh on those poems that continue the eighteenth-century tradition of the poetry of statement.

Thomson urges readers to quit looking for elaborate structure in *In Memoriam*, to appreciate Tennyson's achievement in *Maud* (which he thinks is the best of the long poems), and to understand once and for all that "the large claims which have been made for the *Idylls* are exaggerated" (169). While he seems to appreciate those qualities in Tennyson's poems that link him with successors such as Yeats and Eliot, Thomson is almost Arnoldian in his categorical pronouncements about what constitutes good and bad work in the Tennyson canon.

A more conventional reading is offered by American critic Michael Timko in *Carlyle and Tennyson* (1987). In his opening paragraphs, Timko asserts that Carlyle and Tennyson were the most important literary figures of the Victorian age, and that to understand them is to understand the Victorian temper. Some may be disappointed to find that, rather than trace the relationships between these two giants as Charles R. Sanders does in his 1961 article, Timko deals with them separately, choosing to illustrate their differences metaphorically by identifying them with characters in Tennyson's "Ulysses": Carlyle is the questing Ulysses who clashes with many in his relentless pursuit of the truth, while Tennyson is the Telemachus who concentrates on more mundane matters, opting to win people over more subtly than his more arrogant and adventuresome "father." Although he devotes much more of his work to an analysis of Carlyle, Timko argues that Tennyson was able to reach a wider audience than Carlyle because he took a less controversial stance on most social, political, and religious issues. Tennyson won people over, Timko says, by being deceptive, offering what seemed to his contemporaries like palliatives to their troubles, but actually causing them to confront issues that shook the age to its foundations.

How conventional Timko is in his assessment can be illustrated by comparing his examination of *In Memoriam* to that of Rob Johnson, whose "Strategies of Containment: Tennyson's *In Memoriam*" appeared the same year in *Post-Structuralist Reading of English Poetry* (1987). Johnson engages in a subtle, detailed deconstruction of the rhetoric and language of Tennyson's elegy. His commentary demonstrates how the deliberately ambiguous rhetoric of the poem exploits the "element of difference in language" and allows Tennyson to contain his grief within the formal structure of poetry. In this fashion, Tennyson can play off the ideas of faith and doubt so that neither is given undue prominence. This, in Johnson's view, is exactly what Tennyson intended, as the poet himself vacillated between these two emotional states.

In 1987 Linda K. Hughes, whose articles had established her reputation as a Tennyson scholar of the first rank, and whose annual commentary on Tennyson criticism had graced the pages of *Victorian Poetry* for several years, finally brought together her disparately published work in a comprehensive study of Tennyson's dramatic monologues. *The Manyfacéd Glass* begins with a chapter outlining the distinguishing characteristics of the dramatic monologue, drawing on the work on Ina B. Sessions, Robert Langbaum, and Dwight Culler to demonstrate how Tennyson's monologues differ from those of Browning and other Victorian poets. By reading the monologues, Hughes argues, one can trace Tennyson's poetic development. In his earliest attempts in the genre, he uses dramatic monologue "typically for subjective purposes"; as he became more confident in his craft, he began to use them for "more objective ends" (24-25). One can also see Tennyson becoming more adept at using the form. Hughes's chronological study compares monologues not only with one another but also with other Tennyson lyrics, illustrating how the poet was able to use the appropriate genre for the many subjects and themes with which he dealt during his long career. Her epilogue offers insight into the ways Tennyson influenced modern poets, especially T. S. Eliot — even though many of them, including Eliot, were quick to deny that influence.

A work that will certainly stand among the best to appear in the final decades of the century, and rank with the finest poststructuralist studies of Tennyson's poetry, is Herbert Tucker's *Tennyson and the Doom of Romanticism* (1988). Tucker had signaled the thrust of his argument in three articles in 1982, 1983, and 1984, and in a major article, "Tennyson and the Measure of Doom," in 1983. In a brilliant introduction, he demonstrates how the tendency of modernists and New Critics to denigrate Tennyson was more a matter of taste than critical principles. Tucker's own claims are falsely modest: he intends, he says "to tell the story of the life in Tennyson's texts to midcareer," to "practice specifically *literary* biography" (9). The book is this, but much more: it is a fine study of the creative process, examined through a series of close readings of poems that yield new insights into the ways events of Tennyson's life, aspects of his personality, and observations he gleaned from his readings in literature, science, and other subjects are melded into poetry of exquisite charm and evocative beauty.

From the beginning, Tucker says, Tennyson set out to be a poet, and to examine his work is to examine the steps along his career path. In that light, Tucker's chapters on the 1842 volumes are particularly rich in suggesting readings that both illuminate individual works and demonstrate the poet's commitment to his vocation. Even the death of Arthur Hallam is seen by

Tucker as an impetus for Tennyson to further his career, exploring the theme of fatalism he discovered early in life and which stayed with him as his skills became sharper and his fame increased.

Tucker describes with authority the process Tennyson used to compose his poems, a process of accretion that almost always began with the germ of an idea — sometimes a remark by a friend, at times a comment in a newspaper or a sentence in a work he was reading, sometimes an old poem of his own. He also describes ways Tennyson used framing devices for both artistic and political purposes. Principal among the sources for Tennyson's inspiration, Tucker argues, are the works of Virgil, whose career was a model for the man who would become Victoria's laureate. Tucker celebrates more than any other late-century critic (with the possible exception of Robert Pattison) Tennyson's debt to classical as well as Romantic traditions.

Among the many good things about Tucker's book, the best might be his close readings of individual poems — something not always present in other works launched from a theoretical platform. He pays attention to the technical qualities of the verse, especially Tennyson's use of language, his grammatical constructions, and his use of sound to convey both mood and meaning. Hence, his analyses of poems such as *The Princess, In Memoriam,* and *Maud,* as well as the readings of shorter works, convey the care and attention Tennyson gave to his craft. Reading Tucker gives one a sense of how sophisticated the practice of practical criticism has become in the twentieth century. The interdisciplinary approach to individual poems, mixed with a solid understanding of poetic theory, psychological insight, and political context are hallmarks of this superb work of criticism and scholarship. If one wishes to see how far criticism has come, one need only turn back immediately from *Tennyson and the Doom of Romanticism* to that early staple of critical commentary, Raymond Alden's *Alfred Tennyson: How to Know Him* (1917).

But Tucker is no idolater. Early in his study, he offers an assessment of what one ought to expect from Tennyson: "To the reader willing to tolerate a certain ethical and practical poverty," he says, "Tennyson offers the twin compensations of his richest gifts: the sustained evocation of an emotional atmosphere, and the atmospheric and physical acoustics of one of the most fulfilling voices in English tradition" (19). Tennyson's is "grandly minor music" (434), Tucker concludes; and after reading with care his well-researched and genuinely brilliant analysis of the poet's rise to fame, a reader is almost compelled to accept this judgment without question. Not every devotee of Tennyson will like the conclusion, but Tucker's argument will be hard to contradict.

Like Tucker's study, James Richardson's *Vanishing Lives: Style and Self in Tennyson, D. G. Rossetti, Swinburne, and Yeats* (1988) makes a significant contribution to scholarship through a careful, balanced assessment of Tennyson's style and its relationship to the creation of the poetic self. Like Tucker, Richardson is adept at employing the latest critical techniques to his analysis of Tennyson's poetry. What he especially admires is Tennyson's ability "to say yes and no at the same time" (32) — to maintain two contrary ideas simultaneously — and to create a sense of "absent presence" (34). He succeeds in doing so through specific word choice and composition of scenes that create tensions within readers. "Dimness and sharp particularity," Richardson says, "are states of consciousness held in tension" in poems such as *In Memoriam* (43). Tennyson is "less a poet of subject or object than of circumference, and the looming and fading of details is the looming and fading of the borders of the self" (43). Richardson takes issue with those who call Tennyson an escapist. He is not "in flight from life," but he recognizes that death is the alternative to life. What he fears most, and what he expresses most poignantly, is that all too often, "life escapes us" (75). Better than any other poet, Tennyson is "an elegist of the self," able to depict the transparent, dissolving, and sometimes almost unrememberable aspects of the self (4).

Two critical biographies of Tennyson published in 1988 are also of great value to understanding new critical approaches to the poet. The first, Marion Shaw's *Alfred Lord Tennyson* (1988), is part of the Harvester Wheatsheaf Feminist Series, volumes designed to provide feminist perspectives on major male writers. As Shaw notes in her introduction, "most feminist literary criticism" written since the emergence of feminism "has been and is concerned with women's writing" (1). Shaw was particularly well suited for her task, having published previously on Tennyson and having served with colleague Susan Shatto as coeditor of the Oxford University Press edition of *In Memoriam* (1982). Claiming that Tennyson has been "desexed" by patriarchal criticism, Shaw argues that her feminist reading will "put the sex back into the text" (3). Operating from that premise, she concentrates on those poems that deal with love, demonstrating how feminist theory can be used with great advantage to shed new insight into both major and minor works in the Tennyson canon.

The benefits of Shaw's approach are many. For example, she notes that though Tennyson, like his Victorian contemporaries, idealizes marriage, in his poetry happy marriages are either are prevented by "hostile circumstances" or are spoiled by "a failure of trust and love in one or both of the partners once a marriage has taken place" (37). Significant insights into *The Princess, Maud,* and *Idylls of the King* emerge as Shaw carries out her analysis based on this keen observation. In a similar vein, Shaw demonstrates that there is "a marked scarcity of manly men in Tennyson's poetry" (63). The speaker of *In Memoriam* is more typical of the laureate's male protagonists. While Tennyson initially used female protagonists to examine psychological issues, as he advanced in his career, the "attitudes and neuroses embodied in the female figures in his early work become more consistently located in the young male protagonists of his later poems" (76). Shaw's lengthy analysis of *In Memoriam* demonstrates how Tennyson blurs gender lines in dealing with the loss of Hallam.

Shaw's feminist analysis of Tennyson's King Arthur reveals how the poet's attempt to combine both genders in one character robs the hero of *Idylls of the King* not only of his manhood but also of "moral complexity" (91). Arthur's "asexual self serves to sharpen sexual differences" (97–98) and leads to the downfall of a kingdom where neither women nor men can divest themselves of gender to achieve the kind of perfection Arthur represents.

Claiming that "no English poet has written more about women than Tennyson" (101), Shaw offers detailed, insightful analyses of the female figures in his poetry, relying on the best feminist scholarship to demonstrate how, despite his professed veneration of women, Tennyson emerges as "a misogynist poet" to whom women represent "fear and loathing and, even more invidious, self-loathing" (141). Dividing the women into typical categories — the Madonna, the virgin, the fallen woman — Shaw shows that, as his career progressed, "Tennyson's division of women into good and bad became more pronounced and his conception of the dangerousness of women intensified and darkened" (106). In a provocative investigation of *In Memoriam*, Shaw explains how "Hallam's death provokes a crisis of self-formation" for the poet, who must come to grips with "what makes a man, particularly what makes a man in relation to women" (144). Shaw concludes her study by speculating that Tennyson is actually a precursor of twentieth-century men, unable to hold in balance the duality he sees in women's nature — "polluted morality" and "immaterial potential" for goodness (165).

Shaw's was certainly not the only study of Tennyson to approach his work from a feminist perspective. Beginning with critical comments made about the poet by Kate Millet in *Sexual Politics* (1970), scholars adopted the tools of feminist criticism to offer new perspectives on Tennyson's poems. Among them are Diane Hoeveler, whose "Manly-Women and Womanly-Men" (1981) explores Tennyson's attempts to achieve an androgynous ideal in both *The Princess* and *In Memoriam*. Carol Christ does so in two articles (1977 and 1987) in which she writes about growing tendency in Victorian England toward the "feminization of the poetic ideal" ("Feminine Subject," 395–96). Alan Sinfield discusses at length the idea of Tennyson as an androgynous poet in *The Language of "In Memoriam"* (1981). Finally, James Eli Adams uses feminist critical methodology to explore Tennyson's descriptions of nature in "Woman Red in Tooth and Claw" (1989).

Although also influenced by feminist theory, Elaine Jordan says in *Alfred Tennyson* (1988) that the principal purpose of her study (done for the Cambridge University Press British and Irish Authors Series) is "to listen" to Tennyson's poems "and then come back from that immersion to try and communicate my sense of what they were and how they worked" (ix). Despite her claims to be "entirely innocent and open" (ix), Jordan relies on previous scholarship, including contemporary poststructuralist theory, to develop a portrait of Tennyson as an artist and thinker. After providing a brief sketch of his life, she offers some important background on the poet's understanding of science, religion, and politics as the ontological and epistemological ground from which he writes. Jordan is interested in the various genres with which Tennyson experiments: idyll, dramatic monologue, elegy, and epic. Her study of the poems goes farther than most critics to demonstrate Tennyson's reliance on the visual arts as inspiration for his work. Her careful close readings of individual works reveal Tennyson's debt to his Romantic predecessors while emphasizing the poet's continuing concerns with the power of art to depict reality.

Jordan is particularly strong in explicating *The Princess*, a work she calls both a "political poem" and a "poem of love" (84). Like most twentieth-century feminists, she criticizes Tennyson's decision to emphasize the importance of the woman's role in caring for children, a limitation on the development of womankind which Jordan says he seems to espouse. At the same time, however, she is exceptionally good at demonstrating the wrong-headedness of Lionel Stevenson's reading of the poem in his influential 1948 article "The 'High-Born Maiden' Symbol in Tennyson." Stevenson sees Tennyson's Princess Ida as mere object; Jordan believes this is a travesty of what Tennyson was attempting, namely, "to put the point of view of a woman with a strong will directed to a noble cause" (93). She also challenges R. B. Martin's claim that Tennyson possessed a low level of sexual feeling. "On the contrary," Jordan argues, Tennyson "wrote the best erotic verse since that of the seventeenth century" (107).

Jordan's analysis of *In Memoriam* and *Maud* stresses the importance of external events that shaped Tennyson's development of his themes. Her curious handling of *Idylls of the King*, which loosely follows the order of composition, demonstrates Tennyson's growing pessimism and disillusionment with women. She is less harsh than most critics in seeing some balance in the poet's treatment of gender relationships in the poem, and she is inclusive in seeing multiple themes emerging as Tennyson developed the poem. It is not simply about gender relationships, but also about "the conflict between mystical-religious and humanist-rational accounts of the world" (177). With some demonstrated bravura she dismisses the earlier studies of the poem by John R. Reed (1969) and William Buckler (1984) as being too reductive. In Jordan's view, all of Tennyson's poetry, but especially his Arthurian work, contains levels of complexity that involve gender relations and much more besides.

In contrast to Jordan's feminist study, Kenneth M. McKay's *Many Glancing Colours: An Essay in Reading Tennyson 1809–1850* (1988) might be viewed as a throwback to the earlier forms of criticism practiced by the neohumanists or New Critics. His title is taken from a remark Tennyson made to his son Hallam: "Poetry is like shot silk with many glancing colours" (*Memoir* II: 127). Like shot silk, an expensive weave with an iridescent sheen that appears to be different colors depending on the way one looks at it, poetry is subject to varying interpretation depending on the viewpoint of the reader. McKay has a dual purpose in writing: first, he wants to explain how the intentional indeterminacy of Tennyson's poetry gives it a special strength and appeal, and second, to highlight the inadequacies of previous readings of the laureate's work. Along the way, McKay points out the many parallels that exist between Tennyson's work and that of earlier writers. Far from being a simple source-study (he specifically chastises Tennyson's contemporary Churton Collins for this kind of work), McKay demonstrates how the poet's borrowings and adaptations from earlier writers allow him to establish continuity with literary tradition. Such continuity is imperative for Tennyson, since he sees about him a world where fragmentation and alienation abound. In McKay's view, Tennyson's best poems "are rich and complex in allusion, poems of shot-silk focused on a passion for the past which communicates energy and poetic vision" (73).

Concentrating on more than a dozen poems from the poet's teenage years until the publication of *In Memoriam,* McKay explains how Tennyson modulates between this passion for the past and a need for currency. In doing so he points out interesting parallels among such works as "Oenone," "Ulysses," "The Lady of Shalott," and "Tithonus." More than most twentieth-century critics, McKay sees Tennyson influenced by the ideas of Christianity, if not by the practices of Christian sects; he also acknowledges the debt Tennyson owes to such diverse precursors as Shakespeare, Milton, Spenser, Keats, and Goethe. Nowhere is this more evident than in his extensive discussion of *In Memoriam,* a work that he says is not the product of "some peculiar obsession of Tennyson" (152). More than merely "a tribute to Hallam," the elegy is "a work of art in which some of the deepest possibilities of Tennyson's thought are realized" (153). In two chapters devoted to analyzing the poem, McKay demonstrates how Tennyson moves emotionally from despair to a realization that Love — "the reconciliation of God and Nature" — can be seen in the union of man and woman in marriage (211). The poet shows how it is possible to move through sorrow to a deeper understanding of the human condition. For Tennyson there were no fixed truths, but only "the truth of one's place in time as it can be made out against the forms of the past" (252). Tennyson's chief accomplishment in his own time was to serve as "navigator for the high Victorians," "fixing the modern [i.e., Victorian] position by determining his relation to the different positions of the past" (259).

While McKay is confident in his reading of the poet, he is even more strident in his strictures against the poet's critics. He is openly hostile toward theorists such as Alan Sinfield, whose 1986 Marxist critique he dismisses as "not a serious rereading of Tennyson's poems so much as an effort to manipulate the conventional understanding to accord with the *realpolitikal* demands of current critical theory" (4). Predictably he challenges the work of Nicolson and Auden. He acknowledges the brilliance of T. S. Eliot's insights into *In Memoriam,* but insists that it is necessary to "see through" them or "risk sharing his essential misconstruction" of the poem (189). At one point or another in his study, he takes issue with G. Robert Stange, F. E. L. Priestley, Christopher Ricks, Henry Kozicki, Timothy Peltason, and Kerry McSweeney. One can only assume that McKay intends his work to be the last word, both a corrective to previous misguided readings and a catechism for future students of the Victorian laureate.

Like McKay, Roger Ebbatson also has a thesis to advance in his brief volume on Tennyson in the Penguin Critical Studies series. In the introductory note to *Tennyson* (1988), Ebbatson asserts that he wants to offer a middle way between the "widely divergent critical approaches of Christopher Ricks and Alan Sinfield" (ix). There is throughout all of Tennyson's poetry, Ebbatson says, one unifying theme: "the desire to escape the self, and the equally strong desire to hold on to it" (26). The bulk of his volume is given over to readings of individual poems that illustrate this overriding principle. Unfortunately, most readings are exceptionally brief, and Ebbatson offers no assessment of *Idylls of the King,* claiming space limitations prevent him from doing so.

It may seem surprising that, less than a decade after Ann Colley published her lengthy study of Tennyson's use of madness, another book on the topic should appear. Roger Platizky's *A Blueprint of His Dissent: Madness and Method in Tennyson's Poetry* (1989) complements rather than contradicts Colley's work, however, in that he focuses not on the biographical and historical background for Tennyson's use of madness, but rather on the way "the language of the poetry itself reveals psychological patterns and tensions that are timely as well as historical" (11). Platizky is interested in Tennyson's use of "a variety of methods" to make "the language of his poetry on madness psychologically dynamic," displaying special interest in the tendencies toward conservatism or subversion (12). For his study Platizky examines five poems in detail. His readings of "St. Simeon Stylites," *Maud,* "Romney's Remorse," "Lucretius," and "Rizpah" rely on the pioneering work of psychologists as well as the insights of late-twentieth-century theorists who have extended our understanding of the psychological dimensions of literature. Perhaps not surprisingly, given his grounding in poststructuralism, Platizky finds Tennyson was able to do what many great artists have done before and after him: code in his apparently conservative poetry "a blueprint of his dissent" from mainstream thinking about social, political, and cultural issues (117).

David Goslee's *Tennyson's Characters: "Strange Faces, Other Minds"* (1989) contains an argument remarkably similar to Platizky's, though there has certainly been no direct influence. Interested in the conflict of Self and Other that had become a central concern of theorists in the last decades of the century, Goslee posits that "throughout Tennyson's poetry" there is "an elaborate and remarkably consistent psychomachia, a structural model which not only dramatized the original conflict but shaped it into an elaborate yet flexible pattern of meanings." That model, Goslee says, is of "a centered, cloistered, but still authorial presence . . . threatened by some Other" that "encroaches upon it from the fringes of the poem's imaginative universe." There is, too, almost always a "vatic speaker or preternatural agent" that "mediates between the authorial presence and the Other" (xi).

Goslee traces this pattern throughout Tennyson's career, offering readings of individual poems in chronological order to demonstrate both the consistency of the central pattern and the variations that occurred as circumstances imposed on the poet and determined his choice of subjects. In presenting his thesis, Goslee explains how the arguments of earlier critics such as W. D. Paden, Ralph Rader, E. D. H. Johnson, and R. B. Martin are complemented in his work. While the influence of Derrida and other theorists can be traced throughout Goslee's study, his focus remains on individual poems in which Tennyson struggles with issues of anxiety.

In the tradition established by early twentieth-century critics such as G. K. Chesterton, William Payne, Arnold Smith, and the authors of the *Cambridge History of English Literature,* Paul Turner's sweeping study *English Literature 1832–1890, Excluding the Novel* (1989) provides an end-of-century perspective on the Victorian period that includes a brief survey of Tennyson's career. While his commentary on most individual poems is more a statement of received opinion than new analysis, Turner's comments on *In Memoriam* remind readers how far criticism has come since the days when debates over issues such as evolution and the status of the soul stirred enormous controversy. The subject of the poem, the "conflict between science and religion" was of vital importance to the Victorians. "That problem has generally been shelved, if not solved," he says, "and the poem is valued less as theology than as literature, for its verbal music and its human interest as a convincing study of bereavement" (29). How many general readers would agree with such an assessment at the close of the twentieth century may be open to question, as reactionary movements in world religions still strike out at the primacy of science as a way of viewing the world. Nevertheless, Turner's remarks seem to suggest that, whatever one thinks of Tennyson's science, his ability to explore one of humankind's most universal emotions remains as relevant as it was in 1850.

Another study appearing in 1989 uses the tools of contemporary literary theory to explore Tennyson's lifelong fascination with the genre of the pastoral. Owen Schur's *Victorian Pastoral: Tennyson, Hardy, and the Subversion of Forms* provides detailed, sensitive, and imaginative readings of poems such as "Mariana," "The Lotos-Eaters," "Oenone," and "Ulysses" to illustrate ways the poet struggled to reform the pastoral tradition for his own purposes. These readings provide evidence that Tennyson was not simply reaching back into the literary tradition for subject matter more amenable than the chaotic circumstances of modern life. Rather, his use of tradition — and especially myth — was a conscious poetic strategy that allowed him to test the conventions of the pastoral genre, a form particularly attractive to him because it allowed him to explore concepts of exile and alienation. Taken in this light, Tennyson's work is particularly modern and links him more closely with writers who claimed to be breaking with him in establishing the conventions of modern poetry.

J. B. Bullen's *The Sun is God: Painting, Literature, and Mythology in the Nineteenth Century* (1989) includes an intriguing essay by Isobel Armstrong, a major critic whose passage from formalism to poststructuralism signals the trend among critics of the Victorian period during the last decades of the twentieth century. The better part of "Tennyson's 'The Lady of Shalott': Victorian Mythography and the Politics of Narcissism" is devoted to an explanation of the ways Victorians came to understand the nature of mythology and its uses in literature. Her reading is reminiscent of, and obviously indebted to, the work of Gerhard Joseph, whose articles on Tennyson had been appearing in journals for more than a decade. Using the theoretical framework of de Man, Lacan, and nineteenth-century philologists, Armstrong demonstrates how myth became useful to poets such as Tennyson in supporting or attacking the ideology of conservative politicians. She concludes that "The Lady of Shalott" actually "insists on . . . failure of the conservative *mythos*" (102). One wonders if Tennyson would be pleased or horrified by the work of Armstrong and others, who in a half century, following the lead of E. D. H. Johnson, transformed the poet from the spokesperson for the conservative values of his age into a rebel attacking mainstream society with the one weapon he knew how to use.

Works Cited

Adams, James Eli. "Woman Red in Tooth and Claw: Nature and the Feminine in Tennyson and Darwin." *Victorian Studies* 33:1 (Autumn 1989): 7–27.

Albright, Daniel. *Tennyson: The Muses' Tug-of-War*. Charlottesville: UP of Virginia, 1986.

Alden, Raymond M. *Alfred Tennyson: How to Know Him*. Indianapolis: Bobbs-Merrill, 1917. Reprint, Norwood, PA: Norwood Editions, 1977.

Armstrong, Isobel. *Language as Living Form in Nineteenth-Century Poetry*. London: Routledge, 1982.

———. "Tennyson's 'The Lady of Shalott': Victorian Mythography and the Politics of Narcissism." In *The Sun is God: Painting, Literature, and Mythology in the Nineteenth Century*. Ed. J. B. Bullen. Oxford: Clarendon Press, 1989. 49–107.

Assad, Thomas J. *Tennysonian Lyric: "Songs of the Deeper Kind" and "In Memoriam."* New Orleans, LA: Tulane UP, 1984.

Bloom, Harold, ed. *Alfred Lord Tennyson*. New York: Chelsea House, 1985.

Buckler, William E. *Man and His Myths: Tennyson's "Idylls of the King" in Critical Context*. New York: New York UP, 1984.

———. *The Victorian Imagination: Essays in Aesthetic Exploration*. New York: New York UP, 1980.

Buckley, Jerome H. "The Myth of the Poet." *Nineteenth Century Studies* 6 (1992): 61–71.

———. "The Persistence of Tennyson." In *The Victorian Experience: The Poet*, Ed. Richard A. Levine. Athens: Ohio UP, 1982. 1–22.

———. "Tennyson's Landscapes." *Tennyson Research Bulletin* 6:5 (November 1996): 278–88.

Byatt, A. S. "Insights *Ad nauseum*." *Times Literary Supplement*, 14 November 1986. 1274.

Christ, Carol T. "The Feminine Subject in Victorian Poetry." *ELH* 54 (Summer 1987): 385–401.

———. "Victorian Masculinity and the Angel in the House." In *A Widening Sphere: Changing Roles of Victorian Women*. Ed. Martha Vicinus. Bloomington: Indiana UP, 1977. 146–62.

Colley, Ann C. *Tennyson and Madness*. Athens: U of Georgia P, 1983.

Coslett, Tess. *The "Scientific Movement" and Victorian Literature*. New York: St. Martin's, 1982.

Craft, Chris. "'Descend, Touch, and Enter': Tennyson's Strange Manner of Address." *Genders* 1 (Spring 1988): 83–101.

Dellamora, Richard. "Tennyson, The Apostles, and *In Memoriam*." *Masculine Desire: The Sexual Politics of Victorian Aestheticism*. Chapel Hill: U of North Carolina P, 1990.

Ebbatson, Roger. *Tennyson*. London: Penguin, 1988.

Fletcher, Pauline. *Gardens and Grim Ravines: The Language of Landscape in Victorian Poetry*. Princeton, NJ: Princeton UP, 1983.

Ford, George H. "'A Great Poetical Boa-Constrictor,' Alfred Tennyson: An Educated Victorian Mind." In *Victorian Literature and Society: Essays Presented to Richard D. Altick*. Ed. James R. Kincaid and Albert J. Kuhn. Columbus: Ohio State UP, 1983. 146–67.

———. *Keats and the Victorians: A Study of His Influence and Rise to Fame, 1821–1895*. New Haven, CT: Yale UP, 1944. Reprint, Hamden, CT: Archon Books, 1962. 17–48.

Fulweiler, Howard W. "Tennyson's *In Memoriam* and the Scientific Imagination." *Thought: A Review of Culture and Idea* 59 (1984): 296–318.

Goslee, David. *Tennyson's Characters: Strange Faces, Other Minds*. Iowa City: U of Iowa P, 1989.

Hair, Donald S. *Domestic and Heroic in Tennyson's Poetry*. Toronto: U of Toronto P, 1981.

Hoeveler, Diane L. "Manly-Women and Womanly-Men: Tennyson's Androgynous Ideal." *Michigan Occasional Papers in Women's Studies* 19 (1981): 1–19.

Hughes, Linda K. *The Manyfacéd Glass: Tennyson's Dramatic Monologues*. Athens: Ohio UP, 1987.

Johnson, Rob. "Strategies of Containment: Tennyson's *In Memoriam*." In *Post-Structuralist Readings of English Poetry*. Ed. Richard Machin and Christopher Norris. Cambridge: Cambridge UP, 1987. 308–31.

Jordan, Elaine. *Alfred Tennyson*. Cambridge: Cambridge UP, 1988.

Joseph, Gerhard. "The Homeric Competitions of Tennyson and Gladstone." *Browning Institute Studies* 10 (1982): 105–15.

———. "Tennyson's 'Idylls': Attack and Defense." *Virginia Quarterly Review* 50 (1974): 152–56.

———. "Tennyson's Optics: The Eagle's Gaze." *PMLA* 92 (1977): 420–28.

———. "Tennyson's Parable of Soul Making: A Jungian Reading of *The Princess*." In *CUNY English Forum*, Vol. 1. Ed. Saul N. Brody and Harold Schechter. New York: AMS, 1985. 231–40.

———. "Tennyson's Stupidity." *University of Hartford Studies in Literature* 15 (1983): 55–62.

———. "Tennyson's Three Women: The Thought Within the Image." *Victorian Poetry* 19 (Spring 1981): 1–18.

———. "Victorian Frames: The Windows and Mirrors of Browning, Arnold, and Tennyson." *Victorian Poetry* 16 (1978): 70–87.

Kiernan, Victor. "Tennyson, King Arthur, and Imperialism." In *Culture, Ideology and Politics: Essays for Eric Hobsbawm*. Ed. Raphael Samuel and Gareth Stedman Jones. London: Routledge, 1982. 126–48.

McGann, Jerome J. "Tennyson and the Histories of Criticism." *Review* 4 (1982): 219–53.

McKay, Kenneth. *Many Glancing Colours: An Essay in Reading Tennyson, 1809–1850*. Toronto: U of Toronto P, 1988.

McSweeney, Kerry. *Supreme Attachments: Studies in Victorian Love*. Aldershot, England: Ashgate, 1998. 40–59.

———. *Tennyson and Swinburne as Romantic Naturalists*. Toronto: U of Toronto P, 1981.

Mermin, Dorothy. "Tennyson." *The Audience in the Poem: Five Victorian Poets*. New Brunswick, NJ: Rutgers UP, 1983.

Millett, Kate. *Sexual Politics*. Garden City, NY: Doubleday, 1970.

Peltason, Timothy. *Reading "In Memoriam."* Princeton, NJ: Princeton UP, 1985.

———. "Tennyson, Nature, and Romantic Nature Poetry." *Philological Quarterly* 63:1 (Winter 1984): 75–93.

———. "Tennyson's Philosophy: Some Lyric Examples." In *Philosophical Approaches to Literature: New Essays on Nineteenth and Twentieth Century Texts*. Ed. William E. Cain. Lewisburg, PA: Bucknell UP, 1984. 51–72.

Pinion, F. B. *A Tennyson Companion*. London: Macmillan, 1984.

Platizky, Roger S. *A Blueprint of His Dissent: Madness and Method in Tennyson's Poetry*. Lewisburg, PA: Bucknell UP; London: Associated UP, 1989.

Radford, Colin, and Sally Minogue. "The Logical Richness of Criticism: An Analysis of Ricks on Tennyson." *The Nature of Criticism*. Brighton, England: Harvester; Atlantic Highlands, NJ: Humanities Press, 1981. 84–114.

Reed, John R. *Perception and Design in Tennyson's "Idylls of the King."* Athens: Ohio UP, 1969.

Richardson, James. *Vanishing Lives: Style and Self in Tennyson, D. G. Rossetti, Swinburne, and Yeats*. Charlottesville: UP of Virginia, 1988.

Sanders, Charles R. "Carlyle and Tennyson." *PMLA* 76 (March 1961): 82–97. Reprint, in *Carlyle's Friendships and Other Studies*. Durham, NC: Duke UP, 1977. 192–225.

Schur, Owen. *Victorian Pastoral: Tennyson, Hardy, and the Subversion of Forms.* Columbus: Ohio State UP, 1989.

Sedgwick, Eve Sokofsky. *Between Men: English Literature and Male Homosocial Desire.* New York: Columbia UP, 1985.

Shatto, Susan, and Marion Shaw, eds. *In Memoriam.* Oxford: Oxford UP, 1982.

Shaw, Marion. *Alfred Lord Tennyson.* New York: Harvester Wheatsheaf, 1988.

Sinfield, Alan. *Alfred Tennyson.* Oxford: Basil Blackwell, 1986.

———. "Tennyson and the Cultural Politics of Prophecy." *ELH* 57:1 (Spring 1990): 175–95.

Staines, David. *Tennyson's Camelot: "The Idylls of the King" and Its Medieval Sources.* Waterloo, Ont.: Wilfrid Laurier UP, 1982.

Stevenson, Lionel. "The 'High-Born Maiden' Symbol in Tennyson." *PMLA* 63 (March 1948): 234–43.

Thomson, Alastair W. *The Poetry of Tennyson.* London: Routledge & Kegan Paul, 1986.

———. "Tennyson and Some Doubts." *Essays and Studies* 35 (1982): 84–100.

Timko, Michael. *Carlyle and Tennyson.* Iowa City: U of Iowa P, 1987. Basingstoke, England: Macmillan, 1988.

Tucker, Herbert F. *Tennyson and the Doom of Romanticism.* Cambridge, MA: Harvard UP, 1988.

———. "Tennyson and the Measure of Doom." *PMLA* 98 (1983): 8–20.

Turner, Paul. *English Literature 1832–1890, Excluding the Novel.* Oxford: Clarendon Press, 1989. 18–38.

Wordsworth, Ann. "An Art That Will Not Abandon the Self to Language: Bloom, Tennyson and the Blind World of the Wish." In *Untying the Text: A Post-Structuralist Reader.* Ed. Robert Young. Boston: Routledge, 1981. 207–22.

7: Tennyson *Fin-de-Siècle:* 1990–2000

THE APPROACH OF THE CENTENARY OF Tennyson's death spurred critical activity in the early 1990s, resulting in the appearance of several new major biographical and critical studies. Two helpful, if limited, books deserve brief mention. The first, *A Tennyson Chronology* (1990), is F. B. Pinion's compilation of a chronological listing of events in the poet's life. Issued as one of a series of "Chronologies" by the publishers at Macmillan, Pinion's guidebook is useful for scholars wishing to check facts, but offers little interpretation about the significance of events that shaped Tennyson's art. The second, Roger Simpson's *Camelot Regained* (1990), is less about Tennyson's poetry than about the Arthurian background that informs many of his works, including *Idylls of the King*. Simpson shows that, far from being the initiator of Arthurian studies in England, Tennyson was simply following the lead of other nineteenth-century writers who had resurrected Arthurian tales. Nevertheless, Simpson argues, much of the Arthurian background in Tennyson's work is really the invention of the poet rather than a borrowing from medieval sources.

During the final decade of the century, Tennyson became a figure of significant interest to feminist critics. Two essays on Tennyson are included in Regina Barreca's *Sex and Death in Victorian Literature* (1990). In the first, Gerhard Joseph examines the image of the sword in Tennyson's poetry, demonstrating how this object carries dual significance, serving at once as a symbol of sexual power and of death. Sylvia Manning explores Tennyson's fascination with sex and death in his early poetry, noting that the poet's knowledge of both seemed to be based on secondary experience until the death of Arthur Henry Hallam, when his personal confrontation with death led him to deal more directly and sincerely with the experience. For Thais Morgan's *Victorian Sages and Cultural Discourse* (1990), Linda Shires contributed "Rereading Tennyson's Gender Politics," an essay that "take[s] soundings in Tennyson's poetry in order to discover the changing status and use of the feminine" (50). Though she does not contend that Tennyson was a feminist, Shires finds that "his treatment of subjectivity and his archaeology of masculinity" frequently expose "important gaps" in the male-dominated hegemony he claims to support (50). Certainly, too, Leslie Brisman's "*Maud:* The Feminine as the Crux of Influence" (1992) can be linked with these essays as an attempt to explain Tennyson's handling of the feminine ideal in his poetry.

Antony Harrison and Beverly Taylor include in their *Gender and Discourse in Victorian Literature and Art* (1992) two essays on Tennyson's work: Taylor's "'School-Miss Alfred' and 'Materfamilias': Female Sexuality and Poetic Voice in *The Princess* and *Aurora Leigh*," and Deborah Hooker's "Ambiguous Bodies: Keats and the Problem of Resurrection in Tennyson's 'Demeter and Persephone,'" both heavily influenced by late-century theories of feminism and semiotics, and both offering intriguing revisionist views of selected poems. A later feminist analysis of Tennyson's work is Catherine Maxwell's "Engendering Vision in the Victorian Male Poets" (1997), an article discussing the "fictions of the feminine" that help in "constructing the male poet" (73).

Certainly the most significant study appearing in 1991 was Donald S. Hair's *Tennyson's Language*. The thesis of this work was anticipated in two fine articles, "Tennyson's Faith: A Re-Examination" (1986) and "'Matter-Moulded Forms of Speech'" (1989). Following in the tradition of F. E. L. Priestley and Alan Sinfield, Hair concentrates on the philosophy of language underlying Tennyson's poetry. His aim is to "define Tennyson's own views of language, and to set those views in the context of both the old and new approaches to language study" (3). Hair focuses on the ideological background of the poet's work, demonstrating how Tennyson followed the path set out by Coleridge in treating language as more than an arbitrary system of signs. Instead, language for Tennyson was "linked with a providential view of history," and studying words carefully would gradually reveal to the poet "a dynamic and divinely ordered world" (4). Hair's examination of dozens of poems, especially *In Memoriam* and *Idylls of the King*, not only illustrates the care with which Tennyson chose his words and phrases, but also reveals how well the poet understood the philosophical position behind his philological practice. Hair would continue his study of Tennyson in a 1996 article, "Soul and Spirit in *In Memoriam*." His work on Tennyson's language was extended to examinations of many of the minor poems by Richard Marggraf Turley in "Tennyson and the Nineteenth-Century Language Debate" (1997).

Since its founding in the 1960s, the Tennyson Society had been sponsoring annual meetings at which a distinguished scholar would deliver a lecture on the poet's work. During the 1970s and 1980s, only a few of these were printed by the Society. However, in 1992 — perhaps to celebrate the centenary of Tennyson's death — seven of those not previously published were collected in *Tennyson: Seven Essays* (1992), a volume edited by Philip Collins. These essays are the work of a pantheon of giants in Victorian scholarship: Jerome Buckley, Isobel Armstrong, Aidan Day, John Beer, Norman Page, Collins, and W. W. Robson. Eric Griffiths, whose previous work applying semiotics and speech theory to an analysis of Tennyson's poems had appeared in *The Printed Voice in Victorian Poetry* (1989), is also a contributor.

Collectively, these authors provide insight into the key questions in Tennyson criticism and offer an assessment of the poet's reputation in the closing decades of the century.

The hundredth anniversary of Tennyson's death prompted Simon Haines to take a retrospective look at the poet's reputation. In "Victorian Self-Fashioning: Tennyson One Hundred Years After" (1992), Haines argues that despite the mountain of commentary, no one had yet been able "to effect a real revaluation" (72). He believes that, despite the ups and downs Tennyson's reputation had suffered, the earliest critics' estimates of his "metrical and picturesque genius" (73) had stood for a century. Examining three representative poems, Haines concludes, however, that a dispassionate historian would find Tennyson not a representative of the Victorians, but rather a herald of his age and a "conduit for certain aspects of Romanticism" (75) that survived into the later decades of the nineteenth century.

Also in 1992, a special double issue of *Victorian Poetry* edited by Gerhard Joseph celebrated the centenary of Tennyson's death. This was the second time the journal's editors had devoted an entire issue to criticism of Tennyson (the first in 1980). For the centenary publication, distinguished critics such as James Kincaid, J. Hillis Miller, John R. Reed, U. C. Knoepflmacher, and Herbert Tucker, all of whom had already done much to secure Tennyson's achievement, contributed essays. Six of the selections focus on *Idylls of the King* — something that would simply not have been done by respected critics a half-century earlier. Unquestionably, the century following the poet's death, turbulent as it may have been at times, had finally seen justice done to his entire canon. In a creative introduction cast in the form of a dialogue between the editor and the shade of the poet, Joseph says to Tennyson: "We remember you . . . because you still touch so many of us in so many crucial ways" (195).

Concurrently, Gerhard Joseph brought out his second book on Tennyson, *Tennyson and the Text: The Weaver's Shuttle* (1992). If one wants to see how critical theories popularized during the 1970s and 1980s affected American critics, Joseph's works might be used as textbook examples. His 1969 *Tennysonian Love: The Strange Diagonal* is representative of what had now come to be called orthodox criticism. Much of the argument for the book had been worked out partially in the many articles Joseph had published between 1970 and 1990. The 1992 volume, however, is heavily influenced by writers such as Freud, Derrida, Barthes, de Man, and Lacan. It is also one of the most self-reflexive works published by a Tennyson critic. Joseph constantly calls attention to the processes he uses to judge Tennyson's work and to his own prejudices and predilections.

Joseph argues that the metaphor of weaving explains both Tennyson's method and his own, as he weaves the various strands of psychological analysis, deconstruction, and gender theory to offer a provocative reading of the

Tennyson canon. Beginning with a discussion of Tennyson and Poe as practitioners of a new form of poetry, Joseph explains how both used visual and auditory imagery to create works of beauty. Focusing on the optical quality of the poems, Joseph sees running through Tennyson's work a tension between "the aesthetic of particularity and the aesthetic of vagueness" (47). While he is at times the poet "of the particularized and the proximate," his most interesting work also celebrates "the exotically distanced in space and the remote in time" (56). Joseph believes this technique reflects the poet's epistemology, which he says is "symbolically rendered as bifocal dialectic, as particularized concentration that alternates with blurred and generalized sweep" (73). Rather than offer detailed explications of individual poems, Joseph concentrates on the patterns of representation in Tennyson's texts. In the second part of his study, he examines characters from the classical and Arthurian poems, using gender theory as a ground for his analysis. Throughout he makes clear both his commitment to the tenets of critical theory which, in his view, help explain the continuing fascination readers have in studying the works of the most representative of the Victorians.

Isobel Armstrong, whose work on Tennyson and other Victorians had distinguished her among critics writing at the end of the century, included three essays on Tennyson in her 1993 collection, *Victorian Poetry: Poetry, Poetics, and Politics*. This volume illustrates the movement of Armstrong's criticism away from what had been the orthodox approach when she published her first volume in 1969 to a more politically charged, theory-based analysis of Victorian literature. In *Victorian Poetry: Poetry, Poetics, and Politics*, Armstrong highlights the experimental nature of much of Tennyson's early work. It is not surprising to her that his first critics found him subversive and radical. As he grew older he appeared to become more conservative in his methodology, but Armstrong says it was his conservative political nature that "leads him toward radical questioning" of the social and political policies of his day (283).

Though they appeared a year late, two new full-scale biographies were issued to celebrate the centenary of Tennyson's death. The first, by Michael Thorn, is by far the longer and more detailed. It is also more revisionist in its outlook. In *Tennyson* (1993) Thorn concentrates on telling the story of the poet's life, interweaving literary criticism only lightly to suggest how biography shapes art. With the perspective of a century, Thorn sets out to discriminate between the poet and his age. "More than enough has been said by other writers" on that subject, Thorn says. "Individually such commentaries have been useful," he admits, "but collectively they have erected a heavy barrier between Tennyson and ourselves." It is necessary, Thorn argues, to "peer past the Victorian gauze" if modern readers really want to understand Tennyson's accomplishments (126).

The kind of revisionism that characterizes Thorn's book can be seen in his description of the poet's childhood and his relationship with Arthur Henry Hallam. Thorn argues that Tennyson's childhood was not as bad as it has been portrayed since the publication of Sir Charles Tennyson's biography of his grandfather. Instead, Thorn believes Tennyson exploited his childhood, as he did so many events in his life, for the sake of his art. Perhaps even more controversial is Thorn's assertion that, in the early period of their friendship, there existed between the poet and Arthur Henry Hallam a "significant jealousy which has too often been passed over" (50). Both were aspiring poets, and only when Hallam adopted the role of Tennyson's unofficial agent and promoter did the jealousy subside. Thorn defends Tennyson, however, from charges of homosexuality, claiming that male friendships in the nineteenth century were more openly affectionate than in modern times.

Thorn also takes issue with earlier critics who claim the Cambridge Apostles had coerced Tennyson into abandoning efforts to write aesthetic verse and instead adopt a high moralistic tone in his poetry. To support his claim, Thorn presents evidence of the encouragement the poet received to publish works such as "Anacaona," which was actually a favorite among the Apostles. He acknowledges, however, that the pressure to do something grand — pressure begun during Tennyson's college days and continued even through the 1840s — insured that his poems would eventually "not only be didactic but on a much grander scale" than they had been during the first thirty years of his life.

Thorn has mixed reactions to Tennyson's major poems. He admires Tennyson for breaking with tradition to write about medieval subjects in *The Princess* — something one might not realize in light of the large volume of Victorian poetry about medieval subjects that followed Tennyson's experiments with this genre. His discussion of *In Memoriam* is detailed and insightful, especially his depiction of Tennyson's exploration of the themes of grief and loss that the poet exploited so successfully. Among all of Tennyson's poems, Thorn says, *Maud* is "the most readily accessible to the modern mind" (282) because both its subject and its techniques appeal to modern tastes. In Thorn's opinion the *Idylls* have been devalued in some respects, and critics who believe that Tennyson displays a "sedate and secluded respectability" in the individual idylls are wrong (294). Nevertheless, Tennyson's attempt to write an Arthurian epic eventually fails; *Idylls of the King* is simply not able to live up to either the Victorians' belief that it represents the ideal, nor "more recent attempts to defend [it] as a large-scale achievement" (327). Thorn treats most of Tennyson's later poems with sensitivity, however, claiming the poet produced much of value during the last decades of his life.

More than any other biographer, Thorn speculates extensively on Tennyson's relationships with women, particularly Rosa Baring (whom Thorn insists he loved passionately), Sophie Rawnsley (with whom he was infatuated both before and after his own marriage), Julia Cameron (who dominated him during his years at Farringford), and Emily Sellwood (who would become his soul mate for nearly half a century). Perhaps no other writer has discussed so candidly the growing estrangement between the poet and his wife, an estrangement due in part to her physical condition but more likely due to their wide differences in temperament. Emily Sellwood Tennyson is presented not simply as a helpless invalid, however; on several occasions Thorn shows her acting as the power behind the throne to urge Tennyson to accept honors or conduct business deals in a way that may have been uncomfortable for him were it not for her support. In discussing these relationships, and in assessing Tennyson's many other interactions with family, friends, official figures, and even strangers, Thorn develops a well-rounded portrait of the man behind the Victorian myth that had obscured his value as a poet for much of the twentieth century.

The second major biography to appear in 1993, Peter Levi's *Tennyson*, is intentionally light on critical analysis. Levi, a distinguished British poet and Oxford scholar, consciously ignores "the pure critics" (2) so he can concentrate on telling what he calls Tennyson's fascinating life story. For him, Tennyson is an engaging subject whose early life was fraught with domestic and personal trials, but whose years as England's most celebrated poet were distinguished by his devotion to the family he waited so long to have. Not surprisingly, Levi devotes two-thirds of his study to examining the first forty years of Tennyson's life, those *angst*-filled times when he dealt first with a domineering father, then a hostile press, then the oppressive loss of his closest friend. At the same time, he found himself having to delay marriage to a woman he fell for almost instantly in the 1830s but whom he could wed only when he had become financially secure and her father became convinced that Alfred would not be as difficult a husband for Emily Sellwood as his brother Charles had been for her sister Louisa.

Levi tends to focus on Tennyson's personal relationships, repeating the sights and sounds of places that remained with the exceptionally sensitive poet and found their way into his best poems. His method is to create vignettes of Tennyson's life with family, friends, and others he met in a professional capacity to reveal the character of the man who eventually came to symbolize all things Victorian. Following Jerome Buckley's assessment, however, and in contrast to received opinion from Nicolson to the end of the century, Levi asserts that Tennyson was not unduly influenced by those closest to him, not even the members of the Apostles who pushed him hard to write moralistic treatises on subjects of public importance. In fact, Levi asserts, if "Tennyson had relied really and fully on his friends or his sisters or his mother for criticism, he would have got lost"; instead, "he relied deeply on himself," producing poem after poem that became better for his careful revision (125). In fact, Levi slips out of academic character to take shots at scholars who criticize the poet for his constant complaints of poverty and disinheritance. "These same scholars are salaried, they are fat cats," Levi says (129); they do not realize the depths to which Tennyson's financial status pushed him during the 1820s through the 1840s.

Nevertheless, though he is generous in praising the poet's craftsmanship, Levi tends to align himself with those critics who value the lyrical Tennyson over the poet laureate. "If it is possible to judge such a thing," Levi says, 1842 was "the moment of Alfred Tennyson's supremacy as a poet." If he had not published anything after that year, "and published only what there was then of *In Memoriam*" — most of the shorter lyrics but not the preface and epilogue — "it is arguable that his reputation would stand higher than it does today, at least with the small elite of poets and lovers of poetry who would have pursued him through libraries and antiquarian bookshops" (162). Even more telling is his observation regarding the poet's self-aggrandizement during his years as laureate, when he began comparing himself with Shakespeare. He may have been a master craftsman, Levi admits, "but a poet who has perfect ability to express and nothing to say is in a fatal position" (200).

Surprisingly, Levi praises *The Princess* as "a work of astonishing originality" (184) — but believes the subsequent changes, including the addition of the songs and prince's weird seizures, diminish the poem. He finds *Maud* a poem of great merit, but not a masterpiece. *Idylls of the King* is flawed; despite Tennyson's attempts to piece together individual idylls into some coherent whole, they remain no more than loosely connected, "and that is one of their deepest faults" (228). The best Levi can say of Tennyson's Arthurian poem — which he cannot bring to treat as a single entity — is that the *Idylls* are an "extraordinary *tour de force*" invented and sustained so well by their creator that "they never fall to a disastrous level" (234). Levi's final comments on the poem reveal his true assessment: "It would be unjust to Tennyson to carry over the huge botch of *Idylls of the King* to obscure the rest of his reputation" (247).

Writing with the perspective of a century since Tennyson's death, Levi is able to demonstrate what his contemporaries and many modern critics could not see: the laureate became a harsh critic of his own age, never fully accepting the material values that characterized his century, turning the Idea of Progress on its head in his later work and demanding that there was something more to human existence than the findings of science would suggest. Levi seems delighted to reveal to readers a gifted craftsman, a man of character and principle, and a restless seeker after truth — all wrapped into a single personality whose poetry both represents his age and speaks to ages to come.

In what may have been an unusual decision, the editors of the *New Yorker* commissioned veteran biographer Ian Hamilton to review the Thorn and Levi biographies. Actually, however, "Tennyson, Anyone?" is more than that, for Hamilton uses the occasion to assess Tennyson's reputation a century after his death. While some academic critics might claim that Tennyson's status as one of the greatest poets of all time might be assured, Hamilton claims "a weakness for Tennyson still needs to be explained" (116). While he is hard on critics of earlier decades — T. S. Eliot, Nicolson, and others who helped to explode the Tennyson myth so carefully created by the Victorians and by Tennyson's family — Hamilton himself believes that it is hard to know and appreciate the man behind the laureate's mask. Many of his works are too long and tedious; *Idylls of the King, Maud,* and even *In Memoriam* fall into that category. In Hamilton's review, Tennyson remains "the most skippable and the least skippable of poets," who wrote too much and whose best work needs salvaging. The voices of Nicolson, Eliot, Baum, and others rise in chorus behind Hamilton's summary judgment.

A third major study published in 1993, less detailed than Thorn's or Levi's in providing biographical information but perhaps stronger in scholarly analysis, is Leonée Ormond's *Alfred Tennyson: A Literary Life* (1993). Ormond, a former editor of the *Tennyson Research Bulletin,* offers a series of sound judgments about individual poems in a book organized to demonstrate the relationship of events in Tennyson's life to his work. While she offers no new revelations about the poet's life — one must turn to Levi or especially to Thorn for the latest biographical information — she is especially good in describing ways the landscapes Tennyson visited appear in his work. Ormond is also adept at summarizing the political, economic, religious, and scientific controversies that motivated the poet.

Like Marion Shaw and other feminist writers, Ormond acknowledges how much the young Tennyson "expresses his own feelings by dramatizing the emotions of a woman" (24). She also notes how, as he grew older, his view of women became less idealistic, though his view of men did not necessarily improve. For example, she believes *The Princess* is "not a feminist work," but neither is it "a celebration of masculinity" (99). She is not particularly enlightening regarding Tennyson's relationship with real women, however; her account of his courtship and marriage to Emily Sellwood is handled with exceptional brevity and almost no judgment. In her later chapters, Ormond attempts to demonstrate that Emily was a woman of some capability and judgment, but she does not go as far as other biographers in emphasizing the strains on the marriage caused by Tennyson's exceptional self-centeredness, especially once he became poet laureate. She is not afraid to offer harsh criticism of some of his actions, however, such as calling home his son Hallam when Emily could no longer serve as personal secretary, a move Ormond calls "inexcusable" (176).

Echoing Valerie Pitt, Ormond believes Tennyson gave himself completely to the role of poet laureate, treating the position not simply as a sinecure requiring the composition of occasional verse. Ormond demonstrates how, from his earliest years, Tennyson was conscious of the need to reach a wide audience, and the laureateship gave him the platform from which he could do so. At the same time, she says, Tennyson began to sense that "poetry occupied a less central place in the culture of his own time than it had in the romantic period." His reaction to this phenomenon was to try even harder to be "a link in a chain," a poet speaking to his people (152). Nevertheless, Ormond argues throughout her study that "Tennyson was no intellectual" (14). Though a great poet, he "was alarmingly ordinary in other matters" (146), and in later life he associated with men such as Thomas Woolner and Francis Palgrave, whose intellectual prowess was, in Ormond's view, no greater than his own (167).

In a 1989 essay, "Vocation and Evocation," Herbert Tucker had made a strong case for the importance of "The Two Voices" in the Tennyson canon. In *Critical Essays on Alfred Lord Tennyson* (1993) he collects a baker's dozen essays and chapters from important monographs, giving readers "an ensemble overview of Tennyson's work from the vantage of the 1980s" (xi). The volume includes an overview of Tennyson by veteran scholars Edgar Shannon and Cecil Lang, from their edition of Tennyson's letters; chapters from books by Alan Sinfield, Isobel Armstrong, Eve Kosofsky Sedgwick, Marion Shaw, and Tucker himself; and articles reprinted from important scholarly journals, including Elliot Gilbert's excellent reading of *Idylls of the King* (1982).

In *High Victorian Culture* (1993), David Morse focuses on *In Memoriam* to illustrate the symmetry between the way Tennyson's attempt to work out his personal reaction to Hallam's death and the way the general public struggled to deal with the revelations of science about the nature of the natural world. Morse presents an imaginative and convincing argument that Tennyson was influenced not only by scientific works such as Charles Lyell's *Principles of Geology* and Robert Chambers's *Vestiges of Creation,* but also by the spiritual writings of Augustus and Julius Hare. Their work stressed that humankind has innate potential, yet to be realized, and that the course of history shows a steady progress toward the idealization of human nature. Such an argument, Morse says, would have appealed to Tennyson, since it offered him a way to explain his own loss and help provide a solution to the general feeling of loss among those whose faith was being shaken. The issue of Tennyson's relationship to scientific discovery was taken up two years later, in greater detail, by Patricia O'Neill in "Victorian Lucretius: Tennyson and the Problem of Scientific Romanticism" (1997). Both Morse and O'Neill stress the poet's familiarity with contemporary science, but O'Neill's closing comments seem to express the majority critical opinion regarding Tennyson's use of scientific information: "Tennyson is not interested in refuting the discoveries of science, but in pointing out the limitations of all forms of human knowledge" (118).

An excellent example of the way critical theorists handled Tennyson's major work is Richard Brantley's study of *In Memoriam* in *Anglo-American Antiphonies* (1994). Beginning with the premise that Tennyson and his American contemporary Ralph Waldo Emerson "theologize empiricism" (1), Brantley demonstrates systematically how both link evangelism and empiricism to explore fundamental philosophical questions in their writings. Using *In Memoriam* as his exemplary text, Brantley employs his exceptional skills as an intellectual historian to demonstrate how the poem displays the union of two philosophical concepts normally thought to be antithetical. According to Brantley, Tennyson's aim in the elegy for Arthur Henry Hallam is actually an attempt "to reconcile empiricism with evangelicism" (28). Brantley argues that Tennyson is actually a late Romantic, and that the language of his work demonstrates his close ties to that tradition. He also links Tennyson to two important intellectual predecessors in the evangelical tradition, the American Jonathan Edwards and the Englishman John Wesley, founder of Methodism. In the course of making his case, Brantley answers the objections of postmodernists who find in the poem "only the wan theology of a proto-late-twentieth-century language theory" (123); he also provides an exceptionally fine analysis of commentary from the mid-nineteenth century through the twentieth. As a consequence, his claim that "*In Memoriam* does not so much repudiate as recast its Romantic heritage" (148) rings true.

A second theoretical study published in the same year, Matthew Rowlinson's *Tennyson's Fixations: Psychoanalysis and the Topics of the Early Poetry* (1994) makes extensive use of the writings of Freud, supplemented by the work of Lacan and Derrida. Rowlinson aims to "develop procedures of hermeneutic and formal analysis" for use in examining all nineteenth-century lyric poetry. He selects Tennyson's early poems as texts for study because he finds them excellent examples of "the materiality of language, as manifested . . . in its rhythmic articulations and in its iterability" (vii). His introductory chapter provides the theoretical framework for his examination; the insights of Freud and Lacan, he argues, can help readers understand what lies beneath the surface in Tennyson's disparate acts of writing individual poems. The bulk of Rowlinson's study consists of detailed, speculative readings of "Armageddon," "Timbuctoo," "The Hesperides," "The Lady of Shalott," "Mariana," "Ulysses," and "Tithonus." Like *Anglo-American Antiphonies*, *Tennyson's Fixations* is a good example of ways poststructuralist theories have been used to reinterpret and revalue Tennyson's work.

A more traditional study of influence published in 1995, Andrew Elfenbein's *Byron and the Victorians*, offers new insights into Tennyson's relationship with Byron. Similar to George Ford's 1944 study of Keats and his

Victorian inheritors, Elfenbein's book is an exploration of ways one of the major Romantic poets affected those who grew up, so to speak, on his poetry. As Elfenbein notes, Tennyson had expressed great admiration for Byron, but had modeled his own early work on Wordsworth and Shelley. In fact, much of the young Tennyson's poetry seems to be a reaction against the Byronic hero, despite the Tennyson's tendency to avoid dealing with larger social and moral issues. In later years, however, echoes of Byron emerge, and Elfenbein claims that *Maud* is a Byronic poem. At the end of his assessment of Tennyson's debt to Byron, Elfenbein makes an observation worth noting: Tennyson's early rejection of Byron, and his later return to one of his acknowledged masters, is parallel to the pattern T. S. Eliot followed in first rejecting and then embracing (albeit silently) much of what he found in Tennyson's poetry.

How far theoretical study can be extended to reinterpret Tennyson's works may best be seen, however, in W. David Shaw's *Alfred, Lord Tennyson: The Poet in an Age of Theory* (1996). Shaw's study, completed for the Twayne English Authors Series, is not an updating of James Kissane's 1970 volume in the same series. Rather, it is a brief collection of essays in which Shaw uses a variety of poststructuralist approaches to reexamine some of Tennyson's major and minor poems. By the time this book appeared, Shaw had established himself as one of the two or three preeminent Victorian scholars of his generation. His 1984 study *Tennyson's Style*, discussed above, consolidated the fine work he had done in periodicals during the 1970s and 1980s. During the next decade, he continued to publish prolifically: An article on genre appeared (1985), one contrasting Hopkins and Tennyson (1989), and another focusing on Tennyson's elegies (1993). Criticism of Tennyson's work is included in his 1990 study *Victorians and Mystery: Crises of Representation* and his 1994 monograph *Elegy and Paradox: Testing the Conventions*. His examination of Victorian poetic theory, *The Lucid Veil: Poetic Truth in the Victorian Age* (1987) cites several Tennyson's poems as examples of the continuance of Romantic poetics in the Victorian era. Shaw would go on to write about Tennyson's dramatic monologues in his 1999 study *Origins of the Monologue: The Hidden God*. It is no surprise that Gerhard Joseph, a contemporary practitioner of critical theory, believes that Shaw's work on the Victorians should be compared with that of M. H. Abrams, the great critic of the Romantic poets (*Tennyson and the Text*, 88).

Organized quite differently from most other Twayne books, Shaw's study is divided into three major subdivisions, focusing on the different genres in which Tennyson worked. Ranging from feminism to theories of performance, and exploring the implications of ideas of silent reading and theories of power, Shaw creates bold new readings of Tennyson's dramatic monologues and *Idylls of the King*. His bibliographical essay at the end of the volume provides an excellent summary of the best theoretical studies of

Tennyson's poetry to date. Unquestionably, Shaw's deep appreciation of Tennyson and his sound knowledge of the work of poststructuralists combine to make *Alfred, Lord Tennyson: The Poet in an Age of Theory* a master work in applied criticism.

A 1996 collection of essays edited by Rebecca Stott in the Longman Critical Reader series is similar to Herbert Tucker's 1993 volume both in its breadth of theoretical background and in the quality of contributions. *Tennyson* (1996) contains eleven essays, all previously published either in first-rate journals or as chapters in influential books. The theoretical work of Derrida, Foucault, and Lacan, as well as the best thinking in gender studies, Marxism, and new historicism underpin the work of contributors such as Terry Eagleton, Alan Sinfield, Isobel Armstrong, and Elaine Jordan. Among them the authors discuss several important lyrics and all the major poems except *Idylls of the King*.

One lacuna in the study of Tennyson's work had been criticism of his dramas. The omission may have been appropriate, since the plays had received only lukewarm approval by Tennyson's contemporaries, and few critics had found much merit in them. Consequently, by the end of the century, even biographers were devoting little attention to Tennyson's stage dramas. Nevertheless, Elton Edward Smith found them worthy of a monograph. His *Tennyson's "Epic Drama"* (1997) is written from the premise that "the measure of Tennyson can be taken only by the consideration of all his work" (xi). Smith attempts to make a case for the importance of Tennyson's drama by highlighting the dramatic qualities of his earlier poetry, thereby demonstrating the poet's lifelong interest in drama as an art form. Smith believes Tennyson "would not agree to an easy dismissal of his drama" (129), but few of Smith's contemporaries would agree with him that the laureate was a good judge of his own dramatic work.

Following the principles laid down by Alan Sinfield, John Brannigan considers the dissident qualities of Tennyson's poetry in *New Historicism and Cultural Materialism* (1998), a guide for readers wishing to understand how these theories work to illuminate literary works as cultural texts. Brannigan uses Tennyson's poetry to demonstrate "the uses and the limitations of the critical practices of both" new historicism and cultural materialism (13). Though brief, his commentary on poems such as *In Memoriam* and *Idylls of the King* suggests their complexity as cultural documents; both display not only qualities of the dominant culture, but signs of dissidence that undermine mainstream Victorian ideology. Brannigan's close readings of "Crossing the Bar" and "Ulysses" demonstrate the possibility of multiple readings that may be supported by the same text.

Another important 1998 study, Antony Harrison's *Victorian Poets and the Politics of Culture*, provides a similar analysis of Tennyson's influence on Victorian culture. Harrison, whose provocative analysis of *Maud* had been included in his 1990 study *Victorian Poets and Romantic Poems,* writes in *Victorian Poets and the Politics of Culture* about ways "literary texts" can act as "material forces in the world and mold readers' values, expectations, and behavior" (1). Harrison devotes a chapter to Tennyson's career. Despite Tennyson's early claims that he did not wish to be famous, Harrison explains how the poet fashioned a persona by aligning himself with the Queen in the minds of his countrymen, gaining for himself authority as both spokesperson for middle-class values and eventually prophet and sage. Tennyson achieved success because he "successfully negotiated a number of conflicting Victorian discourses: historicist and transcendentalist; populist and elitist; nationalist and imperialist; positivist and spiritualist; feminist and antifeminist" (49). Harrison's reading of *Idylls of the King* explains why the work appealed to the Victorians, and notes how Tennyson used it to shape attitudes and values. Tennyson remains popular a century after his death, Harrison argues, because his poetry is capable of eliciting multiple responses from different audiences: it appealed to the Victorians because it most often told them "what they already knew and believed"; it speaks to readers in the late twentieth century by telling them "what we can only with difficulty understand" about our Victorian forebears (70).

Colin Graham's *Ideologies of Epic: Nation, Empire, and Victorian Epic Poetry* (1998) contains a major discussion of *Idylls of the King,* offering a revisionist view that places the poem in the epic tradition despite claims by earlier critics that the work is too disjointed structurally to qualify for inclusion in the genre. Relying on the theoretical principles of Mikhail Bahktin, Graham argues that the significance of the poem is not principally in its "modernity," as many earlier twentieth-century critics have claimed (25). Just as its first readers, the Victorians, misunderstood the work because there was at that time "a void in ways of addressing poetic form" (28), so modern critics have missed the significant cultural tensions that are played out beneath the surface Arthurian narrative. Acknowledging that "Tennyson's poetry had a centrality or aptness to contemporary constructions and voicings of the English nation" by the time he became poet laureate (38), Graham demonstrates how the poet's sense of duty to represent his nation led him to construct a work that sings of the glory and warns of the dangers of empire. Because the Arthurian legend was "an already ideologically charged mythology" (43) understood by the Victorians, Tennyson was able to give the story a Victorian context that appealed to his readers. Graham argues that *Idylls of the King* "not only signals how imperialist views of history, nationality and race are formed and maintained; in its unease with the epic form it uncovers the ways in which imperialism formulates, and seeks to prevent, its own decline" (47). His understanding of theory, coupled with his familiarity with Victorian cultural and political milieu, makes Graham's study another fine example of the way theorists can provide deeper appreciation of controversial works of literature.

One of the more intriguing studies to appear near the end of the century is Matthew Campbell's *Rhythm and Will in Victorian Poetry* (1999). One might have thought the role of the will in shaping Victorian values had been adequately examined in earlier works by Isobel Armstrong (*Victorian Poetry: Poetry, Poetics, and Politics,* 1993) and John R. Reed (*Victorian Will,* 1989). But Campbell's provocative combination of rhythm and will adds a new dimension to our understanding of the ways poets used their art to promote the importance of will — and free choice. Tennyson figures prominently in this study, and Campbell accepts his status as spokesperson for his age seemingly without question.

A sampling of articles published near the end of the 1990s indicates the ways literary theories have helped illuminate aspects of Tennyson's poetry that had been simplified by earlier generations of critics. Dino Franco Felluga uses *Idylls of the King* as a test case for examining the shifting tastes of readers and the responses of publishers in "Tennyson's *Idylls,* Pure Poetry, and the Market" (1997). To be successful, Tennyson had to accommodate readers becoming more accustomed to reading novels if he wanted a large audience and favorable reviews. Tennyson accomplished his purposes, Felluga says, by playing up gender stereotypes, especially fears about women's changing roles. In "Poetics, Metaphysics, Genre: The Stanza Form of *In Memoriam,*" Sarah Gates enlists a variety of literary theorists and philosophers to construct a deeper understanding of the apparent contradictions in Tennyson's elegy. In her essay she explains how Tennyson's stanza form helps bridge the gap between the genres of elegy and lyric.

A decidedly political slant is given to Tennyson's handling of Arthurian materials by Richard D. Mallen in "The 'Crowned Republic' of Tennyson's *Idylls of the King*" (1999). Using the political theory of the king's two bodies, Mallen notes how Tennyson creates Arthur as both real man and symbol of authority; Arthur is successful only when his knights act as equal participants in preserving order in society. This method, Mallen says, allows Tennyson to hold onto notions of monarchy (in which he believed) while acknowledging the progress of society toward more democratic forms of government. All three authors, young scholars heavily influenced by the writings of poststructuralists and new historicists, demonstrate how Tennyson's poems can best be understood within larger cultural, political, and literary contexts.

One might imagine from the foregoing paragraphs that, by the end of the century, Tennyson criticism had become the exclusive purview of literary theorists. But R. L. Brett announces at the outset of *Faith and Doubt: Religion and Secularization in Literature from Wordsworth to Larkin* (1997) that the work is intentionally anti-theory, "impertinently biographical and historical" (1). Harkening back to scholarly methods used by critics practicing a century earlier, Brett explores Tennyson's growing pessimism about religious and social issues. He believes that a careful reading of *In Memoriam* and *Idylls of the King,* two poems that share a common philosophy about human nature and the importance of idealism, reveal "the nightmare of chaos" that "runs through a good deal of Tennyson's poetry" (144). Brett's Tennyson is not the subversive darling of late-century theorists, but the conservative crying out against the progress of materialism. Also more reminiscent of earlier forms of critical inquiry is Robert and Laura Lambdin's *Camelot in the Nineteenth Century: Arthurian Characters in the Poems of Tennyson, Arnold, Morris, and Swinburne* (2000). In this work the authors celebrate Tennyson's ability to create characters that vivify his theme. In the Lambdins' view, the poem demonstrates "the impossibility of perfect loves or deaths among people who are unable to live both morally and in moderation" (97).

James Hood's *Divining Desire: Tennyson and the Poetics of Transcendence* (2000) demonstrates that, at the end of the twentieth century, Tennyson still remains for scholars and students the preeminent Victorian. Using techniques of literary theory developed in the last decades of the century, Hood demonstrates how Tennyson's best works "transcend human limitations by forming a dynamic partnership through which poet and reader create what we call a 'poem.'" Each poem becomes "a locus of transcendence . . . precisely because (ironically) it acknowledges limitations and brokenness, even drawing attention to the insufficiencies of language, its own medium" (24–25). Throughout the Tennyson corpus, Hood argues, readers will find the poet preoccupied with issues of eroticism, aesthetics, and epistemology, because in exploring these subjects Tennyson is able to suggest ways humankind can transcend experiential existence to gain some knowledge of realms of being about which it can have no direct experience.

While theoretical arguments can be difficult to follow at times, Hood is particularly good at making his complex analyses understandable and compelling. He uses "The Lover's Tale" to illustrate his methodology before launching into detailed critiques of Tennyson's major work. Concentrated discussions of representative early poems, especially "The Lady of Shalott," precede chapters on *The Princess, In Memoriam, Maud,* and *Idylls of the King.* Rather than offering relativist value judgments on each poem's place in the Tennyson canon, however, Hood treats them as artifacts intended to provide distinct ways of reaching truths about human existence. His discussion of *Idylls of the King* is perhaps the most intriguing, because he argues that Tennyson intends for readers to see that the failure of Arthur to establish a utopian kingdom on earth is actually a sign of his success in becoming a symbol of the unattainable.

In his discussions of individual poems, Hood demonstrates exceptional grasp of recent criticism and a simultaneous appreciation for the critical tradition from the Victorian age to the onset of theoretical analysis that characterizes much of the published work on Tennyson since 1980. There is a certain irony, too, in Hood's conclusions about the value of Tennyson's work. "Tennyson's poetry," he says in his concluding epilogue, "provides one of the most compelling examples of a culture reconfiguring its conception of the transcendent." As such, it "gave voice to the deepest desires of [Victorian] culture" (190). This is the reason Tennyson was so popular with his contemporaries. It appears also to be a sufficient reason for critics of the late twentieth century to continue to study the work of a poet who was once praised, and then denigrated, for being representative of his age.

If one wishes to view a "snapshot" of the status of Tennyson criticism, and of the poet's reputation, at the close of the twentieth century, one need look no farther than Adam Roberts's edition of the poet's work for Oxford University Press. *Alfred Tennyson: A Critical Edition of the Major Works* (2000) is nearly twice as long as the selections prepared by Auden in 1944. *The Princess, In Memoriam,* and *Maud* are reprinted in their entirety; only *Idylls of the King* is excerpted (curiously, some might judge). What is notable, however, is that Roberts's introduction deals honestly with the poet's strengths and weaknesses. There is no special pleading for works that now seem dated, and Roberts's acknowledgement that Tennyson is the Victorian poet most closely tied to his age is stated with the assurance that readers in the twenty-first century will not shrink repugnantly from that judgment. One might say with some certainty that Tennyson has — finally — settled comfortably into his "place" among the great poets of the English language.

Works Cited

Armstrong, Isobel. *Victorian Poetry: Poetry, Poetics, and Politics.* New York: Routledge, 1993.

Barreca Regina, ed. *Sex and Death in Victorian Literature.* Bloomington: Indiana UP, 1990.

Brannigan, John. *New Historicism and Cultural Materialism.* New York: St. Martin's, 1998.

Brantley, Richard E. *Anglo American Antiphony: The Late Romanticism of Tennyson and Emerson.* Gainesville: UP of Florida, 1994.

Brett, R. L. *Faith and Doubt: Religion and Secularization in Literature from Wordsworth to Larkin.* Macon, GA: Mercer UP, 1997. 125–60.

Brisman, Leslie. "*Maud:* The Feminine as the Crux of Influence." *Studies in Romanticism* 31:1 (Spring 1992): 21–43.

Buckley, Jerome H. *Tennyson: The Growth of a Poet.* Cambridge, MA: Harvard UP, 1960. Boston: Houghton Mifflin, 1965.

Campbell, Matthew. *Rhythm and Will in Victorian Poetry*. Cambridge: Cambridge UP, 1999.

Collins, Philip, ed. *Tennyson: Seven Essays*. New York: St. Martin's, 1992.

Elfenbein, Andrew. *Byron and the Victorians*. Cambridge: Cambridge UP, 1995. 169–205.

Felluga, Dino Franco. "Tennyson's *Idylls*, Pure Poetry, and the Market." *SEL: Studies in English Literature, 1500–1900* 37:4 (Autumn 1997): 783–803.

Gates, Sarah. "Poetics, Metaphysics, Genre: The Stanza Form of *In Memoriam*." *Victorian Poetry* 37 (1999): 507–19.

Gilbert, Elliot L. "The Female King: Tennyson's Arthurian Apocalypse." *PMLA* 98:5 (October 1983): 863–78.

Graham, Colin. *Ideologies of Epic: Nation, Empire and Victorian Epic Poetry*. Manchester: Manchester UP, 1998.

Haines, Simon. "Victorian Self Fashioning: Tennyson One Hundred Years After." *Critical Review*. 32 (1992): 69–94.

Hair, Donald S. "'Matter Moulded Forms of Speech.'" *Victorian Poetry* 27:1 (Spring 1989): 1–15.

———. "Soul and Spirit in *In Memoriam*." *Victorian Poetry* 34:2 (Summer 1996): 175–91.

———. "Tennyson's Faith: A Re-Examination." *University of Toronto Quarterly* (Winter 1985–1986): 185–203.

———. *Tennyson's Language*. Toronto: U of Toronto P, 1991.

Hamilton, Ian. "Tennyson, Anyone?" *New Yorker* (22–29 August 1994): 116–21.

Harrison, Antony H. *Victorian Poets and the Politics of Culture: Discourse and Ideology*. Charlottesville: UP of Virginia, 1998.

———. *Victorian Poets and Romantic Poems*. Charlottesville: UP of Virginia, 1990. 69–89.

Harrison, Antony H., and Beverly Taylor, eds. *Gender and Discourse in Victorian Literature and Art*. DeKalb: Northern Illinois Press, 1992.

Hood, James W. *Divining Desire: Tennyson and the Poetics of Transcendence*. Burlington, VT: Ashgate, 2000.

Hooker, Deborah. "Ambiguous Bodies: Keats and the Problem of Resurrection in Tennyson's 'Demeter and Persephone.'" In *Gender and Discourse in Victorian Literature and Art*. Ed. Anthony H. Harrison and Beverly Taylor. DeKalb: Northern Illinois Press, 1992.

Joseph, Gerhard. "Tennyson's Sword: From 'Mungo the American' to *Idylls of the King*." In *Sex and Death in Victorian Literature*. Ed. Regina Barreca. Bloomington: Indiana UP, 1990. 60–68.

Joseph, Gerhard, ed. "Centennial of Alfred, Lord Tennyson." *Victorian Poetry* 30 (Autumn/Winter 1992): 3–4.

———. *Tennyson and the Text: The Weaver's Shuttle*. Cambridge: Cambridge UP, 1992.

———. *Tennysonian Love: The Strange Diagonal*. Minneapolis: U of Minnesota P, 1969.

Levi, Peter. *Tennyson*. New York: Scribner's, 1993.

Lambdin, Laura C., and Robert Thomas Lambdin. *Camelot in the Nineteenth Century: Arthurian Characters in the Poems of Tennyson, Arnold, Morris, and Swinburne* Westport, CT: Greenwood Press, 2000. 13–50.

Mallen, Richard. "The 'Crowned Republic' of Tennyson's *Idylls of the King*." *Victorian Poetry* 37 (1999): 275–89.

Manning, Sylvia. "Death and Sex from Tennyson's Early Poetry to *In Memoriam*." In *Sex and Death in Victorian Literature*. Ed. Regina Barreca. Bloomington: Indiana UP, 1990. 194–220.

Maxwell, Catherine. "Engendering Vision in the Victorian Male Poet." In *Writing and Victorianism*. Ed. J. B. Bullen. London: Longmans, 1997. 73–103.

Morgan, Thais, ed. *Victorian Sages and Cultural Discourse: Renegotiating Gender and Power*. New Brunswick, NJ: Rutgers UP, 1990.

Morse, David. "Keeping the Faith: Newman, F. D. Maurice, Tennyson and Trollope." *High Victorian Culture*. New York: New York UP, 1993. 218–98.

O'Neill, Patricia. "Victorian Lucretius: Tennyson and the Problem of Scientific Romanticism." In *Writing and Victorianism*. Ed. J. B. Bullen. London: Longmans, 1997. 73–103.

Ormond, Leonée. *Alfred Tennyson: A Literary Life*. New York: St. Martin's, 1993.

Pinion, F. B. *A Tennyson Chronology*. London: Macmillan, 1990.

Reed, John R. *Victorian Will*. Athens: Ohio UP, 1989.

Roberts, Adam, ed. *Alfred Tennyson*. Oxford: Oxford UP, 2000.

Rowlinson, Matthew C. *Tennyson's Fixations: Psychoanalysis and the Topics of the Early Poetry*. Charlottesville: UP of Virginia, 1994.

Shaw, W. David. *Alfred Lord Tennyson: The Poet in an Age of Theory*. New York: Twayne; London: Prentice Hall International, 1996.

———. *Elegy and Paradox: Testing the Conventions*. Baltimore: Johns Hopkins UP, 1994.

———. "Impact and Tremor in Tennyson's Elegies: The Power of Genre." *Victorian Poetry* 31 (Summer 1993): 127–42.

———. "Incomprehensible Certainties and Interesting Uncertainties: Hopkins and Tennyson." *Texas Studies in Literature and Language* 31:1 (Spring 1989): 66–84. Reprinted in *Victorians and Mystery: Crises of Representation*. Ithaca, NY: Cornell UP, 1990. 88–106.

———. *The Lucid Veil: Poetic Truth in the Victorian Age*. London: Athlone Press, 1987.

———. *Origins of the Monologue: The Hidden God*. Toronto: U of Toronto P, 1999.

———. "Philosophy and Genre in Victorian Poetics: The Idealist Legacy." *ELH* 52:2 (Summer 1985): 471–501.

Shires, Linda M. "Rereading Tennyson's Gender Politics." In *Victorian Sages and Cultural Discourse: Renegotiating Gender and Power*. Ed. Thais Morgan. New Brunswick, NJ: Rutgers UP, 1990. 46–65.

Simpson, Roger. *Camelot Regained: The Arthurian Revival and Tennyson, 1800–1849*. Cambridge; Wolfeboro, NH: D. S. Brewer, 1990.

Smith, Elton E. *Tennyson's "Epic Drama."* Lanham, MD: UP of America, 1997.

Stott, Rebecca, ed. *Tennyson*. London: Longman, 1996.

Taylor, Beverly. "'School-Miss Alfred' and 'Materfamilias': Female Sexuality and Poetic Voice in *The Princess* and *Aurora Leigh*." In *Gender and Discourse in Victorian Literature and Art*. Ed. Anthony H. Harrison and Beverly Taylor. DeKalb: Northern Illinois Press, 1992.

Tennyson, Hallam. *Alfred Lord Tennyson: A Memoir*. 2 vols. London: Macmillan, 1897.

Thorn, Michael. *Tennyson*. New York: St. Martin's, 1993.

Tucker, Herbert F., ed. *Critical Essays on Alfred Lord Tennyson*. New York: G. K. Hall; Toronto: Maxwell Macmillan Canada, 1993.

———. "Vocation and Evocation: The Dialogue of Genesis in Tennyson's 'The Two Voices.'" In *Victorian Connections*. Ed. Jerome J. McGann. Charlottesville: UP of Virginia, 1989.

Turley, Richard Marggraf. "Tennyson and the Nineteenth Century Language Debate." *Leeds Studies in English* 28 (1997): 123–40

Victorian Poetry 18 (1980). Special Edition devoted to Tennyson's poetry.

8: A Twenty-First Century Prospectus

WHAT IS THE FUTURE OF TENNYSON STUDIES? Any attempt at a definitive answer would be immediately suspect. The foregoing study demonstrates quite clearly that, like so many other great poets, Tennyson has had as many detractors as supporters. One might think his contemporary, Matthew Arnold, had him in mind when he observed in the opening line of his sonnet to Shakespeare: "Others abide our question. Thou art free." Like all the "others," Tennyson has certainly not been free from questions — about his artistry, his politics, his "representativeness" or his individuality. But there is no guarantee that in the next hundred years, scholars will be as interested in Tennyson or the Victorians as their predecessors in the twentieth century had been.

The signs for Tennyson are mixed. In the twenty years that closed the previous century, more than forty emerging scholars chose Tennyson as the subject for their doctoral dissertations. Quite a few of them have published all or part of their work: Richard Mallen, Dino Franco Felluga, A. A. Markley, Andrew Elfenbein, James Hood, Roger Platizky, and Owen Schur. In the first three years of the twenty-first century, Richard Marggraf Turley's *The Politics of Language in Romantic Literature* (2002) and Robert Douglas-Fairhurst's *Victorian Afterlives: The Shaping Influence in Nineteenth-Century Literature* (2002) include lengthy chapters on Tennyson in volumes that demonstrate the ways poststructuralist scholarship can contribute to our understanding of literature and the creative process. Even the Tennyson Society, long a bastion of what might be called traditional scholarship, has begun to publish the work of scholars more sensitive to late-century developments in theoretical criticism. Roger Ebbatson's 2002 Tennyson Society monograph *Tennyson's English Idyls: History, Narrative, Art* offers readings of individual poems that expose Victorian preconceptions and highlight the unspoken social, political, aesthetic, and gender assumptions on which Tennyson and his contemporaries constructed their art. This may bode well for the Society in soliciting manuscripts for its monograph series and the *Tennyson Research Bulletin*; however, the summary of activities conducted by the Society indicates that large groups of scholars are not gathering to discuss Tennyson. The Modern Language Association has not had a session devoted to Tennyson in some time. The trend away from Tennyson should be understandable to anyone who has witnessed the growing link between the (often unspoken) political assumptions underlying literature and its suitability for critical study. Poets and novelists who espouse openly or tacitly political positions right-of-center may be dismissed as unworthy of serious study. If that happens, there is a good chance that, in the coming years, Tennyson studies could become merely a by-water off the mainstream of critical studies.

If that does not happen — and the political pendulum has been known to swing both ways even in academic circles over the past two centuries — scholars who enjoy reading Tennyson will find numerous opportunities for continued critical investigation. Of course, one may have to become critically adventurous and creative to master the interdisciplinary tools required to examine Tennyson's works as cultural artifacts. More can be done to demonstrate how Tennyson as writing subject creates not only his own identity but also recreates his world through his poetry.

There are still opportunities, too, in the realm of scholarship and textual studies. The thirty volumes of Tennyson's papers produced by Christopher Ricks and Aidan Day for Gale Publishers need to be mined. Among the notes, annotations, and variant readings there might be new light shed on the process of composition or on the sources for some of Tennyson's poems. There might be room, too, for new editions, selected and carefully annotated, to supplement Christopher Ricks's 1987 three-volume edition. Susan Shatto and Marion Shaw's work in the 1980s can serve as a useful example for scholars who want to produce tools for scholars interested in works such as *The Princess, Idylls of the King,* and some of the short works that have attracted significant critical attention, such as "Ulysses," "The Gardener's Daughter," and that magical poem that has emerged as a darling of critics at the close of the century, "The Lady of Shalott."

Such study has proven valuable in the past, and if we can move beyond the extremist position held by some theorists that the text is simply an illusion, it may be possible to heed Herbert Tucker's advice that we "fix ourselves to form" and conduct real cultural studies with Tennyson as a fruitful subject for our inquiry (535). As William Buckler reminds us in the introduction to *Man and His Myths: Tennyson's "Idylls of the King" in Critical Context* (1984) reading is a creative activity, and each reader produces his own version of a poem in the act of reading it. If one agrees with him, then there is hope that Tennyson will appeal to future generations, as new readers and new critics discover the joy of recreating works that have stimulated and satisfied generations of readers before them.

Whatever may happen in the future, it seems to me that a review of the criticism about Tennyson and his poems is revealing not only about the poet but about those who choose him as a subject for critical inquiry. As the foregoing study shows, poems that in one age are disparaged become icons for the next generation; one need only to review what has been written about *Idylls of the King* to see the point proven in spades. How we read our own values into his work will determine how we come to value Tennyson's poems.

Works Cited

Buckler, William E. *Man and His Myths: Tennyson's "Idylls of the King" in Critical Context.* New York: New York UP, 1984.

Douglas-Fairhurst, Robert. *Victorian Afterlives: The Shaping Influence in Nineteenth-Century Literature.* Oxford: Oxford UP, 2002.

Ebbatson, Roger. *Tennyson's English Idyls: History, Narrative, Art.* Lincoln, England: Tennyson Society, 2003.

Tucker, Herbert. "The Fix of Form: An Open Letter." *Victorian Literature and Culture* 27:2 (1999): 531–35.

Turley, Richard Marggraf. *The Politics of Language in Romantic Literature.* London: Palgrave Macmillan, 2002.

Works by Alfred Tennyson

Poems by Two Brothers. London: Louth and Jackson, 1827.

Poems, Chiefly Lyrical. London: Effingham Wilson, 1830.

Poems. London: Edward Moxon & Co., 1833.

Poems. 2 vols. London: Edward Moxon & Co., 1842.

The Princess: A Medley. London: Edward Moxon & Co., 1847.

In Memoriam A. H. H. London: Edward Moxon & Co., 1850.

Ode on the Death of the Duke of Wellington. London: Edward Moxon & Co., 1852.

Maud, and Other Poems. London: Edward Moxon & Co., 1855.

Idylls of the King. London: Edward Moxon & Co., 1859.

Enoch Arden and Other Poems. London: Edward Moxon & Co., 1864.

The Holy Grail and Other Poems. London: Strahan & Co., 1869.

Gareth and Lynette, and Other Poems. London: Strahan & Co., 1872.

Queen Mary. London: Henry S. King, 1875.

Harold. London: Henry S. King, 1877.

The Lover's Tale. London: C. Kegan Paul, 1879.

Ballads and Other Poems. London: C. Kegan Paul, 1880.

Becket. London: Macmillan & Co., 1884.

The Cup and the Falcon. London: Macmillan & Co., 1884.

Tiresias and Other Poems. London: Macmillan & Co., 1885.

Locksley Hall Sixty Years After. London: Macmillan & Co., 1886.

Demeter and Other Poems. London: Macmillan & Co., 1889.

The Foresters. London: Macmillan & Co., 1892.

The Death of Oenone, Akbar's Dream, and Other Poems. London: Macmillan & Co., 1892.

The Devil and the Lady. London: Macmillan & Co., 1930.

Works Cited

1850s

Aytoun, W. E. Review of *Maud*. *Blackwood's Edinburgh Magazine* 78 (September 1855): 311–21. Reprinted in *Notorious Literary Attacks*. Ed. Albert Mordell. New York: Boni & Liveright, 1926; Reprint, Freeport, NY: Books for Libraries Press, 1969. 138–61.

1860s

Bagehot, Walter. "Wordsworth, Tennyson, and Browning; or Pure, Ornate, and Grotesque Art in English Poetry." *National Review* n.s. 1 (November 1864): 27–66. Reprinted in *Literary Studies, II*. London: Longmans Green, 1905; London: J. M. Dent, 1911. 305–52.

Brightwell, Daniel B. *A Concordance to the Entire Works of Alfred Tennyson*. London: Moxon, 1869.

1870s

Swinburne, Algernon Charles. *Under the Microscope*. London: White, 1872. 36–45.

Stedman, E. C. *Victorian Poets*. Boston: Osgood, 1875; Boston: Houghton Mifflin, 1887. 150–233.

Bayne, Peter. *Lessons from My Masters: Carlyle, Tennyson, and Ruskin*. London: J. Clark, 1879.

1880s

Gatty, Alfred. *A Key to Tennyson's "In Memoriam."* London, D. Bogue, 1881. Reprint, New York: Haskell House, 1972.

Genung, John F. *Tennyson's "In Memoriam": Its Purpose and Its Structure: A Study*. Boston: Houghton Mifflin, 1884. Reprint, New York: Haskell House, 1970.

Jennings, Henry J. *Lord Tennyson: A Biographical Sketch*. London: Chatto & Windus, 1884. Rev. and enlarged ed. 1892. Reprint, Folcroft, PA: Folcroft Press, 1972.

Swinburne, Algernon Charles. *Miscellanies*. London: Chatto & Windus, 1886. Reprint, 1895.

Whitman, Walt. "A Word About Tennyson." *Critic* 10 (1 January 1887): 1–2. Reprinted in *November Boughs*. Philadelphia: McKay, 1888. 65–67; *Democratic Vistas*. London: Scott, 1888. 125–29; *Rivulets of Prose*. New York: Greenberg, 1928. 92–98.

Chapman, Elizabeth R. *A Companion to "In Memoriam."* London: Macmillan, 1888. 2nd ed.: London: Macmillan, 1901.

Hutton, R. H. *Literary Essays*. London: Macmillan, 1888.

Robertson, J. M. "The Art of Tennyson." *Essays Towards a Critical Method*. London: Unwin, 1889.

1890s

Cheney, John V. *The Golden Guess: Essays on Poetry and the Poets*. Boston: Lee and Shepard, 1892. 161–201.

Jacobs, Joseph. *Tennyson and "In Memoriam": An Appreciation and a Study*. London: Nutt, 1892. Reprint, Folcroft, PA: Folcroft Press, 1974.

Mabie, Hamilton W. "The Influence of Tennyson in America: Its Sources and Extent." *Review of Reviews* (6 December 1892): 553–56.

Parsons, Eugene. *Tennyson's Life and Poetry: And Mistakes Concerning Tennyson*. Chicago: Craig, 1892.

Paul, Herbert W. "Tennyson." *New Review* 7 (November 1892): 513–32.

"Tennyson." *Blackwood's Edinburgh Magazine* 152 (November 1892): 748–66.

Traill, H. D. "Aspects of Tennyson." *Nineteenth Century* 32 (December 1892): 952–66. Reprinted in *Living Age* 196 (11 February 1893): 415–25.

Waugh, Arthur. *Alfred Lord Tennyson: A Study of His Life and Work*. New York: United States Book Co., 1892; London: Heinemann, 1902.

Canton, William. "Tennyson." *In the Footsteps of the Poets*, ed. David Masson. London: Isbister, 1893.

Carpenter, William B. *The Message of Tennyson*. London: Macmillan, 1893.

Gosse, Edmund. "Tennyson — and After." *Questions at Issue*. London: Heinemann, 1893. 175–98.

Innes, Arthur D. *Seers and Singers: A Study of Five English Poets*. London: A. D. Innes, 1893.

Knowles, James T. "Aspects of Tennyson." *Nineteenth Century* 33 (January 1893): 164–88.

Littledale, Harold. *Essays on Lord Tennyson's "Idylls of the King."* London: Macmillan, 1893.

Luce, Morton. *New Studies in Tennyson, Including a Commentary on "Maud."* London: Baker, 1893. Reprint, Folcroft, PA: Folcroft Press, 1973.

Myers, F. W. H. "Tennyson as Prophet." *Science and a Future Life.* London: Macmillan, 1893. 27–65.

Salt, Henry S. *Tennyson as a Thinker.* London: Reeves, 1893. Reprint, 1909.

Walters, J. C. *Tennyson: Poet, Philosopher, Idealist: Studies of the Life, Work, and Teaching of the Poet Laureate.* London: Kegan Paul, Trench, Trubner, 1893. Reprint, New York: Haskell House, 1971.

Brooke, Stopford A. *Tennyson, His Art and Relation to Modern Life.* London: Isbister; New York: G. P. Putnam's Sons, 1894. 5th ed.: London: Isbister; New York: Putnam, 1902. Reprint, New York: AMS Press, 1970.

MacCallum, M. W. *Tennyson's "Idylls of the King" and Arthurian Story from the XVIth Century.* Glasgow: MacLehose, 1894.

Gurteen, Stephen H. V. *The Arthurian Epic: A Comparative Study of the Cambrian, Breton, and Anglo-Norman Versions of the Story and Tennyson's "Idylls of the King."* New York: Putnam, 1895. Reprint, New York: Haskell House, 1965.

Jacobs, Joseph. "Alfred Tennyson." *Literary Studies.* London: Nutt, 1895. 155–71.

Jones, Richard D. *The Growth of the "Idylls of the King."* Philadelphia: J. B. Lippincott, 1895.

Luce, Morton. *A Handbook to the Works of Alfred, Lord Tennyson.* London: Bell, 1895. Reprint, rev., 1914. Reprint, New York: Burton Franklin, 1970.

Oates, John. *The Teaching of Tennyson.* London: J. Bowden, 1895. 2nd ed. 1898. Reprint, New York: Haskell House, 1973.

Saintsbury, George. "Tennyson." *Corrected Impressions: Essays on Victorian Writers.* London: Heinemann, 1895. New York: Dodd, 1895. 21–40.

Walker, Hugh. *The Greater Victorian Poets: Tennyson, Browning, and Arnold.* London: Swan Sonnenschein, 1895.

Dixon, W. M. *A Tennyson Primer: With a Critical Essay.* London: Methuen, 1896. Reprint, New York: Haskell House, 1971.

Saintsbury, George. "Tennyson." *A History of Nineteenth-Century Literature.* London: Macmillan, 1896. 253–68.

Davidson, Thomas. *A Prolegomena to "In Memoriam."* Boston: Houghton Mifflin, 1897.

Farrar, Frederick W. "Lord Tennyson." *Men I Have Known.* New York: Crowell, 1897. 1–41.

Gosse, Edmund. "Life of Tennyson." *North American Review* 165 (November 1897): 513–26.

Rearden, Timothy H. "Alfred Tennyson, Poet Laureate." *Petrarch and Other Essays*. San Francisco: Doxey, 1897. 43–96.

Stanley, Hiram M. "Tennyson's Rank as a Poet." *Essays on Literary Art*. London: Swan Sonnenschein, 1897. 13–24.

Strong, Augustus Hopkins. "Tennyson." *The Great Poets and Their Theology*. Philadelphia: Griffith and Rowland, 1897. 449–524.

Tennyson, Hallam. *Alfred Lord Tennyson: A Memoir*. 2 vols. London: Macmillan, 1897.

Walker, Hugh. *Age of Tennyson*. London: Bell, 1897.

Armstrong, Richard A. "Alfred Tennyson." *Faith and Doubt in the Century's Poets*. New York: Whitman, 1898. 67–90.

Cuthbertson, Evan J. *Tennyson: The Story of His Life*. London: Chambers, 1898. Reprint, Folcroft, PA: Folcroft Press, 1973.

"Reputations Reconsidered: III. Lord Tennyson." *Academy* 53 (8 January 1898): 34–36.

Royce, Josiah. "Tennyson and Pessimism." *Studies of Good and Evil*. New York: Appleton, 1898. Reprint, Hamden, CT: Archon Books, 1964. 76–88.

Van Dyke, Henry. *The Poetry of Tennyson*. Cambridge: Cambridge UP, 1898. New York: Charles Scribner's Sons, 1902. Rev. and reissued as *Studies in Tennyson*. New York: Scribner, 1920. Reprint, Port Washington, NY: Kennikat Press, 1966.

Adams, Francis. "Tennyson." *Essays in Modernity: Criticism & Dialogues*. London: Lane, 1899. 3–39.

Dawson, W. J. *Makers of Modern Poetry*. 7th ed. London: Hodder and Stoughton, 1899. 169–269.

Gwynn, Steven L. *Tennyson: A Critical Study*. London: Blackie, 1899. Reprint, New York: Haskell House, 1974.

1900s

Harrison, Frederic. "Tennyson." *Tennyson, Ruskin, Mill and Other Literary Estimates*. New York: Macmillan, 1900. 1–47.

Horton, Robert F. *Alfred Tennyson: A Saintly Life*. London: Dent, 1900. Reprint, New York: Haskell House, 1973.

Masterman, C. F. G. *Tennyson as a Religious Teacher*. London: Methuen, 1900.

Sneath, Elias H. *The Mind of Tennyson: His Thoughts on God, Freedom, and Immortality*. Westminster: Constable, 1900. Reprint, New York: Gordian Press, 1970.

Yeats, W. B. "The Symbolism of Poetry." *The Dome,* 1900. Reprinted in *Essays and Introductions.* London: Macmillan, 1961. 153–64.

Bradley, A. C. *A Commentary on Tennyson's "In Memoriam."* New York: Macmillan, 1901. 3rd ed., rev. London: Macmillan, 1915.

Lang, Andrew. *Alfred Tennyson.* New York: Dodd, Mead, 1901.

Luce, Morton. *Tennyson.* London: Dent, 1901.

Moore, John M. *Three Aspects of the Late Alfred Lord Tennyson.* Manchester: Marsden, 1901. Reprint, New York: Haskell House Publishers, 1972.

Lyall, Sir Alfred. *Tennyson.* London: Macmillan, 1902. Reprint, New York: Haskell House, 1977.

Rader, William. *The Elegy of Faith: A Study of "In Memoriam."* New York: Crowell, 1902.

Chesterton, G. K., and Richard Garnett. *Tennyson.* London: Hodder and Stoughton, 1903.

Harrison, Frederic. "Tennyson: A New Estimate." *North American Review* 176 (June 1903): 856–67.

Robertson, J. M. "Tennyson." *Browning and Tennyson as Teachers.* London: Brown, 1903. 1–83.

Stevenson, Morley. *Spiritual Teaching of the Holy Grail.* London: Wells, Gardner, and Darton, 1903.

Benson, Arthur C. *Alfred Tennyson.* New York: Dutton, 1904. Reprint, New York: Greenwood Press, 1969.

Lyttleton, Arthur T. "Tennyson." *Modern Poets of Faith, Doubt, and Other Essays.* London: Murray, 1904. 1–32.

Moulton, Charles W., ed. "Alfred, Lord Tennyson." *The Library of Literary Criticism of English and American Authors.* Vol. 8. Buffalo, NY: Moulton, 1904–5. 64–111.

Pallen, Condé B. *The Meaning of "The Idylls of the King": An Essay in Interpretation.* New York: American Book Co., 1904.

Stevenson, Morley. *Spiritual Teaching of Tennyson's "In Memoriam": Six Lenten Addresses.* London: Gardner, Darton, 1904.

Gordon, William C. *The Social Ideals of Alfred Tennyson as Related to His Time.* London: Unwin; Chicago: U of Chicago P, 1906. Reprint, New York: Haskell House, 1966.

Griggs, Edward H. *The Poetry and Philosophy of Tennyson.* New York: Huebsch, 1906.

Warren, T. Herbert. "*In Memoriam* after Fifty Years." *Edinburgh Review* 203 (April 1906): 297–318.

Genung, John F. *The "Idylls" and the Ages: A Valuation of Tennyson's "Idylls of the King," Elucidated in Part by Comparisons between Tennyson and Browning.* New York: Crowell, 1907.

Gunsaulus, Frank W. "Alfred Tennyson." *The Higher Ministries of Recent English Poetry.* New York: Revell, 1907. 107–17.

Jones, Henry. *The Immortality of the Soul in the Poems of Tennyson and Browning.* Boston: American Unitarian Association, 1907.

Payne, William M. "Alfred Tennyson." *The Greater English Poets of the Nineteenth Century.* New York: Holt, 1907. 221–50.

Smith, Arnold. "Tennyson." *The Main Tendencies of Victorian Poetry.* London: Simkin, Marshall, Hamilton, Kent, 1907. 59–104.

Smyser, William E. *Tennyson.* Cincinnati: Eaton and Mains, 1907.

Tennyson, Hallam, ed. *The Works of Alfred, Lord Tennyson.* 9 vols. London and New York: Macmillan, 1907–8.

Shepherd, Henry E. *A Commentary on Tennyson's "In Memoriam."* New York: Neale, 1908.

Cook, E. W. "Appreciations and Depreciations of Tennyson." *Academy* 77 (28 August 1909): 473–74.

Harrison, Frederic. "The Centenary of Tennyson." *Nineteenth Century and After* 66 (August 1909): 226–33. Reprinted in *Among My Books.* New York: Macmillan, 1912. 284–96.

Hayes, J. W. *Tennyson and Scientific Theology.* London: Stock, 1909. Reprint, Brooklyn, NY: Haskell, 1977.

"Is Tennyson's Influence on the Wane?" *Current Literature* 47 (September 1909): 275–78.

Jones, Henry. "Tennyson." *British Academy Proceedings* 4 (1909): 131–45.

Ker, William P. *Tennyson: The Leslie Stephen Lecture.* Cambridge: Cambridge UP, 1909. Reprinted in *Collected Essays of W. P. Ker.* Vol. 1. London: Macmillan, 1925. 258–76.

Magnus, Laurie. *English Literature in the Nineteenth Century.* New York: Putnam, 1909. 224–42, 280–86.

"Our Debt to Tennyson." *Spectator* 103 (14 August 1909): 230–31.

Warren, T. Herbert. *The Centenary of Tennyson, 1809–1909.* Oxford: Clarendon Press, 1909.

1910s

Austin, Alfred. "A Vindication of Tennyson." *The Bridling of Pegasus: Prose Papers on Poetry.* London: Macmillan, 1910. 197–217.

More, Paul Elmer. "Tennyson." *Shelburne Essays*. 7th Series. New York: Putnam, 1910. 64–94. Reprinted in *Modern Essays*. Ed. J. M. Berdan. New York: Macmillan, 1916. 204–28.

Saintsbury, George. "Tennyson and Browning." *A History of English Prosody, from the Twelfth Century to the Present Day*. Vol. 3. London: Macmillan, 1910. 183–217.

Walker, Hugh. *The Literature of the Victorian Era*. Cambridge: Cambridge UP, 1910. 2nd ed. 1921. 287–309, 374–410.

Gingerich, Solomon F. *Wordsworth, Tennyson, and Browning: A Study in Human Freedom*. Ann Arbor. MI: Wahr, 1911. 113–75. Reprint, New York: Gordian Press, 1968.

Lewis, W. D. "Introduction." *Tennyson's "Idylls of the King."* New York: Merrill, 1911.

Tennyson, Hallam, ed. *Tennyson and His Friends*. London: Macmillan, 1911.

Dixon, William Macneile. "Narrative Poetry in the Nineteenth Century — Tennyson, Morris, Arnold." *English Epic and Heroic Poetry*. London: Dent, 1912. Reprint, New York: Haskell House, 1964. 302–29.

Rawnsley, William F. "Tennyson Centenary." *Introduction to the Poets*. London: Routledge, 1912. 243–313.

Chesterton, G. K. "Great Victorian Poets." *The Victorian Age in Literature*. New York: Holt, 1913; London: Williams & Norgate, 1914. 160–69. Reprint, South Bend, IN: U of Notre Dame P, 1963. 79–103.

Johnson, R. Brimley. *Tennyson and His Poetry*. London: Harrap, 1913. Reprint, Port Washington, NY: Kennikat Press, 1970.

Baker, Arthur E. *A Concordance to the Poetical and Dramatic Works of Alfred, Lord Tennyson*. London: Kegan Paul, Trench, Trubner, 1914. Reprint, New York: Barnes & Noble, 1966.

"Tennyson as a Minor Poet." *Literary Digest* 48 (21 March 1914): 619–20.

Bell, A. F. "Tennyson and Browning." *Leaders of English Literature*. London: Bell, 1915. 182–94.

Gray, W. F. "Alfred, Lord Tennyson." *The Poets Laureate of England*. New York: Dutton, 1915. 252–73.

Lounsbury, Thomas R. *The Life and Times of Tennyson: From 1809 to 1850*. London: Oxford UP; New Haven: Yale UP, 1915.

Turnbull, Arthur. *Life and Writings of Alfred, Lord Tennyson*. New York: Scribner, 1915.

Grierson, Herbert J. C. "The Tennysons." In *Cambridge History of English Literature*. Ed. A. W. Ward and A. R. Waller. Vol. 13. Cambridge: Cambridge UP, 1916. 25–53.

Hearn, Lafcadio. "Studies in Tennyson." In *Appreciations of Poetry*. Ed. J. Erskine. New York: Dodd, Mead, 1916. 30–36.

Alden, Raymond M. *Alfred Tennyson: How to Know Him*. Indianapolis: Bobbs-Merrill, 1917. Reprint, Norwood, PA: Norwood Editions, 1977.

Bradley, A. C. *The Reaction Against Tennyson*. London: Oxford UP, 1917. Reprinted in *A Miscellany*. London: Macmillan, 1929. 1–31; and in *English Critical Essays*. Ed. P. M. Jones. New York: Oxford UP, 1933. 59–87.

Hearnshaw, Fossey J. C. "Tennyson Twenty-Five Years After." *Spectator* 119 (6 October 1917): 352–53.

———. "Tennyson Twenty-Five Years After." *Spectator* 119 (10 November 1917): 522.

Meynell, Alice. "Some Thoughts of a Reader of Tennyson." *Hearts of Controversy*. London: Burns & Oates, 1917. 1–22. Reprinted in *Alice Meynell: Prose & Poetry*. London: Jonathan Cape, 1947. 79–89.

Cook, E. T. "The Second Thoughts of Poets." *Literary Recreations*. London: Macmillan, 1918. 246–317. Reprint, Freeport, NY: Books for Libraries Press, 1968.

Palmer, George H. "Alfred Tennyson." *Formative Types in English Poetry*. Boston: Houghton Mifflin, 1918. 233–69.

Hodgson, Geraldine E. "The Legacy of Tennyson." *Criticism at a Venture*. London: Macdonald, 1919. 167–72.

Rice, William North. "The Poet of Science." *The Poet of Science and Other Addresses*. New York: Abingdon, 1919. 11–45.

1920s

Blore, George H. "Alfred Tennyson." *Victorian Worthies*. London: Milford, 1920. 150–75.

Elton, Oliver. "Tennyson." *A Survey of English Literature, 1830–1880*. Vol. 3. London: Arnold, 1920. 330–61. Rev. and reprinted in *Tennyson and Matthew Arnold*. London: Arnold, 1924. Reprint, New York: Haskell House, 1971.

Pyre, James F. A. *The Formation of Tennyson's Style: A Study, Primarily, of the Versification of the Early Poems*. Madison: U of Wisconsin P, 1920. Reprint, New York: Phaeton Press, 1968.

Smith, Jean Pauline. *The Aesthetic Nature of Tennyson*. New York: White, 1920. Reprint, New York: Haskell House, 1971.

Squire, John C. "Tennyson." *London Mercury* 2 (August 1920): 443–55. Reprinted in *Essays on Poetry*. London: Hodder & Stoughton, 1923. 63–87.

Broadus, Edmund K. *The Laureateship*. Oxford: Clarendon Press, 1921. Reprint, Freeport, NY: Books for Libraries Press, 1966. 184–96.

Chesterton, G. K. "Tennyson." *The Uses of Diversity.* New York: Dodd, Mead, 1921. 18–23.

Lynd, Robert. "Tennyson: A Contemporary Criticism." *Art of Letters.* New York: Scribner, 1921. 134–38.

Starnes, De Witt T. "The Influence of Carlyle on Tennyson." *Texas Review* 6 (July 1921): 316–36.

Fausset, Hugh I'Anson. *Tennyson: A Modern Portrait.* London: Selwyn & Blount; New York: Appleton, 1923.

Nicolson, Sir Harold. *Tennyson: Aspects of His Life, Character and Poetry.* London: Constable, 1923; 2nd ed. Boston: Houghton Mifflin, 1925. Reprint, London: Arrow Books, 1960; Garden City, NY: Anchor Books, 1962.

Warren, T. Herbert. "The Real Tennyson." *Nineteenth Century and After* 94 (October 1923): 507–19.

Hoyt, Arthur S. *The Spiritual Message of Modern English Poetry.* New York: Macmillan, 1924. 67–85, 89–112.

Noyes, Alfred. "Tennyson and Some Recent Critics." *Some Aspects of Modern Poetry.* London: Hodder & Stoughton; New York: Stokes, 1924. Reprinted in *Tennyson.* Edinburgh: Blackie, 1932. 153–99.

Hearn, Lafcadio. "*Idylls of the King.*" *Occidental Gleanings.* Vol. 1. New York: Dodd, Mead, 1925. 1–25.

Mackail, John W. "Tennyson." *Studies of English Poets.* London: Longmans, Green, 1926. 227–51.

Hearn, Lafcadio. "Tennyson and the Great Poetry." *A History of English Literature: A Series of Lectures.* Vol. 2. Tokyo: Hokuseido, 1927. 637–46.

Perry, Henry Ten Eyck. "The Tennyson Tragedy." *Southwest Review* 12 (January 1927): 97–112.

Shanks, Edward B. "The Return of Tennyson." *Second Essays on Literature.* London: Collins, 1927. Reprint, Freeport, NY: Books for Libraries Press, 1968. 163–76.

Atkins, Gaius Glenn. *Reinspecting Victorian Religion.* New York: Macmillan, 1928.

Macy, John. "Tennyson, the Perfect Laureate." *Bookman* (NY) 69 (June 1929): 375–86.

Magnus, Laurie. "Tennyson a Hundred Years After." *Cornhill Magazine* n.s. 68 (May 1929): 660–70.

1930s

Bowden, Marjorie. *Tennyson in France.* Manchester, UK: Manchester UP, 1930.

Harstock, E. "Poor Tennyson." *Personalist* 11 (1930): 28–31.

Lucas, F. L. "Tennyson." *Eight Victorian Poets*. New York: Macmillan, 1930. 3–19. Subsequent editions published as *Ten Victorian Poets*.

Scaife, Christopher H. *Poetry of Alfred Tennyson: An Essay in Appreciation*. London: Cobden-Sanderson, 1930.

Wolfe, Humbert. *Tennyson*. London: Faber & Faber, 1930. Reprint, Freeport, NY: Books for Libraries Press, 1969.

Abercrombie, Lascelles. "Tennyson." In Lascelles Abercrombie, Lord David Cecil, G. K. Chesterton, et al. *Revaluations: Studies in Biography*. London: Oxford UP, 1931. 60–76.

Crum, Ralph B. "Nature Red in Tooth and Claw: Tennyson's Problem." *Scientific Thought in Poetry*. New York: Columbia UP, 1931. 157–90.

Ward, A. C. "Introduction." In Lascelles Abercrombie, Lord David Cecil, G. K. Chesterton, et al. *Revaluations: Studies in Biography*. London: Oxford UP, 1931.

Collier, John. "Lord Tennyson." In *The Great Victorians*. Ed. H. J. Massingham and H. Massingham. London: Nicholson & Watson, 1932. 503–16.

Stevenson, Lionel. "Alfred Tennyson." *Darwin Among the Poets*. Chicago: U of Chicago P, 1932. Reprint, New York: Russell & Russell, 1963. 55–116.

Cruse, Amy. *The Victorians and Their Reading*. London: Allen & Unwin, 1935. Boston: Houghton Mifflin, 1935.

Beach, Joseph Warren. "Tennyson." *The Concept of Nature in Nineteenth-Century English Poetry*. New York: Macmillan, 1936. Reprint, New York: Russell & Russell, 1966. 406–34.

Ehrsam, Theodore G., Robert H. Deily, and Robert M. Smith. "Alfred Lord Tennyson." *Bibliographies of Twelve Victorian Authors*. New York: Wilson, 1936. 299–362.

Eliot, T. S. "*In Memoriam*." *Essays Ancient and Modern*. London: Faber & Faber, 1936; New York: Harcourt, 1936. 175–90.

Weygandt, Cornelius. *The Times of Tennyson: English Victorian Poetry as It Affected America*. New York: Appleton, Century, 1936.

Bush, Douglas. "Tennyson." *Mythology and the Romantic Tradition in English Poetry*. Cambridge, MA: Harvard UP, 1937. 197–228.

Routh, H. V. *Towards the Twentieth Century*. New York: Macmillan, 1937.

Groom, Bernard. *On the Diction of Tennyson, Browning, and Arnold*. Oxford: Clarendon Press, 1939. Reprint, Hamden, CT: Archon, 1970.

Young, G. M. *The Age of Tennyson*. London: Oxford UP, 1939.

1940s

De La Mare, Walter. *Pleasures and Speculations*. London: Faber & Faber, 1940.

Evans, B. Ifor. *Tradition and Romanticism*. London: Methuen, 1940. Reprint, Hamden, CT: Archon Books, 1964.

Paden, W. D. "Tennyson and the Reviewers (1829–1835)." *Studies in English in Honor of Raphael Dorman O'Leary and Selden Lincoln Whitcomb*. Lawrence: U of Kansas P, 1940. Reprint, Freeport, NY: Books for Libraries Press, 1968. 15–39.

Chew, Samuel C. "Introduction." *Tennyson: Representative Poems*. New York: Odyssey, 1941: xi–xlii.

Hearn, Lafcadio. *Lafcadio Hearn's Lectures on Tennyson*. Ed. Shigetsugu Kishi. Tokyo: Hokuseido; Pasadena, CA: Perking, 1941. Reprint, Norwood, PA: Norwood Editions, 1978.

Marchand, Leslie A. "Tennyson." *The Athenaeum: A Mirror of Victorian Culture*. Chapel Hill: U of North Carolina P, 1941. Reprint, New York: Octagon, 1971. 267–82.

Nicolson, Harold. "Tennyson: Fifty Years After." *Poetry Review* 33 (November 1942): 333–36.

Paden, William D. *Tennyson in Egypt: A Study of the Imagery in His Earlier Work*. Lawrence: U of Kansas P, 1942.

Quiller-Couch, Arthur. "Tennyson After Fifty Years." *Poetry Review* 33 (1942): 269–71.

Eidson, John O. *Tennyson in America: His Reputation and Influence from 1827 to 1858*. Athens: U of Georgia P, 1943.

Shannon, Edgar F., Jr. "Tennyson and the Reviewers, 1830–1842." *PMLA* 58 (1943): 181–94.

Auden W. H. "Introduction." *A Selection from the Poems of Tennyson*. New York: Doubleday, 1944.

Basler, Roy P. "Tennyson the Psychologist." *South Atlantic Quarterly* 43 (April 1944): 143–59.

Ford, George H. *Keats and the Victorians: A Study of His Influence and Rise to Fame, 1821–1895*. New Haven, CT: Yale UP, 1944. Reprint, Hamden, CT: Archon Books, 1962. 17–48.

Grierson, Herbert J. C., and J. C. Smith. *A Critical History of English Poetry*. London: Chatto & Windus; New York: Oxford UP, 1944.

Bibliographies of Studies in Victorian Literature. 5 vols. Urbana: U of Illinois P. 1945–1985.

Brooks, Cleanth. *The Well Wrought Urn: Studies in the Structure of Poetry.* New York: Harcourt Brace, 1947.

Fausset, Hugh I'Anson. "The Hidden Tennyson." *Poets and Pundits: Essays and Addresses.* New Haven, CT: Yale UP, 1947. 187–91.

Lucas, F. L. "Introduction." *Tennyson, Poetry and Prose.* Oxford: Clarendon Press, 1947.

Baum, Paull F. *Tennyson Sixty Years After.* Chapel Hill: U of North Carolina P, 1948.

Stevenson, Lionel. "The 'High-Born Maiden' Symbol in Tennyson." *PMLA* 63 (March 1948): 234–43.

Priestley, F. E. L. "Tennyson's *Idylls.*" *University of Toronto Quarterly* 19 (October 1949): 35–49.

Tennyson, Charles. *Alfred Tennyson.* New York: Macmillan, 1949.

Turner, Paul. "The Stupidest English Poet." *English Studies* 30 (February 1949): 1–12.

1950s

Bateson, Frederick W. *Romantic Schizophrenia: English Poetry: A Critical Introduction.* New York: Longmans, 1950.

Carr, Arthur J. "Tennyson as a Modern Poet." *University of Toronto Quarterly* 19 (1950): 361–82. Reprinted in *Victorian Literature: Modern Essays in Criticism.* Ed. Austin Wright. New York: Oxford UP, 1961. 311–33.

Davis, Arthur K., Jr. "Mid-Century Tennyson." *Virginia Quarterly Review* 26 (1950): 307–11.

James, David G. "Wordsworth and Tennyson." *British Academy* 36 (1950): 113–20.

Milmed, Bella K. "*In Memoriam* a Century Later." *Antioch Review* 10 (1950): 471–92.

Templeman, W. D. "Tennyson's 'Locksley Hall' and Thomas Carlyle." *Booker Memorial Studies.* New York: Russell & Russell, 1950. 34–58.

Buckley, Jerome H. "Tennyson — The Two Voices." *The Victorian Temper: A Study in Literary Culture.* Cambridge, MA: Harvard UP, 1951. 66–86.

Green, Joyce. "Tennyson's Development During the 'Ten Years' Silence' (1932–1842)." *PMLA* 66 (September 1951): 662–97.

Mattes, Eleanor B. *"In Memoriam": The Way of a Soul.* New York: Exposition, 1951.

McLuhan, H. Marshall. "Tennyson and Picturesque Poetry." *Essays in Criticism* 1 (July 1951): 262–82.

Bush, Douglas. *English Poetry: The Main Currents from Chaucer to the Present.* New York: Oxford UP, 1952.

Johnson, E. D. H. "Tennyson." *The Alien Vision of Victorian Poetry.* Princeton: Princeton UP, 1952. 3–68.

Shannon, Edgar F., Jr. *Tennyson and the Reviewers; A Study of His Literary Reputation and of the Influence of the Critics upon His Poetry, 1827–1851.* Cambridge, MA: Harvard UP, 1952.

Stevenson, Lionel. "The Pertinacious Victorian Poets." *University of Toronto Quarterly* 21 (April 1952): 237–45.

Shannon, Edgar F. Jr. "The Critical Reception of Tennyson's *Maud.*" *PMLA* 68 (June 1953): 397–417.

Esher, Viscount. "Tennyson's Influence on His Times." *Essays by Divers Hands: Being the Transactions of the Royal Society of Literature* n.s. 28 (1954): 35–47.

Evans, B. Ifor. *Literature and Science.* London: Allen & Unwin, 1954. 72–78.

Tennyson, Sir Charles. *Six Tennyson Essays.* London: Cassell, 1954. Reprint, Wakefield: S. R. Publishers, 1971.

House, Humphry. "Tennyson and the Spirit of the Age." *All in Due Time.* London: Rupert Hart-Davis, 1955. 121–29.

Baum, Paull F. "Alfred Lord Tennyson." In *The Victorian Poets: A Guide to Research.* Ed. Frederick E. Faverty. Cambridge, MA: Harvard UP, 1956.

Beck, Warren. "Clouds Upon Camelot." *English Journal* 45 (1956): 447–54.

de Selincourt, Aubrey. "Alfred, Lord Tennyson." *Six Great Poets.* London: Hamilton, 1956.

Millhauser, Milton. "Tennyson: Artifice and Language." *Journal of Aesthetics and Art Criticism* 14 (1956): 333–38.

Willey, Basil. "Tennyson." *More Nineteenth-Century Studies: A Group of Honest Doubters.* London: Chatto & Windus, 1956. 53–105.

Fairchild, Hoxie N. *Religious Trends in English Poetry.* Vol. 4: *1830–1880: Christianity and Romanticism in the Victorian Era.* New York: Columbia UP, 1957. 102–31.

Lucas, F. L. *Tennyson.* London: Longmans, Green, 1957. Reprint, 1961.

Buckley, Jerome H. "Introduction." *Poems of Tennyson.* Cambridge, MA: Riverside Press, 1958: ix–xxi.

Foakes, Reginald A. "The Rhetoric of Faith." *The Romantic Assertion: A Study in the Language of Nineteenth-Century Poetry.* New Haven, CT: Yale UP, 1958. 111–38.

Killham, John. *Tennyson and "The Princess": Reflections of an Age.* London: Athlone Press, 1958.

Duncan, Edgar H. "Tennyson: A Modern Appraisal." *Tennessee Studies in Literature* 4 (1959): 13–30.

1960s

Buckley, Jerome Hamilton. *Tennyson: The Growth of a Poet*. Cambridge, MA: Harvard UP, 1960. Boston: Houghton Mifflin, 1965.

Killham, John, ed. *Critical Essays on the Poetry of Tennyson*. London: Routledge & Paul; New York: Barnes & Noble, 1960.

Daiches, David. "Imagery and Mood in Tennyson and Whitman." *English Studies Today* 11 (1961): 217–32.

Sanders, Charles R. "Carlyle and Tennyson." *PMLA* 76 (March 1961): 82–97. Reprinted in *Carlyle's Friendships and Other Studies*. Durham, NC: Duke UP, 1977. 192–225.

Benziger, James. "Tennyson." *Images of Eternity: Studies in the Poetry of Religious Vision from Wordsworth to T. S. Eliot*. Carbondale: U of Southern Illinois P, 1962. 138–63.

Danzig, Allan. "The Contraries: A Central Concept in Tennyson's Poetry." *PMLA* 77 (December 1962): 577–85.

Davies, Hugh Sykes. "Lord Tennyson." *The Poets and Their Critics*. Vol. 2. London: Hutchinson, 1962. 243–95.

Pitt, Valerie. *Tennyson Laureate*. London: Barrie & Rockliff, 1962. Toronto: U of Toronto P, 1963.

Reeves, James. *A Short History of English Poetry 1340–1940*. London: Dutton, 1962.

Richardson, Joanna. *The Pre-eminent Victorian: A Study of Tennyson*. London: Jonathan Cape, 1962.

Ryals, Clyde de L. "The 'Heavenly Friend': The 'New Mythus' of *In Memoriam*." *Personalist* 43 (Summer 1962): 383–402.

———. "The Poet as Critic: Appraisals of Tennyson by His Contemporaries." *Tennessee Studies in Literature* 7 (1962): 113–25.

Smalley, Donald. "A New Look at Tennyson — and Especially the *Idylls*." *Journal of English and Germanic Philology* 61 (April 1962): 349–57.

Ball, Patricia M. "Tennyson and the Romantics." *Victorian Poetry* 1 (January 1963): 7–16.

Marshall, George O. *A Tennyson Handbook*. New York: Twayne Publishers, 1963.

Rader, Ralph W. *Tennyson's "Maud": The Biographical Genesis*. London: Cambridge UP; Berkeley: U of California P, 1963.

Forsyth, R. A. "The Myth of Nature and the Victorian Compromise of the Imagination." *Journal of English Literary History* 31 (1964): 213–40.

Gransden, K. W. *Tennyson: "In Memoriam."* London: Edward Arnold, 1964.

Ryals, Clyde de L. *Theme and Symbol in Tennyson's Poems to 1850*. London: Oxford UP; Philadelphia: U of Pennsylvania P, 1964.

Smith, Elton Edward. *The Two Voices: A Tennyson Study*. Lincoln: U of Nebraska P, 1964.

Tennyson, Charles. "The Dream in Tennyson's Poetry." *Virginia Quarterly Review* 40 (Spring 1964): 228–48.

Whiting, George W. "The Artist and Tennyson." *Rice University Studies* 50 (1964): 1–84.

Assad, Thomas J. "On the Major Poems of Tennyson's *Enoch Arden* Volume." *Tulane Studies in English* 14 (1965): 29–56.

Fulweiler, Howard W. "Tennyson and the 'Summons from the Sea.'" *Victorian Poetry* 3 (1965): 25–44.

Kissane, James R. "Tennyson: The Passion of the Past and the Curse of Time." *Journal of English Literary History* 32 (1965): 85–109.

Tillotson, Kathleen. "Tennyson's Serial Poem." *Mid-Victorian Studies*. London: Athlone Press, 1965. 80–109.

Preyer, Robert. "Alfred Tennyson: The Poetry and Politics of Conservative Vision." *Victorian Studies* 9:4 (1966): 325–52.

Sendry, Joseph. "'The Palace of Art' Revisited." *Victorian Poetry* 4 (1966): 149–62.

Steane, J. B. *Tennyson*. London: Evans, 1966.

Anderson, Warren D. "Types of the Classical in Arnold, Tennyson, and Browning." In *Victorian Essays: A Symposium*. Ed. Warren D. Anderson and Thomas D. Clareson. Kent, OH: Kent State UP, 1967. 60–70.

Jump, John D., ed. *Tennyson: The Critical Heritage*. London: Routledge & Kegan Paul; New York: Barnes & Noble, 1967.

Ostriker, Alicia. "The Three Modes of Tennyson's Prosody." *PMLA* 82 (1967): 273–84.

Robson, W. W. "The Dilemma of Tennyson." *Critical Essays*. New York: Barnes & Noble, 1967. 191–99.

Ryals, Clyde de L. *From The Great Deep*. Athens: Ohio UP, 1967.

Shaw, W. David. "The Idealist's Dilemma in *Idylls of the King*." *Victorian Poetry* 5 (1967): 41–53.

———. "The Transcendentalist Problem in Tennyson's Poetry of Debate." *Philological Quarterly* 46 (1967): 79–94.

Shmiefsky, Marvel. "*In Memoriam:* Its Seasonal Imagery Reconsidered." *Studies in English Literature, 1500–1900* 7 (1967): 721–39.

Smith, Elton E. "Tennyson Criticism 1923–1966: From Fragmentation to Tension in Polarity." *Victorian Newsletter* 31 (Spring 1967): 1–4.

Solimine, Joseph. "The Burkean Idea of the State in Tennyson's Poetry: The Vision in Crisis." *Huntington Library Quarterly* 30 (1967): 147–65.

Tennyson, Sir Charles, and Christine Fall. *Alfred Tennyson: An Annotated Bibliography*. Athens: U of Georgia P, 1967.

Tennyson Research Bulletin. Lincoln, England: Tennyson Research Centre. 1967–.

Ball, Patricia M. "Inheriting Pegasus: Tennyson, Arnold and Browning." *The Central Self: A Study in Romantic and Victorian Imagination*. London: Athlone, 1968. 166–200.

Chapman, Raymond. "Tennyson and Browning." *The Victorian Debate: English Literature and Society 1832–1901*. London: Weidenfeld & Nicolson; New York: Basic Books, 1968. 194–206.

Donoghoe, Denis. "From Tennyson to Eliot." *The Ordinary Universe: Soundings in Modern Literature*. New York: Macmillan; London: Faber & Faber, 1968. 90–107.

Johnson, E. D. H. "Alfred, Lord Tennyson." In *The Victorian Poets: A Guide to Research*. Ed. Frederic E. Faverty. Cambridge, MA: Harvard UP, 1968. 33–80.

Armstrong, Isobel, ed. *The Major Victorian Poets: Reconsiderations*. London: Routledge & Kegan Paul, 1969.

August, Eugene R. "Tennyson and Teilhard: The Faith of *In Memoriam*." *PMLA* 84 (1969): 217–26.

Brashear, William R. *The Living Will: A Study of Tennyson and Nineteenth-Century Subjectivism*. The Hague: Mouton, 1969.

Gray, J. M. *Man and Myth in Victorian England: Tennyson's "The Coming of Arthur."* Lincoln, England: Tennyson Society Research Centre, 1969.

Joseph, Gerhard. *Tennysonian Love: The Strange Diagonal*. Minneapolis: U of Minnesota P, 1969.

Kaplan, Fred. "Woven Paces and Waving Hands: Tennyson's Merlin as a Fallen Artist." *Victorian Poetry* 7 (1969): 285–98.

Killham, John. "Tennyson (and FitzGerald)." In *The New History of Literature: The Victorians*. Ed. Arthur Pollard. London: Cresset; New York: Bantam, 1969. Reprint, New York: Bedrick, 1987. 361–86.

Kumar, Shiv, ed. *British Victorian Literature: Recent Revaluations*. New York: New York UP, 1969.

Miyoshi, Masao. *The Divided Self: A Perspective on the Victorians.* New York: New York UP, 1969. 107–23, 235–40.

Pollard, Arthur, ed. *The New History of Literature: The Victorians.* London: Cresset; New York: Bantam, 1969. Reprint, New York: Bedrick, 1987.

Reed, John R. *Perception and Design in Tennyson's "Idylls of the King."* Athens: Ohio UP, 1969.

Ricks, Christopher, ed. *The Poems of Tennyson.* London: Longmans, 1969; 2nd ed., rev. 3 vols. Berkeley: U of California P, 1987.

Shaw, W. David. "*Idylls of the King:* A Dialectical Reading." *Victorian Poetry* 7 (1969): 175–90.

Walton, James. "Tennyson's Patrimony: From 'The Outcast' to 'Maud.'" *Texas Studies in Literature and Language* 11 (1969): 733–59.

1970s

Bloom, Harold. "Tennyson, Hallam, and Romantic Tradition." *The Ringers in the Tower: Studies in Romantic Tradition.* Chicago: U of Chicago P, 1970. 145–54.

Colville, Derek. "Tennyson." *Victorian Poetry and the Romantic Religion.* Albany: State U of New York P, 1970. 167–238.

Hunt, John Dixon, ed. *Tennyson, "In Memoriam": A Casebook.* London: Macmillan, 1970.

Kissane, James D. *Alfred Tennyson.* New York: Twayne, 1970.

Langbaum, Robert. "The Dynamic Unity of *In Memoriam*." *The Modern Spirit: Essays on the Continuity of Nineteenth and Twentieth Century Literature.* London: Chatto & Windus; New York: Oxford UP, 1970. 51–75.

Millett, Kate. *Sexual Politics.* Garden City, NY: Doubleday, 1970.

Peckham, Morse. "Escape from Charisma." *Victorian Revolutionaries: Speculations on Some Heroes of a Cultural Crisis.* New York: Braziller, 1970. 8–43.

Pettigrew, John. *Tennyson: The Early Poems.* London: Arnold, 1970.

Scott, P. G. *Tennyson's "Enoch Arden": A Victorian Best-Seller.* Lincoln, England: Tennyson Research Centre, 1970.

Campbell, Nancie, comp. *Tennyson in Lincoln: A Catalogue of the Collections in the Research Centre.* 2 vols. Lincoln, England: Tennyson Society, 1971.

Eggers, John Philip. *King Arthur's Laureate; A Study of Tennyson's "Idylls of the King."* New York: New York UP, 1971.

Gray, J. M. *Tennyson's Doppelganger: Balin and Balan.* Lincoln, England: Tennyson Society, 1971.

Hunt, John D. "Tennyson, 1809–1832." In *English Poetry: Select Bibliographical Guides.* Ed. A. E. Dyson. London: Oxford UP, 1971. 265–83.

Knight, G. Wilson. *Neglected Powers: Essays on Nineteenth and Twentieth Century Literature.* London: Routledge & Kegan Paul; New York: Barnes & Noble, 1971.

Millhauser, Milton. *Fire And Ice: The Influence of Science on Tennyson's Poetry.* Lincoln, England: Tennyson Society, 1971.

Shaw, W. David. "*In Memoriam* and the Rhetoric of Confession." *Journal of English Literary History* 38 (1971): 80–103.

Sinfield, Alan. *The Language of Tennyson's "In Memoriam."* Oxford: Blackwell; New York: Barnes & Noble, 1971.

Southam, B. C. *Tennyson.* Harlow, England: Longman Group, 1971.

Armstrong, Isobel. *Victorian Scrutinies: Reviews of Poetry 1830–1870.* London: Athlone, 1972.

Auden, W. H. "The Poet of No More — W. H. Auden Offers Some Personal Reflections on Tennyson." *Listener* 88 (1972): 181.

Hellstrom, Ward. *On the Poems of Tennyson.* Gainesville: U of Florida P, 1972.

Revel, Peter, and Sian Allsobrook. *A Catalogue of the Tennyson Collection in the Library of University College, Cardiff.* Cardiff, Wales: University College, 1972.

Ricks, Christopher B. *Tennyson.* New York: Macmillan, 1972. 2nd ed., Basingstoke: Macmillan, 1989.

Shaw, W. David. "Imagination and Intellect in Tennyson's 'Lucretius.'" *Modern Language Quarterly* 33 (1972): 130–39.

Joseph, Gerhard. "Poe and Tennyson." *PMLA* 88 (1973): 418–28.

Palmer, D. J., ed. *Tennyson.* London: Bell, 1973. Athens: Ohio University P, 1973.

Pfordresher, John. *A Variorum Edition of Tennyson's "Idylls of the King."* New York: Columbia UP, 1973.

Pratt, Linda R. "The Holy Grail: Subversion and Revival of a Tradition in Tennyson and T. S. Eliot." *Victorian Poetry* 11 (1973): 307–21.

Priestley, F. E. L. *Language and Structure in Tennyson's Poetry.* London: Deutsch, 1973.

Robbins, Tony. "Tennyson's 'Ulysses': The Significance of the Homeric and Dantesque Backgrounds." *Victorian Poetry* 11 (1973): 171–93.

Rosenberg, John D. *The Fall of Camelot: A Study of Tennyson's "Idylls of the King."* Cambridge, MA: Harvard UP, 1973.

Shaw, W. David. "Tennyson's 'Tithonus' and the Problem of Mortality." *Philological Quarterly* 52 (1973): 274–85.

Culler, A. Dwight. "Tennyson, We Cannot Live by Art." In *Nineteenth-Century Literary Perspectives: Essays in Honor of Lionel Stevenson*. Ed. Clyde de L. Ryals. Durham, NC: Duke UP, 1974. 77–92.

Hargrove, Nancy D. "Landscape as Symbol in Tennyson and T. S. Eliot." *Victorians Institute Journal* 3 (1974): 73–83.

Hoge, James O., ed. *The Letters of Emily Lady Tennyson*. University Park: Pennsylvania State UP, 1974.

Joseph, Gerhard. "Tennyson's 'Idylls': Attack and Defense." *Virginia Quarterly Review* 50 (1974): 152–56.

McSweeney, Kerry. "The State of Tennyson Criticism." *Papers on Language and Literature* 10 (1974): 433–46.

Stange, G. Robert. "The 'Voyages' of Tennyson and Baudelaire." In *Nineteenth-Century Literary Perspectives: Essays in Honor of Lionel Stevenson*. Durham, NC: Duke UP, 1974. 93–104.

Tennyson, Sir Charles. *Tennyson and His Times*. Lincoln, England: Tennyson Research Centre, 1974.

Tennyson, Sir Charles, and Hope Dyson. *The Tennysons: Background to Genius*. London: Macmillan, 1974.

Christ, Carol T. *The Finer Optic: The Aesthetic of Particularity in Victorian Poetry*. New Haven, CT: Yale UP, 1975. 17–29 and *passim*.

Gliserman, Susan. "Early Victorian Science Writers and Tennyson's *In Memoriam*: A Study in Cultural Exchange." *Victorian Studies* 18:3 (1975): 277–308; 18:4: 437–59.

Johnson, Wendell Stacy. "Marriage and Divorce in Tennyson." *Sex and Marriage in Victorian Poetry*. Ithaca, NY: Cornell UP, 1975. 110–84.

Kincaid, James R. *Tennyson's Major Poems: The Comic and Ironic Patterns*. New Haven, CT: Yale UP, 1975.

Kozicki, Henry. "The 'Medieval Ideal' in Tennyson's *The Princess*." *Criticism* 17 (1975): 121–30.

———. "Philosophy of History in Tennyson's Poetry to the 1842 *Poems*." *Journal of English Literary History* 42 (1975): 88–106.

Ball, Patricia M. *The Heart's Events: The Victorian Poetry of Relationships*. London: Athlone; Atlantic Highlands, NJ: Humanities Press, 1976.

Bloom, Harold. "Tennyson: In the Shadow of Keats." *Poetry and Repression*. New Haven, CT: Yale UP, 1976. 143–74.

Hunt, John D., and David Palmer. "Tennyson." In *English Poetry*. Ed. Alan Sinfield. London: Sussex, 1976. 130–47.

Shaw, W. David. "Consolation and Catharsis in *In Memoriam*." *Modern Language Quarterly* 37 (1976): 47–67.

———. *Tennyson's Style*. Ithaca, NY: Cornell UP, 1976.

Turner, Paul. *Tennyson*. London: Henley; Boston: Routledge & Kegan Paul, 1976.

Brantlinger, Patrick. *The Spirit of Reform: British Literature and Politics 1832–1867*. Cambridge, MA: Harvard UP, 1977.

Brashear, William R. "The Boundless Deep: Tennyson." *The Gorgon's Head: A Study in Tragedy and Despair*. Athens: U of Georgia P, 1977. 27–48.

Christ, Carol T. "Victorian Masculinity and the Angel in the House." In *A Widening Sphere: Changing Roles of Victorian Women*. Ed. Martha Vicinus. Bloomington: Indiana UP, 1977. 146–62.

Culler, A. Dwight. *The Poetry of Tennyson*. New Haven, CT: Yale UP, 1977.

Joseph, Gerhard. "Tennyson's Optics: The Eagle's Gaze." *PMLA* 92 (1977): 420–28.

Kozicki, Henry. "A Dialectic of History in Tennyson's *Idylls*." *Victorian Studies* 20 (1977): 141–57.

———. "'Meaning' in Tennyson's *In Memoriam*." *Studies in English Literature 1500–1900* 17 (1977): 673–94.

McSweeney, Kerry. "Tennyson's Quarrel with Himself: The Tristram Group of *Idylls*." *Victorian Poetry* 15 (1977): 49–59.

Allen, Peter. *The Cambridge Apostles: The Early Years*. Cambridge: Cambridge UP, 1978.

Eagleton, Terry. "Tennyson: Politics and Sexuality in *The Princess* and *In Memoriam*." In *1848: The Sociology of Literature*. Ed. Francis Barker, et al. Colchester, England: U of Essex P, 1978. 97–106.

Gaskell, Phillip. *From Writer to Reader: Studies in Editorial Method*. London: Oxford UP, 1978. 118–41.

Henderson, Philip. *Tennyson, Poet and Prophet*. London: Routledge & Kegan Paul, 1978.

Hough, Graham. "The Natural Theology of *In Memoriam*." *Selected Essays*. London: Cambridge UP, 1978. 110–25.

Joseph, Gerhard. "Victorian Frames: The Windows and Mirrors of Browning, Arnold, and Tennyson." *Victorian Poetry* 16 (1978): 70–87.

Lerner, Laurence, ed. *The Victorians*. New York: Holmes & Meier, 1978.

Tillotson, Geoffrey A. *A View of Victorian Literature*. London: Oxford UP, 1978. 286–327.

Dawson, Carl. "*In Memoriam:* The Uses of Dante and Wordsworth." *Victorian Noon: English Literature to 1850*. Baltimore: Johns Hopkins UP, 1979. 36–51.

Hagen, June Steffensen. *Tennyson and his Publishers*. London: Macmillan; University Park: Pennsylvania State UP, 1979.

Kozicki, Henry. *Tennyson and Clio: History in the Major Poems*. Baltimore: Johns Hopkins UP, 1979.

Pattison, Robert. *Tennyson and Tradition*. Cambridge, MA: Harvard UP, 1979.

1980s

Buckler, William E. *The Victorian Imagination: Essays in Aesthetic Exploration*. New York: New York UP, 1980.

Francis, Elizabeth A., ed. *Tennyson: A Collection of Critical Essays*. Englewood Cliffs, NJ: Prentice-Hall, 1980.

Gray, J. M. *Thro' The Vision of the Night: A Study of Source, Evolution and Structure in Tennyson's "Idylls of the King."* Edinburgh: Edinburgh UP; Montreal: McGill-Queen's UP, 1980.

Martin, Robert Bernard. *Tennyson: The Unquiet Heart*. London: Faber; Oxford: Clarendon Press; New York: Oxford UP, 1980.

McGhee, Richard D. *Marriage, Duty and Desire in Victorian Poetry and Drama*. Lawrence: U of Kansas P, 1980. 29–66.

Victorian Poetry 18 (1980). Special Edition devoted to Tennyson's poetry.

Christ, Carol T. "T. S. Eliot and the Victorians." *Modern Philology* 79:2 (1981): 157–65.

Hair, Donald S. *Domestic and Heroic in Tennyson's Poetry*. Toronto: U of Toronto P, 1981.

Hoeveler, Diane L. "Many-Women and Womanly-Men: Tennyson's Androgynous Ideal." *Michigan Occasional Papers in Women's Studies* 19 (1981): 1–19.

Hoge, James O., ed. *Lady Tennyson's Journal*. Charlottesville: UP of Virginia, 1981.

Johnston, Eileen T. "Hallam's Review of Tennyson: Its Contexts and Significance." *Texas Studies in Literature and Language* 23 (Spring 1981): 1–26.

Joseph, Gerhard. "Tennyson's Three Women: The Thought Within the Image." *Victorian Poetry* 19 (Spring 1981): 1–18.

Lang, Cecil Y., and Edgar F. Shannon Jr., eds. *The Letters of Alfred Lord Tennyson*. 3 vols. Oxford: Clarendon Press; Cambridge, MA: Harvard UP, 1981–1990.

McSweeney, Kerry. *Tennyson and Swinburne as Romantic Naturalists.* Toronto: U of Toronto P, 1981.

Radford, Colin, and Sally Minogue. "The Logical Richness of Criticism: An Analysis of Ricks on Tennyson." *The Nature of Criticism.* Brighton, England: Harvester; Atlantic Highlands, NJ: Humanities Press, 1981. 84–114.

Wordsworth, Ann. "An Art That Will Not Abandon the Self to Language: Bloom, Tennyson and the Blind World of the Wish." In *Untying the Text: A Post-Structuralist Reader.* Ed. Robert Young. Boston: Routledge, 1981. 207–22.

Armstrong, Isobel. *Language as Living Form in Nineteenth-Century Poetry.* London: Routledge, 1982.

Buckley, Jerome H. "The Persistence of Tennyson." In *The Victorian Experience: The Poets.* Ed. Richard A. Levine. Athens: Ohio UP, 1982. 1–22.

Coslett, Tess. *The "Scientific Movement" and Victorian Literature.* New York: St. Martin's, 1982.

Joseph, Gerhard. "The Homeric Competitions of Tennyson and Gladstone." *Browning Institute Studies* 10 (1982): 105–15.

Kiernan, Victor. "Tennyson, King Arthur, and Imperialism." In *Culture, Ideology and Politics: Essays for Eric Hobsbawm.* Ed. Raphael Samuel and Gareth Stedman Jones. London: Routledge, 1982. 126–48.

McGann, Jerome J. "Tennyson and the Histories of Criticism." *Review* 4 (1982): 219–253.

Shatto, Susan, and Marion Shaw, eds. *In Memoriam.* Oxford: Oxford UP, 1982.

Staines, David. *Tennyson's Camelot: "The Idylls of the King" and Its Medieval Sources.* Waterloo, Ont.: Wilfrid Laurier UP, 1982.

Thomson, Alastair. "Tennyson and Some Doubts." *Essays and Studies* 35 (1982): 84–100.

Colley, Ann C. *Tennyson and Madness.* Athens: U of Georgia P, 1983.

Fletcher, Pauline. *Gardens and Grim Ravines: The Language of Landscape in Victorian Poetry.* Princeton, NJ: Princeton UP, 1983.

Ford, George H. "'A Great Poetical Boa-Constrictor,' Alfred Tennyson: An Educated Victorian Mind." In *Victorian Literature and Society: Essays Presented to Richard D. Altick.* Ed. James R. Kincaid and Albert J. Kuhn. Columbus: Ohio State UP, 1983. 146–67.

Gilbert, Elliot L. "The Female King: Tennyson's Arthurian Apocalypse." *PMLA* 98:5 (October 1983): 863–78.

Joseph, Gerhard. "Tennyson's Stupidity." *University of Hartford Studies in Literature* 15 (1983): 55–62.

Lang, Cecil Y. *Tennyson's Arthurian Psycho Drama*. Lincoln, England: Tennyson Research Centre, 1983.

Mermin, Dorothy. "Tennyson." *The Audience in the Poem: Five Victorian Poets*. New Brunswick, NJ: Rutgers UP, 1983.

Page, Norman, ed. *Tennyson, Interviews and Recollections*. Totowa, NJ: Barnes & Noble Books, 1983.

Tucker, Herbert F. Jr. "Tennyson and the Measure of Doom." *PMLA* 98 (1983): 8–20.

Assad, Thomas J. *Tennysonian Lyric: "Songs of the Deeper Kind" and "In Memoriam."* New Orleans, LA: Tulane UP, 1984.

Beetz, Kirk H. *Tennyson: A Bibliography, 1827–1982*. Metuchen, NJ: Scarecrow Press, 1984.

Buckler, William E. *Man and His Myths: Tennyson's "Idylls of the King" in Critical Context*. New York: New York UP, 1984.

Fulweiler, Howard W. "Tennyson's *In Memoriam* and the Scientific Imagination." *Thought: A Review of Culture and Idea* 59 (1984): 296–318.

Peltason, Timothy. "Tennyson, Nature, and Romantic Nature Poetry." *Philological Quarterly* 63:1 (Winter 1984): 75–93.

———. "Tennyson's Philosophy: Some Lyric Examples." In *Philosophical Approaches to Literature: New Essays on Nineteenth and Twentieth Century Texts*. Ed. William E. Cain. Lewisburg, PA: Bucknell UP, 1984. 51–72.

Pinion, F. B. *A Tennyson Companion*. London: Macmillan, 1984.

Bloom, Harold, ed. *Alfred Lord Tennyson*. New York: Chelsea House, 1985.

Joseph, Gerhard. "Tennyson's Parable of Soul Making: A Jungian Reading of *The Princess*." In *CUNY English Forum*. Vol. 1. Ed. Saul N. Brody and Harold Schechter. New York: AMS, 1985. 231–40.

Peltason, Timothy. *Reading "In Memoriam."* Princeton, NJ: Princeton UP, 1985.

Sedgwick, Eve Sokofsky. *Between Men: English Literature and Male Homosocial Desire*. New York: Columbia UP, 1985.

Shaw, W. David. "Philosophy and Genre in Victorian Poetics: The Idealist Legacy." *ELH* 52:2 (Summer 1985): 471–501.

Albright, Daniel. *Tennyson: The Muses' Tug-of-War*. Charlottesville: UP of Virginia, 1986.

Byatt, A. S. "Insights *Ad nauseum*." *Times Literary Supplement* (14 November 1986): 1274.

Hair, Donald S. "Tennyson's Faith: A Re-Examination." *University of Toronto Quarterly* 55 (Winter 1985–1986): 185–203.

Ricks, Christopher, and Aidan Day, eds. *The Tennyson Archives*. 30 vols. New York: Garland, 1986–.

Shatto, Susan, ed. *Tennyson's "Maud": A Definitive Edition*. Norman: U of Oklahoma P, 1986.

Sinfield, Alan. *Alfred Tennyson*. Oxford: Basil Blackwell, 1986.

Thomson, Alastair W. *The Poetry of Tennyson*. London: Routledge & Kegan Paul, 1986.

Christ, Carol T. "The Feminine Subject in Victorian Poetry." *ELH* 54 (Summer 1987): 385–401.

Clark, Barbara R. "Tennyson across the Atlantic." *Tennyson Research Bulletin* 5:1 (November 1987): 1–8.

Hughes, Linda K. *The Manyfacéd Glass: Tennyson's Dramatic Monologues*. Athens: Ohio UP, 1987.

Johnson, Rob. "Strategies of Containment: Tennyson's *In Memoriam*." In *Post-Structuralist Readings of English Poetry*, ed. Richard Machin and Christopher Norris. Cambridge: Cambridge UP, 1987. 308–31.

Rosenberg, John D. "Tennyson and the Passing of Arthur." *Victorian Poetry* 25:3–4 (Autumn/Winter 1987): 141–50.

Shaw, W. David. *The Lucid Veil: Poetic Truth in the Victorian Age*. London: Athlone Press, 1987.

Timko, Michael. *Carlyle and Tennyson*. Iowa City: U of Iowa P, 1987. Basingstoke, England: Macmillan, 1988.

Craft, Chris. "'Descend, Touch, and Enter': Tennyson's Strange Manner of Address." *Genders* 1 (Spring 1988): 83–101.

Ebbatson, Roger. *Tennyson*. London: Penguin, 1988.

Jordan, Elaine. *Alfred Tennyson*. Cambridge: Cambridge UP, 1988.

McKay, Kenneth. *Many Glancing Colours: An Essay in Reading Tennyson, 1809–1850*. Toronto: U of Toronto P, 1988.

Richardson, James. *Vanishing Lives: Style and Self in Tennyson, D. G. Rossetti, Swinburne, and Yeats*. Charlottesville: UP of Virginia, 1988.

Shaw, Marion. *Alfred Lord Tennyson*. New York: Harvester Wheatsheaf, 1988.

Tucker, Herbert F. *Tennyson and the Doom of Romanticism*. Cambridge, MA: Harvard UP, 1988.

Adams, James Eli. "Woman Red in Tooth and Claw: Nature and the Feminine in Tennyson and Darwin." *Victorian Studies* 33:1 (Autumn 1989): 7–27.

Armstrong, Isobel. "Tennyson's 'The Lady of Shalott': Victorian Mythography and the Politics of Narcissism." In *The Sun is God: Painting, Literature, and Mythology in the Nineteenth Century.* Ed. J. B. Bullen. Oxford: Clarendon Press, 1989. 49–107.

Goslee, David. *Tennyson's Characters: Strange Faces, Other Minds.* Iowa City: U of Iowa P, 1989.

Hair, Donald S. "'Matter Moulded Forms of Speech.'" *Victorian Poetry* 27:1 (Spring 1989): 1–15.

Platizky, Roger S. *A Blueprint of His Dissent: Madness and Method in Tennyson's Poetry.* Lewisburg, PA: Bucknell UP; London: Associated UP, 1989.

Schur, Owen. *Victorian Pastoral: Tennyson, Hardy, and the Subversion of Forms.* Columbus: Ohio State UP, 1989.

Shaw, Marion. *An Annotated Critical Bibliography of Alfred, Lord Tennyson.* London: Harvester Wheatsheaf; NY: St. Martin's Press, 1989.

Shaw, W. David. "Incomprehensible Certainties and Interesting Uncertainties: Hopkins and Tennyson." *Texas Studies in Literature and Language* 31:1 (Spring 1989): 66–84. Reprinted in *Victorians and Mystery.* Ithaca, NY: Cornell UP, 1990. 88–106.

Tucker, Herbert F. "Vocation and Evocation: The Dialogue of Genesis in Tennyson's 'The Two Voices.'" In *Victorian Connections.* Ed. Jerome J. McGann. Charlottesville: UP of Virginia, 1989.

Turner, Paul. *English Literature 1832–1890, Excluding the Novel.* Oxford: Clarendon Press, 1989. 18–38.

1990s

Dellamora, Richard. "Tennyson, The Apostles, and *In Memoriam.*" *Masculine Desire: The Sexual Politics of Victorian Aestheticism.* Chapel Hill: U of North Carolina P, 1990.

Harrison, Antony. *Victorian Poets and Romantic Poems.* Charlottesville: UP of Virginia, 1990.

Joseph, Gerhard. "Tennyson's Sword: From 'Mungo the American' to *Idylls of the King.*" In *Sex and Death in Victorian Literature.* Ed. Regina Barreca. Bloomington: Indiana UP, 1990. 60–68.

Manning, Sylvia. "Death and Sex from Tennyson's Early Poetry to *In Memoriam.*" In *Sex and Death in Victorian Literature.* Ed. Regina Barreca. Bloomington: Indiana UP, 1990. 194–210.

Morgan, Thais, ed. *Victorian Sages and Cultural Discourse: Renegotiating Gender and Power.* New Brunswick, NJ: Rutgers UP, 1990.

Pinion, F. B. *A Tennyson Chronology.* London: Macmillan, 1990.

Shires, Linda M. "Rereading Tennyson's Gender Politics." In *Victorian Sages and Cultural Discourse: Renegotiating Gender and Power.* Ed. Thais Morgan. New Brunswick, NJ: Rutgers UP, 1990. 46–65.

Simpson, Roger. *Camelot Regained: The Arthurian Revival and Tennyson, 1800–1849.* Cambridge; Wolfeboro, NH: D. S. Brewer, 1990.

Sinfield, Alan. "Tennyson and the Cultural Politics of Prophecy." *ELH* 57:1 (Spring 1990): 175–95.

Hair, Donald S. *Tennyson's Language.* Toronto: U of Toronto P, 1991.

Brisman, Leslie. "*Maud:* The Feminine as the Crux of Influence." *Studies in Romanticism* 31:1 (Spring 1992): 21–43.

Buckley, Jerome H. "The Myth of the Poet." *Nineteenth Century Studies* 6 (1992): 61–71.

Collins, Philip, ed. *Tennyson: Seven Essays.* New York: St. Martin's, 1992.

Gerhard, Joseph. *Tennyson and the Text: The Weaver's Shuttle.* Cambridge: Cambridge UP, 1992.

Gerhard, Joseph, ed. "Centennial of Alfred, Lord Tennyson." *Victorian Poetry* 30 (Autumn/Winter 1992): 3–4.

Haines, Simon. "Victorian Self-Fashioning: Tennyson One Hundred Years After." *Critical Review.* 32 (1992): 69–94.

Harrison, Antony, and Beverly Taylor, eds. *Gender and Discourse in Victorian Literature and Art.* DeKalb: Northern Illinois Press, 1992.

Hooker, Deborah. "Ambiguous Bodies: Keats and the Problem of Resurrection in Tennyson's 'Demeter and Persephone.'" In *Gender and Discourse in Victorian Literature and Art.* Ed. Anthony H. Harrison and Beverly Taylor. DeKalb: Northern Illinois Press, 1992.

Millgate, Michael. *Testamentary Acts: Browning, Tennyson, James, Hardy.* Oxford: Clarendon Press; New York: Oxford UP, 1992.

Taylor, Beverely. "'School-Miss Alfred' and 'Materfamilias': Female Sexuality and Poetic Voice in *The Princess* and *Aurora Leigh*." In *Gender and Discourse in Victorian Literature and Art.* Ed. Anthony H. Harrison and Beverly Taylor. DeKalb: Northern Illinois Press, 1992.

Andrew, Aletha. *An Annotated Bibliography and Study of the Contemporary Criticism of Tennyson's "Idylls of the King," 1859–1886.* New York: Peter Lang, 1993.

Hardy, Barbara. *Tennyson and the Novelists.* Lincoln, England: Tennyson Research Centre, 1993.

Levi, Peter. *Tennyson.* New York: Scribner's, 1993.

Morse, David. "Keeping the Faith: Newman, F. D. Maurice, Tennyson and Trollope." *High Victorian Culture.* New York: New York UP, 1993. 218–98.

Ormond, Leonée. *Alfred Tennyson: A Literary Life*. New York: St. Martin's, 1993.

Shaw, W. David. "Impact and Tremor in Tennyson's Elegies: The Power of Genre." *Victorian Poetry* 31 (Summer 1993): 127–42.

Sherbo, Arthur. "Additions to the Beetz Tennyson Bibliography." *Notes and Queries* (England) 40 (December 1993): 482–84.

Thorn, Michael. *Tennyson*. New York: St. Martin's, 1993.

Tucker, Herbert F., ed. *Critical Essays on Alfred Lord Tennyson*. New York: G. K. Hall; Toronto: Maxwell Macmillan Canada, 1993.

Brantley, Richard E. *Anglo American Antiphony: The Late Romanticism of Tennyson and Emerson*. Gainesville: UP of Florida, 1994.

Hamilton, Ian. "Tennyson, Anyone?" *New Yorker* (22–29 August 1994): 116–21.

Rowlinson, Matthew C. *Tennyson's Fixations: Psychoanalysis and the Topics of the Early Poetry*. Charlottesville: UP of Virginia, 1994.

Shaw, W. David. *Elegy and Paradox: Testing the Conventions*. Baltimore: Johns Hopkins UP, 1994.

Elfenbein, Andrew. *Byron and the Victorians*. Cambridge: Cambridge UP, 1995.

Elliott, Philip Lovin. *The Making of the Memoir*. Lincoln, England: Tennyson Society, 1995.

Buckley, Jerome H. "Tennyson's Landscapes." *Tennyson Research Bulletin* 6:5 (November 1996): 278–88.

Hair, Donald S. "Soul and Spirit in *In Memoriam*." *Victorian Poetry* 34:2 (Summer 1996): 175–91.

Shaw, W. David. *Alfred Lord Tennyson: The Poet in an Age of Theory*. New York: Twayne; London: Prentice Hall International, 1996.

Stott, Rebecca, ed. *Tennyson*. London: Longman, 1996.

Brett, R. L. *Faith and Doubt: Religion and Secularization in Literature from Wordsworth to Larkin*. Macon, GA: Mercer UP, 1997.

Felluga, Dino Franco. "Tennyson's *Idylls*, Pure Poetry, and the Market." *SEL: Studies in English Literature, 1500–1900* 37:4 (Autumn 1997): 783–803.

Hill, Alan G. *Tennyson, Wordsworth and the "Forms" of Religion*. Lincoln, England: Tennyson Research Centre, 1997.

Maxwell, Catherine. "Engendering Vision in the Victorian Male Poet." In *Writing and Victorianism*. Ed. J. B. Bullen. London: Longmans, 1997. 73–103.

Smith, Elton E. *Tennyson's "Epic Drama."* Lanham, MD: UP of America, 1997.

Turley, Richard Marggraf. "Tennyson and the Nineteenth Century Language Debate." *Leeds Studies in English* 28 (1997): 123–40.

Brannigan, John. *New Historicism and Cultural Materialism.* New York: St. Martin's, 1998.

Graham, Colin. *Ideologies of Epic: Nation, Empire and Victorian Epic Poetry.* Manchester, UK: Manchester UP, 1998.

Harrison, Antony H. *Victorian Poets and the Politics of Culture: Discourse and Ideology.* Charlottesville: UP of Virginia, 1998.

Kolb, Jack. "Laureate Envy: T. S. Eliot on Tennyson." *ANQ: A Quarterly Journal of Short Articles, Notes, and Reviews* 11:3 (Summer 1998): 29–37.

Campbell, Matthew. *Rhythm and Will in Victorian Poetry.* Cambridge: Cambridge UP, 1999.

Gates, Sarah. "Poetics, Metaphysics, Genre: The Stanza Form of *In Memoriam*." *Victorian Poetry* 37 (1999): 507–19.

Mallen, Richard. "The 'Crowned Republic' of Tennyson's *Idylls of the King*." *Victorian Poetry* 37 (1999): 275–89.

Shaw, W. David. *Origins of the Monologue: The Hidden God.* Toronto: U of Toronto P, 1999.

Tucker, Herbert. "The Fix of Form: An Open Letter." *Victorian Literature and Culture* 27:2 (1999): 531–35.

2000s

Coyle, John, and Richard Cronin. "Tennyson and the Apostles." In *Rethinking Victorian Culture.* Ed. Juliet John and Alice Jenkins. London: Macmillan, 2000.

Hood, James W. *Divining Desire: Tennyson and the Poetics of Transcendence.* Burlington, VT: Ashgate, 2000.

Lambdin, Laura C., and Robert Thomas Lambdin. *Camelot in the Nineteenth Century: Arthurian Characters in the Poems of Tennyson, Arnold, Morris, and Swinburne* Westport, CT: Greenwood Press, 2000

Roberts, Adam, ed. *Alfred Tennyson.* Oxford: Oxford UP, 2000.

Slater, Michael. *Tennyson in the Theater.* Lincoln, England: Tennyson Research Centre, 2000.

Douglas-Fairhurst, Robert. *Victorian Afterlives: The Shaping Influence in Nineteenth-Century Literature.* Oxford: Oxford UP, 2002.

Turley, Richard Marggraf. *The Politics of Language in Romantic Literature.* London: Palgrave Macmillan, 2002.

Ebbatson, Roger. *Tennyson's English Idyls: History, Narrative, Art.* Lincoln, England: Tennyson Society, 2003.

Index

Abercrombie, Lascelles, 76–77, 98, 208
Abrams, M. H., 185
Adams, Francis, 44, 46–47, 59, 202
Adams, James Eli, 165, 171, 222
Albert, Prince, 17
Albright, Daniel, 158–59, 160, 171, 221
Alden, Raymond M., 66, 98, 163, 171, 206
Aldworth (Tennyson home), 72
Alexandrian poets, 139
Allen, Peter, 28, 218
Allsobrook, Sian, 4, 9, 216
Altick, Richard, 81, 98, 152
Anderson, Warren D., 118, 122, 213
Andrew, Aletha, 5, 8, 224
Apostles. *See* Cambridge Apostles
Armstrong, Isobel, 6, 120, 121, 122, 153, 170, 171, 176, 178, 183, 186, 188, 190, 214, 216, 220, 223
Armstrong, Richard A., 43, 59, 202
Arnold, Frances Lucy, 35
Arnold, Matthew, 25, 31, 32, 35, 40, 45, 47, 51, 52, 73, 79, 82, 91, 92, 104, 118, 128, 145, 149, 151, 155, 161, 189, 194
Assad, Thomas J., 117, 122, 156–57, 171, 213, 221
Atkins, Gaius Glenn, 74–75, 98, 207
Auden W. H. (Wystan Hugh), 58, 76, 79–81, 89, 91, 97, 98, 155, 157, 168, 190, 209, 216

August, Eugene R., 117, 123, 214
Augustan poetry, 2
Aurora Leigh (E. B. Browning), 176, 193
Austin, Alfred, 20–21, 22, 27, 28, 46, 160, 204
Aytoun, W. E., 17, 28, 199

Bagehot, Walter, 19, 29, 121, 123, 199
Bahktin, Mikhail, 187
Baker, Arthur E., 3, 8, 205
Ball, Patricia M., 118–19, 123, 129, 145, 213, 214, 217
Baring, Rosa, 14, 110, 144, 179
Barreca, Regina, 175, 190
Barthes, Roland, 160, 177
Basler, Roy P., 83, 98, 209
Bateson, Frederick W., 91, 98, 210
Baudelaire, Charles, 20, 80, 132
Baum, Paull F., 4, 8, 51, 85–86, 99, 104, 144, 182, 210, 211
Bayne, Peter, 22–23, 29, 199
Beach, Joseph Warren, 81, 99, 208
Beck, Warren, 95, 99, 211
Beetz, Kirk H., 5, 7, 8, 221
Bell, A. F., 50–51, 59, 205
Benson, Arthur C., 37–38, 59, 203
Benziger, James, 107, 123, 212
Bergonzi, Bernard, 121
Berkeley, George, 44
Bloom, Harold, 127, 138, 143, 145, 149, 158, 171, 215, 217, 221

Blore, George H., 67, 99, 206
Bowden, Marjorie, 6, 8, 28, 29, 76, 99, 209
Bradley, A. C., 40, 50, 57–58, 129, 157, 203, 206
Brannigan, John, 186, 190, 226
Brantley, Richard E., 184, 190, 225
Brantlinger, Patrick, 138, 145, 218
Brashear, William R., 119, 123, 214, 218
Brett, R. L., 188–89, 190, 225
Brightwell, Daniel B., 3, 8, 199
Brimley, George, 18
Brisman, Leslie, 175, 190, 224
British Broadcasting Company, 78
Broadus, Edmund K., 67, 99, 206
Brooke, Stopford A., 39–41, 46, 58, 59, 201
Brooks, Cleanth, 84–85, 99, 107, 210
Browning, Elizabeth Barrett, 18, 19
Browning, Robert, 18, 19, 24, 25, 26, 39, 43, 45, 48, 49, 51, 52, 75, 82, 92, 118, 121, 128, 137, 155, 162
Buckler, William E., 144–45, 155–56, 166, 171, 195, 196, 219, 221
Buckley, Jerome H., 72, 92, 93, 97, 104–6, 107, 110, 112, 114, 115, 116, 119, 122, 123, 128, 130, 136, 139, 143, 151–52, 159, 160, 171, 176, 180, 190, 210, 211, 212, 220, 224, 225
Bullen, J. B., 170
Bush, Douglas, 80–81, 93–94, 99, 208, 211
Byatt, A. S., 121, 160, 171, 221
Byron, Lord (George Gordon), 11, 22, 184–85

Cambridge Apostles, 28, 71, 104, 121, 158, 179, 180
Cambridge University, 2, 3, 4, 13, 14, 17, 28, 38, 69, 71, 75, 78, 84, 88, 104, 120
Cameron, Julia, 109, 180
Campbell, Matthew, 189, 191, 226
Campbell, Nancie, 4, 8, 215
Canton, William, 34, 59, 200
Carlyle, Thomas, 14, 19, 25, 67–68, 97, 108, 119
Carpenter, William B., 31, 59, 200
Carr, Arthur J., 89–90, 99, 107, 210
Chambers, Robert, 95, 183
Chapman, Elizabeth R., 25, 29, 200
Chapman, Raymond, 118, 123, 214
Chaucer, Geoffrey, 47, 76, 79
Cheney, John V., 26, 29, 200
Chesterton, G. K., 51, 52, 59, 169, 203, 205, 207
Chew, Samuel C., 4, 81, 98, 99, 209
Christ, Carol T., 92, 98, 99, 134–35, 145, 165, 171, 217, 218, 219, 222
"Christopher North." *See* John Wilson
Clark, Barbara R., 6, 8, 222
classical literature, 81, 86, 118, 136, 141, 163, 178
Clough, Arthur Hugh, 51
Cockney School, 12, 13
Coleridge, Samuel Taylor, 11, 19, 47, 83, 127, 145, 176
Colley, Ann C., 154, 168, 171, 220
Collier, John, 76–77, 99, 208
Collins, Churton, 167
Collins, Philip, 176, 191, 224
colonialism, 108, 139, 153

Colville, Derek, 127–28, 146, 215
Cook, E. T., 5, 8, 206
Cook, E. W., 54, 59, 204
Coslett, Tess, 152, 171, 220
Cowper, William, 42
Coyle, John, 28, 29, 226
Craft, Chris, 158, 172, 222
Croker, John Wilson, 12–14, 23
Cronin, Richard, 28, 29, 226
Crum, Ralph B., 78–79, 99, 208
Cruse, Amy, 6, 8, 208
Culler, A. Dwight, 132–33, 138–39, 143, 158, 160, 162, 217, 218
Culler, Jonathan, 160
cultural materialism, 186
Cuthbertson, Evan J., 36, 59, 202

Daiches, David, 26, 29, 212
Dante (Alighieri), 41, 43, 133
Danzig, Allan, 120–21, 123, 212
Darwin, Charles, 43, 67, 78, 81
Davidson, Thomas, 38, 59, 201
Davies, Hugh Sykes, 106–7, 123, 212
Davis, Arthur K., Jr., 89, 100, 210
Dawson, Carl, 140, 146, 219
Dawson, W. J., 42–43, 59, 202
Day, Aidan, 3, 10, 176, 195, 222
De La Mare, Walter, 77, 99, 209
De Man, Paul, 149, 150, 160, 170, 177
de Selincourt, Aubrey, 94, 99, 211
deconstruction (critical methodology), 93, 150, 159, 161, 177
Deily, Robert H., 4, 8, 208
Dellamora, Richard, 158, 172, 223
Derrida, Jacques, 138, 160, 169, 177, 184, 186
Dickens, Charles, 18

Dixon, W. M., 34, 49, 59, 201, 205
Dodsworth, Martin, 121
Donne, John, 40
Donoghoe, Denis, 98, 99, 214
Douglas-Fairhurst, Robert, 194, 196, 226
dramatic monologue, 40–41, 141, 153, 159, 162, 166, 185
Dryden, John, 11, 36
Duke University, 132
Duncan, Edgar H., 96–97, 100, 212
Dyson, A. E., 5, 9, 216
Dyson, Hope, 4, 10, 217

Eagleton, Terry, 138, 146, 159, 186, 218
Ebbatson, Roger, 168, 172, 194, 196, 222, 226
Edwards, Jonathan, 184
Eggers, John Philip, 116, 123, 131, 142, 215
Ehrsam, Theodore G., 4, 8, 208
Eidson, John O., 6, 8, 28, 29, 60, 209
eighteenth-century literature, 84, 129, 154, 161
elegy, 3, 16, 25, 33, 34, 38, 47, 48, 50, 80, 90, 91, 105, 108, 110, 111, 113, 118, 128, 129, 132, 133, 141, 157, 161, 166, 167, 184, 185, 188
Elfenbein, Andrew, 184–85, 191, 194, 225
Eliot, T. S. (Thomas Stearns), 14, 35, 74, 79–80, 82, 84, 89, 91, 94, 95, 98, 100, 107, 109, 112, 114, 116, 128, 129, 130, 140, 142–43, 158, 161, 162, 168, 182, 185, 208
Elliott, Philip Lovin, 36, 60, 225
Elton, Oliver, 68, 100, 206
Emerson, Ralph Waldo, 13, 184
Enlightenment, 130

epic poetry, 1, 18, 22, 35, 38, 39, 42, 49, 55, 84, 88, 107, 116, 130, 132, 141, 142, 166, 179, 187
Esher, Viscount, 94, 100, 211
Evans, B. Ifor, 81–82, 98, 100, 209, 211
evolution, 44, 45, 52, 53, 67, 76, 78–79, 81, 112, 114, 136, 169

Faerie Queene, The, 36, 142
Fairchild, Hoxie N., 95, 100, 211
Fall, Christine, 5, 10, 214
Farrar, Frederick W., 31, 60, 201
Farringford (Tennyson home), 72, 180
Fausset, Hugh I'Anson, 69, 70–72, 73, 74, 75, 79, 84, 85, 91, 93, 97, 100, 118, 207, 210
Felluga, Dino Franco, 186, 191, 194, 225
feminism (feminist movement), 15, 96, 106, 157, 175, 176
feminist criticism, 131, 135, 140, 157, 164, 165–66, 175, 176, 182, 185, 187
First World War, 57, 65, 66, 69, 78, 82
FitzGerald, Edward, 37, 42
Fletcher, Pauline, 154–55, 172, 220
Foakes, Reginald A., 95, 100, 211
Ford, George H., 83–84, 100, 152, 172, 184–85, 209, 220
Forgues, E. D., 13
formalist criticism, 78, 170
Forster, John, 14
Forsyth, R. A., 111, 123, 152, 213
Foucault, Michel, 186
Fox, W. J., 11–12, 14
Francis, Elizabeth A., 142–43, 146, 219
Freud, Sigmund, 138, 177, 184
Freudian psychology, 66, 94, 136

Friswell, J. H., 21
Fuller, Margaret, 13
Fulweiler, Howard W., 117, 123, 152, 172, 213, 221

Garnett, Richard, 52, 59, 203
Gaskell, Phillip, 122, 123, 218
Gates, Sarah, 188, 191, 226
Gatty, Alfred, 25, 29, 199
gender theory (gender studies), 135, 159, 165–66, 177–78, 186
Genung, John F., 25, 29, 49–50, 60, 199, 204
Gilbert, Elliot L., 183, 191, 220
Gingerich, Solomon F., 52–53, 60, 205
Gladstone, William E., 17, 18–19, 155
Gliserman, Susan, 133, 146, 217
Goethe, Johann Wolfgang von, 78, 167
Gordon, William C., 46, 60, 203
Goslee, David, 169, 172, 223
Gosse, Edmund, 26, 31–32, 36, 60, 200, 201
Graham, Colin, 187–88, 191, 226
Gransden, K. W., 111–12, 123, 213
Gray, J. M., 121, 124, 142, 146, 153, 215, 219
Gray, Thomas, 11
Gray, W. F., 55, 60, 205
Green, Joyce, 28, 29, 210
Grierson, Herbert J. C., 56–57, 58, 60, 97, 100, 205, 209
Griggs, Edward H., 54, 60, 203
Groom, Bernard, 82, 100, 208
Gunsaulus, Frank W., 45, 60, 204
Gurteen, Stephen H. V., 38–39, 60, 201
Gwynn, Steven L., 36, 60, 202

Hagen, June Steffensen, 140–41, 146, 219

Haines, Simon, 177, 191, 224
Hair, Donald S., 150–51, 158, 172, 176, 191, 219, 221, 223, 224, 225
Hallam, Arthur Henry, 11, 12, 14, 15, 17, 28, 32, 41, 47, 50, 69, 71, 80, 87, 88, 90, 91–92, 97, 105, 108, 110, 111, 114, 121, 122, 129, 130, 131, 138, 139, 157, 162, 165, 167, 175, 179, 183, 184
Hamilton, Ian, 182–83, 191, 225
Hardy, Barbara, 122, 124, 224
Hardy, Thomas, 84
Hare, Augustus, 183
Hare, Julius, 183
Hargrove, Nancy D., 98, 100, 217
Harrison, Antony, 176, 186–87, 191, 223, 225, 226
Harrison, Frederic, 46, 48–49, 53, 61, 202, 203, 204
Harstock, E., 76, 100, 208
Hayes, J. W., 44, 58, 61, 204
Hazlitt, William, 12
Hearn, Lafcadio, 20, 29, 56, 58, 61, 206, 207, 209
Hearnshaw, Fossey J. C., 65, 100, 206
Hellstrom, Ward, 131, 146, 216
Henderson, Philip, 139–40, 146, 218
Hill, Alan G., 122, 125
Hobbes, Thomas, 44
Hodgson, Geraldine E., 66, 101, 206
Hoeveler, Diane L., 165, 172, 219
Hoge, James O., 3, 8, 217, 219
Holland, John, 158
Homer, 41, 43, 133, 142
Hood, James W., 189–90, 191, 194, 226
Hopkins, Gerard Manley, 19–20, 185

Horne, R. H., 14
Horton, Robert F., 7, 9, 45–46, 61, 202
Hough, Graham, 84, 101, 107, 218
House, Humphry, 90–91, 101, 211
Hoyt, Arthur S., 73, 101, 207
Hughes, Linda K., 4, 162, 172, 222
Hunt, John Dixon, 5, 9, 128, 138, 146, 215, 216, 217
Hunt, Leigh, 12, 14
Hutton, R. H., 23–24, 29, 200
Huxley, Aldous, 84

Ibsen, Henrik, 84
idealism, 1, 16, 33, 90, 107, 160, 182, 189
idyl(l), 14, 15, 20, 85, 112, 113, 141–42, 143, 144, 150, 166
imperialism, 83, 108, 152–53, 187
Innes, Arthur D., 38, 61, 200
Irving, Henry, 24

Jacobs, Joseph, 34–35, 38, 61, 200, 201
James, David G., 90, 101, 210
James, Henry, 24
Jennings, Henry J., 23, 29, 199
Johnson, E. D. H., 4, 9, 92–93, 101, 169, 170, 211, 214
Johnson, R. Brimley, 54–55, 61, 205
Johnson, Rob, 161–62, 172, 222
Johnson, Samuel, 7, 9, 79, 134
Johnson, Wendell Stacy, 135, 146, 217
Johnston, Eileen T., 28, 29, 219
Jones, Henry, 39, 53, 61, 204
Jones, Richard D., 38, 61, 201
Jordan, Elaine, 165–66, 172, 186, 222

Joseph, Gerhard, 15, 29, 119–20, 124, 155, 170, 172, 175, 177–78, 186, 191–92, 214, 216, 217, 218, 219, 220, 221, 223
Joyce, James, 89
Jump, John D., 4, 27, 29, 213
Jungian psychology, 136, 155

Kant, Immanuel, 44, 119
Kaplan, Fred, 118, 124, 214
Keats, John, 11, 12, 14, 19, 22, 42, 83–84, 119, 138, 152, 167, 176, 184
Ker, William P., 53, 61, 204
Kiernan, Victor, 152–53, 173, 220
Killham, John, 96, 101, 107, 121, 124, 211, 212, 214
Kincaid, James R., 133–34, 136, 146, 177, 217
Kingsley, Charles, 16, 18
Kishi, Shigetsugu, 58, 61, 209
Kissane, James R., 128, 143, 146, 185, 213, 215
Knight, G. Wilson, 83, 101, 216
Knowles, James T., 22, 31, 61, 73, 200
Kolb, Jack, 98, 101, 226
Kozicki, Henry, 141, 146, 168, 217, 218, 219
"Kubla Khan," 83
Kumar, Shiv, 120, 121, 124, 214

Lacan, Jacques, 138, 160, 170, 177, 184, 186
Lambdin, Laura C., 189, 192, 226
Lambdin, Robert Thomas, 189, 192, 226
Lang, Andrew, 41, 61, 203
Lang, Cecil Y., 3, 9, 122, 124, 158, 183, 219, 221
Langbaum, Robert, 128–29, 147, 158, 162, 215
Lerner, Laurence, 140, 147, 218

Leslie Stephen Lecture, 53
Levi, Peter, 180–82, 192, 224
Levine, Richard A., 151
Lewes, George, 16
Lewis, W. D., 54, 62, 205
Littledale, Harold, 39, 62, 200
Locke, John, 44
Lounsbury, Thomas R., 5, 9, 11, 29, 55–56, 62, 205
Lowell, James Russell, 13
Lowell Lecture, 73
Lowes, John Livingston, 83, 96, 101
Lucas, F. L., 78, 84, 98, 101, 208, 210, 211
Luce, Morton, 34, 62, 201, 203
Lyall, Sir Alfred, 36–37, 49, 62, 203
Lycidas, 16
Lyell, Charles, 95, 183
Lynd, Robert, 68–69, 101, 207
lyric (lyric poetry), 15, 24, 27, 35, 37, 42, 52, 53, 58, 70, 75, 77, 78, 81, 82, 128, 132, 160, 181, 184, 188
Lyttleton, Arthur T., 31, 62, 203

Mabie, Hamilton W., 6, 9, 38, 62, 200
MacCallum, M. W., 39, 62, 88, 116, 201
Mackail, John W., 69, 101, 207
Macy, John, 75, 101, 207
Magnus, Laurie, 50–51, 62, 95, 101, 204, 207
Mallarmé, Stéphane, 20
Mallen, Richard, 188, 192, 194, 226
Malory, Sir Thomas, 39, 40, 48, 74, 153
Mann, R. J., 18
Marchand, Leslie A., 5, 9, 209
Marshall, George O., 2–3, 9, 156, 212
Marston, J. W., 15, 16

Martin, Robert Bernard, 30, 143–44, 147, 166, 169, 219
Masson, David, 34
Masterman, C. F. G., 44–45, 48, 62, 202
materialism, 45, 78, 81, 108, 121, 186, 189
Mattes, Eleanor B., 28, 30, 91, 101, 157, 210
Maxwell, Catherine, 176, 192, 225
McGann, Jerome J., 149, 158, 173, 220
McGhee, Richard D., 135, 147, 219
McKay, Kenneth, 166–68, 173, 222
McLuhan, H. Marshall, 92, 101, 107, 158, 210
McSweeney, Kerry, 6, 9, 133, 147, 151, 168, 173, 217, 218, 220
medieval literature, 19, 20, 23, 39, 159, 175, 179
Meredith, George, 40
Mermin, Dorothy, 153–54, 173, 221
Metaphysical poets, 40, 79
Meynell, Alice, 65, 102, 206
Mill, John Stuart, 13, 14, 18, 48
Miller, J. Hillis, 177
Millett, Kate, 165, 173, 216
Millgate, Michael, 35, 62, 224
Millhauser, Milton, 121–22, 124, 211, 216
Milmed, Bella K., 90, 102, 210
Milsand, Joseph, 16
Milton, John, 16, 18, 19, 28, 33, 36, 43, 47, 76, 167
Minogue, Sally, 150, 173, 220
Miyoshi, Masao, 120, 124, 215
Modern Language Association, 194
modernism, 2, 52, 97, 105, 114, 115, 127, 129, 144, 162

Montegut, Émile, 20
Moore, John M., 36, 62, 203
More, Paul Elmer, 53–54, 58, 62, 205
Morris, William, 40, 189
Morse, David, 183, 192, 224
Morte D'Arthur, 40, 74, 153
Moulton, Charles W., 6, 9, 203
Myers, F. W. H., 24, 27, 30, 201

narrative (narrative poetry), 11, 16, 21, 23, 24, 25, 41, 49, 57, 69, 75, 76, 77, 78, 79–80, 82, 84, 94, 128, 137, 140, 160
natural selection. *See* evolution
New Criticism, 18, 84, 137, 149
new historicism, 186, 188
Nicolson, Sir Harold, 22, 30, 35, 38, 41, 48, 51, 58, 66, 69–71, 72, 73, 74, 75, 76, 78, 79, 80, 82–83, 84, 85, 87, 91, 93, 97, 102, 104, 107, 113, 118, 127, 130, 168, 180, 182, 207, 209
Nietzsche, Friedrich, 19
Noyes, Alfred, 73–74, 102, 207

Oates, John, 43, 62, 201
Ormond, Leonée, 1, 9, 182–83, 192, 225
Ostriker, Alicia, 117, 124, 213
Owen, Wilfrid, 113
Oxford University, 53, 180, 190

Pacific Theological Seminary, 65
Paden, W. D., 5, 9, 83, 102, 169, 209
Page, Norman, 4, 9, 176, 221
Pallen, Condé B., 49, 62, 203
Palmer, D. J., 133, 138, 146, 147, 216, 217
Palmer, George H., 65–66, 102, 206
pantheism, 78
Paradise Lost, 25, 33, 43, 142
Parsons, Eugene, 26, 30, 200

pastoral (pastoral poetry), 150, 170
Patmore, Coventry, 16, 77, 135
Pattison, Robert, 141–42, 147, 163, 219
Paul, Herbert W., 31, 62, 200
Payne, William M., 50–51, 62, 169, 204
Peckham, Morse, 127, 147, 215
Peltason, Timothy, 157, 160, 168, 173, 221
performance theory, 185
Perry, Henry Ten Eyck, 72–73, 102, 207
Pettigrew, John, 127, 147, 215
Pfordresher, John, 117, 124, 216
Pinion, F. B., 156, 174, 175, 193, 221, 223
Pitt, Valerie, 107–9, 113, 124, 182, 212
Platizsky, Roger S., 168–69, 173, 194, 223
Poe, Edgar Allan, 15, 56, 178
"Poetic Principle, The," 15
Pope, Alexander, 11, 36, 42, 55, 129
poststructuralism (literary methodology), 7, 73, 93, 145, 149–70
Pratt, Linda R., 98, 102, 216
Prelude, The, 90, 142
Pre-Raphaelite poets, 138
Preyer, Robert, 115, 125, 213
Priestley, F. E. L., 86, 89, 93, 102, 107, 113, 114, 125, 131–32, 137, 143, 147, 168, 176, 210, 216
Principles of Geology (Charles Lyell), 183
psychological criticism, 70, 73, 83, 143, 168
Pyre, James F. A., 67, 102, 117, 125, 137, 147, 206

queer theory, 158–59

Quiller-Couch, Arthur, 82, 102, 209

Rader, Ralph W., 110, 125, 169, 212
Rader, William, 50, 63, 203
Radford, Colin, 150, 173, 220
Rasselas, 7, 134
Rawnsley, Drummond, 53
Rawnsley, Sophie, 180
Rawnsley, W. F., 53, 63, 205
reaction against Tennyson, 20, 21, 22, 27, 48, 49, 53, 54, 57–58, 65, 66, 68, 69, 72, 73, 82, 84, 96, 151, 152
Rearden, Timothy H., 38, 63, 202
Reed, John R., 115–16, 125, 130, 142, 155, 166, 173, 177, 188, 192, 215
Reeves, James, 106, 125, 212
Renaissance, 21, 141
Renaissance literature, 136, 141
Revel, Peter, 4, 9, 216
Rice, William North, 67, 103, 206
Richardson, James, 163–64, 173, 222
Richardson, Joanna, 1, 10, 109–10, 125, 212
Ricks, Christopher, 3, 7, 10, 13, 30, 122, 125, 129–31, 143, 147, 150, 156, 158, 159, 160, 168, 195, 215, 216, 222
Ring and the Book, The (Browning), 142
Road to Xanadu, The (Lowes), 183
Roberts, Adam, 190, 192, 226
Robertson, J. M., 48, 63, 200, 203
Robson, W. W., 96, 102, 176, 213

Romance (literary genre), 39, 68, 117, 132, 133, 134, 142, 150, 153
Romantic poets, 26, 68, 69, 70, 71, 84, 90, 93, 95, 104–5, 108, 112, 118–19, 127–28, 132, 137, 145, 152, 154, 158, 166, 184, 185
Romanticism (Romantic movement), 55, 59, 70, 80–82, 85, 90, 91, 95, 107, 111, 118–19, 127–28, 129, 135, 144, 151, 157, 158, 161, 162–63, 177, 183, 184, 185, 187
Rosenberg, John D., 116–17, 125, 142, 143, 148, 155, 216, 223
Rossetti, Christina, 77
Rossetti, Dante Gabriel, 163
Routh, H. V., 81, 102, 208
Rowlinson, Matthew C., 184, 192, 225
Royce, Josiah, 26, 30, 202
Ruskin, John, 37, 48
Russell, G. W. E., 35
Ryals, Clyde de L., 6, 10, 112–14, 115, 116, 125, 130, 132, 155, 212, 213

Saintsbury, George, 31, 42, 63, 201, 205
Salt, Henry S., 27, 30, 56, 63, 201
Sanders, Charles R., 97, 161, 173, 212
Scaife, Christopher H., 75, 102, 208
Schopenhauer, Arthur, 119
Schur, Owen, 170, 174, 194, 223
Scott, P. G., 122, 125, 215
Scott, Sir Walter, 2, 11, 22
Second World War, 82
Sedgwick, Eve Sokofsky, 157–58, 174, 183, 221

Sellwood, Emily. *See* Tennyson, Emily Sellwood
Sellwood, Louisa, 180
semiotics, 129, 176
Sendry, Joseph, 4, 117, 125, 213
Sessions, Ina B., 162
Shakespeare, William, 16, 19, 21, 24, 41, 47, 74, 119, 167, 181, 194
Shanks, Edward B., 74, 103, 207
Shannon, Edgar F., Jr., 3, 5, 9, 10, 13, 28, 30, 183, 209, 211, 219
Shatto, Susan, 3, 10, 28, 30, 160, 164, 174, 195, 220, 222
Shaw, Marion, 3, 5, 10, 28, 30, 155, 164–65, 174, 182, 183, 195, 220, 222, 223
Shaw, W. David, 137, 143, 148, 185–86, 192–93, 213, 215, 216, 217, 218, 221, 222, 223, 225, 226
Shelburne Lecture, 53
Shelley, Percy Bysshe, 11, 12, 14, 19, 42, 159, 185
Shepherd, Henry E., 50, 63, 204
Sherbo, Arthur, 5, 10, 225
Sherer, Edmund, 20
Shires, Linda M., 175, 193, 224
Shmiefsky, Marvel, 175, 125, 214
Simpson, Roger, 176, 193, 224
Sinfield, Alan, 121, 129, 137, 143, 148, 159–60, 165, 168, 174, 176, 183, 186, 216, 217, 222, 224
Slater, Michael, 122, 125, 226
Smalley, Donald, 106, 125, 212
Smith, Arnold, 50, 51, 63, 169, 204
Smith, Elton Edward, 6, 10, 110–11, 125, 186, 193, 213, 214, 225
Smith, J. C., 58, 60, 209
Smith, Jean Pauline, 66–67, 103, 206

Smith, Robert M., 4, 8, 208
Smyser, William E., 45, 48, 63, 204
Sneath, Elias. H., 44, 63, 202
Solimine, Joseph, 117, 126, 214
Somersby (England), 14, 23, 71, 110
Southam, B. C., 127, 148, 216
Spedding, James, 11, 14
Spengler, Oswald, 119
Spenser, Edmund, 13, 16, 36, 167
Spinoza, Baruch, 44
Spitzer, Leo, 107
Squire, John C., 69, 103, 206
Staines, David, 153, 174, 220
Stanley, Hiram M., 42, 63, 202
Starnes, De Witt T., 67–68, 103, 207
Steane, J. B., 114–15, 126, 213
Stedman, E. C., 25, 26, 30, 199
Sterling, John, 14
Stevens, Wallace, 116, 138
Stevenson, Lionel, 78–79, 92, 103, 107, 132, 166, 174, 208, 210, 211
Stevenson, Morley, 39, 63, 203
Stott, Rebecca, 186, 193, 225
Strong, Augustus Hopkins, 43–44, 63, 202
Swinburne, Algernon Charles, 21–22, 24, 26, 28, 30, 40, 151, 160, 163, 189
symbolist poets, 20, 27, 117, 129
Symonds, Arthur, 40

Taine, Hippolyte, 20
Taylor, Beverly, 176, 191, 193, 224
Templeman, W. D., 4, 68, 103, 210
Tennyson, Alfred, works by:
  "Amphion," 118
  "Anacaona," 179
  "Ancient Sage, The," 90

"Armageddon," 184
Becket, 24
"Brook, The," 150
"Charge of the Light Brigade, The," 55
"Crossing the Bar," 186
"Enoch Arden," 1, 24, 33, 76, 85, 144, 150
Enoch Arden and Other Poems, 19, 117, 122
"Epic, The," 139
"Gardener's Daughter, The," 195
"Hands All Round," 55
"Hesperides, The," 184
Idylls of the King, 1, 5, 18–22, 23–24, 26, 27, 33, 34, 36, 37, 38–39, 40, 41, 42, 43, 45, 47, 48, 49, 51, 53, 54, 55, 57, 58, 66, 68, 70, 71–72, 73, 74, 75, 76, 84, 85–86, 88–90, 93–94, 95, 98, 105–6, 107, 108–9, 110, 113–14, 115–17, 119, 120, 121, 122, 127, 130, 131, 132, 133, 134, 135, 136, 137, 138, 139–40, 141–42, 143, 144, 150–51, 152, 153, 154, 155–56, 159, 161, 164, 165, 166, 168, 175, 176, 177, 179, 181, 182, 183, 185, 186, 187, 188, 189, 190, 195
In Memoriam A. H. H., 1, 3, 6, 15, 16–17, 18, 20, 23, 24, 25, 28, 33, 34, 37, 38, 39, 40, 41, 42, 43, 45, 47, 48, 49, 50, 51, 53, 54, 55, 56, 57, 58, 60, 70, 71, 72, 73, 74, 75, 76, 78, 79–80, 81, 82, 84, 85, 86, 90, 91–92, 93–95, 97, 98, 105, 106, 107, 108, 110, 111–12, 113, 114, 115, 117, 118, 119, 121, 127, 128, 129, 130,

131, 132, 133, 134, 136, 137, 138, 139, 140, 141, 142–43, 144, 149–50, 152, 153, 156, 157, 158, 159, 161, 163, 164, 165, 166, 167, 168, 169, 176, 179, 181, 182, 183, 184, 186, 188, 189, 190
"Kraken, The," 161
"Lady of Shalott, The," 85, 133, 167, 170, 184, 189, 195
"Locksley Hall," 20, 68, 75, 110, 138, 144
"Locksley Hall Sixty Years After," 25–26, 41
"Lotos Eaters, The," 144, 170
"Lover's Tale, The," 128, 154, 189
"Lucretius," 24, 79, 137, 168
"Mariana," 127, 170, 184
Maud, 1, 3, 17–18, 20, 23, 27, 28, 33, 34, 37, 41, 48, 58, 68, 70, 72, 75, 76, 77, 80, 83, 84, 86, 96, 105, 108, 110, 115, 116, 118, 119, 121, 130, 131, 133, 134, 136, 137, 138, 139, 141, 143, 144, 151, 154, 155, 159, 161, 163, 174, 166, 168, 175, 179, 181, 182, 185, 186, 189, 190
Maud, and Other Poems, 1
"Miller's Daughter, The," 150
"Northern Farmer," 41
"Ode on the Death of the Duke of Wellington," 17, 33, 55
"Oenone," 144, 150, 167, 170
Poems (1833), 5, 6, 12–13, 16, 32, 66, 112, 127, 143
Poems (1842), 6, 11, 14, 15, 16, 23, 67, 71, 85, 105, 112, 127, 143, 162, 181
Poems by Two Brothers (1827), 83, 127

Poems, Chiefly Lyrical (1830), 5, 6, 11–12, 13, 16, 32, 66, 112, 127, 143
Princess, The, 1, 6, 15, 32, 33, 34, 37, 40, 41, 55, 58, 71, 75, 84, 85, 88, 94, 96, 105, 107, 120, 121, 130, 133, 134, 135, 136, 138, 139, 140, 141, 143, 144, 150, 151, 155, 157, 159, 163, 164, 165, 166, 176, 179, 181, 182, 189, 190, 195
Queen Mary, 24
"Recollections of the Arabian Nights," 127
"Riflemen, Form!" 55
"Rizpah," 22, 41, 168
"Romney's Remorse," 168
"Sea Dreams," 150
"St. Simeon Stylites," 154, 168
"Talking Oak, The," 158
"Tears, Idle Tears," 84–85, 91, 107, 157
"Timbuctoo," 75, 184
"Tithon," 159
"Tithonus," 24, 154, 157, 159, 167, 184
"Two Voices, The," 40, 72, 110, 116, 133, 183
"Ulysses," 14, 15, 24, 86, 96, 107, 133, 154, 157, 159, 161, 167, 170, 184, 186, 195
"Will Waterproof's Lyrical Monologue," 158
Tennyson, Charles (the poet's brother), 180
Tennyson, Charles (the poet's grandson), 4, 5, 10, 86–89, 92, 94, 98, 109, 110, 122, 126, 130, 139, 144, 179, 214, 217
Tennyson, Emily Sellwood (the poet's wife), 3, 35, 130, 180, 182

Tennyson, George Clayton (the poet's father), 1, 143
Tennyson, Hallam (the poet's son), 2, 4, 10, 16–17, 30, 35–36, 37, 41, 46, 52, 56, 64, 86–87, 167, 182, 193, 202, 204, 205
Tennyson d'Eyncourt, Charles (the poet's cousin), 1
Tennyson Research Bulletin, 6, 98, 121, 152, 182, 194
Tennyson Research Centre, 3
Tennyson Society, 6, 121–22, 176, 194
ten-years' silence, 15, 28, 32, 105
"Theodicaea Novissima" (Arthur Henry Hallam), 91
Thomson, Alastair W., 160–61, 174, 220, 222
Thorn, Michael, 178–80, 181–82, 193, 225
Tillotson, Geoffrey A., 140, 148, 218
Tillotson, Kathleen, 113, 126, 140, 148, 213
Timko, Michael, 161, 174, 222
Traill, H. D., 31, 64, 200
Trench, R. C., 158
Trinity College (Cambridge University), 2, 3
Troilus and Criseyde (Chaucer), 142
Tucker, Herbert F., Jr., 162–63, 164, 174, 177, 183, 186, 193, 195, 196, 221, 222, 223, 225, 226
Turley, Richard Margraaf, 176, 193, 194, 196, 225, 226
Turnbull, Arthur, 55, 56, 64, 205
Turner, Paul, 135–36, 148, 169, 174, 210, 218, 223

Union Club (Cambridge University), 18, 28

Van Dyke, Henry, 38, 64, 202
Verlaine, Paul, 20
Vestiges of Creation (Robert Chambers), 183
Victoria (Queen), 1, 17, 92, 187
Victorians, 1, 2, 4, 16–17, 18, 19, 21, 22, 23, 24, 25, 31, 32–33, 34, 37, 38, 40–41, 44, 45, 46, 47, 49, 50, 52, 55, 57, 65, 68, 70, 71, 72, 74, 75, 76, 77, 81, 82, 83, 85, 90, 81, 92, 93, 95, 97, 107, 108, 109, 110, 112, 116, 117, 118, 119, 120, 127–28, 129, 130–31, 135, 136, 144, 145, 151, 157, 159, 161, 165, 167, 169, 177, 179, 180, 182, 185, 186, 187, 188, 190, 194
Virgil, 43, 48, 163
Virginia, University of, 89, 158

Wagner, Richard, 114
Walker, Hugh, 51, 52, 64, 201, 202, 205
Walters, J. C., 33, 64, 201
Walton, James, 118, 126, 215
Ward, Wilfrid, 24
Warren, T. Herbert, 50, 53, 64, 73, 103, 203, 204, 207
Warton Lecture, 82, 90
Waugh, Arthur, 30, 32–33, 34, 64, 200
Wesley, John, 184
Westminster Abbey, 81
Weygandt, Cornelius, 76, 103, 208
Whiting, George W., 112, 126, 213
Whitman, Walt, 25–26, 29, 30, 45, 138, 200
Willey, Basil, 94–95, 103, 211
Wilson, John, 12, 13, 23
Wolfe, Humbert, 77, 80, 103, 208
Wordsworth, Ann, 150, 174, 220

Wordsworth, William, 11, 17, 19, 21, 42, 43, 47, 52, 76, 90, 96, 111, 121, 122, 127, 140, 156, 185, 188

Yale University, 55, 138
Yeats, W. B., 27, 30, 64, 89, 109, 116, 129, 138, 161, 163, 203
Young, G. M., 82, 103, 107, 158, 208
Young, Robert, 149, 150, 174, 220

PR 5587.3
.M39
2004